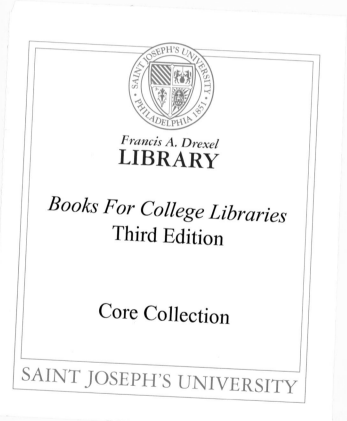

Francis A. Drexel
LIBRARY

Books For College Libraries
Third Edition

Core Collection

INSTRUCTIONS FOR PRACTICAL LIVING AND OTHER NEO-CONFUCIAN WRITINGS BY WANG YANG-MING

Number LXVIII of the Records of Civilization: Sources and Studies
Edited under the auspices of the
Department of History, Columbia University

Prepared for the Columbia College Program of Translations from
the Oriental Classics,
Wm. Theodore de Bary, Editor

WANG YANG-MING
MING DYNASTY PORTRAIT IN THE COLLECTION
OF HUANG CHIEH (1874-1935): PHOTOGRAPH BY
PROFESSOR KUSUMOTO MASATSUGU

INSTRUCTIONS
FOR PRACTICAL LIVING
AND OTHER
NEO-CONFUCIAN
WRITINGS
BY WANG YANG-MING

Translated, with Notes, by
Wing-tsit Chan

Columbia University Press

NEW YORK AND LONDON

The addition to the "Records of Civilization: Sources and Studies" of a group of translations of Oriental historical materials, of which this volume is one, was made possible by funds granted by Carnegie Corporation of New York. That Corporation is not, however, the author, owner, publisher, or proprietor of this publication, and is not to be understood as approving by virtue of its grant any of the statements made or views expressed therein.

UNESCO COLLECTION OF REPRESENTATIVE WORKS
CHINESE SERIES

This work has been accepted in the Chinese Translation Series of the United Nations Educational, Scientific and Cultural Organization (UNESCO).

To
Shao Chang Lee
PIONEERING CHINESE PROFESSOR WHO HAS
FOR FORTY YEARS INSTRUCTED AMERICAN STUDENTS
IN CHINESE HISTORY AND CULTURE

Foreword

This volume containing the major works of Wang Yang-ming is one of a group of publications, the Translations from the Oriental Classics, through which the Committee on Oriental Studies has sought to transmit to Western readers representative works of the Oriental traditions in thought and literature. In its volumes of source readings forming the " Introduction to Oriental Civilizations," the Committee has provided a broad selection of excerpts from influential thinkers in India, China, and Japan, discussing the great problems of their times in historical sequence. Insofar as a reading of what Asian peoples have written for their own delight and edification may give us a sympathetic insight into their alien traditions, the present series fulfills the same purpose. Where it differs from any survey, however—and differs also from drugstore anthologies which present the East always in aphorism or epigram— is that it makes major works or authors available in something more substantial than excerpts, and in accurate, readable translations prepared for the general reader as well as the scholar.

There are good reasons why these writings have not been accessible before: they are often formidable works for both translator and reader. But if we have thought them worth presenting here in spite of such difficulties, it is because the admiration in which they have been held for centuries, by both popular and sophisticated audiences in the East, compels our own attention. It is time for more of us to learn why they should have enjoyed such esteem; it is time to face the challenge and gain the rewards of conquering—or being conquered by—these imposing masters.

Wang Yang-ming, we must admit, is no popular writer nor has he been universally esteemed. He writes in the classical style, in a distinctive Confucian context. And the place he has won in the high tradition, instead of rendering him immune from attack, has ensured that he would be at the center of intellectual controversy ever since. Yet what he has to say—concerning man's moral sense, the inner springs of human motivation, the integrity of the individual in thought and action, human nature and man's place in the

universe—has found a deep response in the lives of educated
Japanese and Koreans as well as Chinese. Both samurai officers of
Imperial Japan and Sun Yat-sen's republican revolutionaries, both
Chiang Kai-shek and some of his severest intellectual critics, have
acknowledged Wang Yang-ming as their chief philosophical
inspiration.

Now with the help of Professor Chan's faithful translation,
Western readers may judge if they too would wish to acknowledge
him, not as a Chinese sage, but as a teacher from whom they have
learned something about themselves.

WM. THEODORE DE BARY

Preface

The *Instructions for Practical Living* (*Ch'uan-hsi lu*) has been chosen for translation for the simple reason that no one can adequately understand Chinese thought without having read this work in its entirety. This embodiment of Wang Yang-ming's philosophy is indisputably the most important Chinese philosophical classic since the early thirteenth century. It has developed Confucian doctrines to new heights and has carried them to new frontiers. Like other Neo-Confucian works, it is by no means merely a de luxe edition of the Confucian *Analects* or the *Book of Mencius,* in spite of the fact that it quotes from them on almost every page and that its moral values are largely confined to ancient ideals.

As every student of Chinese thought knows, Neo-Confucianism, which developed and transformed Confucianism under the influence of Buddhism and Taoism, has dominated Chinese thought for some eight hundred years. The philosophy of Ch'eng I and Chu Hsi represents the rationalistic wing of that movement while that of Lu Hsiang-shan and Wang Yang-ming represents the idealistic wing. It is in the *Instructions for Practical Living* that the idealistic tendency has reached its full bloom.

Since Chu Hsi's rationalistic philosophy ruled supreme in the Chinese intellectual scene for centuries and its influence continued to some degree until our own time, it is necessary to understand its idealistic counterpart.

Wang's philosophy did not merely play the role of opposition, however. It overshadowed Chu Hsi's philosophy for over a hundred years and because of its emphasis on sincere purpose and concrete action, the need of which was keenly felt in China's troubled times, it has in recent decades exercised considerable influence on Chinese intellectuals and social and political leaders alike. In Japanese history it provided the leaders of the Meiji Restoration with inspiration and impetus and has thereby contributed substantially to the reawakening and revitalization of Japan.

I have also translated here the *Inquiry on the "Great Learning,"* which embodies the essential ideas of the *Instructions for Practical Living* in a somewhat systematic manner, and seven documents dealing with social and political problems which show tò some extent the way in which Wang's doctrines were put into practice.

A general introduction has been provided for Wang's philosophy. There are separate introductions for certain sections and essays.

I wish to thank the Committee on Oriental Studies of Columbia University for the grant which provided me with time and assistance to undertake and complete this translation. I am particularly indebted to its Chairman, Professor Wm. Theodore de Bary, for his strong encouragement and support. As Editor of Translations from the Oriental Classics, he is doing much to further the spread of knowledge and increase in understanding of Asian thought. He has read through my manuscript and made many valuable suggestions for improvement. Miss Elisabeth L. Shoemaker, Editor, Columbia University Press, has given me tremendous help on the format and literary expression of the work.

I wish also to thank the Harvard-Yenching Library and its Librarian, Dr. Kaiming A. Chiu; the East Asiatic Library of Columbia University and its Librarian Mr. Howard P. Linton; and the staff of Baker Library of Dartmouth College, especially the members of its Reference Division, for their generous assistance. Miss Naomi Fukuda, Librarian of the International House of Japan, has been ever ready to locate Japanese works for me and to secure microfilms of them. My colleague Professor Arthur Dewing has been most patient and sympathetic in helping me find suitable expressions and translations. Dartmouth College has given me financial aid in the preparation of the manuscript, and Mrs. Alice W. Weymouth has kindly typed it. I am grateful to all of them.

Above all, I am indebted to my wife. This work has heen made possible only by her patience, understanding, and wholehearted support.

Dartmouth College
September, 1962
W.T.C.

Translator's Note

This is a new translation of the *Ch'uan-hsi lu,* plus a few short works which supplement it. A previous translation by Frederick Goodrich Henke (*The Philosophy of Wang Yang-ming,* 1916) contains too many mistakes to be of any use. The translator rearranged the text and omitted many sections for no justifiable reason.

The present translation is complete, except for passages from Chu Hsi's works which Wang selected and included in the *Appendix* and Yüan Ch'ing-lin's short postscript. The *Wang Wen-ch'eng Kung ch'üan-shu* (Complete works of Wang Yang-ming) of the Ssu-pu ts'ung-k'an edition is used. It is a photographic reproduction of the edition of 1572 which is the oldest and is considered the most authentic. I have not translated the title literally. The term "ch'uan-hsi" comes from the *Analects* 1:4 and means "what has been transmitted [from the teacher] and is to be learned well [and to be practiced]" or, according to another interpretation, "to transmit those doctrines which one has already learned well or put into practice himself." Wang's pupil Hsü Ai used the term as the title for his records of conversations with his teacher. Most annotators have emphasized the idea of learning, especially through recitation. But Wang denounced book learning and advocated practice instead. I believe that the title *Instructions for Practical Living* expresses better the meaning and the spirit of the original. The word *lu* (records) has been omitted.

I have used the name Wang Yang-ming, an honorific, instead of the philosopher's private name Shou-jen or his courtesy name Po-an. Although in most cases I have used people's private names, I have not hesitated to make exceptions in cases where a courtesy name or an honorific is much better known, as in the case of Lu Hsiang-shan. Since the generally used names of ancient philosophers are mostly not private names, and Chinese abounds in such well-established names as Sun Yat-sen, absolute consistency is impossible anyway. Chinese and Japanese names are given in the Chinese order, that is, with the family name first, except for some contemporaries who (like myself) follow the Western order. Birth and death dates are provided, where known, in all cases except those of Western and contemporary Asian writers and of Confucius, Mencius, and the outstanding Neo-Confucians, whose dates, to avoid needless repetition, are given only in the Introduction.

The Chinese calendar year has been equated with its corresponding year in the Western calendar, even though the two do not exactly coincide. I have made an exception in the case of Wang's death, however. He died in the seventh year of Chia-ching. Ordinarily this would be equated with 1528. But since his death occurred on the twenty-ninth day of the eleventh month of the seventh year of Chia-ching, which happened to correspond to January 10, 1529, the year 1529 is used instead. In reference to age, when Wang is said to be fifty, for example, it means that he was in his fiftieth year.

Almost every Chinese philosophical term is used in the *Instructions for Practical Living*. Insofar as possible, these terms have been translated consistently. Many sayings and phrases occur again and again. These, too, have been translated consistently except where slight adjustments are unavoidable. Sources of quotations, which are numerous, have been traced. This is not an easy task, especially in the case of quotations from Neo-Confucian sources, of which there are many. In the absence of indexes and concordances and often without any indication as to whose saying a quotation is, where it is from, or whether it is a quotation at all, it is sometimes necessary to go through a whole work to locate it. Japanese annotations are helpful but inadequate. Their references to Neo-Confucian works, by no means complete, are to an anthology instead of original works. The work of the two Chinese annotators is useless. (See Bibliographical and Historical Notes on the *Ch'uan-hsi lu*.) But the identification of sources enables the reader to see the historical and philosophical connections between Wang and his predecessors and to check the context of the quotations whenever desired.

Wang quoted freely, often paraphrasing or changing a word or two. Most of these liberties have not been pointed out since they do not alter the original meanings. In a few cases where Wang did twist the meaning this fact is indicated in footnotes.

There are many variations of individual words in different editions and selections. Except in a few cases, none affects the sense of the sentences involved. I have not deemed it necessary to note all these variations except where emendation is called for. Some anthologies contain additional conversations not included in the 1572 edition. These have not been translated because their authenticity is questionable. In any case they contain nothing of special significance. (See Bibliographical and Historical Notes on the *Ch'uan-hsi lu*.) Section numbers have been provided for convenient reference.

All Chinese and Japanese titles have been translated in the List of Chinese and Japanese Works. English titles are given in full when first cited in each section of footnotes and thereafter are abbreviated. Specific editions referred to are given in the List of Chinese and Japanese Works. Transliterations follow the Wade-Giles system except for a few well-known geographical names. The glossary includes Chinese characters for all Chinese and Japanese words except well-known geographical names and names of dynasties.

Abbreviations

PNP   Pai-na-pen (Choice works) edition
SPPY   Ssu-pu pei-yao (Essentials of the four libraries) edition
SPTK   Ssu-pu ts'ung-k'an (Four-library series) edition

Contents

Introduction

The philosophy of Wang Yang-ming is a vigorous philosophy born of serious searching and bitter experience. It is no idle speculation or abstract theory developed for the sake of intellectual curiosity. Rather, it is intended to provide a fundamental solution to basic moral and social problems. It calls for firm purpose and earnest effort, and for the actual practice and concrete demonstration of values. The intellectual and political situations of the time demanded just such a system.

Intellectually, the light of Neo-Confucianism, which arose in the eleventh century and gave Confucianism a new life, was in the fifteenth century dim if not extinguished. The rationalistic Neo-Confucianism of Ch'eng I (Ch'eng I-ch'uan, 1033-1107) and Chu Hsi (1130-1200) had dominated the Chinese intellectual world since the twelfth century. But its doctrine of the Principle of Nature, aimed at promoting good and removing evil, was overcome by selfish human desires. Its doctrine of humanity, advocating love for all, gave way to mutual jealousy and rivalry. And its doctrine of the investigation of things, intended as a means to a clear and penetrating understanding of the things investigated, was now replaced by memorization, recitation, philological and textual studies, and the writing of flowery compositions. The civil service examination system, through which government officials were selected, and which had rendered remarkable service since its formal establishment almost a thousand years before, had become an avenue for personal fame and success. The Sung Neo-Confucians had honored the Confucian Classics with great authority, as an expression of natural law providing a set of standards for social life and moral action. But now the Classics were being used to restrict creativity and freedom of thought. In 1313 Chu Hsi's and Ch'eng I's interpretations of the Classics were declared the official doctrines and in 1415 the *Ssu-shu ta-ch'üan* and the *Wu-ching ta-ch'üan* (Great collections of commentaries on the Four Books and Five Classics)[1] were made the

---

[1] The *Ssu-shu ta-ch'üan* and the *Wu-ching ta-ch'üan*, compiled by imperial decree, were completed in 1415. The Four Books are the *Analects*, the *Great Learning*, the

basis for the examinations. The domination of Chu's philosophy in the intellectual scene was now absolute. But it was a domination that at best encouraged a concern with fragmentary and isolated details and with nonessentials, and at worst led to the habits of memorization and recitation instead of the search for meanings and values. Thus the Ch'eng-Chu philosophy, losing the moral strength it originally had possessed, became pure scholasticism. With such a philosophy as the only channel to public service and personal success, critical spirit, creative thought, and moral purpose and vitality gradually disappeared.

The government at this time was exceedingly corrupt and impotent. The Cheng-te emperor was a playboy who spent much time in horse riding and in dog chasing inside the palace. What was worse, he left the government to eight eunuchs, one of whom, Liu Chin (d. 1510), was particularly powerful and wicked. Liu prevented scholar officials who wanted to have him removed from having audience with the emperor; he intercepted memorials demanding his execution. As was often the case in China when eunuchs were in power, there was disorder in the government and chaos throughout the land. Hundreds of square miles of territory in many provinces, especially in Kiangsi, Fukien, Kwangtung, and Kwangsi in central and south China, were under the control of rebels and bandits. Many of them had held power for several decades, and even government officials had to take orders from them. The moral decay, political degeneration, and economic crisis were such that intellectual and social collapse was imminent. Nothing except a complete spiritual revolution could save the day. The Chu Hsi philosophy, now itself decadent, was in no position to offer a solution.

Some scholar officials risked their lives in an attempt to remedy the situation. The number of brave souls who were willing to suffer beating and imprisonment, or even death for protesting against the evil-doing of the eunuchs and the emperor was impressive. But the source of the trouble lay in the fact that Confucianism, the very ideology of government and the basic philosophy of life, had now been so suffocated by traditional thought and the restrictive examination system that it had become "dry wood and dead ashes."

Doctrine of the Mean, and the *Book of Mencius.* The Five Classics are the books of *History Odes, Changes,* and *Rites* (since the tenth century replaced by the *Rites of Chou*), and the *Spring and Autumn Annals.* A sixth Classic, the *Book of Music,* is no longer extant.

Government corruption and social chaos were but symptoms of that disease. Clearly an injection of new vigor and fresh life into the Confucian system was necessary. The man who provided this was Wang Yang-ming.

Wang's private name was Shou-jen and his courtesy name Po-an.[2] He was born on the thirtieth day of the ninth month in the eighth year of Ch'eng-hua (1472) in Yüeh, a place in the Yü-yao district southeast of Hangchow in modern Chekiang. His ancestry has been traced to the famous calligrapher Wang Hsi-chih (321-79). His father, Wang Hua, a "presented scholar" of 1481, was minister of civil personnel in Nanking. It is said that Wang Yang-ming could not talk until he was five. At eleven he joined his father in Peking and stayed there until he was sixteen. It was during this sojourn, when he was thirteen, that his mother Madame Cheng died. When he was fifteen, he visited the passes in the Chü-yung Mountain in the present Hopei Province in North China. Both the *Nien-p'u* (Chronological biography) and the *Hsing-chuang* (Biography) claim that he volunteered to fight against the rebellion of Liu Ch'ien-chin and others and withdrew only after a stern admonition by his father. But as Mao Ch'i-ling (1623-1716) has pointed out in his most authoritative *Wang Wen-ch'eng chuan-pen* (Basic materials for the biography of Wang Yang-ming),[3] this rebellion occurred far away from the Chü-yung Mountain, six years before Wang's

[2] Sources for Wang's biography are: *Nien-p'u*, written by Wang's favorite and outstanding disciple Ch'ien Te-hung, and constituting ch. 32 of the *Wang Wen-ch'eng Kung ch'üan-shu; Hsing-chuang*, written by another disciple, Huang Wan, and included in ch. 37 of the *Wang Wen-ch'eng Kung ch'üan-shu; Ming shih*, ch. 195; and *Ming shih kao*, ch. 185, biography 80. The biography in Huang Tsung-hsi, *Ming-ju hsüeh-an*, contains an excellent account. Mao Ch'i-ling's *Wang Wen-ch'eng chuan-pen* is indispensable to any critical study. Yü Ch'ung-yao in his *Yang-ming Hsien-sheng chuan-tsuan* has made good use of Mao's work and has compared the above sources, examined their inconsistencies, and selected the most reliable facts, thus making his book the best full-length biography in Chinese. The best in Japanese is Takase Takejirō's *Ōyōmei shōden*. It offers nothing new and contains some mistakes (such as saying, on p. 54, that Wang visited Lou Liang in 1507 although Lou died in 1491) but is a systematic narrative and has helpful explanations. In English there is Frederick Goodrich Henke's biography in his *The Philosophy of Wang Yang-ming*, pp. 3-44. It is an uncritical and abridged translation of the *Nien-p'u*, which retains legendary materials such as the account of Wang's living in a grotto and escaping by boat (pp. 10-11), omits essential materials like the famous conversation on the "Doctrine in Four Axioms" (p. 36), and makes many mistakes in translation, such as calling the office to select and regulate government personnel the office "regarding letters received" (p. 15).

[3] *Wang Wen-ch'eng chuan-pen*, p. 2b.

birth. However, the visit did arouse the boy's interest in the frontiers, as his later activities were to show. At seventeen he went to Hung-tu[4] to take a wife, a Miss Chu whose father was then a state counselor in the provincial government. On the evening of the wedding day, when he passed by a Taoist temple and saw a Taoist priest sitting cross-legged, he sat down with him to talk about nourishing everlasting life, and was so absorbed that he neglected to go home until he was fetched the next morning. In the following year, when he was on his way home to Yü-yao with his wife, he called on the prominent scholar Lou Liang (1422-91) who was then sixty-eight. Lou acquainted him with Chu Hsi's doctrine of the investigation of things and told him that sagehood could be attained through learning. Both the *Nien-p'u* and the *Hsing-chuang* say that he was strongly convinced by Lou.[5] Whether this is true or not, evidently the conviction did not have any immediate effect, for in the following year, at nineteen, he became much interested in military tactics and archery. However, two years later (in 1492), after having received the "recommended person" degree in his native provincial examination, he studied Chu Hsi's doctrine of the investigation of things in real earnestness, searching widely for Chu Hsi's writings. One day while Wang was with his father in Peking he decided to investigate the principles of bamboos. Since Chu Hsi had taught that principles are inherent in things, Wang and a friend sat in front of bamboos and tried hard to investigate their principles. His friend gave up after three days and he after seven, both having become ill.[6] Thoroughly disillusioned in the search, he devoted himself to the writing of flowery compositions, which, however, did not enable him to pass the national civil service examinations either in 1493 or in 1496. Now he turned his attention back, first to military crafts and not long afterwards to the Taoist techniques of nourishing everlasting life. He actually contemplated entering a Taoist retreat in some mountain to search for immortality.

---

[4] Now Nan-ch'ang in Kiangsi Province.

[5] Both the *Ming shih* and the *Ming shih kao* place this interview in his seventeenth year.

[6] See *Instructions for Practical Living*, sec. 319. All section numbers in the footnotes refer to this work. Some scholars argue that Wang's father could not have been in the capital in 1492 because he was at home mourning the death of Wang's grandfather, and that this episode therefore must have taken place when Wang was with his father in Peking before 1492. There is no reason, however, why he and his father could not have returned to Peking in the latter part of 1492 after having observed mourning.

These must have been years of intense spiritual and intellectual struggle, for he was not able to make a definite choice between Taoism and Confucianism, or between flowery compositions and military arts. If anything, he was still traveling on the traditional path by taking civil service examinations leading to government service. In 1499, when he was twenty-eight, he passed the examinations for the "presented scholar" degree, ranking second.

Immediately after that Wang was appointed a member of the department of public works. At that time China was invaded in the northwest by semi-nomadic tribes. He presented a memorial to the throne recommending eight measures for national defense and security.[7] Although his recommendations were not accepted, his fame grew because of his brilliant ideas on strategy, finance, and morale, and in the following year he was made divisional executive assistant in the Yunnan division of the department of justice, quite a responsible position for a young man of twenty-nine. A year later he was ordered to check the records of prisoners. He reversed many convictions. Without doubt an active life and public responsibility helped him to realize the errors of Taoism and Buddhism. He also came to frown upon flowery compositions. Because his health became poor, he returned home to Yüeh for recuperation. He built a small house in Yang-ming-tung in the Hui-chi Mountain and called himself Yang-ming Tzu or Philosopher of Yang-ming, from which came the honorific Master Yang-ming.[8]

After he recovered his health he went to Peking again in 1504 and was, at thirty-three, appointed to conduct the provincial examinations in Shantung. The questions he asked revealed such profound knowledge of the evils of Buddhism and Taoism, the reasons for the decline of Confucianism, governmental and social systems, and civil personnel that his reputation soared.[9] Later in the year, he was transferred to be divisional executive assistant of the military personnel division of the department of military affairs. A year later disciples first began to gather around him, thus giving him fresh interest and new enthusiasm and opening for him a broad

[7] This memorial is found below, pp. 284-92.

[8] As Mao Ch'i-ling has pointed out, there is no grotto in the Hui-chi Mountain. The stories about Wang's lecturing in a grotto, visiting the Yü cave (Yü-hsüeh), receiving instructions from a Taoist hermit in a cave, etc., are products of the imagination. See *Wang Wen-ch'eng chuan-pen*, p. 2a.

[9] For these documents see *Wang Wen-ch'eng Kung ch'üan-shu*, ch. 31B.

and clear horizon. He had found his direction and was moving forward with sure conviction and firm purpose. He lectured on the primary importance of making up one's mind to become a sage, and he severely attacked the habits of recitation and flowery composition. This did not please the conservative scholars, who felt he was resorting to strange doctrines in order to fish for fame. One man, however, thought highly of Wang. This was Chan Jo-shui (1466-1560), then an Honored Academician in the Han-lin Academy.[10] They became fast friends and took it upon themselves to clarify and spread the true doctrines of Confucius.

Wang's intellectual and spiritual progress now gained momentum. Nevertheless, had his life been smooth and uneventful, he might have become a highly respected lecturer with many followers but with no important effect on Chinese history. Fortunately, an extremely significant although painful event now took place. The eunuch Liu Chin had usurped the power of the emperor. In 1506, when Policy Review Adviser Tai Hsien and others protested, Liu put them in prison. Wang immediately presented a memorial in their defense.[11] This angered the eunuch and Wang was ordered to be beaten forty strokes before the emperor. In addition, he was banished to Lung-ch'ang in modern Kuei-chou, which was then inhabited by the barbarian Miao tribes, to become an insignificant executive in a dispatch station, whose duty it was to provide horses for rapid transportation. He started the journey in the spring of 1507 and arrived a year later, stopping over on the way to visit his father. Liu's agents pursued him and he escaped assassination only by throwing his clothing away by the Ch'ien-t'ang River near Hangchow, thus suggesting suicide. Some accounts, to make the event more dramatic, have him escape by sea from Hangchow to Fukien and thence to Kuei-chou. More reliable chronicles, however, have recorded his trip overland from Hangchow to Kuei-chou. In Kuei-chou he taught the Miao aboriginals to build houses and live in them.[12]

----

[10] See below, sec 201, n. 3.

[11] In *Wang Wen-ch'eng Kung ch'üan-shu*, ch. 9.

[12] These accounts are corroborated by the *Nien-p'u*, *Hsing-chuang*, *Ming shih*, and *Ming shih kao*. The *Nien-p'u*, however, has fantastic stories like that of the escape by boat, and the *Hsing-chuang* says that at first Wang lived in a cave and that later the Miaos, inspired by the gods, built several houses for him.

Life was rugged and difficult. At times Wang had to gather fuel, fetch water, and cook meals for his subordinates as well as for himself. But the trying situation turned out to be a blessing in disguise. Having to face in isolation all sorts of hardship — political, natural, and cultural—he was driven back to search within his own mind. One night in 1508, when he was thirty-seven, he suddenly understood the Confucian doctrines of the investigation of things and the extension of knowledge. After another year of thought he began in 1509 to pronounce the doctrine of the unity of knowledge and action. Wang had now come into his own.

When his term at Kuei-chou was up in 1510 he was promoted to be the magistrate of Lu-ling in modern Kiangsi, where he built up a remarkable record in seven months of service. After an audience with the emperor later in the year he was raised to be divisional executive assistant in the Szechuan division of the department of justice at Nanking. A number of promotions followed—to divisional executive assistant in the inspections division of the department of civil personnel, to assistant chief of the civil personnel division (both in 1511), and to chief of the merits division, all in Peking, then to junior lord of the bureau of imperial stables (1512) and to senior lord of the bureau of state ceremonies (1514), both in Nanking. Before he assumed his new duties in Nanking he went home to Yüeh for a visit. His disciple Hsü Ai (1487-1517) rode in the same boat with him. It was here that the conversations which are recorded in Part I of the *Instructions for Practical Living* took place. In these Nanking days (1514-16), his fame spread and many scholars, including one of his superior officials, became his followers. At the same time his radical doctrines, including his insistence on following the old text of the *Great Learning* instead of the one rearranged by Chu Hsi, attracted more and more criticism. Devotion to him as a great teacher and attacks on him as a heretic grew simultaneously. And even among his followers, there were some who violated his teachings and some who enjoyed irresponsible high-sounding talk.

At this point another political event occurred that ultimately forced him to explore new intellectual frontiers and thus to add new dimensions to his philosophy. When in 1516 repeated campaigns failed to suppress rebels and bandits in Kiangsi and Fukien, Wang was promoted, on the recommendation of Minister Wang Ch'iung (d. 1532) to be senior censor in the censorate and also governor of an area bordering Kwangtung, Kiangsi, and Fukien, charged with the pacification of that area. He arrived in Kan-chou in southern Kiangsi early in 1517 and immediately proceeded to recruit able-bodied fighters, reorganize the armed forces, institute the ten-family joint registration system,[13] and restore social order.[14] The situation in Chang-chou, Fukien, suddenly became critical. He directed his forces there and succeeded in subduing the rebellion in two months. He took measures to rehabilitate "new citizens" or former bandits[15] and petitioned for the establishment of a magistracy for better security and the reorganization of the salt gabelle for better economy. At the end of the year rebels in Heng-shui, T'ung-kang, Ta-mao, and Li-t'ou in southern Kiangsi were rampant. In five months' time Wang suppressed all of them, so that by the fourth month of 1518 he was able to start reconstruction measures, such as establishing primary schools,[16] and to petition for the establishment of a new county.[17] Two months later, in recognition of his spectacular success, he was promoted to be the right assistant censor, and his son was appointed an imperial guard with the income of one hundred families which was to be hereditary.[18] In the tenth month of the year he instituted the famous Community Compact.[19]

In the summer of 1519 Wang was ordered to go to suppress a rebellion in Fukien. While he was on the way, an emergency call came for him to subdue the rebellion of Chu Ch'en-hao, who was Prince Ning, in Kiangsi. Prince Ning, nephew of the emperor, had plotted rebellion for years. He had bribed the eunuch Liu Chin, who was executed in 1510. Now he declared himself head of state, calling his orders sacred edicts. He intended to capture Nanking and establish a new dynasty.

With Prince Ning strongly entrenched and supported by a huge army, Wang faced great odds. But through both political and

---

[13] For this system, see below, pp. 293-94; 306-9.
[14] See below, p. 295, for his moral teachings to the populace.
[15] For his instructions to them, see below, pp. 296-97.
[16] For his philosophy and program of primary education, see below, pp. 182-86.
[17] For this petition, see below, pp. 297-98.
[18] This was originally his cousin's son, whom his father had adopted for him in 1516 since neither he nor his brothers had any son. Wang's wife died in 1525. Three years later he married a Miss Chang and a son was born of this marriage.
[19] For this Compact, see below, pp. 298-306.

military maneuvers he captured the prince after ten days of fighting.

Toward the end of the year Wang was made governor of Kiangsi. In the following year, 1520, he carried out the various reforms once more.

By all precedents Wang's brilliant success should have been an occasion for extensive celebration and generous rewards. Unfortunately several things prevented this. The emperor had been urged by his favorites to lead the expedition himself, obviously so that he could claim credit for himself and his close subordinates. Wang, however, had bluntly advised him not to come. Furthermore, his capture of the prince caught the emperor and his circle in embarrassing surprise. In addition, in gratitude to the department of military affairs for the operation of the campaign, in his report Wang gave credit to its officials, especially Minister Wang Ch'iung, and ignored the inner circles of the court. Most damaging of all, prior to the prince's open rebellion, he and the prince had exchanged messengers. The prince had sent Liu Yang-cheng, a scholar with ardent admiration for Wang, to visit him and Wang had dispatched his disciple Chi Yüan-heng[20] to the prince. Angered and jealous, Wang's political enemies now charged that he and the prince had conspired together and that he had turned against the prince only because circumstances had become unfavorable to him. Chi was tortured and imprisoned, and died only five days after he was cleared and released. In his defense of Chi, Wang said that Chi was sent to Prince Ning only to dissuade him from rebellion and, if that should fail, to spy on him.[21] Nevertheless, some official documents actually state that Wang conspired with the prince through Liu. Mao Ch'i-ling, however, has authoritatively concluded that the whole charge is absurd.[22] At any rate, Wang became virtually *persona non grata* to the court. It was not until the spring of 1521, when the Chia-ching emperor ascended the throne, that rewards were recommended. Even then, because of the opposition of his enemies, he was only appointed minister of military affairs at Nanking, and then only in the capacity of adviser and planner. He was also awarded the title Earl of Hsin-chien with a salary of

---

[20] See below, sec. 118, n. 58.
[21] *Wang Wen-ch'eng Kung ch'üan-shu,* 17:54b.
[22] *Wang Wen-ch'eng chuan-pen,* Supplement 4b-5b.

1,000 piculs[23] of rice for three generations and an imperial certificate exempting his descendants from criminal punishment. Neither the salary nor the certificate was issued, however.

From 1521 to 1527, when Wang was in virtual retirement in his native place Yüeh, hostility toward him became more and more intense. He was ridiculed and attacked. His teachings were sometimes prohibited. Ironically, it was in this period that his following grew in numbers and in enthusiasm. Well-known scholars both in and out of government became his pupils. Whenever he lectured there were several hundred scholars from all parts of China to sit around him.[24] His philosophy had attained maturity. Most of his important letters, including the one containing the famous essay "Pulling Up the Root and Stopping Up the Source," were written during this time. So were most of the conversations recorded in Part III of the *Instructions for Practical Living*. Most important of all, it was in 1521, when he was fifty, that he arrived at the doctrine of the extension of innate knowledge, which culminated his whole philosophy. This was a period of searching thought. During these six years he was never appointed to office.

In 1527 rebellions spread in Ssu-en and T'ien-chou in Kwangsi. Wang, in the capacity of left censor, was called to suppress them. On the eve of his departure in the fall, he and his most outstanding disciples Wang Chi and Ch'ien Te-hung[25] engaged in the famous conversation concerning the celebrated "Doctrine in Four Axioms."[26] It was at about the same time that the *Inquiry on the "Great Learning,"* which embodies his most essential ideas, was written down. He pacified Kwangsi early in 1528. As before he promoted education and restored social order.

His coughing had bothered him for years, and now he was very ill. Part of the time during this campaign he had to handle military affairs while going about in carriages.[27] On his way home he died in Nan-an in modern Kiangsi on the twenty-ninth day of the eleventh month in the seventh year of Chia-ching (January 10, 1529).

Because the antagonism among government officials toward both Wang himself and his teachings was still very bitter, Minister

---

[23] One picul is 133½ pounds.
[24] See below, sec. 316.
[25] See below, preface to sec. 130, n. 1, and sec. 257, n. 15.
[26] See below, sec. 315.
[27] See below, secs. 184-85.

of Rites and Senior Academician Kuei O memorialized the throne and recommended that because Wang left his post without permission, his earldom should be taken away. Kuei and his associates condemned Wang for not respecting ancient traditions, for propagating strange doctrines, and for opposing Chu Hsi's theory of the investigation of things, and also charged that his disciples were either reckless or irresponsible. The result was that all hereditary privileges were revoked. Those who protested were dismissed.

However, in 1567, thirty-eight years after Wang's death, when a new emperor came to the throne, Wang was given the title of Marquis of Hsin-chien and honored with the posthumous title of Wen-ch'eng (Completion of Culture). In the following year his son was given the hereditary title of Earl of Hsin-chien. In 1584 an imperial decree was issued that Wang should be offered sacrifice in the Confucian temple, the highest honor a person could ever expect to receive. Only four scholars were so honored during the entire Ming period.[28]

The honor was well deserved, not only because, after he subdued the rebels, the Ming dynasty enjoyed a century of peace, free of rebellions and banditry, but far more importantly as a recognition of the significance of his philosophy. Certainly he was, except for Chu Hsi, the most influential philosopher in China since the fifteenth century. His philosophy dominated the remainder of the Ming period and his influence was felt in Japan.

According to Huang Tsung-hsi (1610-95), in his learning Wang went through three stages. First he indulged in flowery compositions. Then, after reading Chu Hsi's works and attempting to investigate the principles of bamboos according to Chu Hsi's formula, which he found wanting, he went in and out of the Buddhist and Taoist schools for a long time.[29] Finally, as the difficult life in Kuei-chou during banishment hardened his character and stimulated his mind, he suddenly awoke to the Confucian doctrines of the investigation of things and the extension of knowledge (1508). This keen observation shows clearly the stages of Wang's struggle. Huang added that in the development of his own philosophy Wang also went through three stages. In the first stage, before

---

[28] The others are Hsüeh Hsüan (1392-1464) and Hu Chü-jen (1434-84), both leaders of the Ch'eng-Chu School, and Ch'en Hsien-chang (Ch'en Po-sha, 1428-1500), leader of the idealistic Neo-Confucian movement, teacher of Chan Jo-shui.

[29] According to Wang himself, it was some thirty years. See below, sec. 124.

the Kiangsi days, that is, before 1517 (when Wang was forty-six),
he aimed at acquiring a foundation through sitting in meditation
and calming the mind in order to attain the equilibrium before the
feelings are aroused which is prerequisite for the harmony after the
feelings are aroused. After his Kiangsi days he concentrated on
teaching the doctrine of the extension of innate knowledge (*liang-
chih*), in which neither sitting in meditation nor calming the mind
is necessary because, as innate knowledge is extended, there is
neither a distinction between the equilibrium before the feelings
are aroused and the harmony after the feelings are aroused nor a
distinction between action and knowledge. Finally, after he returned
to Yüeh in 1522 when he was fifty-one, at all times he knew the
right to be right and the wrong to be wrong and whatever he said
was dictated by the original nature of his mind.[30]

These are eminently sound accounts of Wang's spiritual progress.
It should be pointed out, however, that Wang had propounded
the doctrine of unity of knowledge and action in 1509 and not after
1517 as Huang seems to suggest. Huang also gives the impression
that Wang's final stage of philosophical development was a matter
of state of mind, above and beyond the extension of innate knowledge. The fact is that Wang's philosophy reached its zenith in the
doctrine of the extension of innate knowledge in 1521 and that
from then until his death it remained the foundation stone of his
teachings. His emphasis was on extension, that is, action, and not
merely on a state of mind. This spirit was clearly expressed by his
disciple Ch'ien Te-hung. Actually Huang's accounts are a derivation
and a modification of Ch'ien's, according to which Wang went
through three stages in his learning. In his teachings, Ch'ien said,
Wang also went through three stages. In his Kuei-chou days he
taught his followers the doctrine of unity of knowledge and action.
From 1510 to 1517 he often taught them sitting in meditation. In
his Kiangsi days he concentrated on teaching the doctrine of the
extension of innate knowledge.[31] The important point here is that to
the end Wang emphasized the act of extending innate knowledge.
His own spiritual development may have culminated in a certain
state of mind but in his teaching he stressed the extension of innate
knowledge to the very end.

[30] *Ming-ju hsüeh-an,* 10:3b-4a.
[31] Ch'ien's preface to the *Yang-ming Hsien-sheng wen-lu,* in the *Wang Wen-ch'eng Kung
ch'üan-shu,* Introduction, p. 13a.

As already noted, Wang was utterly disappointed in Chu Hsi's theory, and opposed him at almost every point. The central issue was the doctrine of investigation of things. This was the issue that led Wang to return to the old text of the *Great Learning* as it is found in the *Book of Rites*. In this old text, the chapter on the sincerity of the will comes first. Chu Hsi shifted certain chapters to precede this chapter, saying that they represented the idea of the investigation of things and the extension of knowledge, an idea which was now lost, and he wrote a passage to "amend" the treatise. In other words, Chu Hsi put the investigation of things ahead of the sincerity of the will. Wang, however, claimed that the sincerity of the will was the necessary foundation on which investigation and extension must be based.[32] According to Ch'eng I, every blade of grass and every tree possesses principle and therefore should be investigated.[33] In his amendment of the *Great Learning,* Chu Hsi said, "We must investigate the principles of all things we come into contact with, for the intelligent mind of man is certainly formed to know, and there is not a single thing in which its principles do not inhere.... For this reason, the first step in the education of the adult is to instruct the learner, in regard to all things in the world, to proceed from what knowledge he has of their principles, and investigate further until he reaches the limit. After exerting himself in this way for a long time, he will one day achieve a wide and far-reaching penetration."

For more than two centuries this was accepted as an unalterable formula in the process of learning. Wang, however, rejected the investigation of all things as a hopeless task.[34] Moreover, Chu Hsi's theory was that the mind should go to things to investigate principles. This is to consider principles as external, an idea entirely unacceptable to Wang.[35] He stated that it is absurd to say that the principle of filial piety, for example, exists in the parents for, if that were true, that principle would cease to be as soon as the parents die.[36] This doctrine is all the more objectionable because it separates the mind from principles. As Wang said, "To investigate the prin-

---

[32] See below, sec. 129. For Wang's other criticisms of Chu Hsi's rearrangement, see below, sec. 173.

[33] *I-shu,* 18:9a.

[34] See below, sec. 318.

[35] See below, secs. 173 and 201.

[36] See below, sec. 135.

ciples in things to the utmost as we come into contact with them
means to look in each individual thing for its so-called definite
principles. This means to apply one's mind to each individual thing
and look for principles in it. This is to divide the mind and
principle into two."[37] In Wang's view, this is absolutely contrary
to the truth, for according to him mind and principle are one.[38]
This theme, that mind is principle, recurs many times in the *Instructions for Practical Living*. Wang admitted that Chu Hsi also
considered principle to be in the mind when he said, "Although
principles are distributed throughout the ten thousand things . . .
actually they are not outside one's mind." But Wang then pointed
out that "these are but the two aspects of concentration and diversification" and that Chu Hsi's interpretation inevitably "opened the
way to the defect among scholars of regarding the mind and principles as two separate things."[39]

Moreover, as there is no principle outside the mind, there is no
thing outside it. To Wang a thing is nothing but the functioning
of the will. "When the will functions in the service of parents, then
serving parents is a thing (an actuality).... Wherever the will is
applied, there cannot be nothing. Where there is a particular will,
there is a particular thing corresponding to it, and where there is
no particular will, there will be no particular thing corresponding
to it."[40]

We can readily see that Wang and Chu are diametrically opposed.
To Chu there must be the principle of filial piety before there can be
the mind to practice it. Wang, on the other hand, held that the
principle of filial piety is nothing but the exercise of the mind and
therefore there must be first of all the mind.[41] Chu Hsi believed that
principles exist independently of the mind, whereas Wang insisted
that principles and the mind are identical. Actually, of course, Chu Hsi
was talking about principles of natural objects as well as moral action,
while Wang thought of moral actions alone. To Chu Hsi the
investigation of things requires an objective method, including both
induction and deduction, whereas Wang takes the investigation
of things to mean moral awakening. This is the reason why he

[37] *Ibid.*
[38] See below, secs. 32 and 140.
[39] See below, sec. 133.
[40] See below, sec. 137; see also sec. 6. The word *shih* means both "thing" and "event,"
"affair," or "matter."
[41] See below, secs. 133 and 135.

interpreted the word *ko* in the phrase *ko-wu* (the investigation of things) not as study and inquiry as Chu Hsi understood it but as "rectification," that is, "to eliminate what is incorrect in the mind and to preserve the correctness of the original substance."[42] In short, to investigate things is to do good and to remove evil.[43]

Philosophically Wang's position is weak because it entirely neglects objective study and confuses reality with value. Readers of the *Instructions for Practical Living* will realize that Wang's idealism is very naïve indeed. When he was asked, if nothing is external to the mind, what blossoming trees on the high mountains have to do with it, he merely said, "Before you look at these flowers, they and your mind are in the state of silent vacancy. As you come to look at them, their colors at once show up clearly."[44] But if Wang's philosophy is short in logical acumen, it is long in moral insight. To him the separation of the mind and the principle of things was not only a fallacy in theory but a moral calamity, because it led to "the devotion to external things and the neglect of the internal." Scholars who followed that doctrine were concerned only with "fragmentary, isolated details and broken pieces." Although they might become broad, they certainly lacked the essentials. They trifled with things and lost their purpose in life. This, to him, was the reason for the decline of the Confucian doctrine, which in turn brought on intellectual, political, and moral decay.[45]

These criticisms of Chu Hsi's system were not entirely new. They had been offered by Chu Hsi's own friend Lu Hsiang-shan (Lu Chiu-yüan, 1139-93).[46] The difference between Lu and Wang is that with Lu the dispute was chiefly academic, whereas with Wang it was an actual struggle to solve acute problems. This gives Wang's theory a vital and dynamic character which Lu's lacked. Lu and Wang are often spoken of together. The idealistic tendency in Neo-Confucianism which they present is often called the Lu-Wang School, in contrast to the rationalistic Neo-Confucianism of Ch'eng-

[42] See below, secs. 7, 85, and 174.
[43] See below, sec. 315.
[44] See below, sec. 275; see also sec. 337.
[45] See below, secs. 135 and 137.
[46] See *Hsiang-shan ch'üan-chi*, 2:7b-11b; 34:4b-5a, 24a-b. On the controversy between Chu and Lu, see Fung Yu-lan, *A History of Chinese Philosophy*, II, 585-92; Carsun Chang, *The Development of Neo-Confucian Thought* (New York, Bookman Associates, 1957), pp. 296-301; Huang Siu-chi, *Lu Hsiang-shan, a Twelfth Century Chinese Idealist Philosopher* (New Haven, American Oriental Society, 1944), pp. 75-86.

Chu. As a broad characterization this is correct. They both insisted that mind and principle are one, and they both emphasized knowing fundamentals as opposed to isolated details, it is true. Wang recognized that Lu taught that one should "devote one's effort to the area of human feelings and human affairs"[47] When he was asked what he thought of Lu, he said that since the eleventh century "there has been only Lu Hsiang-shan. But he was still somewhat crude."[48] He did not explain why Lu was crude, but the fact that he did not follow Lu blindly is quite clear. He almost never quoted Lu. However, he did publish Lu's works and, when he was a government official in Lu's native district, he ordered Lu's descendants exempt from conscript service and awarded them scholarships. This indicates that Wang held a great admiration for him. But where ideas were concerned, he told a friend that he both agreed and differed with Lu.[49] When he was asked about the controversy between Chu and Lu, he replied that it was more important to discuss wherein oneself is right or wrong than wherein Chu or Lu was right or wrong.[50] We cannot help but sense here Wang's spirit of independence. In fact, he once remarked that "the way of learning . . . is the task of creating something from nothing."[51] In a large measure he did just that, notably in his doctrines of the unity of knowledge and action and of the extension of innate knowledge.

The relationship between knowledge and action had been a perennial topic for discussion in the Confucian tradition. In the *Book of History* it is said that "it is not difficult to know but difficult to act."[52] Throughout his teachings Confucius (551-479 B.C.) had stressed the correspondence and equal importance of knowledge and action.[53] Ch'eng I also said that the extension of knowledge and actual demonstration should proceed simultaneously.[54] Chu Hsi, too, recognized the mutual dependence of knowledge and action. He said, "Knowledge and action always require each other. It is like a person who cannot walk without legs although he has eyes,

---

[47] See below, sec. 37.
[48] See below, sec. 205.
[49] *Wang Wen-ch'eng Kung ch'üan-shu*, 6:13a.
[50] See below, sec. 149.
[51] See below, sec. 115.
[52] "The Charge to Yüeh," pt. 2. Cf. trans. by Legge, *Shoo King*, p. 258.
[53] *Analects*, 5:9; 13:4; 14:4; 15:5; 18:8.
[54] *Ts'ui-yen*, 1:16a-b; also *I-shu*, 18:4a.

and who cannot see without eyes although he has legs."[55] He also said, "The efforts of both knowledge and action must be exerted to the utmost. As one knows more clearly, he acts more earnestly, and as he acts more earnestly, he knows more clearly."[56] But Wang struck a new note in declaring that they are not only closely related but are identical. He said, "Knowledge in its genuine and earnest aspect is action, and action in its intelligent and discriminating aspect is knowledge. At bottom the task of knowledge and action cannot be separated.... Knowledge is what constitutes action and unless it is acted on it cannot be called knowledge."[57] For evidence to support his contentions, he refers to such experiences as not knowing pain unless one suffers it or not knowing the taste of food until one actually eats it. "As soon as one sees that beautiful color," he said, "he has already loved it. It is not that he sees it first and then makes up his mind to love it.... Suppose we say that so-and-so knows filial piety and so-and-so knows brotherly respect. They must have actually practiced filial piety and brotherly respect before they can be said to know them. It will not do to say that they know filial piety and brotherly respect simply because they show them in words."[58]

The type of knowledge he referred to is clearly limited to personal experience and does not exhaust the whole realm of knowledge. But on his major premise that knowledge is a function of the will and that the will is action, the conclusion that knowledge is action is inevitable. As he said, "A man must have the desire for food before he knows the food. This desire to eat is the will; it is already the beginning of action."[59]

The radical difference between Wang and his predecessors, then, is that while they considered knowledge and action to be two things, he identified them as one. Chu Hsi, for example, clearly said that in terms of time knowledge is prior to action although in terms of value action is more important.[60] In contrast, Wang said, "I have said that knowledge is the direction for action and action the effort of knowledge, and that knowledge is the beginning of action and

---

[55] *Chu Tzu yü-lei*, 9:1a.
[56] *Ibid.*, 14:30a.
[57] See below, sec. 133.
[58] See below, sec. 5.
[59] See below, sec. 132.
[60] *Chu Tzu yü-lei*, 9:3a.

action the completion of knowledge."[61] The words "beginning" and "completion" may suggest a sequence in time, but Wang was careful to add that knowledge and action "should not be separated."[62] For as soon as there is the will, action has already begun, and if the will is sincere all that can be carried out is already contained in it. This is why the sincerity of the will is the foundation and must precede the investigation of things. If the will is sincere, the knowledge will naturally and easily be extended to the fullest extent. This is the doctrine of the extension of innate knowledge.

This doctrine is Wang's supreme philosophical achievement. It was attained at the age of fifty after several years of fighting the rebels and facing his political enemies. It was a product of painful experience and thorough soul-searching. As he himself said, "It was achieved from a hundred deaths and a thousand sufferings."[63] It is not merely a combination of the teaching of the extension of knowledge in the *Great Learning* and Mencius' (371-289 B.C.?) doctrine of innate knowledge.[64] It is a new understanding that the extension of knowledge is the very nature of man.

Wang describes innate knowledge in various terms. It is "the original substance of the mind," "the Principle of Nature," "the pure intelligence and clear consciousness of the mind," and the mind that is "always shining" and reflects things as things come without being stirred.[65] It is "the equilibrium before the feelings are aroused," "the substance that is absolutely quiet and inactive," and "the state of being broad and extremely impartial."[66] It is "where the Principle of Nature is clear and intelligent."[67] It is "man's root which is intelligent and is grown by nature. It naturally grows and grows without cease."[68] It is the "spirit of creation" and it "produces heaven and earth, spiritual beings, and the Lord."[69] Since it permeates and penetrates all existence, even trees and grass possess it.[70]

---

[61] See below, sec. 5.
[62] See below, sec. 26,
[63] *Wang Wen-ch'eng Kung ch'üan-shu,* Prefaces, p. 15a.
[64] *Great Learning,* ch. 5; *Book of Mencius,* 7A:15.
[65] See below, secs. 152, 135, 137, and 151, respectively.
[66] See below, sec. 155.
[67] See below, sec. 169.
[68] See below, sec. 244.
[69] See below, sec. 261.
[70] See below, sec. 274.

It depends on nothing outside[71] and it "does not come from hearing and seeing."[72]

While these descriptions do not define innate knowledge, it can simply be equated with the Principle of Nature. And the Principle of Nature, from the Sung Neo-Confucians down, simply means the principle of right and wrong. In the "Doctrine in Four Axioms" it is stated that "the faculty of innate knowledge is to know good and evil."[73] To extend innate knowledge therefore means to be "completely identified with the Principle of Nature" so that without being in the least influenced by selfish desires one knows right to be right and wrong to be wrong instantly and spontaneously. When Wang was asked how to extend innate knowledge, he replied, "Your innate knowledge is your own standard. When you direct your thought your innate knowledge knows that it is right if it is right and wrong if it is wrong. You cannot keep anything from it. Just don't try to deceive it but sincerely and truly follow it in whatever you do. Then the good will be preserved and evil will be removed. What security and joy there is in this! This is the true secret of the investigation of things and the real effort of the extension of knowledge."[74]

The instantaneous realization may seem similar to the sudden enlightenment of Zen Buddhism. Wang once said that what the Buddhists call the original nature at the time when one thinks of neither good nor evil is what the Confucian school calls innate knowledge.[75] In the "Doctrine in Four Axioms"[76] he said that in the original substance of the mind there is no distinction of good and evil. Forty or more Buddhist expressions and stories appear in the *Instructions for Practical Living*. Moreover, at one stage in his teaching Wang advocated sitting in meditation, and later some of his followers drifted into Zen Buddhism. For these reasons Wang has been accused of being a Buddhist in Confucian disguise. Actually, although his attitude toward Buddhism was not as hostile as that of other Neo-Confucians, his criticism of it is nonetheless severe. He not only attacked the Buddhists for their escape from social responsi-

[71] See below, sec. 8.
[72] See below, sec. 168.
[73] See below, sec. 315.
[74] See below, sec. 206.
[75] See below, sec. 162.
[76] See below, sec. 315.

bilities, for their inability to handle human affairs, and for their selfishness;[77] he also criticized their failure to handle the mind itself. In spite of all their protestations, Wang said, the Buddhists can never get away from attachment to phenomena. He said, "The Taoist talk about vacuity is motivated by a desire for nourishing everlasting life, and the Buddhist talk about non-being is motivated by the desire to escape from the sorrowful sea of life and death. In both cases certain selfish ideas have been added to the original substance [of the mind], which thereby loses the true character of vacuity and is obstructed."[78] Thus he attacked the very foundation of Buddhism.

The extension of innate knowledge is also different from the method of moral cultivation of the Sung Neo-Confucians. Their formula may be summed up by the dictum, "Seriousness is to straighten the internal life. Righteousness is to square the external life," which Ch'eng I used as the basis of his philosophy and which other Sung and Ming Neo-Confucians accepted as a sacred formula.[79] This is essentially a quietistic process. In fact, most Sung and Ming Neo-Confucians practiced sitting in meditation along with efforts at seriousness and righteousness. Quite aside from the separation of the internal and the external,[80] a separation which Wang would never tolerate, its quietistic character makes the Sung Neo-Confucian effort quite different from Wang's. His extension of knowledge not only requires absolute sincerity of the will, which may be equated with seriousness, and the sense of right and wrong, which may be equated with righteousness; it also calls for vigorous and active effort. It requires self-mastery and self-examination. It requires making up the mind. Most important of all, it requires "polishing and training in the actual affairs of life." One must be alert and vigilant all the time, and there must be a sense of urgency and earnest exertion of effort at every instant. This is what is meant by seeing to it that "one must always be doing something."[81] In this task, one should not lean forward or backward, or be perturbed or

[77] See below, secs. 101, 162, 236, and 270.
[78] See below, sec. 269. For a discussion of this question, see Wing-tsit Chan, "How Buddhistic Is Wang Yang-ming?", Philosophy East and West, XII (no. 2, 1962).
[79] Book of Changes, commentary on hexagram no. 2. Cf. trans. by Legge, Yi King, p. 420. For Ch'eng, see I-shu, 1:1b, 2A:9a, 11:1a, 7b, etc.
[80] Ch'eng nevertheless claimed that they were combined. Ibid., 11:2a.
[81] Book of Mencius, 2A:2.

hindered by an instant of evil thought. When the will is completely sincere and innate knowledge is fully extended, the moral and social life will be developed to its fullest extent. When this point is reached, one will become a sage, who "forms one body with all things."

This idea of forming one body with all things is a continuation of a long Chinese tradition. Many ancient philosophers taught it and it became especially strong among the Sung Neo-Confucians. Chang Tsai (Chang Heng-ch'ü, 1020-77) in his *Hsi-ming* (Western inscription) calls Heaven and Earth father and mother and all men brothers.[82] Ch'eng Hao (Ch'eng Ming-tao, 1032-85) said, "The man of humanity forms one body with all things without any differentiation."[83] His brother Ch'eng I also said, "The man of humanity regards Heaven and Earth and all things as one body."[84] From the time of Chang Tsai on, all Neo-Confucians have elaborated on or at least repeated the idea. But the strongest champion of the doctrine was Wang. He said, "The great man regards Heaven and Earth and the myriad things as one body. He regards the world as one family and the country as one person. As to those who make a cleavage between objects and distinguish between the self and others, they are small men. That the great man can regard Heaven, Earth, and the myriad things as one body is not because he deliberately wants to do so, but because it is natural to the humane nature of his mind that he does so."[85] This is the opening passage of the *Inquiry on the "Great Learning*," which, along with the "Doctrine in Four Axioms" and the essay on "Pulling Up the Root and Stopping Up the Source,"[86] constitutes one of the three important works which crown Wang's philosophy. The idea of forming one body with all things is equally central in the latter essay. In fact, this conception is even more vital and concrete here, for it concerns not only ethics, but government and history, as well. The difference between Wang's idea of forming one body and that of the Sung Neo-Confucians is that in his case the idea is tied up with the actual human situation and has a dynamic force behind it.

[82] *Hsi-ming,* in the *Chang Heng-ch'ü chi,* 1:1a-b.
[83] *I-shu,* 2A:3a.
[84] *Ts'ui-yen,* 1:7b.
[85] See below, "Inquiry on the *Great Learning*," second paragraph.
[86] See below, secs. 142-43, and 315, and "Inquiry on the *Great Learning*"; see also the special introductions to these sections and to the "Inquiry."

What did Wang's philosophy accomplish? It presented the Chu Hsi philosophy with a strong challenge, which contributed not a little to its health. It set Chinese thought free. It created a new philosophy and it restored Confucianism to its central emphasis on purpose and action. Wang's followers spread over all parts of China and his system dominated China for some 150 years, to the end of Ming.

Unfortunately the movement contained certain elements of weakness. There was never any unity among his followers. In his accounts of the Yang-ming school, Huang Tsung-hsi divided them into seven different branches.[87] Diversity should lead to development, but among the Wang followers there was mostly confusion. Take the interpretation of innate knowledge, for example. Each follower understood it in his own way, so that the central basis of the Wang philosophy lacked unity and thereby strength. Furthermore, toward the end of the movement there were some who justified their irresponsibility as the extension of their innate knowledge. Since having the desire was considered action, the lazy defended themselves by saying that action was already complete in the mind. Instead of adhering to firm purpose and vigorous effort to do good, they gave free rein to their passions. Drunkards were considered sages. Thus forming one body with all things came to mean acceptance of everything without any standard. By the seventeenth century, when the empirical and critical philosophy emerged, the Yang-ming movement was eclipsed.

However, Wang's philosophy was too dynamic and too challenging to disappear from the scene completely. Its emphasis on sincere purpose and concrete action never ceased to inspire the Chinese, and in the twentieth century it has exerted considerable influence on such leaders as Sun Yat-sen (1866-1925) and such thinkers as Liang Ch'i-ch'ao (1873-1929) and Hsiung Shih-li (1885-   ).[88]

Wang's philosophy was introduced into Japan by a Japanese monk, Keigo Ryōan (1425-1515), who visited Wang about 1513.

---

[87] *Ming-ju hsüeh-an,* chs. 10-36.

[88] For Wang's influence on modern thinkers, see O. Brière, *Fifty Years of Chinese Philosophy, 1898-1950* (London, Allen and Unwin, 1956) *passim*; Chu Chi-hsien, *A Study of the Development of Sun Yat-sen's Philosophical Ideas* (Ann Arbor, University Microfilms, 1950), pp. 106-33; Clarence Burton Day, *The Philosophers of China, Classical and Contemporary* (New York, Philosophical Library, 1962), pp. 263-73, 323-30; and Wing-tsit Chan, *Religious Trends in Modern China* (New York, Columbia University Press, 1953), pp. 30-43.

There it grew to be a prominent branch of Neo-Confucianism through the work of such great thinkers as Nakae Tōju (1608-48), Kumazawa Banzan (1619-91), and Sakuma Shōzan (1811-64).[89] Although it never matched the prestige or influence of the Chu Hsi School (*Shushigaku*), nevertheless because of the simplicity and easiness of its philosophy, its emphasis on direct action and sharpness of mind, and its spirit of dedication, it had a special attraction for the Japanese, who admired these qualities because of their Zen Buddhist and military traditions. Furthermore, Wang's brilliant career was envied by those who had dedicated themselves to the building of a glorious and strong Japan. Consequently the school (*Yōmeigaku*) attracted considerable following and produced such leaders as Saigō Takamori (1827-77) and Ōkubo Toshimichi (1830-78),[90] who transformed their country and laid the foundation for modern Japan. They are shining examples of how a dynamic philosophy could be translated into noble achievements when applied in the right way.

All of Wang's fundamental doctrines are contained in the *Instructions for Practical Living*. This is a collection of conversations and letters in three parts compiled by Wang's disciples, Nan Ta-chi and Ch'ien Te-hung. Comments on its importance, its history, its title, and its text are given elsewhere,[91] as are separate introductions to two of its sections, namely, "Pulling Up the Root and Stopping Up the Source" (secs. 142-43) and "Doctrine in Four Axioms" (sec. 315). Suffice it to say that the conversations and letters are intimate and vital communications between teacher and disciple, between friend and friend. They are meant to be carried out in action.

[89] For the ideas of these men, see Ryusaku Tsunoda, Wm. Theodore de Bary, and Donald Keene, eds., *Sources of Japanese Tradition* (New York, Columbia University Press, 1958), pp. 378-92, 603-16.

[90] See *ibid.*, pp. 654-62.

[91] See above, Preface, and Translator's Note; see below, Ch'ien Te-hung's preface preceding sec. 130, and postscript following sec. 343. See also, below, Bibliographical and Historical Note on the *Ch'uan-hsi lu*.

Instructions for Practical Living

Instructions for Practical Living, Part I

CONVERSATIONS RECORDED BY HSÜ AI[1]
(Sections 1-14)

Introduction by Hsü Ai

Concerning the doctrine of the investigation of things and so forth in the *Great Learning*,[2] our Teacher has in all cases regarded what is set forth in the old text[3] as correct, the text which former scholars[4] thought to be wrong.[5] I was shocked when I first heard him, then became skeptical, then devoted all my energy and thought to it,

---

[1] His courtesy name was Yüeh-jen and his literary name was Heng-shan. He was born in 1487 and died in 1518 according to the chronology in the *Wang Wen-ch'eng Kung ch'üan-shu*, or in 1517 according to the *Ming-ju hsüeh-an*, 11:3a. He was the husband of Wang's sister. When Wang was released from prison and was about to leave for his post in primitive Kuei-chou in 1507, Hsü became his first pupil. He rose to be an assistant divisional chief in the department of public works. The following conversations took place in 1512-13, when he accompanied Wang on his trip home for a visit before taking up new official duties at Nanking. In this period Wang's teaching aimed at restraint and discipline and therefore stressed sitting in meditation and calm thinking. Hsü faithfully put these doctrines into practice although he did not theorize about them. However, even though Wang had not yet preached his cardinal doctrine of "extending one's innate knowledge of the good to the utmost," Hsü mentioned the subject in sec. 8, thus indicating that he understood his master even before his thoughts were fully developed. No wonder he has often been compared with Yen Hui (521-490 B.C.), the most understanding pupil of Confucius. Yen Hui died at thirty-two; Hsü at thirty-one. For an account of Hsü, see *Ming-ju hsüeh-an*, 11:3a-4b.

[2] For English translations, see "The Great Learning," trans. by E. R. Hughes, in his *The Great Learning and the Mean-in-Action* (New York, Dutton, 1943), pp. 105-44; "The Great Learning," trans. by James Legge, in his *The Chinese Classics*, I, 355-81; or "The Great Learning," trans. by Lin Yutang, in his *The Wisdom of Confucius* (New York, The Modern Library, 1938), pp. 100-34.

[3] Traditionally constituting a chapter of the *Book of Rites*. Its chapter order was rearranged by Ch'eng I and Chu Hsi, the order followed in both Lin's and Legge's translations, while Hughes follows the chapter order of the old text, that is, ch. 42 of the *Book of Rites*. See below, sec. 129.

[4] Notably Ch'eng I (Ch'eng I-ch'uan, 1033-1107) and Chu Hsi (1130-1200).

[5] And rearranged the order of its chapters.

examining it with extensive reference and consultation and raising questions with our Teacher, and finally came to realize that the doctrines of our Teacher are as true as water is cold and as fire is hot, and can surely "wait a hundred generations for a sage to confirm them without a doubt."⁶

Our Teacher is endowed with intelligence and wisdom. But he is at peace, happy, self-possessed, and simple, and pays no attention to his appearance. Because as a young man he was unrestrained and unconventional, drifted into the practice of writing flowery compositions, and studied Buddhism and Taoism off and on, when people suddenly heard this theory of his, they all looked upon it as an attempt to be novel and different, without careful deliberation. They did not realize that after having been in a barbarous land for [nearly] three years,⁷ living in hardship and nourished by tranquillity, our Teacher has achieved a refinement and singleness of mind⁸ which has definitely penetrated the sphere of the sages and has arrived at the point of great perfection and absolute correctness. I have been exposed to his teachings day and night. I can only see that the way of our Teacher, in our immediate contact with it, seems to be easy, but the more we look up toward it, the higher it becomes. Look at it and it seems crude, but the more you go into it, the more refined it is. Approach it and it seems near, but the more you try to accomplish it, the more inexhaustible it becomes. After more than ten years I have not been able to penetrate its depth. And yet many gentlemen of the day, who have had no more than a casual acquaintance with our Teacher, or who have not even heard his voice, or who have already made up their minds to belittle him and to be angry with him, imagine things and draw prejudiced conclusions on the basis of a chance conversation or hearsay. How will that do? As to our Teacher's followers, when they heard his teachings, they

⁶ *Doctrine of the Mean*, ch. 29. For English translations, see "Central Harmony," trans. by Ku Hung-ming, in Lin Yutang, ed., *The Wisdom of Confucius*, pp. 104-34; "The Golden Mean of Tsesze," in Lin Yutang, ed., *The Wisdom of China and India* (New York, Random House, 1942), pp. 845-65; "The Doctrine of the Mean," trans. by James Legge, in his *The Chinese Classics*, I, 382-434; or "The Mean-in-Action," trans. by E. R. Hughes, in his *The Great Learning and The Mean-in-Action*, pp. 145-66.

⁷ As a punishment Wang was banished to primitive Kuei-chou in remote southwest China to be a minor official from 1508 to 1510.

⁸ Referring to the *Book of History*, "Counsels of the Great Yü." Cf. trans. by James Legge, *The Shoo King*, p. 61.

often got only a third of them and missed the rest, seeing, as it were, only the sex and color of the horse while overlooking its capacity of a thousand *li*.[9] I have therefore recorded what I have heard from him over the years, to show privately to like-minded friends, to compare notes and to correct what I have taken down, so that, I believe, we shall not do injustice to our Teacher's teachings.

Pupil Hsü Ai

1. I asked: "Chu Hsi said that the phrase 'in loving the people' (*ch'in-min*) in the *Great Learning* should read 'in renovating the people' (*hsin-min*). Since in a later section of the book it says, 'arouse the people to become new,'[1] he seems to have some evidence for his contention. Do you also have evidence for believing that the phrase 'in loving the people' in the old text should be followed?"

The Teacher said, "The word *hsin* in the phrase 'arouse the people to become new (*hsin*)' means the people become new themselves. It is different in meaning from the same word in the phrase 'in renovating the people.' How can it be accepted as evidence? The term 'arouse the people to become' parallels the term 'love' but does not mean the same. The passages that follow in the text on bringing order to the state and peace to the world do not amplify the meaning of renovation. On the contrary, these passages in the text— 'Rulers deemed worthy what they deemed worthy and loved what they loved, while the common people enjoyed what they enjoyed and benefited from their beneficial arrangements', 'Act as if you were watching over an infant', and the ruler 'likes what people like and dislikes what the people dislike. That is what is

---

[9] A *li* is about one third of a mile. The story about the horse is found in the *Huai-nan Tzu*, 12:9a-b. According to the account there, Duke Mu (r. 659-619 B.C.) of Ch'in, on the recommendation of his minister, sent an expert in search of a steed. After three months the expert returned, saying that he had found a yellow male. When the horse came, it proved to be a black female. The duke was displeased and asked his minister about it. The minister replied, "What the expert saw was the secret of Nature. He grasped the essential factor and ignored the coarse element." The horse proved to be a horse of a thousand *li*. See Evan Morgan, trans., *Tao, the Great Luminant* (Shanghai, Kelly and Walsh, 1934), p. 119.

[1] *Great Learning*, ch. 2. Although it was opposed by Wang Yang-ming, Chu Hsi's chapter order instead of the order in the old text is used in these footnotes, because many of Chu Hsi's commentaries are referred to here.

meant by being a parent of the people'[2] —all express the meaning of love. The meaning of 'loving the people' is the same as in Mencius' saying, 'The superior man is affectionate to his parents and humane to all people.'[3] To love is the same as to be humane. Because the common people did not love one another, Emperor Shun[4] appointed Hsieh to be minister of education and to institute with great seriousness the five teachings.[5] This was Emperor Shun's way to love the people. The sentence 'He was able to manifest his lofty character'[6] means the same as 'manifesting the clear character,' and the statements there, 'to love the nine classes of his kindred,' 'to have harmony,' and 'to have unity and accord,'[7] mean the same as 'loving the people' and 'manifesting the clear character to the world.' Also, Confucius said, 'The superior man cultivates himself so as to give the common people security and peace.'[8] Cultivating oneself means manifesting the clear character and giving the common people security and peace means loving the people. Reading the phrase as loving the people expresses both the ideas of educating and feeding the people. Reading it to mean renovating the people, however, seems to be one-sided."

2. I said, "With reference to the sentence, 'Only after knowing what to abide in can one be calm' in the *Great Learning*, Chu Hsi considered that "all events and things possess in them a definite principle."[9] This seems to contradict your theory."

The Teacher said, "To seek the highest good [the abiding point] in individual events and things is to regard righteousness as external.[10]

[2] *Ibid.*, chs. 3, 9, 10 respectively.
[3] *Book of Mencius*, 7A:45.
[4] Legendary sage-emperor of the third millennium B.C.
[5] For the father to be righteous, the mother to be affectionate, the older brother to be friendly, the younger brother to be respectful, and the son to be filially pious. See *Book of History*, "Canon of Shun." Cf. trans by Legge, *Shoo King*, p. 44.
[6] *Ibid.*, "Canon of Yao." Cf. trans. by Legge, *Shoo King*, p. 17.
[7] *Ibid.*
[8] *Analects*, 14:45.
[9] The text of the *Great Learning*, and Chu Hsi's *Ta-hsüeh huo-wen*, 1702 ed., p. 15a.
[10] *Book of Mencius*, 6A:4. Throughout the *Instructions for Practical Living*, Wang attacks again and again the doctrine that righteousness and other moral principles are to be found in external things, a doctrine advocated by Kao Tzu (c. 420-c. 350 B.C.), whom Mencius vigorously denounced.

The highest good is the original substance of the mind. It is no other than manifesting one's clear character to the point of refinement and singleness of mind. And yet it is not separated from events and things. When Chu Hsi said in his commentary that [manifesting the clear character is] 'the realization of the Principle of Nature to the fullest extent without an iota of selfish human desire,'[11] he got the point."

3. I said, "If the highest good is to be sought only in the mind, I am afraid not all principles of things in the world will be covered."

The Teacher said, "The mind *is* principle. Is there any affair in the world outside of the mind? Is there any principle outside of the mind?"

I said, "In filial piety in serving one's parents, in loyalty in serving one's ruler, in faithfulness in intercourse with friends, or in humanity in governing the people, there are many principles which I believe should not be left unexamined."

The Teacher said with a sigh, "This idea has been obscuring the understanding of people for a long time. Can they be awakened by one word? However, I shall comment along the line of your question. For instance, in the matter of serving one's parents, one cannot seek for the principle of filial piety in the parent. In serving one's ruler, one cannot seek for the principle of loyalty in the ruler. In the intercourse with friends and in governing the people, one cannot seek for the principles of faithfulness and humanity in friends and the people. They are all in the mind, that is all, for the mind and principle are identical. When the mind is free from the obscuration of selfish desires, it is the embodiment of the Principle of Nature, which requires not an iota added from the outside. When this mind, which has become completely identical with the Principle of Nature, is applied and arises to serve parents, there is filial piety; when it arises to serve the ruler, there is loyalty; when it arises to deal with friends or to govern the people, there are faithfulness and humanity. The main thing is for the mind to make an effort to get rid of selfish human desires and preserve the Principle of Nature."

I said, "Having heard what you said, sir, I begin to understand.

[11] Chu Hsi, *Ta-hsüeh chang-chü*, commenting on the opening sentence of the text of the *Great Learning*.

However, the old theory still lingers in my mind, from which I cannot entirely get away. Take, for example, the matter of serving one's parents. The filial son is to care for their comfort both in winter and summer, and to inquire after their health every morning and evening.[12] These things involve many actual details. Should we not endeavor to investigate them?"

The Teacher said, "Why not endeavor to investigate them? The main thing is to have a basis. The main thing is to endeavor to investigate them by ridding the mind of selfish human desires and preserving the Principle of Nature. For instance, to investigate the provision of warmth for parents in the winter is none other than the extension of the filial piety of this mind to the utmost, for fear that a trifle of human selfish desires might creep in, and to investigate the provision of coolness for parents in the summer is none other than the extension of the filial piety of this mind to the utmost, for fear that a trifle of selfish human desires might creep in. It is merely to investigate this mind. If the mind is free from selfish human desires and has become completely identical with the Principle of Nature, and if it is the mind that is sincere in its filial piety to parents, then in the winter it will naturally think of the cold of parents and seek a way to provide warmth for them, and in the summer it will naturally think of the heat of parents and seek a way to provide coolness for them. These are all offshoots of the mind that is sincere in its filial piety. Nevertheless, there must first be such a mind before there can be these offshoots. Compared to the tree, the mind with sincere filial piety is the root, whereas the offshoots are the leaves and branches. There must first be roots before there can be leaves and branches. One does not seek to find leaves and branches and then cultivate the root. The *Book of Rites* says, 'A filial son who loves his parents deeply is sure to have a peaceful disposition. Having a peaceful disposition, he will surely have a happy expression. And having a happy expression, he will surely have a pleasant countenance.'[13] There must be deep love as the root and then the rest will naturally follow like this."

[12] Quoting the *Book of Rites*, "Summary of Ceremonies." Cf. trans. by Legge, *Li Ki*, ch. 1, p. 67.

[13] *Book of Rites*, "The Meaning of Sacrifices." Cf. trans. by Legge, *Li Ki*, ch. 21, pp. 215-16.

4. Cheng Chao-shuo[14] said, "In some cases the highest good must be sought in events and things."

The Teacher said, "The highest good is none other than the mind which has completely identified with the Principle of Nature in its fullest extent. What is the need for seeking it in things and events? Suppose you cite some instances."

Chao-shuo said, "Take serving parents. What the details in providing warmth or coolness for them are and what the proper ways of supporting them are[15] must be investigated and the correct answers found. Only then will the highest good be achieved. This is why the effort to study extensively, to inquire accurately, to think carefully, and to sift clearly is necessary."[16]

The Teacher said, "If it were only the details of providing warmth or coolness or the proper way of support, they can be entirely discussed in a day or two. What is the need to study, inquire, think, and sift? However, in order for the mind to be completely identified with the Principle of Nature in its fullest extent, when providing parents with warmth or coolness or when supporting them, there must be this effort to learn, ask, think, and sift. Otherwise, an infinitesimal mistake in the beginning will lead to an infinite error at the end. This is why even a sage needs the teachings of refinement and singleness of mind. If the highest good means no more than having the details correct, then dressing like an actor and acting out these details correctly on the stage would be called the highest good."

I gained further understanding on that day.

5. I did not understand the Teacher's doctrine of the unity of knowledge and action and debated it back and forth with Huang Tsung-hsien[17] and Ku Wei-hsien[18] without coming to any conclu-

---

[14] His name was I-ch'u. He obtained a "presented scholar" degree in 1505.

[15] Words of Ch'eng I quoted by Chu Hsi in his *Ta-hsüeh huo-wen*, p. 50a-b.

[16] These steps are taught in the *Doctrine of the Mean*, ch. 20. In these footnotes, Chu Hsi's chapter order is used. See n. 1, above.

[17] The courtesy name of Huang Wan (1477-1551), whose literary name was Chiu-an. A grandson of a vice-minister, he obtained a "presented scholar" degree and later became minister of rites. His daughter was married to Wang Yang-ming's son. For an account of Huang Wan, see *Ming-ju hsüeh-an*, 13:5b-6b, where his courtesy name is given as Shu-hsien.

[18] The courtesy name of Ku Ying-hsiang (1483-1565), whose literary name was Lo-hsi. He obtained a "presented scholar" degree in 1505. Introduced by

sion. Therefore I took the matter to the Teacher. The Teacher said,
"Give an example and let me see." I said, "For example, there are
people who know that parents should be served with filial piety
and elder brothers with respect but cannot put these things into
practice. This shows that knowledge and action are clearly two
different things."

The Teacher said, "The knowledge and action you refer to are
already separated by selfish desires and are no longer knowledge
and action in their original substance. There have never been people
who know but do not act. Those who are supposed to know but
do not act simply do not yet know. When sages and worthies taught
people about knowledge and action, it was precisely because they
wanted them to restore the original substance, and not simply to do
this or that and be satisfied. Therefore the *Great Learning* points to
true knowledge and action for people to see, saying, they are 'like
loving beautiful colors and hating bad odors.'[19] Seeing beautiful
colors appertains to knowledge, while loving beautiful colors
appertains to action. However, as soon as one sees that beautiful
color, he has already loved it. It is not that he sees it first and then
makes up his mind to love it. Smelling a bad odor appertains to
knowledge, while hating a bad odor appertains to action. However,
as soon as one smells a bad odor, he has already hated it. It is not
that he smells it first and then makes up his mind to hate it. A person
with his nose stuffed up does not smell the bad odor even if he sees
a malodorous object before him, and so he does not hate it. This
amounts to not knowing bad odor. Suppose we say that so-and-so
knows filial piety and so-and-so knows brotherly respect. They must
have actually practiced filial piety and brotherly respect before they
can be said to know them. It will not do to say that they know filial
piety and brotherly respect simply because they show them in words.
Or take one's knowledge of pain. Only after one has experienced
pain can one know pain. The same is true of cold or hunger. How
can knowledge and action be separated? This is the original sub-

Huang Tsung-hsien, he visited and became a pupil of Wang Yang-ming.
After the campaign to suppress a rebellion, he became minister of justice and
was very famous. An expert in mathematics and astronomy, he died at the age
of eighty-three. As Huang Tsung-hsi (1610-95) has remarked in his *Ming-ju
hsüeh-an*, 14:4a, Ku Ying-hsiang departed from the teaching of Wang Yang-
ming in holding that knowledge and action were not identical.

[19] *Great Learning*, ch. 6.

stance of knowledge and action, which have not been separated by selfish desires. In teaching people, the Sage insisted that only this can be called knowledge. Otherwise, this is not yet knowledge. This is serious and practical business. What is the objective of desperately insisting on knowledge and action being two different things? And what is the objective of my insisting that they are one? What is the use of insisting on their being one or two unless one knows the basic purpose of the doctrine?"

I said, "In saying that knowledge and action are two different things, the ancients intended to have people distinguish and understand them, so that on the one hand they make an effort to know and, on the other, make an effort to act, and only then can the effort find any solution."

The Teacher said, "This is to lose sight of the basic purpose of the ancients. I have said that knowledge is the direction for action and action the effort of knowledge, and that knowledge is the beginning of action and action the completion of knowledge. If this is understood, then when only knowledge is mentioned, action is included, and when only action is mentioned, knowledge is included. The reason why the ancients talked about knowledge and action separately is that there are people in the world who are confused and act on impulse without any sense of deliberation or self-examination, and who thus only behave blindly and erroneously. Therefore it is necessary to talk about knowledge to them before their action becomes correct. There are also those who are intellectually vague and undisciplined and think in a vacuum. They are not at all willing to make the effort of concrete practice. They only pursue shadows and echoes, as it were. It is therefore necessary to talk about action to them before their knowledge becomes true. The ancient teachers could not help talking this way in order to restore balance and avoid any defect. If we understand this motive, then a single word [either knowledge or action] will do.

"But people today distinguish between knowledge and action and pursue them separately, believing that one must know before he can act. They will discuss and learn the business of knowledge first, they say, and wait till they truly know before they put their knowledge into practice. Consequently, to the last day of life, they will never act and also will never know. This doctrine of knowledge first and action later is not a minor disease and it did not come about only yesterday. My present advocacy of the unity of knowledge and action is precisely the medicine for that disease. The doctrine is not my baseless imagination, for it is the original substance of knowledge and action that they are one. Now that we know this basic purpose, it will do no harm to talk about them separately, for they are only one. If the basic purpose is not understood, however, even if we say they are one, what is the use? It is just idle talk."

6. I said, "Yesterday when I heard your teaching about abiding in the highest good, I realized I had some grasp of this task. But I still feel that your teaching does not agree with Chu Hsi's doctrine of the investigation of things."

The Teacher said, "The investigation of things is the work of abiding in the highest good. Once we know what the highest good is, we know how to investigate things."

I said, "Yesterday when I examined Chu Hsi's doctrine of the investigation of things in the light of your teaching, I seemed to understand it in general. But I am still not clear in my mind, because Chu Hsi's doctrine, after all, has the support of what is called 'refinement and singleness of mind' in the *Book of History*, 'extensive study of literature and self-restraint by the rules of propriety' in the *Analects*, and 'exerting one's mind to the utmost and knowing one's nature' in the *Book of Mencius*."[20]

The Teacher said, "Tzu-hsia [507-420 B.C.] had strong faith in the Sage whereas Tseng Tzu [505-c.436 B.C.] turned to seek the highest good in himself.[21] It is good to have strong faith, of course, but it is not as real and concrete as seeking in oneself. Since you have not understood this idea, why should you cling to Chu Hsi's old tradition and not seek what is right? Even with Chu Hsi, while he respected and believed in Master Ch'eng I, he would not carelessly follow him whenever he came to something he could not understand.[22] The teachings of refinement and singleness, extensive study and self-restraint, and exerting the mind to the utmost are basically harmonious with my doctrine. Only you have not thought about it.

"Chu Hsi's teaching on the investigation of things is forced,

---

[20] Referring to the *Book of History*, "Counsels of the Great Yü." Cf. trans. by Legge, *Shoo King*, p. 61; *Analects*, 6:25, and *Book of Mencius*, 7A:1 respectively.

[21] Quoting Chu Hsi, *Meng Tzu chi-chu*, ch. 3, comment on *Book of Mencius*, 2A:2.

[22] See, for example, *Chu Tzu yü-lei*, 69:22a.

arbitrary, and far-fetched, and is not what the investigation of things originally meant. Refinement is the work of achieving singleness and extensive study the work of achieving restraint. Since you already understand the principle of the unity of knowledge and action, this can be explained in one word. As to exerting one's mind to the utmost, knowing one's nature, and knowing Heaven, these are the acts of those who are born with such knowledge and practice it naturally and easily. Preserving the mind, nourishing one's nature, and serving Heaven are the acts of those who learn them through study and practice them for their advantage. To maintain one's single-mindedness regardless of longevity or brevity of life, and to cultivate one's personal life while waiting for fate to take its own course, are the acts of those who learn through hard work and practice them with effort and difficulty.[23] But Chu Hsi wrongly interpreted the doctrine of the investigation of things. Because he reversed the above order, and thought that the higher attainments of exerting one's mind to the utmost and knowing one's nature are equivalent to the investigation of things and the extension of knowledge, he required the beginner to perform the acts of those who are born to know and who practice naturally and easily. How can that be done?"

I asked, "Why are exerting the mind to the utmost and knowing one's nature the acts of those who are born to know and who practice naturally and easily?"

The Teacher said, "Our nature is the substance of the mind and Heaven is the source of our nature. To exert one's mind to the utmost is the same as fully developing one's nature. Only those who are absolutely sincere can fully develop their nature and 'know the transforming and nourishing process of Heaven and Earth.'[24] Those who merely preserve their minds, on the other hand, have not yet exerted them to the utmost. Knowing Heaven is the same as knowing the affairs of a district or a county, which is what the titles prefect and magistrate mean. It is a matter within one's own function, and it means that one in his moral character has already become one with Heaven. Serving Heaven, on the other hand, is like the serving of the parents by the son and the serving of the ruler by the minister. It must be done seriously and reverently to please them if

---

[23] Quoting alternately from the *Book of Mencius*, 7A:1, and the *Doctrine of the Mean*, ch. 20.

[24] Quoting the *Doctrine of the Mean*, ch. 22.

it is to be perfect. Even then, one is still separated from Heaven. This is the difference between a sage [who exerts the mind to the utmost and knows Heaven] and the worthies [who preserve their minds and serve Heaven].

"As to allowing no double-mindedness regardless of longevity or brevity of life, it is to teach the student to do good with single-mindedness, and not to allow success or failure, longevity or brevity of life, to shake his determination to do good, but instead to cultivate his personal life and wait for fate to take its own course, realizing that success and failure, or longevity and brevity of life, are matters of fate and one need not unnecessarily allow them to disturb his mind. Although those who serve Heaven are separated from Heaven, they nevertheless already see Heaven right in front of them. Waiting for fate to take its own course, however, means that one has not yet seen Heaven but is still waiting for it, so to speak. It is the beginner's first step in making up his mind, involving a certain amount of effort and difficulty. But Chu Hsi reversed the order, so that the student has no place to start."

I said, "Yesterday when I heard your teaching, I vaguely realized that one's effort must follow this procedure. Now that I have heard what you said, I have no further doubt. Last night I came to the conclusion that the word 'thing' (*wu*) in the phrase 'the investigation of things' (*ko-wu*) has the same meaning as the word 'event' (*shih*), both referring to the mind."

The Teacher said, "Correct. The master of the body is the mind. What emanates from the mind is the will. The original substance of the will is knowledge, and wherever the will is directed is a thing. For example, when the will is directed toward serving one's parents, then serving one's parents is a 'thing.' When the will is directed toward serving one's ruler, then serving one's ruler is a 'thing.' When the will is directed toward being humane to all people and feeling love toward things, then being humane to all people and feeling love toward things are 'things,' and when the will is directed toward seeing, hearing, speaking, and acting, then each of these is a 'thing.' Therefore I say that there are neither principles nor things outside the mind. The teaching in the *Doctrine of the Mean* that 'Without sincerity there would be nothing,'[25] and the effort to manifest one's clear character described in the *Great Learning* mean

---

[25] *Doctrine of the Mean*, ch. 25.

nothing more than the effort to make the will sincere. And the work of making the will sincere is none other than the investigation of things."

7.   The Teacher further said, "The word *ko* in *ko-wu* is the same as the *ko* in Mencius' saying that 'A great man rectified (*ko*) the ruler's mind.'²⁶ It means to eliminate what is incorrect in the mind so as to preserve the correctness of its original substance. Wherever the will is, the incorrectness must be eliminated so correctness may be preserved. In other words, in all places and at all times the Principle of Nature must be preserved. This is the investigation of principles to the utmost. The Principle of Nature is clear character, and to investigate the principle of things to the utmost is to manifest the clear character."

8.   He further said, "Knowledge is the original substance of the mind. The mind is naturally able to know. When it perceives the parents, it naturally knows that one should be filial. When it perceives the elder brother, it naturally knows that one should be respectful. And when it perceives a child fall into a well, it naturally knows that one should be commiserative.²⁷ This is innate knowledge of good (*liang-chih*) and need not be sought outside. If what emanates from innate knowledge is not obstructed by selfish ideas, the result will be like the saying 'If a man gives full development to his feeling of commiseration, his humanity will be more than he can ever put into practice.'²⁸ However, the ordinary man is not free from the obstruction of selfish ideas. He therefore requires the effort of the extension of knowledge and the investigation of things in order to overcome selfish ideas and restore principle. Then the mind's faculty of innate knowledge will no longer be obstructed but will be able to penetrate and operate everywhere. One's knowledge will then be extended. With knowledge extended, one's will becomes sincere."

9.   I said, "You regard the extensive study of literature (*wen*) as the work of restraining oneself with rules of propriety.²⁹ I have

---

²⁶ *Book of Mencius*, 4A:20. Cf. sec. 85, below.
²⁷ *Ibid.*, 2A:6.
²⁸ *Ibid.*, 7B:31.
²⁹ Referring to the *Analects*, 6:25.

thought over the matter carefully and have not been able to understand. Kindly enlighten me."

The Teacher said, "The word *li* (meaning propriety, ceremonies) means the same as *li* (meaning principle). When principles become manifested and can be seen, we call them patterns (*wen*, also meaning literature) and when patterns are hidden and abstruse and cannot be seen, we call them *li* (principle). They are the same thing. Restraining oneself with rules of propriety means that this mind must become completely identified with the Principle of Nature. In order to become completely identified with the Principle of Nature, one must direct one's effort to wherever principle is manifested. For example, if principle is manifested in the serving of one's parents, one should learn to preserve it in the very act of serving one's parents. If principle is manifested in the serving of one's ruler, one should learn to preserve it in the very act of serving one's ruler. If principle is manifested in one's living in riches or poverty or in noble or humble station, one should learn to preserve it in these situations. And if principle is manifested in one's being in difficulty and danger or being in the midst of barbarous tribes, one should learn to preserve it in these situations.[30] And one should do the same whether working or resting, speaking or silent. No matter where principle may be manifested, one should learn right then and there to preserve it. This is what is meant by the extensive study of literature. This is the work of restraining oneself with the rules of propriety. To study literature extensively means to be refined in one's mind and to restrain oneself with the rules of propriety means to have singleness in one's mind."

10.   I said, " 'The moral mind is always the master of the person, and the human mind always obeys the moral mind.'[31] When examined in the light of your teaching of refinement and singleness of mind, these words seem to be wrong."

The Teacher said, "Right. There is only one mind. Before it is mixed with selfish human desires, it is called the moral mind, and after it is mixed with human desires contrary to its natural state, it is called the human mind.[32] When the human mind is rectified it is

---

[30] Referring to the *Doctrine of the Mean*, ch. 14.
[31] Chu Hsi, in Preface to the *Chung-yung chang-chü*.
[32] See n. 20, above.

called the moral mind and when the moral mind loses its correctness, it is called the human mind. There were not two minds to start with. When Master Ch'eng I said that the human mind is due to selfish desires while the moral mind is due to the Principle of Nature,[33] it sounds like dividing the mind into two, but his idea is really correct. But to say that the moral mind is the master and the human mind obeys it is to say that there are two minds. The Principle of Nature and selfish human desires cannot coexist. How can there be the Principle of Nature as the master and at the same time selfish human desires to obey it?"

11. I asked about Wang T'ung [Wen-chung Tzu, 584-617][34] and Han Yü [768-824].[35]

The Teacher said, "Han Yü was only a giant among literary men, whereas Wang T'ung was a worthy scholar. People have glorified Han Yü only because of his literary accomplishment, but he was really far, far inferior to Wang T'ung."

I asked, "Why did Wang T'ung make the mistake of imitating the Classics?"[36]

The Teacher said, "I am afraid imitating the Classics should not be totally condemned. Suppose you state the difference in objectives between Wang T'ung's imitating the Classics and the writings of later scholars."

I said, "There have been scholars who wrote with an eye on reputation, but their main purpose was to illuminate the doctrine, whereas imitating the Classics seems to be entirely for the sake of reputation."

The Teacher said, "Whom have they followed in writing to illuminate the doctrine?"

[33] *I-shu*, 19:7a.

[34] Wang T'ung was probably the greatest Confucian between the third and the seventh centuries. He wrote treatises and supplements (now lost) to the Six Classics, considering himself comparable to Confucius. Later Confucians have never excused him for this presumptuousness.

[35] Han was an even greater Confucian than Wang T'ung, and he was regarded by Confucians as representing the direct transmission of Confucian orthodoxy from Mencius on. He attacked Buddhism and Taoism vigorously, advocating burning their books and making Buddhist monks "human beings once more." He is generally considered a forerunner of Neo-Confuciansim. As a writer, he ranks with China's best.

[36] By writing the *Supplement to the Book of History*, etc.

I said, "Confucius abridged and transmitted the Six Classics for the purpose of illuminating the doctrine."

The Teacher said, "Isn't imitating the Classics also following Confucius?"

I said, "The scholars' writings contributed something to illuminate the doctrine. But I am afraid Wang T'ung's imitation of the Classics merely seems to imitate the external manifestations without adding anything to the doctrine."

The Teacher said, "By illuminating the doctrine, do you mean returning to simplicity and purity and revealing them in concrete practice, or writing flowery speeches aimed at making noise and creating argument? The great disorder of the world is due to the popularity of conventional, meaningless literature and the decline of actual practice of moral values. If the doctrine had been illuminated throughout the world, there would have been no need to transmit the Six Classics. Confucius abridged and transmitted them only because he had to. From the time of Fu-hsi [legendary emperor of great antiquity] who devised the Eight Trigrams to the time of King Wen [1171-1122 B.C.] and Duke Chou [d. 1094 B.C.], a countless number of books such as the *Lien-shan* (Mountain range) and the *Kuei-ts'ang* (Reservoir)[37] was written on the doctrine of Changes, and consequently the doctrine of Changes became highly confused. Believing that the atmosphere of superficial writing was becoming thicker and realizing there would be no end to theorizing, Confucius took hold of the doctrine of King Wen and Duke Chou and clarified it as the only way of getting at its foundation. As a result, the various theories were all overthrown and a unanimity of interpretation was reached among the expositors of the *Book of Changes*.

"It was the same with the cases of the books of *History*, *Odes*, *Rites*, and *Music*, and the *Spring and Autumn Annals*. Following the first four chapters of the *Book of History* and the first two books of the *Book of Odes*, there had been thousands such as the *Pa-su* (Eight inquiries) and the *Chiu-ch'iu* (Nine mounts) and all those licentious verses. Names, varieties, and systems of ceremonies and music, too, became innumerable. Confucius edited, made deletions, and put them all in order, and only then were the speculative theories overthrown. He did not add a word to the books of *History*, *Odes*,

---

[37] Two versions of the *Book of Changes*, according to the *Chou-li*, ch. 3.

Rites, and *Music*. The various doctrines contained in the present *Book of Rites* all consist of far-fetched interpretations of later scholars and not of Confucius' original teachings. As to the *Spring and Autumn Annals*, although it is supposed to have been written by Confucius, actually it is the original text of the history of Lu. What is meant by Confucius' writing down is that he wrote down the original, and what is meant by his eliminating is that he eliminated the superfluous. Thus what he did was to reduce but not to add. When Confucius transmitted the Six Classics, he feared that superfluous writing was creating a chaos in the world, and he lost no time in making the Classics simple so that people might avoid the superfluous words and find out the real meaning; he did not intend to teach through mere words.

"After the Ch'un-ch'iu period [722-481 B.C.] superfluous writing became more abundant and the world became more chaotic. The First Emperor of Ch'in [r.246-210 B.C.] burned the books and has been condemned because he did so from a selfish motive, and he should not have burned the Six Classics. Had his intention been to illuminate the doctrine, and to burn all those books opposed to the Classics and violating principle, it would have conformed, by implication, to Confucius' intention of editing and transmitting the Classics. From the time of Ch'in and Han [206 B.C.-A.D. 220], literary productions daily increased in number. It would be impossible to discard all of them even if we wanted to. One should only follow the example of Confucius, by recording those that are approximately correct and making them known. The various perverse doctrines will then gradually disappear by themselves. I do not know what Wang T'ung's purpose was when he imitated the Classics, but I rather strongly approve it, believing that if Confucius had lived again, he would not have done otherwise.

"The reason the world is not in order is because superficial writing is growing and concrete practice is declining. People advance their own opinions, valuing what is novel and strange, in order to mislead the common folks and gain fame. They merely confuse people's intelligence and dull people's senses, so that people devote much of their time and energy to competing in conventional writing and flowery compositions in order to achieve fame; they no longer remember that there are such deeds as honoring the fundamental, valuing truth, and returning to simplicity and purity. All this trouble was started by those who wrote [extensively and superficially]."

I said, "Some writing is perhaps indispensable. For example, in the case of the *Spring and Autumn Annals*, if there were not the writing, the *Tso chuan* (Tso's commentary),[38] I am afraid it would be difficult to understand."

The Teacher said, "To say that the *Spring and Autumn Annals* can only be illuminated with a commentary is to regard it as a puzzle with the last part left out. Why should Confucius write in such difficult and abstruse terms? Much of the *Tso chuan* is from the original text of the history of Lu. If the *Spring and Autumn Annals* depends on it to be understood, then why should Confucius have abridged it?"

I said, "Ch'eng I said, 'The commentary contains cases. The Classic contains judgments.'[39] For example, in the *Spring and Autumn Annals* it is recorded that so-and-so murdered his ruler or such-and-such a feudal lord invaded such-and-such a state. It would be difficult to judge unless the facts supplied by the commentary are known."

The Teacher said, "I-ch'uan probably repeated what famous but mediocre scholars had said; he did not appreciate Confucius' purpose in writing the *Spring and Autumn Annals*. When he recorded that so-and-so murdered his ruler, the murder in itself was a crime. What is the need of inquiring into its details? Military expeditions against the feudal state should proceed from the king. When he recorded that such-and-such a feudal lord invaded a state, the invasion in itself was a crime. What is the need of inquiring into its details? The primary purpose of Confucius' transmitting the Six Classics was purely to rectify people's minds, to preserve the Principle of Nature, and to eliminate selfish human desires. He did discuss these matters. Sometimes when people asked him, he would talk to them according to their capacity to understand. But even then he would not talk much, for he was afraid that people would try to seek truth in words only. This is why he said, 'I do not wish to say anything.'[40] How could he be willing to tell people in detail all these things that would release selfish human desires and destroy the Principle of Nature? That would be to promote disorder and induce wickedness. This is the reason Mencius said, 'None of Confucius'

[38] Attributed to Tso Ch'iu-ming, probably Confucius' contemporary. See trans. by Legge, *The Ch'un Ts'ew, with the Tso Chuen*.
[39] *I-shu*, 15:16b.
[40] *Analects*, 17:19.

pupils spoke about the affairs of the despots Duke Huan [r. 685-643 B.C.] and Duke Wen [r. 636-628 B.C.], and therefore they have not been transmitted to posterity.'⁴¹ This is the special and private way of the Confucian school. Famous but mediocre scholars of today talk only about the type of learning suitable for a despot. Therefore they want to learn all kinds of secret and crafty schemes. Their objective is purely success and profit, an aim diametrically opposed to the Sage's purpose in writing the Classics. How can they understand?"

Thereupon the Teacher sighed and added, "It is not easy to talk about this thing with people except those who understand the character of Heaven."⁴²

The Teacher further said, "Confucius said, 'When I was young, a historian would still leave something unsaid,'⁴³ and Mencius said, 'It would be better to have no *Book of History* than to believe all of it. In its "Completion of War" section,⁴⁴ I accept only two or three passages.'⁴⁵ In abridging the book Confucius retained only a few chapters to cover the four or five odd centuries of the T'ang, Yü, and Hsia periods. Weren't there any more events to record? The fact that he confined himself to what he did ought to show us his intention—he merely wanted to eliminate superfluous writing. On the contrary, later scholars have only wanted to add."

I said, "When Confucius produced the Classics, he merely wanted to get rid of selfish human desires and preserve the Principle of Nature, and did not want to tell people in detail about affairs from the time of the Five Despots⁴⁶ down. It is true enough. But why should he have been so brief about the events before Yao and Shun?" [legendary emperors of the T'ang and Yü periods].

The Teacher said, "In the period of Fu-hsi and the Yellow Emperor [preceding Yao and Shun] events were few and far between. Few of them have been transmitted to us. Nevertheless

---

⁴¹ *Book of Mencius*, 1A:7.
⁴² Referring to the *Doctrine of the Mean*, ch. 32.
⁴³ *Analects*, 15:25.
⁴⁴ See trans. by Legge, *Shoo King*, pp. 306-19.
⁴⁵ *Book of Mencius*, 7B:3.
⁴⁶ These despots were: Duke Huan of Ch'i (r. 685-643 B.C.), Duke Wen of Chin (r. 636-628 B.C.), Duke Mu of Ch'in (r. 659-619 B.C.), King Chuang of Ch'u (r. 613-589 B.C.), and Duke Hsiang of Sung (r. 650-635 B.C.). See *Book of Mencius*, 6B:7.

we can imagine that at that time life was perfectly pure, lofty, simple, and plain, without any air of being ornamental. This is the peace and order of great antiquity, not to be matched by later ages."

I said, "Histories like those of Fu-hsi, Shen-nung, and the Yellow Emperor had been handed down. Why did Confucius discard them?"

The Teacher said, "Even if it was true that there were such histories, they would not be good for later ages which have gradually undergone change. As customs and manners became complicated, ornament and embellishment became more prevalent. Even by the end of the Chou [1111-256 B.C.], it was impossible to reinstate the customs of Hsia [2183-1752 B.C.?] and Shang [1751-1112 B.C.] times, let alone the times of Yao and Shun and the times of Fu-hsi and the Yellow Emperor which were further back. However, while their governments were different, the principle is the same with them all. Consequently, Confucius transmitted the doctrines originally handed down by Yao and Shun and adopted and promoted as a model the social and religious laws of King Wen and King Wu [r. 1211-1116 B.C.]. These regulations, in essence, were no different from the principles of Yao and Shun, but because government had to be adjusted to the times, governmental measures and institutions naturally were different. Even the undertakings of the Hsia and the Shang would not be applicable to the Chou. For this reason, 'Duke Chou,[47] wanting to combine the good works of the founders of the Hsia, the Shang, and the Chou, found certain things inapplicable and had to think hard day and night [to make the adjustment].'[48] How much more difficult would it be to reinstate the governments of high antiquity! Naturally Confucius reduced its record to the minimum."

The Teacher further said, "Merely to engage in taking no action, to be unable to adjust the government according to the time as did the three kings, and to insist on practicing the customs of high antiquity is the way of Buddhist and Taoist learning. To adjust the government according to the times but not to be able to base it on the principle [handed down by Yao and Shun] as the three kings did, and instead to exercise government with the motive of success and profit, is the enterprise of the despots and those since them. Later scholars have talked and talked and talked, but all they have talked about is the technique of despotism."

---

[47] Who established the social and governmental institutions of the Chou.
[48] See *Book of Mencius*, 4B:20.

12. The Teacher further said, "The governmental systems before the times of Yao and Shun cannot be reinstated in later ages. They should be ignored. The government after the Three Dynasties [Hsia, Shang, and Chou] is not worth following. The records should be abridged. Only the governments of the Three Dynasties are practicable. Unfortunately people who discuss the Three Dynasties do not understand the fundamental and merely concern themselves with the secondary, and consequently that system cannot be restored either."

13. I said, "Former scholars said that among the Six Classics the *Spring and Autumn Annals* is history. Since history is purely to record events, I am afraid that in the final analysis it is somewhat different in form and content from the other five Classics."

The Teacher said, "A history deals with events while a classic deals with principles. However, events are really principles and principles are really events. Thus the *Spring and Autumn Annals* also is a classic, while the other five Classics are also histories. The *Book of Changes* is the history of Fu-hsi, the *Book of History* is the history of the period from the time of Yao and Shun on, and the books of *Rites* and *Music* are the histories of the Three Dynasties. Inasmuch as the events and principles discussed in these Classics are the same, is there anything wherein that can be said to be different?"

14. The Teacher further said, "The Five Classics are also history, and no more. The principle of history is to distinguish good and evil and to give instructions to do good and warnings against evil. The Classics retain those facts that are good and useful for instruction in order to serve as models for us. As to the facts that are evil but can serve as warning, they retain the warning but eliminate the facts, so as to prevent wickedness."

I said, "To retain the facts in order to show us the model is of course a way of preserving the Principle of Nature as it originally is. Is elimination of the facts to prevent wickedness likewise a way of suppressing selfish desires when they are about to be aroused?"

The Teacher said, "This is of course the purpose of the Sage in producing the Classics. However, one should not take the records too literally."

I further asked, "If, in the case of those evil events that can be taken as warning, the Classics retain the warning but eliminate the facts in order to prevent wickedness, why in the case of the *Book of Odes* alone have the [licentious parts] of the odes of the states of Cheng and Wei not been expunged? A former scholar said, 'Evil can serve to correct one's indolence.'[49] Is that correct?"

The Teacher said, "The *Book of Odes* is not the original work of the Confucian school. Confucius said, 'Banish the songs of Cheng.... They are licentious,'[50] and again said, 'I hate the way in which the songs of Cheng confound the classical songs.'[51] 'The songs of Cheng and Wei are songs of declining states.'[52] This is the position of the Confucian school. The three hundred odes selected by Confucius were all classical. They were all qualified to be sung in sacrifices to Heaven and imperial ancestors as well as in community rites. They were all intended to promote peace and cultivate virtue. For the sake of social reform, should the songs of Cheng and Wei be tolerated? To tolerate them would be to promote lewdness and induce wickedness. Most certainly after the burning of books by the Ch'in[53] famous but mediocre scholars arbitrarily added these songs of Cheng and Wei to the Classic in order to make up three hundred odes. For among the popular masses most people enjoy singing licentious songs. You can hear them in every alley. To say that evil can serve to correct one's indolence is to make an excuse after having failed to find a satisfactory explanation."

Postscript. Because the original doctrine has disappeared, I was shocked and hesitant when I first heard our Teacher's instructions, and did not know where to begin. Later on as I heard him more and more, I gradually realized that his teachings are to be applied to one's life and to be concretely demonstrated, and then I came to believe that they represent the direct heritage of the Confucian school, and that all the rest is but byways, small paths, and dead ends. His theories that the investigation of things is the effort to make the will sincere, that manifesting goodness is the effort to make one's personal life sincere, that the investigation of the principles of things to the utmost is the effort to develop one's nature

---

[49] Chu Hsi, in his *Lun-yü chi-chu*, ch. 1, commentary on *Analects*, 2:2.

[50] *Analects*, 15:10.

[51] *Ibid.*, 17:18.

[52] *Book of Rites*, "The Record of Music." Cf. trans. by Legge, *Li Ki*, ch. 17, p. 94.

[53] In 213 B.C., when some of the odes Confucius had selected were lost.

completely, that the pursuit of study and inquiry is the effort to honor the moral nature, that to study literature extensively is the effort to restrain oneself with rules of propriety, and that to be refined in mind is the effort to achieve single-mindedness—these and others at first seemed hardly harmonious with one another. But after I thought them over long enough, I was so happy that I danced with my hands and feet.

CONVERSATIONS RECORDED BY LU CH'ENG[1]
(Sections 15-94)

15. I asked, "With reference to the effort of concentrating on one thing, suppose in reading books one's mind is concentrated on reading books, and in entertaining guests one's mind is concentrated on entertaining them. Can these be regarded as concentrating on one thing?"

The Teacher said, "Suppose in loving sex one's mind is concentrated on loving sex and in loving money one's mind is concentrated on loving money. Can these be regarded as concentrating on one thing? These are not concentrating on one thing; they are chasing after material things. Concentrating on one thing means the absolute concentration of the mind on the Principle of Nature."

16. I asked about making up the mind. The Teacher said, "It is simply the resolution, in every thought, to preserve the Principle of Nature. If one does not neglect this, in due time it will crystallize in one's mind and become what the Taoists call 'the mystical conception of a sage.' If the thought of the Principle of Nature is always retained, then the gradual steps to the levels of the beautiful man, the great man, the sage, and the spirit man[2] are all but the cultivation and extension of this one thought.

---

[1] His name was Yüan-ching. He obtained a "presented scholar" degree in 1517 and became a divisional executive assistant in the department of justice. When the emperor planned to confer the posthumous title "August Ancestor" on his father instead of his uncle, Yüan-ching criticized the emperor's decision, and was dismissed from office. Later he repented, but was not reinstated because the emperor charged that he lacked integrity. At a later date, when officials were about to suppress Wang Yang-ming's teachings, he memorialized the throne in their defense. For an account of him, see *Ming-ju hsüeh-an*, 14:3a-b.

[2] *Book of Mencius*, 7B:25.

17.   [The Teacher said,] "If during the day one feels work becoming annoying, one should sit in meditation. But if one feels lazy and not inclined to read, then he should go ahead and read. To do this is like applying medicine according to the disease."

18.   [The Teacher said,] "Friends, in dealing with each other, should try to be humble toward one another, for that will benefit them. If they try to be superior to each other, it will hurt them."

19.   Meng Yüan[3] has the defects of regarding himself as always right and of loving fame. The Teacher has admonished him many times. One day just after such an admonition, a friend of his told the Teacher of his recent efforts and asked for correction. Standing by the side of the Teacher, Yüan said, "What he has found is my old stuff."

The Teacher said, "Your defect comes up again."

Yüan's face paled and he was about to argue.

The Teacher said, "Your defect comes up again," and he went on to teach him, saying, "This is the root of the great trouble of your whole life. Suppose you plant this big tree in a square. The nutrition from rain and the energy from the soil are barely sufficient to support it. If you want to plant some good grains around it, they will be covered by its branches above and wrapped up by its roots below. How can they grow? The tree must be removed, leaving not even a tender root, before good grains can be planted. Otherwise, no matter how much you cultivate them and enrich the soil, all the nourishment will go to this tree."

20.   I said, "Scholars of later generations have written a great deal. I am afraid some of it has confounded correct learning."

The Teacher said, "The human mind and the Principle of Nature are undifferentiated. Sages and worthies wrote about them very much like a portrait painter painting the true likeness and transmitting the spirit. He shows only an outline of the appearance to serve as the basis for people to seek and find the true personality. Among one's spirit, feelings, expressions, and behavior, there is that which cannot be transmitted. Later writers have imitated and copied what the sages have drawn. They have erroneously mutilated

[3] Little is known of him except that his courtesy name was Po-sheng.

it and have added to it in their own way in order to show off their own tricks. In this way the original is further and further lost."

21. I asked, "A sage's response to changing conditions is unlimited. Does he have to study beforehand?"

The Teacher said, "How can he study everything? The mind of the sage is like a clear mirror. Since it is all clarity, it responds to all stimuli as they come and reflects everything. There is no such case as a previous image still remaining in the present reflection or a yet-to-be-reflected image already existing there. Scholars of later generations propagate such a doctrine, and therefore they have greatly violated the teachings of the Sage. Duke Chou instituted ceremonies and established musical systems to provide the world with a culture. These are things that all sages are capable of doing. Why didn't Yao and Shun do all of them instead of leaving them to Duke Chou? Confucius edited and transmitted the Six Classics as guidance for ten thousand generations. This is also a thing that any sage can do. Why didn't Duke Chou do it instead of leaving it for Confucius? From these we know that a sage does a thing when the time comes. The only fear is that the mirror is not clear, not that it is incapable of reflecting a thing as it comes. The study of changing conditions and events is to be done at the time of response. However, a student must be engaged in brightening up the mirror. He should worry only about his mind's not being clear, and not about the inability to respond to all changing conditions."

I said, "If so, how about the saying, 'Empty, tranquil, and without any sign, and yet all things are luxuriantly present.'?"[4]

---

[4] Ch'eng I, *I-shu*, 15:8a. Many Japanese historians of Chinese philosophy have asserted that this saying is of Buddhist origin but none has given any direct reference. Yamazaki Ansai (1618-82), in his essay on the saying (*Zoku Yamazaki Ansai zenshū*, pt. 2, pp. 78-86), listed all quotations of this saying and discussions on it by Neo-Confucians but did not say a word about its Buddhist origin. The *Daikanwa jiten*, the fullest dictionary of its kind so far, gives Ch'eng I, rather than any Buddhist, as its author. However, terms like "indefinite," "boundless," and "without any sign" are of Taoist origin, and as Ōta Kinjō (1765-1825) has pointed out (*Gimon roku*, 1831 ed., pt. 1, p. 20b), the second half of the sentence is virtually the same as that in the *Cheng-tao ko* by Zen Master Chen-chiao (d. 712) of Yung-chia, in *Ching-te ch'uan-teng lu*, 30:11a.

The Teacher said, "This theory is fundamentally good. But if it is not understood correctly, there will be trouble."

22. [The Teacher said,] "Moral principles exist in no fixed place and are not exhaustible. Please do not think that, when you have gotten something from conversations with me, that is all there is to it. There will be no end if we talk for ten, twenty, or fifty more years." Some days later, he said again, "Emperors Yao and Shun were the height of sageness and yet goodness goes beyond them indefinitely. Kings Chieh [r. 1802-1752 B.C.?] and Chou [r. 1175-1112 B.C.][5] represented the height of evil, and yet evil goes beyond them indefinitely. If Chieh and Chou had not died when they died, would their wickedness be limited to what it actually was? If there is a limit to goodness, how is it that even Sage-king Wen looked for the Way as if he could not see it?"[6]

23. I said, "One's feelings seem to be all right when one is quiet. However, when something happens, they become different. Why is it?"

The Teacher said, "This is because one only knows how to cultivate oneself in quietness and does not exert effort to master oneself. Consequently when something happens one turns topsy-turvy. One must be trained and polished in the actual affairs of life. Only then can one stand firm and remain calm whether in activity or in tranquillity."[7]

24. I asked about the way of "penetrating on the higher [transcendental] level."[8] The Teacher said, "In their way of teaching people, as soon as they get to anything refined or subtle, scholars of later generations say that it belongs to penetrating on the higher level and should not be pursued, and that it is better to turn to studies on the lower [empirical] level. This is to separate the two levels. Now what the eye can see, what the ear can hear, what the mouth can say, and what the mind can think of are all matters of

[5] Whose wickedness caused the downfall of the Hsia and Shang dynasties, respectively.

[6] Quoting the *Book of Mencius*, 4B:20. *Erh* in the text is interchangeable with *ju* (as though).

[7] Quoting Ch'eng Hao's celebrated saying in the *Wen-chi*, 3:1a.

[8] *Analects*, 14:37.

learning on the lower level, whereas what the eye cannot see, what the ear cannot hear, what the mouth cannot say, and what the mind cannot think of are matters of penetration on the higher level. For example, providing a tree with care and water is learning on the lower level, whereas the activity of the vegetative life day and night and the tree's smooth and luxuriant growth are penetration on the higher level. How can human efforts have any part of it? Therefore whatever human effort can do and whatever can be talked about represent learning on the lower level. But penetration on the higher level is implicit in learning on the lower level. All that the Sage said, although absolutely refined and subtle, is a matter of lower learning. A student should direct his effort to this, and penetration on the higher level will naturally follow. There is no need to seek a separate and distinct way of higher penetration."

(To hold the will firm is like having a pain in the heart. As the whole mind is concentrated on the pain, how can there be time for idle talk or being a busybody?)[9]

25. I asked what efforts are to be made in achieving refinement and singleness of mind.

The Teacher said, "Singleness is the goal of refinement and refinement is the effort to achieve singleness. It is not that outside of refinement there is another thing called singleness. Since the word refinement (*ching*) has the radical meaning rice, let us take rice as an example. Singleness means having the rice absolutely pure and white. However, this state cannot be achieved without the work of refining, such as winnowing, sifting, and grinding. These are the work of refining, but their purpose is no more than to make rice absolutely pure and white, that is all. To study extensively, to inquire accurately, to think carefully, to sift clearly, and to practice earnestly[10] are all efforts of refinement for the sake of singleness of mind. As to the rest, to study literature extensively is the effort to be restrained by the rules of propriety, to investigate things and to extend knowledge are efforts to make the will sincere, to pursue study and inquiry is the effort to honor one's moral nature, and to manifest

---

[9] This whole passage is also found below in sec. 95. It is obviously an interpolation here.

[10] Quoting the *Doctrine of the Mean*, ch. 20.

goodness is the effort to make the personal life sincere. This is the only way to put it."

26. [The Teacher said,] "Knowledge is the beginning of action and action is the completion of knowledge. Learning to be a sage involves only one effort. Knowledge and action should not be separated."

27. [The Teacher said,] "[When Confucius advised Ch'i-tiao K'ai (540- c.450 B.C.) to become an official] the latter said, 'I do not yet have the confidence to do so.' Confucius was pleased.[11] When Tzu-lu [542-480 B.C.] got Tzu-kao [b.521 B.C.] appointed governor of Pi, Confucius said, 'You are doing an injury to someone's son.'[12] When Tseng Tien [father of Tseng Tzu, 505-c.436 B.C.] expressed his wish,[13] Confucius gave his approval. From these we can see what the Sage had in mind."

28. I asked, "When one's mind is preserved in peace and tranquillity, can it be called the state of 'equilibrium before one's feelings are aroused'?"[14]

The Teacher said, "Nowadays when people preserve their mind, only their vital force is calm. When they are peaceful and tranquil, it is only their vital force that is peaceful and tranquil. That cannot be considered as the state of equilibrium before feelings are aroused."

"If it is not equilibrium, isn't it perhaps the way to achieve it?"

"The only way is to get rid of selfish human desires and preserve the Principle of Nature. When tranquil, direct every thought to removing selfish human desires and preserving the Principle of Nature, and when active, direct every thought to doing the same. One should never mind whether or not one is at peace and tranquil. If he depends on that peace and tranquillity, not only will there be the fault of gradually becoming fond of quietness and tired of activity, but there will be many defects latent in that state of mind. They cannot be eliminated but will grow as usual when something happens. If one regards following principle as fundamental, when is

---

[11] *Analects*, 5:5.
[12] *Ibid.*, 11:24.
[13] *Ibid.*, 11:25. See below, secs. 29 and 257.
[14] A quotation from *Doctrine of the Mean*, ch. 1.

it that one will not be peaceful and tranquil? But if one regards peace and tranquillity as fundamental, he is not necessarily able to follow principle."

29. I asked, "When Confucius' disciples expressed their wishes, Tzu-lu and Jan Ch'iu [522-*c*. 462 B.C.] chose governmental positions and Kung-hsi Hua [b. 509 B.C.] chose ceremonies and music. How practical they were! But when Tseng Tien expressed his wishes, they seemed to be frivolous. And yet Confucius approved of him.[15] What does it mean?"

"The three other disciples were opinionated and dogmatic.[16] When one is opinionated and dogmatic, one inevitably becomes one-sided. He may be able to do one thing but not the other. The attitude of Tseng Tien shows that he was neither opinionated nor dogmatic. It means that he 'does what is proper to his position and does not want to go beyond it. If he is in the midst of barbarous tribes, he does what is proper in the midst of barbarous tribes. In a position of difficulty and danger, he does what is proper in a position of difficulty and danger. He can find himself in no situation in which he is not at ease with himself.'[17] The other three disciples may be described as utensils, that is, specific and therefore limited in their usefulness. Tseng Tien's indication was that he was not such a utensil. Nevertheless, the three disciples' talents were all outstanding and excellent; they were unlike people of today who lack substance but have only empty words. This is why Confucius approved of all of them."

30. I asked, "What should one do when he finds no progress in knowledge?"

The Teacher said, "In study there must be a source. One must work from the source and gradually move forward. When the Taoist seekers after immortality talk about an infant[18] it is a good analogy. When the baby is still in its mother's womb, it is only pure material force. What knowledge has it? After its birth, at first it can cry, then it can laugh, then it can recognize its parents and

---

[15] *Analects*, 11:25. See below, sec. 257.
[16] Two great defects in the eye of Confucius. See *Analects*, 9:4.
[17] *Doctrine of the Mean*, ch. 14.
[18] Meaning that spiritual training is similar to the growth of an infant.

brothers, then it can stand, walk, hold things, and carry things on its back, and finally it can potentially do everything in the world. This is all due to the fact that as refined material force is increasingly sufficient, its strength and energy become increasingly strong and its intelligence becomes increasingly developed. All this is not to be found or accomplished on the day of birth. Therefore there must be a source. When the sage cultivates his moral qualities to such a point as to enable a happy order to prevail throughout heaven and earth and all things to flourish, his training begins with the state of equilibrium before the feelings of pleasure, anger, sorrow, and joy are aroused. Later scholars fail to understand the doctrine of the investigation of things. Seeing that the sage knows everything and can do everything, they forthwith want to study everything at the very beginning. How can that be done?"

The Teacher again said, "To make up one's mind and to exert effort are like planting a tree. At first there are only roots and sprouts but not yet the trunk. When there is a trunk there are not yet branches. When there are branches then come the leaves and when there are leaves then come the flowers and fruits. When the root is first planted, one should only care for it and water it and should not think of branches, leaves, flowers, or fruits. What good is it to engage in fantasy? So long as one does not neglect the care of the plant, there is no fear that there will be no branches, leaves, flowers, or fruits."

31.   I asked, "I read books and do not understand. Why?"

[The Teacher said,] "This is because you only seek the meaning through words. This is why you do not understand. This is not as good as to pursue old-style learning. People who pursue old-style learning read the texts over and over and understand them. Although they understand the text perfectly, however, to the end of their lives they achieve nothing. One's effort must be directed to the substance of the mind. Whenever one does not understand a thing or cannot put it into practice, one must return to oneself and in his own mind try to realize it personally. He will then surely understand. For what the Four Books and Five Classics[19] talk about does not go beyond this substance of the mind. This substance of the mind is the Way. When the substance of the mind is understood, the

---

[19] See above, Introduction, n. 1.

Way is understood. They are not two different things. This is the basis of learning."

32. [The Teacher said,] "The original mind is vacuous [devoid of selfish desires], intelligent, and not beclouded. All principles are contained therein and all events proceed from it.[20] There is no principle outside the mind; there is no event outside the mind."

33. Someone asked, "Master Hui-an said that 'man's object of learning is simply mind and principles.'[21] What do you think of this saying?"

The Teacher said, "The mind is the nature of man and things, and nature is principle. I am afraid the use of the word 'and' makes inevitable the interpretation of mind and principle as two different things. It is up to the student to use his good judgment."

34. Someone said, "All people have this mind, and this mind is identical with principle. Why do some people do good and others do evil?"

The Teacher said, "The mind of the evil man has lost its original substance."

35. I asked, " 'Split it [principle] up and you will find it extremely refined and not confused; then put it together again and you will find it extremely great and all inclusive.'[22] What do you think of this saying?"

The Teacher said, "I am afraid that is not entirely correct. Does

---

[20] The two sentences are paraphrases of Chu Hsi's *Ta-hsüeh chang-chü*, commentary on the text. According to Ōta Kinjō (*Gimon roku*, p. 15a), the phrase "vacuous, intelligent, and not beclouded" comes from the *Ta-chih-tu lun* (*Mahāprajñāpāramitā śāstrā*), and was also used by Fa-tsang (643-712), but Ōta gave no specific reference. The phrase is probably derived from the common Buddhist phrase "intelligent, knowing, and not beclouded," which was uttered by Zen Masters like Ch'eng-kuan (c. 760-838) (see *Ching-te ch'uan-teng lu*, 30:8b). The terms "intelligent and knowing" and "not beclouded" were also used by Tsung-mi (780-841) in his *Ch'an-yüan chu-ch'üan chi tu-hsü* (*Taishō daizōkyō*, 48:404-5). Chu Hsi considered the Buddhist concept too abstract and added the second sentence. See *Chu Tzu yü-lei*, 14:17a.

[21] This is a reference to *Ta-hsüeh huo-wen*, 60a-b. Hui-an was Chu Hsi's literary name.

[22] Chu Hsi, *ibid.*, p. 24b.

principle permit any splitting up? And what is the need of putting it together again? What the Sage said about refinement and singleness of mind of course describes it completely."

36. [The Teacher said,] "Self-examination is preserving the mind and nourishing the nature while engaged in activity. Preserving the mind and nourishing the nature are self-examination when one is not engaged in activity."

37. I once asked about Lu Hsiang-shan's [Lu Chiu-yüan, 1139-93] doctrine that one should devote one's effort to the area of human feelings and human affairs.[23]

The Teacher said, "There is no event outside of human feelings and human affairs. Are pleasure, anger, sorrow, and joy not human feelings? Seeing, hearing, speaking, and acting, wealth and noble station, poverty and humble station, misfortune, calamity, death and life are all human affairs. Human affairs are within the realm of human feelings. The important point is to achieve the state of equilibrium and harmony, and achieving equilibrium and harmony depends primarily on being watchful over oneself when alone."

38. I said, "Humanity, righteousness, propriety, and wisdom are so called because they express the qualities of the mind after the feelings are aroused."

The Teacher said, "Correct."

On a later occasion I said, "Are the sense of commiseration, the sense of shame and dislike, the sense of deference and compliance, and the sense of right and wrong manifestations of man's nature?"

The Teacher said, "Humanity, righteousness, propriety, and wisdom are also manifestations. Nature is one. As physical form or body it is called nature. As master of the creative process it is called the Lord. In its universal operation it is called destiny. As endowment in man it is called man's nature. As master of man's body it is called the mind. When it emanates from the mind we have filial piety when it is applied to the father, loyalty when it is applied to the ruler, and so on to infinity. All this is only one nature. Similarly, man is only one. He is called the son with respect to the father, or the father with respect to the son, and so on to infinity.

---

[23] See *Hsiang-shan ch'üan-chi*, 34:5a.

Man is only one. We must direct our effort to our nature. If we distinctly understand what nature is, all the ten thousand principles will become crystal clear."

39.   One day the business of study was discussed. The Teacher said, "In teaching people, don't insist on a particular, one-sided way. In the beginning, one's mind is like a restless monkey and his feelings are like a galloping horse. They cannot be tied down. His thoughts and deliberations mostly tend to the side of selfish human desires. At that point, teach him to sit in meditation and to stop those thoughts and deliberations. Wait a long time till his mind becomes somewhat settled. If, however, at this time he merely remains quiet in a vacuum, like dry wood and dead ashes, it is also useless. Rather, he must be taught self-examination and self-mastery. There is no letup in this work. It is like getting rid of robbers and thieves. There must be the determination to wipe them out thoroughly and completely. Before things happen, each and every selfish desire for sex, wealth, and fame must be discovered. The root of the trouble must be pulled up and thrown away so that it will never sprout again. Only then can we feel fine. At all times be like a cat trying to catch a rat, with eyes single-mindedly watching and ears single-mindedly listening.[24] As soon as an evil thought begins to arise, overcome it and cast it away. Be as decisive as in cutting a nail or slicing a piece of iron. Do not tolerate it or give it any consideration. Do not harbor it and do not allow it any way out. Only efforts such as these can be considered serious and concrete. Only then can selfish desires be thoroughly and completely wiped out. When there are no more evil desires to be overcome, one will then automatically arrive at the state of a king who merely folds his hands and sits erect.[25] Although 'What is there to think about; what is there to deliberate about?'[26] is not the business of a beginner, he must be thinking of self-examination and self-mastery, that is, of sincerity. One has only to think of the

---

[24] A Buddhist story referred to in *Chu Tzu wen-chi*, SPPY ed., entitled *Chu Tzu ta-ch'üan*, 71:6b. The words are by Zen Master Tsu-hsin (*fl.* 1060) of Huang-lung Mountain. See *Wu-teng hui-yüan*, ch. 17, in *Zokuzōkyō*, 1st collection, pt. 2, B, case 11, p. 335a; also *Lien-teng hui-yao*, ch. 15, in *Zokuzōkyō*, 1st coll., pt. 2, B, case 9, p. 339b.

[25] And all is well with his kingdom.

[26] *Book of Changes*, "Appended Remarks," pt. 2, ch. 5. Cf. trans. by Legge, *Yi King*, p. 389.

Principle of Nature. When the mind becomes completely identified with the Principle of Nature, that is the state of 'what is there to think about; what is there to deliberate about?'."

40.   I asked, "Someone is afraid of evil spirits at night. How about it?"

The Teacher said, "This is because in his daily life he has not accumulated righteousness,[27] and his mind is timid about something. That is why he is afraid. If his ordinary conduct is in harmony with the gods, what has he to fear?"

Ma Tzu-hsin[28] said, "One need not be afraid of upright spirits. I am afraid, however, that evil spirits pay no attention to whether a man has done right or wrong. Consequently one cannot but be afraid."

The Teacher said, "Can an evil spirit delude an upright man? This fear itself shows that the mind is not upright. Therefore if anyone is deluded it is not any spirit that deludes him. He is deluded by his own mind. For example, if a man is fond of sex, it means that the spirit of lust has deluded him. If he is fond of money, it means that the spirit of money has deluded him. When he is angry at something at which he should not be angry, it means that the spirit of anger has deluded him. And when he is afraid of something of which he should not be afraid, it means the spirit of fear has deluded him."

41.   [The Teacher said,] "Calmness is the original substance of the mind. It is the Principle of Nature. It is the state in which activity and tranquillity are united."

42.   I asked about the similarity and difference between the *Great Learning* and the *Doctrine of the Mean*. The Teacher said, "Tzu-ssu [492-431 B.C.] incorporated the fundamental ideas of the *Great Learning* in the first chapter of the *Doctrine of the Mean*."

---

[27] As taught in the *Book of Mencius*, 2A:2.

[28] This was his courtesy name. His private name was Ming-heng. He obtained a "presented scholar" degree in 1517 and became a censor in 1524. As he came from Fukien, he was instrumental in the spread of Wang's doctrines in that part of China.

43. I asked, "[When Tzu-lu asked Confucius what he would do first of all if he were to serve under the ruler of Wei, who was then actually hoping that Confucius would do so], Confucius replied that the first thing was the rectification of names (that is, a son should be a true son, etc.).[29] A former scholar said that [since the heir-apparent of Wei, K'uei-wai, attempted matricide and had to flee and since his own son, Ch'e, who was eventually made the duke, opposed his return to Wei, both as sons were not true to the name of a son, and Confucius, being true to his doctrine of the rectification of names,] would report to the Son of Heaven above and inform the regional feudal lords below, remove Ch'e, and put the original ruler's younger son Ying in his place.[30] What is the meaning of this?"

The Teacher said, "This, I am afraid, would be difficult to do. Is it correct that, when a ruler shows his respect and extends his courtesy to the utmost in waiting for a person to serve in his government, the first thing the person should do is to remove the ruler? Is this in conformity with human feelings and the Principle of Nature? Since Confucius was willing to serve under Ch'e, it must have been that Ch'e had wholeheartedly trusted Confucius with all the affairs of the state and listened to his advice, that the Sage, with his eminent virtue and perfect sincerity, had influenced and transformed him, making him realize that none could be counted a man who refused to recognize his father, and that Ch'e would surely cry bitterly and run to welcome his father back. Love of father and son is based on Heaven-endowed human nature. If Ch'e could truly repent like this, could K'uei-wai fail to be moved and delighted by a good deed? When K'uei-wai had returned, Ch'e would forthwith entrust the state to him and beg to be punished by death. Since K'uei-wai would then have been influenced by his son, and furthermore, since Grand Master Confucius, with his perfect sincerity, would have mediated, the father would surely decline to accept but would order Ch'e to continue to rule. All the ministers and the people would then surely want to have Ch'e as their ruler. Ch'e, on the other hand, would voluntarily reveal his own sin, petition the Son of Heaven and inform the feudal lords of regions and states, and insist on entrusting the state to his father. At the same time, K'uei-wai, all the ministers, and the people would also publicize the

---

[29] *Analects*, 13:3.
[30] This is the opinion of Hu Hung (1100-55), quoted by Chu Hsi in his commentary on the above passage of the *Analects* in his *Lun-yü chi-chu*, ch. 7.

excellence of Ch'e's repentance, humanity, and filial piety, petition the Son of Heaven and inform the feudal lords of regions and states, and insist on having Ch'e as their ruler. Consequently, the Mandate of Heaven to rule would center on Ch'e, ordering him to serve again as the ruler of the state of Wei. Ch'e would have no recourse except to do as the Grand Emperor of a later age [when the Emperor Kao-tsu honored his father with the title of Grand Emperor in 201 B.C.],[31] lead all the ministers and the people to honor K'uei-wai as the grand duke, make ample provision for his support, and then step back and resume his position. In that way, according to the Confucian doctrine that the ruler should be a true ruler, the minister a true minister, the father a true father, and the son a true son,[32] the names would be correct and language would be in accord with the truth of things, and then in one stroke one would be able to govern the world. The meaning of Confucius' doctrine of the rectification of names is perhaps this."

44. While I was living temporarily[33] in the bureau of state ceremonials I unexpectedly received a letter saying that my son was seriously ill. My sorrow was unbearable. The Teacher said, "This is the time for you to exert effort. If you allow this occasion to go by, what is the use of studying when nothing is happening? People should train and polish themselves at just such a time as this. A father's love for his son is of course the noblest feeling. Nevertheless, in the operation of the Principle of Nature there is the proper degree of equilibrium and harmony. To be excessive means to give rein to selfish thoughts. On such an occasion most people feel that according to the Principle of Nature they should be sorrowful. Thus they keep on with sorrow and distress. They do not realize that they are already 'affected by worries and anxieties and their minds will not be correct.'[34]

"Generally speaking, the influence of the seven emotions is in the majority of cases excessive, and only in the minority of cases insufficient. As soon as it is excessive, it is not in accord with the original substance of the mind. It must be adjusted to reach the mean before

---

[31] *Ch'ien-Han shu*, ch. 1, 6th yr. See trans. by Homer H. Dubs, *The History of the Former Han Dynasty* (Baltimore, Waverly Press, 1948), II, 115.

[32] *Analects*, 12:11.

[33] *Ts'ang-chü*. Another interpretation is "living in a granary."

[34] *Great Learning*, ch. 7.

it becomes correct. Take the case of the death of parents. Is it not true that the son desires to mourn until death before he feels satisfied? Nevertheless it is said, 'The self-inflicted suffering should not be carried out to such an extent as to destroy life.'[35] It is not that the Sage tries to restrict or suppress it. It is because the original substance of the Principle of Nature has its proper limits that should not be exceeded. People need only to understand the substance of the mind and then automatically not an iota can be added to or subtracted from it."

45. [The Teacher said,] "It should not be said that all ordinary persons have attained the state of equilibrium before the feelings are aroused. For 'substance and function come from one source.'[36] Given the substance, there is the function, and given the equilibrium before the feelings are aroused, there is the harmony in which the feelings are aroused and all attain due measure and degree.[37] Since people of today do not possess this harmony, accordingly we should know that they have not completely attained equilibrium."

46. [The Teacher said,] "The explanation of Change in the sentence 'In the first nine [or the lowest line of the hexagram which is symbolic of the positive element yang, one sees its subject as] the dragon [which is also symbolic of yang] lying in the deep and there-fore [one should lie low and be on guard] for it is not the time for action.'[38] The symbol is [not the dragon, as former theories have held, but] the lowest line. The operation of Change [is not to be found elsewhere but] right in the line itself in accordance with which changes take place. To tell fortune or misfortune according to the Change is [not to use the dragon as the symbol and merely the phrase 'not the time for action' as the explanation but] to use the whole sentence as explanation."

47. [The Teacher said,] "The phrase 'the restorative power of the night'[39] refers to ordinary people. If a student can apply his effort,

---

[35] *Book of Rites*, "The Four Principles Underlying the Dress of Mourning"; cf. trans. by Legge, *Li Ki*, ch. 46, p. 466.

[36] A famous saying by Ch'eng I, preface to the *I ch'uan*.

[37] Quoting the *Doctrine of the Mean*, ch. 1.

[38] *Book of Changes*, the text of hexagram no. 1. Cf. trans. by Legge, *Yi King*, p. 57.

[39] *Book of Mencius*, 6A:8.

then whatever does or does not happen in the daytime is an occasion for this power to gather and to grow. As for the sage, it is unnecessary to talk about the restorative power of the night."

48. I asked about the chapter saying, "Hold it fast and you preserve it. Let it go and you lose it."[40]

The Teacher said, "Although when the passage adds that 'it goes out and comes in at no definite time and without anyone's knowing its direction,' it refers to the mind of the common man, the student must realize that the original substance of the mind is basically like this. The effort of holding fast and preserving the mind is then free from any defects. One should not readily say that when the mind goes out it is lost and when it comes in it is preserved. If we talk about the original substance, in fact it neither goes out nor comes in. If we talk about going out and coming in, then the mind's thoughts, deliberations, and operations are the going out. However, the master is always obviously present. Where is there any going out? And if there is no going out, where is there any coming in? When Master Ch'eng Hao [Ch'eng Ming-tao, 1032-85] talked about 'the hollow place [that fills] the whole body,'[41] he referred to nothing other than the Principle of Nature. Although one may be engaged in social intercourse all day long, if he is able not to depart from the Principle of Nature, it is tantamount to his remaining inside this body. Only when he departs from the Principle of Nature can he be said to have let the mind go or lost it."

He again said, "To go out or come in is no more than activity and tranquillity. Neither activity nor tranquillity has any beginning. Do they have any direction?"

49. Wang Chia-hsiu[42] asked, "The Buddhists lure people into their way of life by the promise of escape from the cycle of life and death, and the Taoists who seek immortality do so with the promise of everlasting life. But in their hearts they do not wish people to do evil. In the final analysis, they also see the upper section of the Way of

[40] *Ibid.*, where this saying is attributed to Confucius.
[41] *I-shu*, 3:3a.
[42] His courtesy name was Shih-fu. He became Wang's pupil after Wang returned from Kuei-chou. He was much interested in Buddhism and Taoism.

the Sage.[43] But their paths to attainment are not correct. It is like the ways of becoming an official today. Some attain positions through civil service examinations, some through recommendations by local officials, and some through connections with palace officials. They all become high officials, but, after all, these are not the proper ways of becoming officials, and the superior man does not follow them. Reduced to fundamentals, the Buddhists and Taoists are somewhat similar to the Confucians. However, they have only the upper section and neglect the lower section,[44] and in the end are not as perfect as the Sage. Nevertheless we cannot deny that they are similar in the upper section.

"On the other hand, Confucians of later generations have only the lower section of the Sage's doctrine. They mutilated it and lost its true nature and degenerated into the four schools of recitation and memorization, the writing of flowery compositions, the pursuit of success and profit, and textual criticism, and thus at bottom are no different from the heterodox schools. People of these four schools work hard throughout their lives and benefit their bodies and minds not a bit. They seem to compare unfavorably with the Buddhists and Taoists, whose minds are pure, whose desires are few, and who are free from the worldly bondage of fame and profit. Nowadays students need not first of all attack Taoism and Buddhism. Rather, they should earnestly fix their determination on the doctrine of the Sage. As the doctrine of the Sage is made clear to the world, Buddhism and Taoism will disappear of themselves. Otherwise, I am afraid what we want to learn will not be considered worth while by Buddhists and Taoists. In that case would it not be difficult to expect them to condescend and come to our fold? This is my humble opinion. What do you think of it, sir?"

The Teacher said, "What you have said is essentially correct. As to what are called the upper section and the lower section, they are one-sided points of view. The way of the Sage is the great mean and perfect correctness, penetrating both the higher and the lower levels, being one thread that runs through all. What is there to be called the upper section or the lower section? 'The successive movement of the active element yang and the passive element yin

---

[43] That is, matters of the mind and the nature; the refined and subtle aspects of the Way.

[44] That is, matters of fact; the obvious and the immediate aspects of the Way.

constitutes the Way.... The man of humanity sees it and calls it humanity. The man of wisdom sees it and calls it wisdom. And the common people act according to it daily without knowing it. In this way the Way of the superior man is fully realized.'[45] Should humanity or wisdom not be called the Way? Only if one's view of it is one-sided will there be trouble."

50.   [The Teacher said,] "The use of stalks of plants for divination is of course a system of [finding out the operation of] the Change. But the use of tortoise shells is also a system of the Change."[46]

51.   I said, "Confucius said that King Wu was not perfectly good.[47] It seems that Confucius was not satisfied with him."
The Teacher said, "Under the circumstances, King Wu could not have been otherwise."
I said, "If King Wen had not died, what would have happened?"
The Teacher said, "Before King Wen died, the House of Chou had already possessed two thirds of the empire. If King Wen had been alive when King Wu sent a military expedition to punish King Chou of Shang, he probably would not have resorted to military force. Certainly the remaining third would have come and submitted to him. King Wen would have handled King Chou skillfully so that he would not have indulged in evil, that is all."

52.   I asked[48] about Mencius' saying, "Holding the mean without allowing for special circumstances is like holding on to one particular thing."[49]
The Teacher said, "The mean is nothing but the Principle of Nature; it is the Change. It changes according to the time. How can

---

[45] *Book of Changes*, "Appended Remarks," pt. 1, ch. 5. Cf trans. by Legge, *Yi King*, pp. 355-56. The Chinese character here translated as "fully" is *hsien*, which in this context should not be understood in its ordinary meaning of "few."
[46] The former system tells fortunes by counting the number of stalks, thus emphasizing number, while in the latter the shells are burned and fortunes are told by the pattern of their cracks, thus emphasizing form.
[47] *Analects*, 3:25.
[48] In Shih Pang-yao's (1585-1644) *Yang-ming Hsien-sheng chi-yao*, this question is ascribed to Chi Wei-ch'ien (Chi Yüan-heng).
[49] *Book of Mencius*, 7A:26.

one hold it fast? One must act according to the circumstance. It is difficult to fix a pattern of action in advance. Later scholars insist on describing principles in their minute details, leaving out nothing, and prescribing a rigid pattern for action. This is the exact meaning of holding on to one particular thing."

53. T'ang Hsü[50] asked, "Does making up the mind mean retaining good thought at all times and wanting to do good and remove evil?"

The Teacher said, "When a good thought is retained, there is the Principle of Nature. The thought itself is goodness. Is there another goodness to be thought about? Since the thought is not evil, what evil is there to be removed? This thought is comparable to the root of a tree. To make up one's mind means always to build up this good thought, that is all. To be able to follow what one's heart desires without transgressing moral principles[51] merely means that one's mind has reached full maturity."

54. [The Teacher said,] "Generally speaking, the fundamental principle should be that of collecting and concentrating one's spirit, moral character, speech, and action. Only under unavoidable circumstances should they be allowed to be diffused. This is true of man, heaven, earth, and things."

55. I asked what sort of a person Wen-chung Tzu was.[52] The Teacher said, "He can just about be described as 'complete in all respects but not great.'[53] It is regrettable that he died young."

I asked, "Then why has he been criticized for imitating the Classics [by writing supplements to them]?"

The Teacher said, "It is not entirely wrong to imitate the Classics."

"Please explain."

After a long while the Teacher said, "I realize all the more that 'the mind of an expert is singularly distressed.' "[54]

---

[50] Nothing is known of him.
[51] As Confucius said he was able to do at seventy. *Analects*, 2:4.
[52] See above, sec. 11.
[53] Quoting the *Book of Mencius*, 2A:2.
[54] For he is likely to be misunderstood. From a poem by Tu Fu (712-70), *Tu Kung-pu chi*, ch. 4.

56. [The Teacher said,] "Hsü Lu-chai's [Hsü Heng, 1209-81][55] theory that the first thing a scholar should do is to secure a livelihood is harmful."

57. I asked about the concepts of the prime force, the prime spirit, and the prime essence of those Taoists who seek after immortality. The Teacher said, "They are all one. In its universal operation it is force. In its condensation and concentration it is essence, and in its wonderful functioning it is spirit."

58. [The Teacher said,] "The original substance of pleasure, anger, sorrow, and joy is naturally in the states of equilibrium and harmony. As soon as one attaches a bit of his own idea to them, they will become excessive or deficient; they will be selfish."

59. I asked about Confucius' not singing on the day of mourning when he wept.[56] The Teacher said, "Because of the substance of the Sage's mind he was naturally like this."

60. [The Teacher said,] "In trying to master oneself, every selfish thought must be thoroughly and completely wiped out without leaving even an iota. If an iota remains, many evils will come one leading the other."

61. I asked about the *Lü-lü hsin-shu* (New book on pitch pipes).[57] The Teacher said, "The student should be earnestly devoted to what is of the greatest importance. Even if one becomes thoroughly familiar with these calculations, they may not necessarily be of any use. It is necessary that the mind should first possess the fundamentals of ceremonies and music. For example, according to the book, usually a series of pitch pipes is used [for the twelve semitones,

---

[55] One of the most outstanding Confucians in the Yüan dynasty. While he adhered to the rationalistic Neo-Confucianism of Chu Hsi, he emphasized the practical need of economic security. See *Hsü Lu-chai chi*, 6:8b. For an account of him, see *Sung-Yüan hsüeh-an*, ch. 90.

[56] *Analects*, 7:9.

[57] The *Lü-lü hsin-shu*, by Chu Hsi's pupil Ts'ai Yüan-ting (1135-98). It deals with musical pitch, weather, etc., and was highly praised by Chu Hsi. According to the *Ssu-k'u ch'üan-shu tsung-mu t'i-yao*, ch. 38, probably Chu Hsi and Ts'ai collaborated in writing it.

filled with reed ashes, buried in the ground in an enclosed room with one end of the pipes exposed] and we then wait for the response of material force to the weather [to determine the correct pitch. If the ashes in a tube fly off at the proper time of its corresponding month, it will show that material force responds to the proper weather and the pitch will therefore be correct. For example, when the ashes fly off during the first two-hour period of the winter solstice, the pitch for the fundamental tone, approximately 'F', is correct]. But at the winter solstice the ashes may fly off just a moment earlier or later. How can we know to what moment of the winter solstice the pipe should correspond? We must first understand in our mind what the exact moment of the winter solstice should be. This is where the book does not make sense. The student must first direct his effort to acquiring the fundamentals of ceremonies and music."

62. Hsü Ai said, "The mind is like a mirror. The sage's mind is like a clear mirror, whereas that of the ordinary person is like a dull mirror. The theory of the investigation of things in recent times[58] says that it works like a mirror reflecting things and the effort is to be directed toward the [passive] role of reflecting. They don't realize that the mirror is still dull. How can it reflect? The investigation of things in our Teacher's theory is like polishing the mirror to make it clear. The effort is to be directed toward the [active] role of polishing. When the mirror is clear, it does not cease to reflect."[59]

63. I asked about the refinement or coarseness of the Way. The Teacher said, "The Way is neither refined nor coarse. It is so only from man's point of view. Take this room. When a person at first comes in, he sees only a large form. After some time he sees clearly the columns, the walls, and so forth, one by one. Still later he sees minute details such as ornaments on the columns if there are any. But the room is just a room."

64. The Teacher said, "When we have seen each other in recent days, you gentlemen have not asked many questions. Why? If a

[58] In the Chu Hsi school.
[59] It is interesting to note that this is the only independent saying by a disciple of Wang's in the whole book.

person does not exert effort, he will think that he already knows the way of learning and that all he has to do is to follow it out in action. He does not realize that one's selfish desires grow day by day, like dirt piling up on the ground. If for one day it is not swept out, another layer will be accumulated. If one exerts serious and concrete effort, he will see that the Way is infinite. The more one reaches for it, the deeper it becomes. In pursuing the Way, one must be as thorough as in grinding rice until it is refined and white, without neglecting the least bit."

65. I asked, "Only after knowledge has been extended to the utmost can we talk about the sincerity of the will. Now since we do not yet know all about the Principle of Nature and selfish human desires, how can we exert any effort on self-mastery?"

The Teacher said, "If a person exerts effort with all seriousness and with personal concern, and does so without stop, he will gradually, day by day, see the refinement and subtlety of the Principle of Nature in his mind. He will also gradually, day by day, see the minuteness and subtlety of selfish desires in his mind. If he does not exert the effort of self-mastery, then all day long he does nothing but talk. The Principle of Nature never reveals itself. Nor do selfish desires. It is like walking on the road to go somewhere. As one walks one section of the road, he recognizes the next section. When he comes to a fork, and is in doubt, he will ask and then go on. Only then can he gradually reach his destination. People today are not willing to preserve as much of the Principle of Nature as they already know, nor to get rid of the selfish human desires they already know, but merely worry about not knowing all of them. They just talk idly. What good is this? Let one wait till he has mastered himself to the point of having no more selfish desires to overcome and then worry about not knowing all. It will still not be too late."

66. I asked, "The Way is one.[60] In discussing it the ancients often disagreed. Are there some essential points about searching for it?"

The Teacher said, "The Way has neither spatial restriction nor physical form, and it cannot be pinned down to any particular. To seek it by confining ourselves to literal meanings would be far off

[60] A quotation from the *Book of Mencius*, 3A:1.

the mark. Take those people today who talk about Heaven. Do they actually understand it? It is incorrect to say that the sun, the moon, wind, and thunder constitute Heaven. It is also incorrect to say that man, animals, and plants do not constitute it. Heaven is the Way. If we realize this, where is the Way not to be found? People merely look at it from one corner and conclude that the Way is nothing but this or that. Consequently they disagree. If one knows how to search for the Way inside the mind and to see the substance of one's own mind, then there is no place nor time where the Way is not to be found. It pervades the past and present and is without beginning or end. Where do similarity and difference come in? The mind is the Way, and the Way is Heaven. If one knows the mind, he knows both the Way and Heaven."

He again said, "If you gentlemen want to understand the Way definitely, you must personally realize it in your own minds, without depending on any search outside. Only then will it be all right."

67. I asked, "Should names, varieties, and systems of things be investigated first of all?"

The Teacher said, "It is necessary only for a person fully to realize the substance of his own mind, and then its functions will be found right in its midst. If one should nourish the substance of his mind so that there is really equilibrium before the feelings are aroused, then naturally when they are aroused they will attain harmony in due measure and degree, and wherever it may be applied it will be correct. On the other hand, if there is no such mind, even if one may have gone into many names, varieties, and systems of things, they really have nothing to do with him but are merely ornaments. Naturally, when the time comes to use them they are of no use. I do not mean to neglect the names, varieties, and systems completely. I merely point out that if we know that first things must come first, then we can approach the Way."

He again said, "One must accomplish according to his ability. Ability is what one can do, like the ability of K'uei, Emperor Shun's minister, to institute musical systems, and the ability of Shun's Minister Chi to institute agriculture.[61] These were the original endowments of their nature. Their accomplishment was due to the fact

---

[61] See *Book of History*, "Canon of Shun." Cf. trans. by Legge, *Shoo King*, pp. 44, 47.

that the substance of their minds became completely identified with the Principle of Nature, so that whatever its function might be it issued from the Principle of Nature. Only this can be called ability. When the point is reached that the mind becomes completely identified with the Principle of Nature, one's ability is not restricted to any particular thing. If K'uei and Chi had exchanged places, they would have been able to accomplish each other's tasks also."

He again said, "Take for example the superior man. In a position of wealth and in noble station he does what is proper to a position of wealth and to noble station, and in a position of difficulty and danger he does what is proper to a position of difficulty and danger.[62] In all these he is not restricted to any particular thing. Only those who have correctly nourished the substance of their mind can do so."

68.   [The Teacher said,] "It is better to be a small body of water in a well which comes from a spring than a large body of water in a pond which comes from no source. The water in the well has the spirit of life that is inexhaustible." It is said that when the Teacher said so, he was sitting by a well next to a pond. Therefore he used this analogy to enlighten his students.

69.   I asked, "Civilization declines further and further. How can we see the condition of great antiquity again?"

The Teacher said, "A single day is no different from a period of 129,600 years.[63] When one gets up early in the morning and sits down, he has not yet come into contact with the influence of the material world. His mind is pure and clear, and this condition makes him feel as though he is living at the time of Fu-hsi of great antiquity."

70.   I asked, "When the mind is inclined to chase after material things, what can be done?"

The Teacher said, "When a ruler folds his arms, sits erect, and is at leisure and at peace, and each of his chief ministers[64] attends to

[62] Quoting the *Doctrine of the Mean*, ch. 14.

[63] According to Shao Yung (1101-77), a *yüan* is a period of 129,600 years, at the end of which heaven and earth perish and a new cycle begins. See his *Huang-chi ching-shih shu*, 6:14a.

[64] Of the six departments : personnel, population, rites, military affairs, justice, and public works.

his duties, the state will be in order. The mind should command the five sense organs in the same way. But if when the eye wants to see, the mind itself pursues the color, or when the ear wants to hear, the mind itself pursues the sound, it will be as though a ruler himself occupied the position of the minister of personnel when he wanted officials selected or the position of the minister of military affairs when he wanted an army transferred. When he does so not only is the true nature of a ruler gone; the six departments cannot function either."

71. [The Teacher said,] "When a good thought arises, recognize it and develop it fully. When an evil thought arises, recognize it and stop it. It is the will that recognizes the thought and develops or stops it; it is intelligence (that is, innate knowledge of the good) endowed by Heaven. This is all a sage has. A student must preserve it."

72. I said, "The love of sex, wealth, and fame is of course selfish desire. But why are idle and sundry thoughts also regarded as selfish desires?"

The Teacher said, "In the final analysis they grow from such roots as the love of sex, wealth, and fame. You will see if you get at the root. You surely know in your own mind that you have no thought of stealing. Why? Because at bottom you do not have such thought. If you eliminate all thoughts of sex, wealth, fame, and so forth, just as you have no thought of becoming a thief, there will be nothing but the original substance of the mind. What idle thoughts can there be? This pure state is 'the state of absolute quiet and inactivity,'[65] 'the equilibrium before the feelings are aroused,'[66] and 'broad and extremely impartial.'[67] The natural effect will be that 'when acted on, it immediately penetrates all things,'[68] 'when the feelings are aroused, each and all attain due measure and degree,'[69] and 'it responds spontaneously to all things as they come.' "[70]

---

[65] *Book of Changes*, "Appended Remarks," pt. 1, ch. 10. Cf. trans. by Legge, *Yi King*, p. 370.

[66] *Doctrine of the Mean*, ch. 1.

[67] Ch'eng Hao, *Wen-chi*, 3:1a.

[68] *Book of Changes*, "Appended Remarks," pt. 1, ch. 10. Cf. trans. by Legge, *Yi King*, p. 370.

[69] *Doctrine of the Mean*, ch. 1.

[70] Ch'eng Hao. *Wen-chi*, 3:1a.

73. I asked about "The will is the highest and the vital force comes next."[71] The Teacher said, "It means that wherever the will goes, so does the vital force. It does not mean that the will is the ultimate chief whereas the vital force is subordinate to it.[72] If the will is held firm, the vital force will also be properly cultivated and nourished, and if no violence is done the vital force, the will will also be held firm. Mencius corrected Kao Tzu's mistake of being one-sided and therefore emphasized both the nature and the will equally."

74. I asked, "A former scholar said, 'The sage necessarily takes his doctrine down to a low position [so people can approach it] while a worthy lifts his words to a higher position [so the doctrine of the sage may be respected].'[73] What do you think of it?"

The Teacher said, "It is wrong. To do so would be insincere. The sage is comparable to Heaven. It is everywhere. Up where the sun, moon, and stars are, it is Heaven, and deep down under ground it is also Heaven. When has Heaven descended to a lower position? A sage is one who is great and is completely transformed [to be goodness itself].[74] A worthy may be compared to a high mountain peak. He has only to maintain this lofty position. But a mountain of 1,000 feet cannot stretch to become 10,000 feet, and a mountain of 10,000 feet cannot stretch to become 100,000 feet. The worthy does not extend himself to achieve a lofty position. To do so would be insincere."

75. I asked, "I-ch'uan [Ch'eng I] said that we should not seek equilibrium before the feelings of pleasure, anger, sorrow, and joy are aroused.[75] Yen-p'ing [Li T'ung, 1088-1158], however, taught people to watch for the disposition before such feelings are aroused.[76] What do you say about them?"

---

[71] *Book of Mencius*, 2A:2.
[72] This is Chu Hsi's commentary on the passage. See his *Meng Tzu chi-chu*, ch. 3.
[73] Ch'eng I, quoted by Chu Hsi in his *Lun-yü chi-chu*, ch. 5, comment on *Analects*, 9:7.
[74] As described in the *Book of Mencius*, 7B:25.
[75] *I-shu*, 18:14b.
[76] Yen-p'ing was Li T'ung's honorific name. He was Chu Hsi's teacher. It was through him that the teachings of Ch'eng were transmitted to Chu Hsi. He emphasized sitting in meditation and tranquillity of mind. The teaching here referred to is found in the *Li Yen-p'ing chi*, 2:16a-b. See below, sec. 94.

The Teacher said, "They are both right. I-ch'uan was afraid lest people seek equilibrium before the feelings are aroused, regarding equilibrium as separate and distinct, like what I previously described as trying to attain equilibrium after one's vital force is calmed down.[77] He therefore told people to make the effort of seeking equilibrium right in self-cultivation and self-examination. Yen-p'ing, on the other hand, was afraid lest people have no place to start. He therefore told them at all times to look for the disposition before the feelings are aroused. He wanted them to direct all attention to this condition when they open their eyes directly to look or turn their ears attentively to listen. This is the work of not waiting to see things before becoming cautious or to hear things before becoming apprehensive.[78] In both cases the teachers of the past could not help teaching people in the ways they did."

76. I asked, "Ordinary people of course do not possess the totality of equilibrium before the feelings of pleasure, anger, sorrow, and joy are aroused and of harmony after they are aroused. But suppose there is a small matter that should arouse one's pleasure or anger. If ordinarily he does not have the mind of pleasure or anger, and when the matter occurs, he can also attain a due measure and degree of pleasure or anger, can that be called the state of equilibrium and harmony?"

The Teacher said, "He may be said to attain equilibrium and harmony in connection with a particular affair or occasion, but cannot be said to have acquired the great foundation or to be following the universal way. The nature of all men is good. They all originally possess the qualities of equilibrium and harmony. How can we say that they are without them? However, since the mind of the ordinary man is obscured and darkened to some extent, although its original substance reveals itself from time to time, nevertheless it appears one moment and disappears the next. It is not the mind in its total substance and great functioning. Only when the mind attains equilibrium at all times can it be said to have a great foundation, and only when it attains harmony at all times can it be said to be following the universal way. Only those who are perfectly sincere can establish the great foundation for humanity."[79]

[77] See above, sec. 28.
[78] Paraphrasing the *Doctrine of the Mean*, ch. 1.
[79] *Ibid.*, ch. 32.

I said, "I still do not understand the meaning of equilibrium."

The Teacher said, "It must be personally realized in one's own mind. It cannot be explained in words. Equilibrium is nothing but the Principle of Nature."

"What is the Principle of Nature?"

"One recognizes it when he has gotten rid of selfish human desires."

"Why is the Principle of Nature called equilibrium?"

"Because it is balanced and impartial."

"What is the condition of that?"

"It is like a bright mirror. It is entirely clear, without a speck of dust attached to it."

"To be partial is to be attached. When one is attached to the love of sex, wealth, fame, and so forth, it is clear that he is unbalanced. However, before the feelings are aroused, the mind is not yet attached to the love of sex, wealth, fame, and so forth. How can we know that it is unbalanced?"

"Although there is not yet any attachment, nevertheless in one's everyday life one's mind is not entirely free from such love. Since it is not free from it, it means that it is present in the mind. This being so, it cannot be said that the mind is not partial. Take a person sick with intermittent fever. Although at times the illness does not appear, so long as the root of the disease has not been eliminated, the person cannot be said to be free from the disease. Only when all such selfish desires as the love for sex, wealth, fame, and so forth in one's daily life are completely wiped out and cleaned up, so that not the least bit is retained, and the mind becomes broad in its total substance and becomes completely identified with the Principle of Nature, can it be said to have attained the equilibrium before the feelings are aroused and to have acquired the great foundation of virtue."

77. I asked, "You said that 'after Yen Hui [Confucius' favorite pupil] passed away, the doctrine of the Sage died out.'[80] I cannot help being dubious about that."

The Teacher said, "Yen Hui alone understood the Way of the Sage in its entirety. You can see that from the fact that he heaved a sigh.[81] When he said, 'The Master, by good order, skillfully leads

---

[80] *Wang Wen-ch'eng Kung ch'üan-shu*, 7:7a.
[81] In admiration of the master's doctrine. See *Analects*, 9:10.

a man along and teaches him. He taught me to broaden myself with literature and restrain myself with rules of propriety,'[82] he said so after he had thoroughly understood the Way. How skillful it is in leading and teaching people to broaden them with literature and restrain them with rules of propriety! The student must think it over. It was difficult even for the Sage to tell people about the Way in its total reality. The student must study and come to understanding by himself. When Yen Hui wished to follow the Way but could not find it,[83] he said so in the same spirit [of humility and devotion] as King Wen who looked for the Way as if he could not see it.[84] I believe that to look for the Way as if one cannot see it is to see it perfectly. Since Yen Hui's death the orthodox doctrine of the Sage has not continued in its totality."

78. I asked, "The mind is the master of the body. Knowledge is the intelligence of the mind. The will is knowledge in operation. And a thing is that to which the will is directed. Is this correct?"
The Teacher said, "Generally correct."

79. [The Teacher said,] "To preserve one's mind and see to it that it is always present is itself learning. What is the use of thinking of past and future events? In doing so one merely loses his mind."

80. [The Teacher said,] "When one speaks without proper order, we can see that his mind is not preserved."

81. Hsüeh Shang-ch'ien[85] asked, "Does the 'unperturbed mind' Mencius talked about differ from that of Kao Tzu?"[86]

---

[82] *Ibid.*
[83] *Ibid.*
[84] *Book of Mencius*, 4B:20.
[85] His name was K'an, and he died in 1545. A holder of the "presented scholar" degree of 1517, he followed Wang for four years in Kiangsi. In 1531 he aroused the anger of the emperor because of his memorial and was imprisoned. Later he lectured for many years in a Buddhist temple in a famous mountain some sixty miles from Canton, and was a staunch defender of Wang against critics. For an account of him, see *Ming-ju hsüeh-an*, 30:3a-8b. For conversations recorded by him, see below, secs. 95-129.
[86] *Book of Mencius*, 2A:2.

The Teacher said, "Kao Tzu forcefully controlled his mind and kept it from being perturbed. Mencius, on the other hand, accumulated righteousness to the point where the mind naturally is unperturbed." The Teacher added, "In its original substance the mind is not perturbed. The original substance of the mind is one's nature, and one's nature is principle. Both human nature and principle are originally unperturbed. The accumulation of righteousness means returning to the original substance of the mind."

82.   [The Teacher said,] "At the time when all things are luxuriantly present, reality is also empty, tranquil, and without any sign. And when reality is empty, tranquil, and without any sign, it is the same as when all things are luxuriantly present.[87] The state of being empty, tranquil, and without any sign is the father of singleness [for all things are produced from this state], and the state of all things' being luxuriantly present is the mother of refinement [since all things embrace principle]. Singleness involves refinement and refinement involves singleness."

83.   [The Teacher said,] "There is no thing [or event] outside the mind. For instance, when a thought rises in my mind to serve my parents filially, then serving my parents filially is a thing [or event]."

84.   The Teacher said, "Nowadays, people who pursue what I call the learning of the investigation of things still for the most part fall into mere talking and listening. How much less can those who pursue learning by talking and listening return to the investigation of things? The refinement and subtlety of the Principle of Nature and selfish human desires are such that one must make a constant effort at self-examination and self-mastery before he can gradually see it. Now if one just talks, even though he talks only about the Principle of Nature, without his realizing it, there is already in his mind, even for a short moment, a certain amount of selfish desire, for it does secretly arise without our knowing it. It is not easy to discover even if one examines it with great effort. How can one expect to know all by merely talking? Now if we merely talk about the Principle of Nature, leave it there and do not follow it, and talk about selfish human desires, leave them there and do not get

[87] Paraphrasing Ch'eng I, *I-shu*, 15:8a. See above, n. 4.

rid of them, is that the learning of the investigation of things and the extension of knowledge? Even at its best, the learning of later generations has only reached its point of achievement through incidental acts of righteousness."[88]

85.   I asked about the investigation of things. The Teacher said, "To investigate (*ko*) is to rectify. It is to rectify that which is incorrect so it can return to its original correctness."[89]

86.   I said, "Abiding by the highest good means to know that the highest good is inherent in my mind and originally not outside. Only then can the will be calm."

The Teacher said, "Right."

87.   I asked, "The time to exert effort to investigate things is the time when one is active. Is that correct?"

The Teacher said, "It makes no difference whether one is active or tranquil. There are also things when one is tranquil. Mencius said, 'Always be doing something.'[90] Thus one is always doing something whether one is active or tranquil."

88.   [The Teacher said,] "The difficult part of our effort lies entirely in the investigation of things and the extension of knowledge. This is precisely the matter of the sincerity of the will. If the will is sincere, then, to a large extent, the mind is naturally rectified, and the personal life is also naturally cultivated. However, effort is also required to rectify the mind and cultivate the personal life. The cultivation of the personal life is the part after the feelings are aroused, whereas the rectification of the mind is the part before the feelings are aroused. If the mind is rectified, there will be equilibrium. If the personal life is cultivated, there will be harmony."

89.   [The Teacher said,] "The various steps from the investigation of things and the extension of knowledge to the bringing of peace to the world[91] are nothing but manifesting the clear character. Even loving

---

[88] A reference to the *Book of Mencius*, 2A:2.
[89] Cf. secs. 7, above, and 137, below.
[90] *Book of Mencius*, 2A:2.
[91] As taught in the *Great Learning*, the text.

the people is also a matter of manifesting the clear character. The clear character is the character of the mind; it is humanity. The man of humanity regards Heaven and Earth and all things as one body.[92] If a single thing is deprived of its place, it means that my humanity is not yet demonstrated to the fullest extent."

90.   [The Teacher said,] "Merely to talk about manifesting the clear character and not to talk about loving the people would be to behave like the Taoists and Buddhists."

91.   [The Teacher said,] "The highest good is the nature. Originally the nature has not the least evil. Therefore it is called the highest good. To abide by it is simply to recover the nature's original state."

92.   I asked, "If one knows that the highest good is his nature, that his nature is completely contained in his mind, and that his mind is where the highest good abides, then he will not seek it outside in a confused manner as in the past, and his will will be calm. Being calm, it will not be disturbed. Not being disturbed, it will be tranquil. Being tranquil, it will not act foolishly and will then be in peaceful repose. To be in peaceful repose is to concentrate the mind and the will right here. In all the thousands and thousands of thoughts, the desire is surely to achieve this highest good. This means he can deliberate and the end can be attained.[93] Is this theory correct?"
       The Teacher said, "It is generally correct."

93.   I said, "Master Ch'eng Hao said that 'the man of humanity regards Heaven, Earth, and all things as one body.'[94] How is it that Mo Tzu's [fl. 479-438 B.C.] doctrine of universal love[95] is not considered one of humanity?"
       The Teacher said, "It is very difficult to say. You gentlemen must find it out through personal realization. Humanity is the principle of unceasing production and reproduction. Although it is prevalent

[92] A famous saying by Ch'eng Hao. See I-shu, 2A:2a.
[93] Paraphrasing the Great Learning, ch. 1.
[94] I-shu, 2A:2a.
[95] Mo Tzu was strongly attacked by Mencius because he did not acknowledge the special affection due to a father. Book of Mencius, 3B:9. For Mo Tzu's doctrine, see Mo Tzu, chs. 14-16, English trans. by Y. P. Mei, The Works of Motse (London, Probsthain, 1928), pp. 78 ff.

and extensive and there is no place where it does not exist, nevertheless there is an order in its operation and growth. That is why it is unceasing in production and reproduction. For example, at the winter solstice the first yang[96] grows. There must be the growth of this first yang before all the six stages of yang[97] gradually grow. If there were not the first yang, could there be all the six? It is the same with the yin.[98] Because there is order, so there is a starting point. Because there is a starting point, so there is growth. And because there is growth, it is unceasing. Take a tree, for example. When in the beginning it puts forth a shoot, there is the starting point of the tree's spirit of life. After the root appears, the trunk grows. After the trunk grows, branches and leaves come, and then the process of unceasing production and reproduction has begun. If there is no sprout, how can there be the trunk, branches, or leaves? The tree can sprout because there is the root beneath. With the root the plant will grow. Without it, the plant will die, for without the root, how can it sprout?

"The love between father and son and between elder and younger brothers is the starting point of the human mind's spirit of life, just like the sprout of the tree. From here it is extended to humaneness to all people and love to all things. It is just like the growth of the trunk, branches, and leaves. Mo Tzu's universal love makes no distinction in human relations and regards one's own father, son, elder brother, or younger brother as being the same as a passer-by. That means that Mo Tzu's universal love has no starting point. It does not sprout. We therefore know that it has no root and that it is not a process of unceasing production and reproduction. How can it be called humanity? Filial piety and brotherly respect are the root of humanity.[99] This means that the principle of humanity grows from within."

94. I asked, "Li Yen-p'ing said, 'Be in accord with principle and have no selfish mind.'[100] What is the difference between being in accord with principle and having no selfish mind?"

The Teacher said, "The mind is principle. To have no selfish mind

[96] The active cosmic force.
[97] The six months between December and June.
[98] The passive cosmic force.
[99] A saying in *Analects*, 1:2.
[100] *Li Yen-p'ing chi*, 2:24a. Also see above, sec. 76.

is to be in accord with principle, and not to be in accord with principle is to have a selfish mind. I am afraid it is not good to speak of the mind and principle as separate."

I asked further, "The Buddhists are [internally] free from all kinds of selfishness of lust in the world and thus appear not to have a selfish mind. But externally they discard human relations and thus do not appear to be in accord with principle."

The Teacher said, "These are the same kind of thing, all building up a mind of selfishness."

CONVERSATIONS RECORDED BY HSÜEH K'AN[1] (Sections 95-129)

95. I asked, "To hold the will firm is like having a pain in the heart. As the whole mind is concentrated on the pain, how can there be time for idle talk or being a busybody?"[2]

The Teacher said, "This is good as an initial effort. But the student must be made to understand that the spiritual intelligence of the mind comes in and goes out at no definite time and without anyone's knowing its direction,[3] and that it is originally this way. Only in this way can one's effort find a solution. If one merely holds his will rigidly, I am afraid his effort will encounter trouble."

96. I asked, "If one confines his effort entirely to self-cultivation and does not devote himself to study, one is likely to mistake his desires for the Principle of Nature. What can be done?"

The Teacher said, "One must understand the true meaning of learning. To study is nothing but self-cultivation. Not to study merely means that one's will to self-cultivation is not sufficiently serious or concrete."

"What is meant by understanding the true meaning of learning?"

"Suppose you tell me what learning is for, and what there is to learn."

"I have heard you teach us saying that to learn is to learn to preserve the Principle of Nature, that the original substance of the

[1] See above, sec. 81, n. 85.
[2] This passage also appears between secs. 24 and 25.
[3] *Book of Mencius*, 6A:8, quoting Confucius.

mind is the Principle of Nature, and that in order personally to realize this, it is merely necessary to have no selfish wishes in one's mind."

"Then it is only necessary to overcome and get rid of selfish wishes. Why worry about not understanding principle and desires?"

"I am simply afraid that the selfish wishes are not truly recognized."

"It is all because the will is not yet serious or concrete. If it is, all the eye sees and the ear hears will be directed toward the selfish desires. How is it possible that they cannot be truly recognized? All people have the sense of right and wrong. One need not seek it outside. To study merely means personally to realize what one's mind has seen. It is not to look for something to be seen outside the mind."

97. The Teacher asked friends who were present about their recent progress in learning. One friend mentioned the idea of the mind's being clear, calm, and free from material desires. The Teacher said, "This refers to the condition of learning."

Another friend spoke about the similarity and difference of past and present efforts in learning. The Teacher said, "This refers to the effect of learning."

The two friends did not know what to say and asked for explanation.

The Teacher said, "Our effort today consists in being genuine and concrete in our determination to do good. If our determination is genuine and concrete, we will immediately advance to do good whenever we see it and immediately correct ourselves whenever we make a mistake.[4] Only in this way do we have genuine and concrete effort. Then selfish human desires will gradually decrease and the Principle of Nature will be increasingly understood. If we merely go after the condition or the effect of learning, we are not making a real effort but are committing the error of forcing the growth of the mind and pursuing external things."

98. When friends studied, many selected Hui-an [Chu Hsi] for criticism. The Teacher said, "This is purposely to find disagreement. It is wrong. When at times my ideas are different from those of

[4] *Book of Changes*, commentary on hexagram no. 42. Cf. trans. by Legge, *Yi King*, p. 319.

Hui-an, it is because I had to argue for my position, so that the student may not make an infinitesimal mistake in the beginning and end up with an infinite error. But my ultimate purpose and that of Hui-an are not different. For the rest, where his statements and explanations are clear and appropriate, why does a single word of his need to be altered?"

99. Ts'ai Hsi-yüan[5] asked, "Sagehood can be achieved through learning. But the abilities[6] and efforts of sages Po-i and I-yin[6] are after all different from those of Confucius. Why are they all called sages?"

The Teacher said, "The reason the sage has become a sage is that his mind has become completely identified with the Principle of Nature and is no longer mixed with any impurity of selfish human desires. It is comparable to pure gold, which attains its purity because its golden quality is perfect and is no longer mixed with copper or lead. A man must have reached the state of being completely identified with the Principle of Nature before he becomes a sage, and gold must be perfect in quality before it becomes pure.

"However, the abilities of sages differ in degree, just as the several pieces of gold quantitatively differ in weight. The sage-emperors Yao and Shun may be compared to 10,000 pounds; King Wen and Confucius to 9,000 pounds; Kings Yü [r. 2183-2175 B.C.?], T'ang, [r. 1751-1739 B.C.?], Wen, and Wu, 7 or 8,000 pounds; and Po-i and I-yin, 4 or 5,000 pounds. Their abilities and efforts differ, but in being completely identified with the Principle of Nature they were the same and all may be called sages. It is just like the several pieces of pure gold, which may be so called because they are qualitatively perfect although quantitatively different. Mix a 5,000 pound piece

---

[5] His private name was Tsung-yen. Holder of a "presented scholar" degree, he was one of Wang's first disciples. He was secretary in the state department of education in Szechuan. For a brief account of him, see *Ming-ju hsüeh-an*, 11:5a-b.

[6] According to tradition, when King Wen, founder of the Chou, launched an expedition against Shang, Po-i, out of loyalty to the Shang dynasty, pleaded with him not to do so. When King Wen finally conquered Shang, Po-i refused to eat the grains of Chou, lived on berries in the mountains, and eventually starved to death. I-yin, who was a minister of King T'ang, founder of the Shang, helped him to bring about peace and prosperity and later banished T'ang's successor who failed in his duties but restored him after he repented. See the *Book of Mencius*, 5B:1. Also cf. sec. 286, below.

of gold with a 10,000 pound piece, and their quality remains the same. Put Po-i and I-yin beside Yao and Confucius, and their complete identification with the Principle of Nature is the same. For to be pure gold depends not on quantity but on perfection in quality, and to be a sage depends not on ability or effort but on being completely identified with the Principle of Nature. Therefore even an ordinary person, if he is willing to learn so as to enable his mind to become completely identified with the Principle of Nature, can also become a sage, in the same way that although a one ounce piece, when compared with a 10,000 pound piece, is widely different in quantity, it is not deficient in perfection in quality. This is why it is said that 'every man can become Yao and Shun.'[7]

"In learning to become a sage, the student needs only to get rid of selfish human desires and preserve the Principle of Nature, which is like refining gold and achieving perfection in quality. If the deficiency in purity is not substantial, the work of refining is simple and success is easily attained. The lower the proportion of purity is, the more difficult the work becomes. In the matter of purity and impurity of physical nature, some men are above average and some are below. With reference to the Sage's doctrines, some are born with the knowledge of them and can practice them naturally and easily, while others learn them through study and practice them for their advantage.[8] Those below the average must make one hundred efforts where others make one, and one thousand efforts where others make ten.[9] But the success of all of them is the same. Later generations do not realize that the foundation for becoming a sage is to be completely identified with the Principle of Nature, but instead seek sagehood only in knowledge and ability. They regard the sage as knowing all and being able to do all, and they feel they have to understand all the knowledge and ability of the sage before they can succeed. Consequently they do not direct their efforts toward the Principle of Nature but merely cripple their spirit and exhaust their energy in scrutinizing books, investigating the names and varieties of things, and imitating the forms and traces [of the acts of the ancients]. As their knowledge becomes more extensive, their selfish desires become more numerous, and

[7] *Book of Mencius*, 6B:2.
[8] Paraphrasing the *Doctrine of the Mean*, ch. 20.
[9] *Ibid.*, ch. 19.

as their abilities become greater and greater, the Principle of Nature becomes increasingly obscured from them. Their case is just like that of a person who, seeing someone else with a piece of pure gold of 10,000 pounds, does not take steps to refine his own so that in the quality of purity his will not yield to that of the other person, but foolishly hopes to match the 10,000 pound piece in quantity. He throws in mixed elements of pewter, lead, brass, and iron with the result that the greater the quantity, the lower the degree of purity. In the end it is no longer gold at all."

At that time Hsü Ai was by the side of the Teacher and remarked, "This analogy of yours will effectively destroy the delusions of famous but mediocre scholars who advocate the study of isolated details and is a great help to us students."

The Teacher further said, "In making effort, we want to diminish every day rather than to increase every day. If we reduce our selfish human desire a little bit, to that extent we have restored the Principle of Nature. How enjoyable and how free! How simple and how easy!"

100. Yang Shih-te[10] asked, "The theory of the investigation of things as you taught it is clear, simple, and easy. Everyone can understand it. How is it that Wen Kung [Chu Hsi][11] failed to understand the theory although he was unsurpassed in intelligence?"

The Teacher said, "Wen Kung's mental energy and vigor were great. Because from the beginning, when he was young, he had already made up his mind to continue the heritage of the past and to enlighten future generations, all along he directed his efforts only to intellectual investigation and writing. Naturally he would have had no time for these if he had given priority to self-cultivation with a sense of genuine and personal concern. After he had reached the state of eminent virtue, if he had really worried lest the doctrine not be made clear to the world, and, following the example of Confucius' retiring to edit the Six Classics, had eliminated superfluous works and confined himself to the simple and essential in order to enlighten later scholars, in general it would not

[10] His private name was Chi. He was at first a disciple of Chan Kan-ch'üan (see below, sec. 201, n. 3) but later followed Wang.

[11] Chu Hsi was honored with the posthumous title, *Wen*, meaning "culture."

have required him to do much investigation. When he was young he wrote many books and then repented doing so in his old age. That was doing things upside down."

Shih-te said, "He repented in his old age. For instance, he said that he realized the mistake of adhering to the traditionally accepted text of the *Great Learning*,[12] that 'book reading did not help his task,'[13] and that his task 'had nothing to do with holding on to books or adhering rigidly to words.'[14] These statements show that when he reached old age he began to regret the mistakes of his previous effort and to direct his new effort toward self-cultivation in the spirit of genuine and personal concern."

The Teacher said, "Correct. This is where we cannot match Wen Kung. His energy being great, once he regretted he immediately turned around. Unfortunately before long he passed away, not living long enough to correct the many mistakes he had made during his lifetime."

101. I was pulling weeds out from among the flowers and there-upon said, "How difficult it is in the world to cultivate good and remove evil!"

The Teacher said, "Only because no effort is made to do so." A little later, he said, "Such a view of good and evil is motivated by personal interest and is therefore easily wrong." I did not understand. The Teacher said, "The spirit of life of Heaven and Earth is the same in flowers and weeds. Where have they the distinction of good and evil? When you want to enjoy flowers, you will consider flowers good and weeds evil. But when you want to use weeds, you will then consider them good. Such good and evil are all products of the mind's likes and dislikes. Therefore I know you are wrong."

I asked, "In that case, there is neither good nor evil, is that right?"

The Teacher said, "The state of having neither good nor evil is that of principle in tranquillity. Good and evil appear when the

[12] Letter in answer to Huang Chih-ch'ing, in *Chu Tzu wen-chi*, 46:30b. Actually the phrase *ting-pen* [accepted edition] does not appear in the letter. At any rate, Chu's regret was over the rigid study of details and has nothing to do with the *Great Learning*. For "Chu Hsi's Final Conclusions Arrived at Late in Life," see below, pp. 263-67.
[13] Letter to Lü Tzu-yüeh, in *ibid.*, 47:29a.
[14] Letter to Ho Shu-ching, in *ibid.*, 40:27a.

vital force is perturbed. If the vital force is not perturbed, there is neither good nor evil, and this is called the highest good."

I asked, "The Buddhists also deny the distinction between good and evil. Are they different from you?"

The Teacher said, "Being attached to the non-distinction of good and evil, the Buddhists neglect everything and therefore are incapable of governing the world. The sage, on the other hand, in his non-distinction of good and evil, merely makes no special effort whatsoever to like or dislike, and is not perturbed in his vital force. As he pursues the kingly path and sees the perfect excellence,[15] he of course completely follows the Principle of Nature and it becomes possible for him to assist in and complete the universal process of production and reproduction and apply it for the benefit of the people."[16]

"If weeds are not evil, they should not be removed."

"This, however, is the view of the Buddhists and Taoists. If they are harmful, what is the objection to your removing them?"

"That would be a case of making a special effort to like or to dislike."

"Not making a special effort to like or to dislike does not mean not to like or dislike at all. A person behaving so would be devoid of consciousness. To say 'not to make a special effort' merely means that one's likes and dislikes completely follow the Principle of Nature and that one does not go on to attach to that situation a bit of selfish thought. This amounts to having neither likes nor dislikes."

"How can weeding be regarded as completely following the Principle of Nature without any attachment to selfish thought?"

"If weeds are harmful, according to principle they should be removed. Then remove them, that is all. If for a moment they are not removed, one should not be troubled by it. If one attaches to that situation a bit of selfish thought, it will be a burden on the substance of his mind, and his vital force will be much perturbed."

[15] Quoting the *Book of History*, "Great Norm." Cf. trans. by Legge, *Shoo King*, p. 331.

[16] Quoting the *Book of Changes*, commentary on hexagram no. 11. Cf. trans. by Legge, *Yi King*, p. 281.

"In that case, good and evil are not present in things at all."

"They are only in your mind. Following the Principle of Nature is good, while perturbing the vital force is evil."

"After all, then, things are devoid of good and evil?"

"This is true of the mind. It is also true of things. Famous but mediocre scholars fail to realize this. They neglect the mind and chase after material things, and consequently get a wrong view of the way to investigate things. All day long they restlessly seek principle in external things. They only succeed in getting at it by incidental deeds of righteousness. All their lives they act in this way without understanding it and do so habitually without examination."[17]

"How about loving beautiful color and hating bad odor?"

"This is all in accord with principle. We do so by the very nature of the Principle of Nature. From the beginning there is no selfish desire to make a special effort to like or dislike."

"How can the love of beautiful color and the hatred of bad odor not be regarded as one's own will?"

"The will in this case is sincere, not selfish. A sincere will is in accord with the Principle of Nature. However, while it is in accord with the Principle of Nature, at the same time it is not attached in the least to selfish thought. Therefore when one is affected to any extent by wrath or fondness, the mind will not be correct.[18] It must be broad and impartial. Only thus is it in its original substance. Knowing this, you know the state of equilibrium before feelings are aroused."

Meng Po-sheng[19] said, "You said that if weeds are harmful, according to principle they should be removed. Why should the desire to remove them be motivated by personal interest?"

"You must find this out yourself through personal realization. What is your state of mind when you want to remove the weeds? And what was the state of mind of Chou Mao-shu [Chou Tun-i, 1017-73] when he would not cut down the grass outside his window?"[20]

---

[17] A quotation from the *Book of Mencius*, 7A:5.

[18] According to the *Great Learning*, ch. 7.

[19] Nothing is known of him except that his name was Yüan.

[20] His courtesy name was Mao-shu and his honorific name Master Lien-hsi. He was generally considered the founder of Neo-Confucianism. Aside from his doctrine of the Great Ultimate which laid the foundation for Neo-Confucianism he was noted for his love of life. The fact that he would not even cut the grass is recorded in the *I-shu*, 3:2a.

102. The Teacher said to students, "When one devotes himself to study, he must have a basis. Only then can his effort lead to any solution. Even though his effort may not be uninterrupted, he will have a definite direction like a boat with a rudder. The mere mention of the subject will immediately wake him up. Otherwise, although he devotes himself to study, he can only accomplish something through the incidental accumulation of righteousness. He will only act without understanding and do so habitually without examination.[21] This is neither a great foundation nor the universal way of virtue."

He again said, "If one understands, no matter how he says it, he is right. If what he says is right in one respect but not in another, it is because he has not understood."

103. Someone said, "For the sake of parents, a student cannot avoid the burden of preparing for the civil service examination."

The Teacher said, "If taking the examinations for the sake of parents is a burden to one's study, then is farming for the sake of parents also a burden to study? A former elder said, 'The danger of the civil service examination lies in its destroying one's will to study.'[22] The only fear is that one's will to study may not be genuine."

104. Ou-yang Ch'ung-i[23] asked, "Ordinarily one's mind is much flustered. It is so whether we are occupied or not. Why?"

The Teacher said, "In the dynamic operation of the material force of the universe there is from the beginning not a moment of rest. But there is the master. Consequently the operation has its regular order and it goes on neither too fast nor too slowly. The master [that is, the wonderful functioning of creation] is always calm in spite of hundreds of changes and thousands of transformations. This process makes it possible for man to live. If, while the

[21] A quotation from the *Book of Mencius*, 7A:5.

[22] Ch'eng I, *Wai-shu* 11:5a. The examination emphasized memorization and lacked stimulation.

[23] His name was Te and his courtesy name Nan-yeh (1495-1554). Holder of a "presented scholar" degree of 1523, he became senior lord of the bureau of state ceremonies, vice-minister of the department of rites, etc. He was outspoken in opposing certain governmental measures. In 1543-44, he lectured by imperial decree on the doctrine of innate knowledge of the good. A thousand scholars gathered to listen to him, setting a record for such a gathering that stood for several hundred years. For an account of him, see *Ming-ju hsüeh-an*, 17:1a-2b.

master remains calm, the mind is ceaseless as heavenly movements are ceaseless, it will always be at ease in spite of countless changes in its dealings with things. As it is said, 'The original mind remains calm and serene, and all parts of the body obey its command.'[24] If there is no master, the vital force will simply run wild. How can the mind not be flustered?"

105. The Teacher said, "The great trouble of students is to be found in the love of fame."

I said, "A year or so ago, I thought this trouble of mine had decreased. Upon careful examination recently, I found that it has not done so at all. It is not necessarily striving for external things or acting to satisfy others. The mere fact that I am happy when I hear words of praise and depressed when I hear words of criticism shows that the trouble occurs."

"Quite right. Name [fame] and actuality are opposed to each other. When devotion to actuality increases a little, to that extent the devotion to name decreases. If one devotes his mind entirely to actuality, he will have no mind to devote to name. If one is devoted to the search for actuality, just as one seeks food when hungry and drink when thirsty, how can he also have time to love fame?"

He again said, " 'A superior man dislikes the thought of his name's not being mentioned after his death.'[25] The word *ch'eng* (to mention) is read in the departing tone [thus meaning to weigh or balance]. It is the same idea as 'a superior man is ashamed of a reputation beyond his merits.'[26] If in reality one is not equal to his fame, the situation can be remedied if he is still living. It will be too late, however, after death. In 'if one reaches the age of forty or fifty and nothing is heard of him'[27] the phrase 'heard of' means his hearing of the Way, not his being heard of. Confucius said, '[To be heard of through the country] is merely to be known. It is different from being distinguished.'[28] How could Confucius be satisfied with the hope of people merely to be known?"

[24] In Chu Hsi's *Meng Tzu chi-chu*, ch. 11, comment on the *Book of Mencius*, 6A:15, where he quotes Fan Chün's (*fl.*1146) *Hsin-chen.*
[25] *Analects*, 15:19.
[26] *Book of Mencius*, 4B:18.
[27] *Analects*, 9:22.
[28] *Ibid.*, 12:20.

106. I often have regrets. The Teacher said, "To have regrets and to realize one's mistakes is comparable to medicine. It gets rid of the disease. But it is better to correct one's mistake. If the mistake is allowed to remain, you have a condition in which disease arises because of the medicine."

107. Te-chang[29] said, "I hear that you compare pure gold to the sage, the quantity to the sage's ability, and the work of refining to the student's effort to learn.[30] The comparison is most profound and keen. But I am afraid it is not quite satisfactory to say that Yao and Shun were, as it were, 10,000 pounds of gold whereas Confucius was only 9,000 pounds."

The Teacher said, "Again this thought is occasioned by the viewing of a person in terms of the body, and therefore you contend about the quantity in behalf of the Sage. If you are not thinking of the body, then 10,000 pounds is not too much for Yao and 9,000 pounds not too little for Confucius. The 10,000 pounds of Yao and Shun belong to Confucius and the 9,000 pounds of Confucius belong to Yao and Shun. There is really no difference as to whether it was his or theirs. What is called sagehood depends only on the refinement and singleness of mind and not on quantity. As long as people are equal in their complete identification with the Principle of Nature, they are equally sages. As to ability, power, and spiritual energy in handling affairs, how can all people be equal in them? Later scholars have confined their comparison to quantity and have therefore drifted into the doctrine of success and profit. If everybody gets rid of the idea of comparing quantity and devotes his energy and spirit entirely to the effort of becoming completely identified with the Principle of Nature, everyone will become self-contained and everyone will be perfectly realized.[31] The great will become

---

[29] Nothing is known of this man.

[30] Cf. sec. 99, above.

[31] Miwa Shissai (1669-1744) in his commentary, *Hyōchū denshū roku*, said that the saying is by Bodhidharma (*fl.* 460-534) and comes from the *Liu-men chi*. Other Japanese annotators have followed him. Quite aside from the fact that the authorship of the *Liu-men chi* is by no means certain, the saying is found neither in the complete text in the *Taishō daizōkyō* 48:365-76, nor in its partial text in the *Zokuzōkyō*, 1st collection, pt. 2, case 8, vol. 5. In his *Denshū roku kōgi*, Azuma Keiji said that the saying comes from the *Liu-ming chi* and that Bodhidharma's words were: "As everyone is self-sufficient and everyone will be

great and the small will become small, each being self-sufficient without depending on the pursuit of external things. This is the real and concrete task of manifesting the good and making the personal life sincere. Later scholars do not understand the doctrines of the Sage, they do not know how to realize their innate knowledge and innate ability directly through personal experience and extend them in their own minds, but instead seek to know what they cannot know and do what they cannot do. They hope single-mindedly only for exalted position and they admire greatness. They do not know they have the evil mind of the wicked kings Chieh and Chou and at every turn they attempt to undertake the task of the sage-emperors Yao and Shun. How could they succeed? They toil year in and year out until they die in old age, and I don't know what they will have accomplished. What a pity!"

108. I asked, "A former scholar considered the mind in its tranquil state as substance and the mind in its active state as function.[32] What about it?"

The Teacher said, "The substance and function of the mind cannot be equated with its tranquil and active states. Tranquillity and activity are matters of time. When we speak of substance as substance, function is already involved in it, and when we speak of function as function, substance is already involved in it. This is what is called 'Substance and function coming from the same source.'[33] However, there is no harm in saying that the substance of

perfectly realized, there is inherent in everyone's mind a way to achieve perfection." I suspect that *ming* is a misprint for *men*, for there is no work entitled *Liu-ming chi*. The saying, "Everyone is self-sufficient and everyone will be perfectly realized," which is slightly different from that quoted by Wang but has essentially the same meaning, is found in the *Ch'u-shih Fan-ch'i Ch'an-shih yü-lu* of Zen Master Fan-ch'i, also called Ch'u-shih (1290-1370), ch. 7, in *Zokuzōkyō*, 1st collection, pt. 2, case 29, 1:66b. (I owe this earliest reference to Professor Yanagida Seizan through the kind help of the Reverend Mrs. Ruth Sasaki of the First Zen Institute, Kyoto.) Fan-ch'i, however, was probably quoting an earlier source. In a personal letter, Dr. D. T. Suzuki doubts Bodhidharma's authorship of the *Liu-men chi*, thinks that Bodhidharma was not the first one to use the saying, and says he can't remember who was the first one to use the dictum, which, according to him, is not confined to the Zen school.

[32] Ch'eng I, *Wen-chi*, 5:12a. Wang Yang-ming said the same thing in the *Wang Wen-ch'eng Kung ch'üan-shu*, 5:6a.

[33] Ch'eng I, preface to his *I chuan*. See below, sec. 156, n. 11.

the mind is revealed through its tranquillity and its function through its activity."

109.   I asked, "Why can't the most intelligent and the most stupid be changed?"[34]

The Teacher said, "It is not that they cannot be changed. It is merely that they are unwilling to change."

110.   I asked about the chapter in the *Analects* in which the pupils of Tzu-hsia asked Tzu-chang [503-c.450 B.C.] about the principles of friendship.[35]

The Teacher said, "When Tzu-hsia said ['to associate with those who are fit for you and avoid those not fit for you'], he was talking about the friendship of young people. When Tzu-chang said that [the superior man honors the worthy and gets along with all and praises the good and pities the incompetent], he was talking about the friendship of adults. If followed carefully, both are correct."

111.   Tzu-jen[36] asked, " 'Is it not a pleasure to learn and to repeat or practice from time to time what has been learned?'[37] A former scholar regarded learning as following the conduct of those who are the first to be enlightened.[38] What do you think?"

The Teacher said, "To learn is to get rid of selfish human desires and to preserve the Principle of Nature. If we devote ourselves to getting rid of selfish human desires and preserving the Principle of Nature, we will naturally be as correct as those who are the first to be enlightened. When we go into the ancient meaning of the term 'learning,' in its derived meaning, it involves questioning, the sifting of ideas, thinking, deliberation, the preservation of the mind, self-examination, self-mastery, and other efforts. But all these are no more than the effort to get rid of selfish human desires from the mind and preserve the Principle of Nature in the mind. To say that it is to follow the conduct of those who are the first to be enlightened is to mention only one item of the process of learning, and one

[34] *Analects*, 17:3.
[35] *Ibid.*, 19:3.
[36] It is not clear whether his family name was Lüan and his private name Hui or his family name Lin and his private name Ch'un.
[37] *Analects*, 1:1.
[38] Chu Hsi, *Lun-yü chi-chu*, ch. 1, comment on *Analects*, 1:1.

seems to be seeking it entirely outside himself. To 'learn with a constant perseverance and application' does not mean, in the case of 'sitting like a boy impersonating an ancestor in a sacrifice,'[39] for example, merely to practice how to sit, but to practice the attitude of mind while sitting, and in the case of 'standing reverently as in sacrificing,'[40] does not mean merely to practice standing, but to practice the attitude of mind while standing. The word pleasure is the same word as in Mencius' saying that 'moral principles please our minds.'[41] The human mind by nature delights in moral principles very much as the eye delights in beauty and the ear in music. If they do not, it is only because they are blinded and spoiled by selfish human desires. Now as selfish human desires are gradually removed, the mind will be increasingly harmonious with moral principles. How can it help being delighted?"

112. Kuo-ying[42] said, "Although Tseng Tzu was genuine in daily examining himself on three points,[43] I am afraid these examinations were undertaken because he had not heard of the doctrine of one thread (*i-kuan*) that runs through all the teachings of Confucius."[44]

The Teacher said, "Confucius told Tseng Tzu about the one thread because he realized that Tseng Tzu had not found the essentials of moral cultivation. If the student can really devote himself to conscientiousness and altruism, are they not the one thread running through all? The 'one' is comparable to the roots of a tree and the 'thread' to its branches and leaves. If the roots have not been cultivated, how can there be branches and leaves? Substance and function come from the same source. If substance is not firmly established, how can function proceed? When [Chu Hsi] said that 'Tseng Tzu had in the sphere of function carefully examined matters as they came along and practiced them vigorously, but had

---

[39] *Book of Rites*, "Summary of Ceremonies." Cf. trans. by Legge, *Li Ki*, ch. 1, p. 62.
[40] *Ibid.*
[41] *Book of Mencius*, 6A:7.
[42] Nothing is known of him except that his family name was Ch'en.
[43] Whether in working for others he was loyal, whether in dealing with friends he was faithful, and whether in giving instructions to others he had practiced what he was taught. See *Analects*, 1:4.
[44] *Ibid.*, 4:15.

not realized their substance as one,'[45] I am afraid he was not in complete accord with truth."

113. Huang Ch'eng-fu[46] asked about the chapter in the *Analects* where Confucius asked Tzu-kung [520-*c.*450 B.C.], "Whom do you consider superior, yourself or Yen Hui?"[47]

The Teacher said, "Tzu-kung learned much and was well informed. He devoted his efforts to what was to be seen and heard. Yen Hui, on the other hand, devoted his effort to the mind. Therefore Confucius enlightened Tzu-kung by asking him the question. But in his reply he confined himself only to matters of knowledge and observation. Therefore Confucius sighed. He did not approve of him."

114. [The Teacher said,] "Yen Hui did not transfer his anger nor repeat his mistakes.[48] He could behave as he did only because he possessed the equilibrium before the feelings are aroused."

115. [The Teacher said,] "As he who grows a tree must nourish the roots, so he who cultivates virtue must nourish his mind. If the tree is to grow, the many branches must be trimmed when it is young. Likewise, if virtue is to become eminent, the love of external things must be eliminated when the student first begins to learn. If one loves such external things as poetry and flowery essays, his mental energy will gradually be dissipated in poetry and literary essays. The same is true of all love of external things."

He further said, "The way of learning I am now talking about is the task of creating something from nothing. You gentlemen

---

[45] *Lun-yü chi-chu*, ch. 2, commenting on *Analects*, 4:15.

[46] His name was Tsung-ming (d. 1536). Holder of a "presented scholar" degree, he served in various official capacities, including that of vice-minister of the department of military affairs. He was dismissed from office because he dared urge the emperor to cancel his proposed pleasure-seeking tour. Later he was restored but was eventually banished to be an official in Fukien because he recommended the impeachment of an evil but powerful official. Ultimately he became a vice-minister of the department of rites. For an account of him, see *Ming-ju hsüeh-an*, 14:4a-b.

[47] *Analects*, 5:8. Tzu-kung's answer was that Yen Hui was superior because, while Yen Hui knew all about a subject upon hearing one part of it, he himself knew only one fifth.

[48] *Ibid.*, 6:2.

must believe me. All depends on making up the mind. If the student makes up his mind to have one thought to do good, his mind will be like the seed of a tree. If only he neither forces it to grow nor neglects it,[49] but keeps on cultivating and nourishing it, it will naturally grow larger every day and night. Its vitality will be increasingly great and its branches and leaves more luxuriant. When the tree first begins to grow, it shoots forth many branches. These must be cut before the roots and trunk may grow large. This is also true when one begins to learn. Therefore in making up one's mind single-mindedness is highly valued."

116. We happened to be talking about the followers of our Teacher, that so-and-so devotes his effort to self-cultivation, and so-and-so devotes his effort to knowledge. The Teacher said, "Those who concentrate on self-cultivation increasingly realize their insufficiency, while those who concentrate on knowledge increasingly believe that they have a superabundance. Actually the former increasingly have a superabundance whereas the latter increasingly have an insufficiency."

117. Liang Jih-fu[50] asked, "Dwelling in seriousness (*ching*) and the investigation of the principles of things to the utmost are two different things. You consider them as one. Why?"

The Teacher said, "There is only this one thing in the world. Where do you find two? If you are thinking of the ten thousand multiplicities, then there are three hundred rules of ceremony and three thousand rules of conduct.[51] Are there only two? Sir, suppose you tell me what dwelling in seriousness and investigating principle to the utmost are."

"Dwelling in seriousness is the work of preserving and nourishing, while investigating principle to the utmost is investigating the principle of things and events to the utmost."

"Preserving and nourishing what?"

---

[49] Paraphrasing the *Book of Mencius*, 2A:2.

[50] His name was Ch'o and he was a native of Canton and a "presented scholar" degree holder of 1514. In 1519, when he urged the emperor to cancel his pleasure-seeking tour, he was punished by beating. It was primarily because of him that Wang Yang-ming's teachings spread to the Canton area.

[51] Quoting the *Doctrine of the Mean*, ch. 27.

"Preserving and nourishing the Principle of Nature in the mind."

"In that case, it is no more than the investigation of the principle of things to the utmost. Suppose you tell me how to investigate the principle of things to the utmost."

"It means that in serving parents, for example, one must investigate the principle of filial piety to the utmost, and in serving the ruler one must investigate the principle of loyalty to the utmost."

"Are the principles of filial piety and loyalty to be found in the person of the parents and the ruler or in one's own mind? If they are to be found in one's own mind, it will also be no more than the investigation of the principles of the mind to the utmost. Please tell me what dwelling in seriousness is."

"It is merely concentration on one thing."

"What do you mean by concentration on one thing?"

"It means, for example, to concentrate the mind on reading when one is reading, and to concentrate the mind on handling affairs when one is handling affairs."

"In that case it would mean to concentrate on drinking when one is drinking and to concentrate on enjoying sex when one is enjoying sex. That would be chasing after material things. How can it amount to any effort to dwell in seriousness?"

Jih-fu asked for an explanation. The Teacher said, "By the one thing is meant the Principle of Nature, and by concentrating on one thing is meant to concentrate the mind on the Principle of Nature. If one only knows how to concentrate on one thing and does not know that the one thing is the same as the Principle of Nature, he will be chasing after material things when he is busy and his mind will become a blank when he is at leisure. Precisely because one's mind completely devotes its efforts to the Principle of Nature, whether one is busy or at leisure, the way to dwell in seriousness is no different from the investigation of principles to the utmost. Dwelling in seriousness is the investigation of principle in its aspect of concentration, and the investigation of principle is dwelling in seriousness in its aspect of thoroughness and care. It is not that after dwelling in seriousness there is another mind to investigate principle, nor that at the time of the investigation of principle there is another mind to dwell in seriousness. Although they differ in name, their task is one. Take the saying in the *Book of Chan es*, 'Seriousness is to straighten the internal life. Righteousness is to square the external life.'[52] Thus seriousness is righteousness when applied to the time of inactivity and righteousness is seriousness when applied to the time of activity. The two sayings together refer to one thing. When Confucius mentioned 'cultivating oneself with seriousness,'[53] for example, it was not necessary for him to mention righteousness, and when Mencius talked about accumulating righteousness,[54] it was not necessary for him to talk about seriousness. If the fact that they are really one is understood, it does not matter how one talks about them, for their task is the same. If one is too rigidly literal and does not understand the fundamental principle, one will be occupied with fragmentary and isolated details and broken pieces and his task will have no solution."

"Why is the investigation of principle the same as the full development of one's nature?"

"The nature of man is the substance of his mind. It is the same as principle. In investigating the principle of humanity to the utmost, one must really extend the humanity [in one's action] to the ultimate of humanity, and in investigating the principle of righteousness to the utmost, one must really extend the righteousness [in one's action] to the ultimate of righteousness. Humanity and righteousness are inherent in one's nature. Therefore to investigate principle to the utmost is fully to develop one's nature. Mencius said that if a man gives full development to his feeling of commiseration, his humanity will be more than he can ever put into practice.[55] This is the work of the investigation of principle to the utmost."

Jih-fu said, "A former scholar said that 'Every blade of grass and every tree possesses principle and should be examined.'[56] What do you say to that?"

The Teacher said, "I have no time for that.[57] You had better understand your own nature and feeling first. It is necessary to develop one's own nature to the fullest extent before one can fully develop the nature of things."

Terrified, Jih-fu achieved some understanding.

---

[52] *Book of Changes*, commentary on hexagram no. 2. Cf. trans. by Legge, *Yi King*, p. 420.
[53] *Analects*, 14:45.
[54] *Book of Mencius*, 2A:2.
[55] *Ibid.*, 7B:31.
[56] Ch'eng I, *I-shu*, 18:9a.
[57] Quoting the *Analects*, 14:31.

118. Chi Wei-ch'ien[58] asked, "How is it that knowledge is in the original substance of the mind?"

The Teacher said, "Knowledge is principle made intelligent. In terms of its position as master [of the body], it is called the mind. In terms of its position as endowment, it is called our nature. All infants know how to love their parents and respect their elder brothers. The simple truth is that when the intelligent faculty is not obstructed by selfish desires, but is developed and extended to the limit, it is then completely the original substance of the mind and can identify its character with that of Heaven and Earth.[59] From the sage downward, none can be without obstruction. Therefore all need to investigate things so as to extend their knowledge."

119. Shou-heng[60] asked, "The task of the *Great Learning* consists only in making the will sincere and the task of making the will sincere consists only in the investigation of things. The cultivation of the personal life, the regulation of the family, the bringing of order to the state and peace to the world[61] are all covered by the sincerity of the will. How is it that there is also the task of the rectification of the mind, in which one's mind will not be correct if one is affected to any extent by wrath and fondness?"[62]

The Teacher said, "You have to think and find out for yourself. If you understand this, you will understand the equilibrium before the feelings are aroused."

Shou-heng asked several times for an explanation.

The Teacher said, "There are grades in the task of study. In the beginning, if one does not earnestly use his will to love good and

[58] This is the courtesy name of Chi Yüan-heng (d. 1521). As a "presented scholar" degree holder, he became the disciple of Wang Yang-ming when the latter was banished to become an official in Kuei-chou. He was sent by Wang to Prince Ning, who was plotting a revolt, ostensibly to lecture on Confucian doctrines but actually to spy on the prince. After the revolt had been suppressed, he was accused of conspiracy with the prince. Although he denied this even after torture, he was imprisoned together with his wife and daughter. When he was finally cleared and set free, he died five days afterward. For an account of him, see *Ming-ju hsüeh-an*, 28:6b-7a.

[59] Quoting the *Book of Changes*, commentary on hexagram no. 1. Cf. trans. by Legge, *Yi King*, p. 417.

[60] Nothing is known of him.

[61] *Great Learning*, the text.

[62] *Ibid.*, ch. 7.

hate evil, how can he do good and remove evil? This earnest use of the will is to make the will sincere. However, if one does not realize that the original substance of mind is devoid of all things [that is, completely pure and open], and attaches his mind solely to loving good and hating evil, he will merely add to his mind this much of his own will and therefore his mind will not be broad and impartial.[63] Only when one does not make any special effort whatsoever to like or dislike, as described in the *Book of History*,[64] can the mind be in its original substance. It is therefore said that if one is affected to any extent by wrath and fondness, one's mind will not be correct. The rectification of the mind is merely the inside of the effort to make the will sincere. Realize the substance of the mind through personal experience at all times and see to it that it is as clear as a mirror and as even as a balance. Then you will find the equilibrium before the feelings are aroused."

120. Huang Cheng-chih[65] asked, "When one does not know a thing, his task is to be apprehensive. When one alone knows it, his task is to be watchful over himself.[66] What do you think of this theory?"

The Teacher said, "Both are the same task. When nothing happens, of course [what is going on in one's mind] is privately known to him. But when things do happen, it is also privately known to him. If people do not exert effort toward what is privately known to them and exert it only toward what is publicly known, this is to act hypocritically and to 'disguise themselves when they see a superior man.'[67] This condition of private knowledge is the root of sincerity. Hence all thoughts, whether good or evil, are genuine. If one step is correct here, all the following steps will be correct, but if one mistake is made here, a hundred mistakes will follow. It is the point of departure between the kingly way of moral principles and the despotic way of power, between righteousness and profit,

---

[63] Ch'eng Hao, *Wen-chi*, 3:1a.

[64] *Book of History*, "Great Norm." Cf. trans. by Legge, *Shoo King*, p. 331.

[65] He was Huang Hung-kang (1492-1561), whose literary name was Lo-ts'un. A faithful disciple of Wang's, he did not serve in the government until several years after Wang's death. He became a divisional executive assistant in the department of justice. For an account of him, see *Ming-ju hsüeh-an*, 19:11a-13a.

[66] As set forth in Chu Hsi's *Chung-yung chang-chü*, ch. 1.

[67] *Great Learning*, ch. 6.

between sincerity and insincerity, and between good and evil. If at this point one makes a firm stand, then the foundation will be correct and the source will be pure. This means that sincerity has been established. Here lies all the spirit and life of many of the efforts of the ancients to make the personal life sincere. Truly, nothing is more visible than the hidden and more manifest than the subtle, and in all places and at all times and from the beginning to the end, this [making the personal life sincere] is the only task. Now if apprehension is taken separately as appertaining to a situation when things are not privately known, the task will be one of fragmentary and isolated details, and will also be interrupted. To be apprehensive implies that one already knows the situation. If one does not know, who is it that is apprehensive? The view as you stated it inevitably leads to the Buddhist meditation that cuts off all events."

"You said that all thoughts, whether good or evil, are genuine. In the area of private knowledge, aren't there moments without thought?"

"To be apprehensive is also thought. The thought of apprehension never ceases. If it is not preserved in any way, it will become either dull and stupid or evil. From morning to evening, and from youth to old age, if one wants to be without thought, that is, not to know anything, he can't do so unless he is sound asleep or dead like dry wood or dead ashes."[68]

121. Chih-tao[69] asked, "Hsün Tzu [*fl.* 298-238 B.C.] said that 'to nourish the mind there is nothing better than sincerity.'[70] But a former scholar said he was wrong.[71] Why?"

The Teacher said, "He should not be regarded too lightly as wrong. Sincerity is sometimes interpreted as a task rather than as a state of mind. Sincerity is the original substance of the mind. To try to restore this original substance is the work of thinking how to be sincere. When Ch'eng Ming-tao said, 'to preserve it [humanity]

---

[68] See *Chuang Tzu*, ch. 2, SPTK ed., 1:18a. Cf. trans. by Herbert Giles, *Chuang Tzu* (London, Allen and Unwin, 1961), p. 34.
[69] Nothing is known of him.
[70] *Hsün Tzu*, ch. 3, SPTK ed., 2:6a; not translated in Homer H. Dubs's *Works of Hsüntze* (London, Probsthain, 1928).
[71] Ch'eng Hao, *Wai-shu*, 2:4b.

with sincerity and seriousness,'[72] he meant this. The *Great Learning* says, 'Those who wished to rectify their minds would first make their wills sincere.'[73] Though there are many defects in what Hsün Tzu said, one should not seize upon one incident in order to find fault with him. Generally speaking, if in examining the sayings of anyone one has a preconceived opinion, he will be wrong. Though the saying, 'He who seeks to be rich will not be humane,'[74] was uttered by the wicked official Yang Hu [*fl.* 505 B.C.], Mencius quoted it just the same. This shows how impartial sages and worthies are."

122. Hsiao Hui[75] asked, "It is difficult to overcome one's selfish desires. What can be done about them?"

The Teacher said, "Give me your selfish desires. I shall overcome them for you."

He continued, "Before one can master himself, he must first have the determination to do something for himself, and before one can fully realize himself, he must master himself."

Hsiao Hui said, "To a certain extent, I, too, have the determination to do something for myself, but I don't know why I cannot master myself."

The Teacher said, "Please tell me what you mean by having the determination to do something for yourself."

After a long while, Hui said, "Having made up my mind to be a good man, I thought I had the determination to do something for myself. As I think of it, I realize that I merely wanted to do something for my bodily self, not for my true self."

The Teacher said, "Has the true self ever been separated from the bodily self? I am afraid you have not even done anything for your bodily self. Tell me, is not what you call the bodily self ears, eyes, mouth, nose, and the four limbs?"

Hui said, "Precisely, for the eye I desire color, for the ear, sound, for the mouth, taste, and for the four limbs, comfort. For these reasons I cannot master myself."

[72] *I-shu*, 2A:3a.
[73] *Great Learning*, the text.
[74] *Book of Mencius*, 3A:3.
[75] Details about him are not known. It is interesting to note that in the conversations recorded by Hsüeh K'an, secs. 95-129, in the case of Hsiao alone he used his private name instead of his courtesy or literary name, perhaps because he was a very young man.

The Teacher said, "Beautiful color causes one's eyes to be blind. Beautiful sound causes one's ears to be deaf. Good taste causes one's palate to be spoiled, and racing and hunting cause one to be mad.[76] All these are harmful to your ears, eyes, mouth, nose, and four limbs. How can this be considered as doing something for them? If you are really doing something for them, you must reflect upon the manner in which the ears listen, the eyes look, the mouth speaks, and the four limbs move. If it is not in accord with the rules of propriety, you must not look, listen, speak, or move. Only then can you fully realize the function of eyes, ears, mouth, nose, and the four limbs, and only in this way can you do something for them. Now all day long you chase after external things and direct yourself to fame and profit. All this is for things external to the body. When you want to do something for your ear, eye, mouth, nose, and four limbs, and will not look, listen, speak, move out of accord with the rules of propriety, are your ears, eyes, mouth, nose, and four limbs themselves capable of not doing so? The ability must come from your mind. These activities of seeing, listening, speaking, and moving are all of your mind. The sight of your mind emanates through the channel of the eyes, the hearing of your mind through the channel of the ears, the speech of your mind through the channel of the mouth, and the movement of your mind through the channel of your four limbs. If there were no mind, there would be no ears, eyes, mouth, or nose. What is called your mind is not merely that lump of blood and flesh. If it were so, why is it that the dead man, whose lump of blood and flesh is still present, cannot see, listen, speak, or move? What is called your mind is that which makes seeing, listening, speaking, and moving possible. It is the nature of man and things; it is the Principle of Nature. Only with this nature can there be the principle of regeneration, which is called *jen* (humanity, also meaning seed). When this creative principle of the nature of man and things emanates through the eye, the eye can see; through the ear, the ear can hear; through the mouth, the mouth can speak; and through the four limbs, they can move. All this is the growth and development of the Principle of Nature. In its capacity as the master of the body, it is called the mind. Basically the original substance of the mind is none other than the Principle of Nature, and is never out of accord with propriety. This is your

[76] Paraphrasing *Lao Tzu* (*Tao-te-ching*), ch. 12.

true self. This true self is the master of the body. If there is no true self, there will be no body. Truly, with the true self, one lives; without it, one dies. If you really want to do something for your bodily self, you must make use of this true self, always preserve its original substance, and be cautious over things not yet seen and apprehensive over things not yet heard of,[77] for fear that the true self be injured, even slightly. Then whenever the least desire to act out of accord with the rules of propriety germinates and becomes active, you will feel as though cut with a knife and stuck with a needle; the feeling will be unbearable, and will not stop until the knife and the needle are removed. Only then may you be said to have the determination to do something for yourself. Only then can you master yourself. But now when you treat a thief as a son[78] why do you say that you cannot master yourself even though you have the determination to do something for yourself?"

123. One student had eye trouble and was exceedingly worried. The Teacher said, "You have a high regard for your eye but a low regard for your mind."

124. Hsiao Hui was fond of Buddhism and the Taoist search for immortality. The Teacher warned him and said, "From youth I was also earnestly devoted to the two systems. I thought I had learned something and thought the Confucian system was not worth studying. Later while I lived in barbarous territory for [nearly] three years, I realized how simple, easy, extensive, and great the doctrines of the Sage are, and then I sighed and regretted having wasted my energy for thirty years. In general, the excellence of the two systems differs from that of the Sage only in an infinitesimal amount. But what you have learned from them is their dregs, and you are so self-confident and self-satisfied. You are really like an owl which has stolen the rotten carcass of a rat!"[79]

Hui begged to ask about the excellence of the two systems. The Teacher said, "I have just mentioned how simple, easy, extensive,

[77] *Doctrine of the Mean*, ch. 1.
[78] This parable comes from the *Leng-yen ching* (*Śūraṅgama sūtra*), ch. 1, in *Taisho daizōkyō*, 19:108. The idea is that to treat beautiful colors, etc., as being for the sake of the eye, etc., is comparable to treating a thief as a son.
[79] A parable from the *Chuang Tzu*, ch. 17, SPTK ed., 6:28a. Cf. trans. by Giles, *Chuang Tzu*, p. 171.

and great the doctrines of the Sage are. You choose not to ask me about what I have realized but only about what I have regretted!"

Hui was ashamed, apologized, and begged to ask about the doctrines of the Sage.

The Teacher said, "You only understand the pursuit after commonplace social affairs. Wait till you have acquired the real determination to become a sage and then I shall talk with you."

Hui asked him again and again. The Teacher said, "I have told you all in one sentence and you still don't comprehend yourself."

125. Liu Kuan-shih[80] asked, "What is the equilibrium before the feelings are aroused?"

The Teacher said, "You will naturally understand if you will only be cautious over things not yet seen and apprehensive over things not yet heard, and nourish the mind until it becomes completely identified with the Principle of Nature."

Kuan-shih asked the Teacher to describe the condition of equilibrium somewhat. The Teacher said, "I cannot tell you any more than a dumb man can tell you about the bitterness of the bitter melon he has just eaten.[81] If you want to know the bitterness, you have to eat a bitter melon yourself."

At that time Hsü Ai was by the side of the Teacher. He said, "This is exactly a case where true knowledge and action are identical."

All the friends present attained a certain enlightenment all at once.

126. Hsiao Hui asked about the principle of life and death. The Teacher said, "If you understand day and night you will understand life and death."

Hui asked about day and night. The Teacher said, "If you understand the day, you will understand the night."

"Is there something about the day that we don't understand?"

The Teacher said, "You understand the day! You rise up with all stupidity and eat with all foolishness. You act without understanding and do so habitually without examination.[82] All day long it is dark to you. You merely dream about the day. Only when you can nourish something at every moment and preserve something in

---

[80] Liu came from the same district as Wang. Otherwise nothing is known of him.

[81] A parable from the *Pi-yen lu*, a collection of Zen stories, no. 3.

[82] Quoting the *Book of Mencius*, 7A:5.

every instant[83] and thus this mind is thoroughly awake and clear, so that the Principle of Nature is not interrupted for a moment, can you be said to understand the day. This is the character of Heaven. This is the knowledge that penetrates the course of day and night.[84] Where does [the knowledge of] life and death come in?"

127. Ma Tzu-hsin[85] asked, "With regard to the doctrine that education consists in cultivating the Way [as set forth in the *Doctrine of the Mean* attributed to Tzu-ssu],[86] the traditional interpretation has been that the Sage regulated and restricted the nature with which he was originally endowed so that he could be a model to the world, his regulations and restrictions resulting in things like ceremonies, music, laws, and governmental measures.[87] What do you think of such an idea?"

The Teacher said, "The Way is nature and is also destiny. It is complete in itself. Nothing can be added to or subtracted from it, and it requires no touching up. What need is there for the Sage to regulate and restrict? To do so would imply that nature is not perfect. Since ceremonies, music, laws, and governmental measures are means to govern the empire, they of course may be regarded as education, but the main objective of Tzu-ssu does not lie in these. If we accept the interpretation of the former scholar [Chu Hsi], how is it that in the passage following the statement that education consists in cultivating the Way, the Sage's methods of education through ceremonies, music, laws, and governmental measures are not mentioned but instead there is a whole section on the effort to be cautious and apprehensive? [If Chu Hsi is correct] then the Sage's teaching [about being cautious and apprehensive] would have been devised in vain!"

Tzu-hsin asked for an explanation. The Teacher said, "When Tzu-ssu talked about nature, the Way, and education, he did so from the point of view of their fundamental source. When Heaven has conferred something on man, that which is conferred is called man's nature. When man acts in accord with his nature, that nature

[83] A quotation from Chang Tsai (1020-77), *Cheng-meng*, ch. 12; *Chang Heng-ch'ü chi*, 3:35 b.
[84] *Book of Changes*, "Appended Remarks," pt. 1, ch. 4. Cf. trans. by Legge, *Yi King*, p. 354.
[85] See above, sec. 40, n. 28.
[86] *Doctrine of the Mean*, ch. 1.
[87] Chu Hsi, *Chung-yung chang-chü*, ch. 1.

becomes the Way. And when man cultivates the Way and learns, the Way becomes education. To be in accord with his nature is the task of a sincere man. It is what is stated as 'It is due to our nature that enlightenment results from sincerity.'[88] To cultivate the Way is the way of one who attains sincerity. It is what is stated as 'It is due to education that sincerity results from enlightenment.'[89] As the sage acts in accord with his nature, the Way obtains. People below the sage in moral quality are not yet able to act in accord with the Way and at times deviate from the mean. Therefore they need to cultivate the Way. By cultivating the Way the worthy and wise will avoid going too far and the stupid and unworthy will avoid not going far enough. They all have to follow the Way and thus the Way is education. This word 'education' is the same as in the saying, 'The way of Heaven is perfect education. All wind and rain, frost and dew are education.'[90] The phrase 'cultivating the Way' is the same as in the saying, 'The cultivation of the Way is to be done through humanity.[91] Only with the cultivation of the Way can one avoid violating the Way and restore the original substance of his nature. When that point is reached, his Way will be the same as that in accord with which the sage acts. Being cautious and being apprehensive, referred to in the later passage, are efforts to cultivate the Way. When the original substance of the nature is restored, there will be equilibrium and harmony. As the Book of Changes says, "Investigate principle to the utmost and fully develop one's nature until destiny is fulfilled.'[92] When equilibrium and harmony exist in perfection, a proper order prevails in the universe and all things attain their full growth and development.[93] That is the full development of the nature and the fulfillment of destiny."

128.   Huang Ch'eng-fu[94] asked, "Confucius' answer to Yen Hui's question about government[95] was regarded by a former

---

[88] Doctrine of the Mean, ch. 21.
[89] Ibid.
[90] Book of Rites, "Confucius at Home at Leisure." Cf. trans. by Legge, Li Ki, ch. 26, p. 281. The first saying in the quotation is Wang's own.
[91] Doctrine of the Mean, ch. 20.
[92] Book of Changes "Remarks on the Trigrams," ch. 1. Cf. trans. by Legge, Yi King, p. 422.
[93] Doctrine of the Mean, ch. 1.
[94] See above, sec. 113, n. 46.
[95] To use the calendar of the Hsia dynasty, to ride in the state carriages of the

scholar[96] as setting up the system for ten thousand generations to follow. What do you think of that?"

The Teacher said, "Yen Hui had all the qualities of a sage. In regard to the great foundation and fundamental source of running the government, he was perfect. Confucius knew that very well all along, and therefore he did not need to speak about them. He talked about social systems and moral conduct only to indicate that these things are not to be neglected, and that only in this way can things be perfect. Also, Confucius did not want him to be negligent about being on guard simply because his ability was sufficient, but wanted him to banish the songs of Cheng and keep away the petty flatterers. For Yen Hui was a man of self-mastery and one who devoted his heart to internal virtues. Confucius was afraid lest he might be negligent in minor details of external conduct. Therefore he helped Yen Hui where he was deficient. With others, it would be necessary to tell them that the conduct of government depends on man, that the right men are obtained by means of the ruler's personal character, that to cultivate his personal character the ruler must follow the Way, and that the cultivation of the Way is to be done through cherishing humanity. It is also necessary to tell them about the universal path of human relations and the nine universal standards[97] and the many tasks of making the will sincere. Only then can this [the fundamental way of government] be achieved. And only then can we have the system to be followed for ten thousand generations. Otherwise, if the ruler merely proceeds to use the calendar of the Hsia, to ride in the state carriages of the Shang, to wear the ceremonial caps of the Chou, and to promote the dance music of *shao*, will the empire be well governed? Because people of later generations knew only that Yen Hui was the best pupil in the Confucian school and that even he asked how to govern, they considered this as important a thing as Heaven."

[96] Chu Hsi, *Lun-yü chi-chu*, ch. 8, comment on *Analects*, 15:10.

[97] Namely, cultivating personal character, honoring worthy men, having affection toward relatives, having respect toward the high ministers, treating the whole body of public affairs kindly and considerately, treating the common people as their children, encouraging and attracting all classes of artisans, showing tenderness to men from afar, and taking interest in the welfare of the princes of the empires. See *Doctrine of the Mean*, ch.20.

129. Ts'ai Hsi-yüan[98] said, "In Wen Kung's [Chu Hsi's] new arrangement of the *Great Learning*,[99] the section on the investigation of things precedes that on the sincerity of the will. It seems that such an order agrees with the main text [on which the sections that follow are commentaries and in which it is said that, wishing to make the will sincere, one must first extend his knowledge to the utmost]. According to your insistence on following the original arrangement, then the section on sincerity of the will would precede that on the investigation of things. This still bothers me."

The Teacher said, "The task of the *Great Learning* consists in manifesting the clear character. To manifest the clear character is none other than to make the will sincere, and the task of making the will sincere is none other than the investigation of things and the extension of knowledge. If one regards the sincerity of the will as the basis and from there proceeds to the task of the investigation of things and the extension of knowledge, only then can the task have a solution. Even doing good and removing evil are nothing but the work of the sincerity of the will. But according to Chu Hsi's new arrangement the first step is to investigate the principles of things to the utmost. In that case one will be drifting and be at a loss and there will not be any solution at all. It will then be necessary to add the task of seriousness before the investigation of things can be related to one's person and mind. Even then there will be no foundation. If it is necessary to add the task of seriousness[100] why did the Confucian school leave out a most important item and wait more than a thousand years for someone to make the correction? The fact is that if the sincerity of the will is taken as the basis, the addition of seriousness is unnecessary. The reason why the sincerity of the will is singled out for discussion is precisely because it is the basis of learning. If this is not understood, the result will be, as the saying goes, that an infinitesimal mistake in the beginning will lead to an infinite mistake at the end.[101] Generally speaking, according to the *Doctrine of the Mean* the task consists purely in making the personal life sincere. When making the personal life sincere reaches

---

[98] See above, sec. 99, n. 5.

[99] See above, Introduction (to secs. 1-14) by Hsü Ai, n. 3.

[100] Ch'eng I said that self-cultivation requires seriousness and the pursuit of learning depends on the extension of knowledge. *I-shu*, 18:5b.

[101] *I-wei t'ung-kua-yen*, pt. 1, 5b.

the highest degree, that is perfect sincerity. According to the *Great Learning*, however, the task consists purely in making the will sincere. When making the will sincere reaches the highest degree, there is the highest good. The two tasks are really the same. To add the word seriousness here and the word sincerity there is as superfluous as to draw a snake and add feet."

Instructions for Practical Living, Part II

Preface by Ch'ien Te-hung :[1]

When Nan Yüan-shan[2] published[3] the *Instructions for Practical Living* in Yüeh,[4] it consisted of two stitched volumes, the second of

[1] His name was Hsü-shan, and his courtesy name Hung-fu (1496-1574). He was a native of the same district as Wang Yang-ming. As a young man he was attracted to Chu Hsi's philosophy and was skeptical when he read the *Instructions for Practical Living*. However, after Wang suppressed the rebellion of Prince Ning in 1520, Ch'ien Te-hung became Wang's disciple. He and Wang Chi were Wang's most outstanding disciples, and the hundreds of scholars who came to Wang from all parts of China were first instructed by these two star pupils and went to the Master only for his final conclusions. While Master Wang was away suppressing a rebellion in Kwangsi in 1527-28, Ch'ien and Wang Chi maintained his center of learning in Chekiang. While they were on their way to the capital to take the civil service examinations they heard of Wang's death and turned back. It was not until 1532 that the two friends went for the examinations and obtained the "presented scholar" degree.

Occupying a series of official posts, Ch'ien reached the position of a divisional chief in the department of justice. Because he offended the emperor by memorializing the throne and criticizing a bad official, he was imprisoned. After he was freed, for some thirty years he taught and lectured on the Confucian doctrine, and institutes for him to lecture in were established throughout Central and South China. When a new emperor came to the throne in 1567, Ch'ien was appointed as a high official at court and in 1573, when another emperor ascended the throne, he was promoted.

Although he and Wang Chi were Wang's two outstanding disciples, their philosophies were quite different. (See below, sec. 315, for their famous conversation with their Master.) As Huang Tsung-hsi has correctly pointed out in his *Ming-ju hsüeh-an*, 11:6a, while Wang Chi emphasized using the mind in its original nature as a source of intuition, Ch'ien stressed training and polishing in the actual affairs of life. Wang excelled in spiritual awakening, while Ch'ien excelled in moral cultivation. While at the end Wang drifted into Zen Buddhism, Ch'ien never departed from Confucian standards, although his contribution to Confucian thought was small. No wonder later Confucian scholars praised him but condemned Wang.

[2] His private name was Ta-chi and his literary name Jui-ch'üan (1487-1541). He was a native of Shensi. Holder of a "presented scholar" degree of 1511, he became a divisional chief. As a prefect, he offended the authorities and was dismissed. He established an academy and propagated Master Wang's doctrines and was instrumental in their spread in Shensi. His own philosophy emphasized the doctrine of the extension of knowledge and being watchful over oneself when alone. For an account of him, see *Ming-ju hsüeh-an*, 29:11a-b.

[3] In 1524, according to Ch'ien Te-hung's *Nien-p'u*. Nan's preface gives the same date.

[4] A place in modern Chekiang.

which contained a selection of eight letters written by our late Teacher.[5] Concerning the two letters in reply to Hsü Ch'eng-chih,[6] our Teacher felt that inasmuch as people had for a long time concluded that Chu Hsi was right and that Lu Hsiang-shan was wrong,[7] it was difficult to reverse the trend overnight. The two letters were meant as a compromise so that people can think for themselves and reach their own conclusions. I believe Yüan-shan had the same idea when he included them at the beginning of the second stitched volume. Now the debate between Chu Hsi and Lu Hsiang-shan has for a long time made clear to the world [that Chu Hsi was wrong]. When I published our Teacher's *Wen-lu* (Literary works)[8] I placed the two letters among the additional works because they do not represent the complete views. I have therefore not included them here.

Among the other six letters, the ideas on the original substance of knowledge and action are most fully expressed in the four letters in reply to someone about learning,[9] to Chou Tao-t'ung,[10] to Lu Yüan-ching,[11] and to Ou-yang Ch'ung-i.[12] The idea that in the investigation of things the effort of the student gradually shows

[5] The first part was the same as the present Part I.

[6] Probably a pupil of Wang's. The *Wang Wen-ch'eng Kung ch'üan-shu* contains only one letter to him, in 4:2a-3a, dated 1511.

[7] Chu Hsi and Lu Hsiang-shan were diametrically opposed in their philosophy and methodology. Chu Hsi claimed that principles are in things and emphasized study and inquiry. Lu Hsiang-shan claimed that principles are in the mind and emphasized honoring the moral nature. To Chu Hsi, the law of being, principle (*li*), and the element, material force (*ch'i*), that gives being its substance and corporeal form are different. To Lu, they are the same. To Chu Hsi, mind is the function of human nature and human nature is identical with principle. To Lu, however, mind *is* principle. For Chu Hsi, the investigation of things means investigating the principle in things. For Lu, investigation means investigating the principle in the mind, for, according to him, all principles are inherent and complete in the mind. Chu advocated inquiry and study with full respect for details. Lu, on the contrary, advocated the simple, easy, and direct method of recovering one's originally good nature and coming to grips with fundamentals.

[8] This was *Yang-ming wen-lu*, published in 1536, consisting of letters, essays, memorials, other official documents, and poems. It now forms chs. 4-25 of the *Wang Wen-ch'eng Kung ch'üan-shu.*

[9] See below, secs. 130-43.

[10] See below, secs. 144-50.

[11] See below, secs. 151-67.

[12] See below, secs. 168-71.

effect is most fully discussed in the letter in reply to Lo Cheng-an.[13]

Throughout his life our Teacher was the object of attack and of attempts to destroy him. He had only one chance in ten thousand to live. Yet he always kept himself busy and never relaxed his effort to expound the doctrine lest we might fail to hear it and drift into the pursuit of success and profit and opportunistic cunning, and degenerate to the level of barbarians and criminals without realizing it. Because of his desire to form one body with all things, he talked and taught all his life and did not stop until death. This is the bitter decision of self-sacrifice on the part of all sages and worthies, from Confucius and Mencius on down, and not even his disciples have been able to console him. His feeling is most fully expressed in the first letter in reply to Nieh Wen-yü.[14]

All these six letters are reproduced as Yüan-shan recorded them. I have added the second letter in reply to Wen-yü[15] because it most fully elucidates the doctrine that always to be doing something is the task of extending the innate knowledge of the good to the utmost. It does so in such a clear, simple, and concrete manner that people are enabled to carry the doctrine into practice as soon as they hear it.

Yüan-shan was at the time very busy and yet he was able personally to demonstrate the doctrine. When at last he encountered enemies and was attacked [as a member of the Wang school which was then severely condemned] he, with all gentleness and ease, regarded the opportunity to learn the doctrine as the greatest fortune in his life, and had not the least feeling of resentment or anger. People know that his publication of the letters was a great contribution to like-minded friends but do not realize the extremely difficult situation he was in. In retaining six of the eight letters and omitting two, I do not mean to add or subtract anything from them without regret. In view of the new developments,[16] it is the proper thing to do.

---

[13] See below, secs. 172-77.

[14] See below, secs. 178-84.

[15] See below, secs. 185-94.

[16] Of the Teacher's doctrine, and the fact that the Teacher's attempt to compromise is now outdated.

LETTER IN REPLY TO KU TUNG-CH'IAO[1]

130. Your letter says, "Recent scholars have devoted themselves to external things and neglected the internal. They become broad but lack essentials. For this reason, you, sir, have purposely advocated the idea of the sincerity of the will [to probe into the fundamental]. You are punching the needle into the most vital part of the body, as it were. This is indeed a great benefit to us."

In so saying you have clearly seen the defects of the present time. How shall we remedy them? As a matter of fact, you have fully expressed in one sentence what I have in mind. What more shall I say? What more shall I say? As to the doctrine of the sincerity of the will, it is of course the first principle which the Confucian school teaches people so that they may know how to go about their task, but recent scholars have regarded it as of secondary importance. For this reason I have to some extent pointed out the importance of sincerity. It is not something I am propagating for my own purpose.

131. Your letter says, "But I am afraid your doctrine is too idealistic and the task involved too abrupt. In studying and transmitting it, the younger generation will misunderstand and be mistaken and will not be able to help falling into the Buddhist method of understanding the mind, seeing one's own nature, attaining calmness and wisdom, and achieving sudden enlightenment. No wonder those who hear your views are skeptical."

My humble views on the investigation of things, the extension of knowledge, the sincerity of the will, and the rectification of the mind are directed toward the student's task of personal examination and actual demonstration in matters concerning his own mind and daily affairs. They involve many steps and much cumulative effort. They are directly opposed to the Buddhist doctrine of sudden

---

[1] Ku Lin (1476-1545). Holder of a "presented scholar" degree of 1496, he became a minister in the department of justice. He was also a renowned poet. Like many scholars of the time, he was imprisoned for his criticism of the government and was eventually dismissed from office. For a brief account of him, see the *Ming shih*, 286:18b-20a. It is said that Ku was a close friend of Wang's when Wang was devoted to literary compositions in his younger days. According to the *Nien-p'u*, this letter was written from Chekiang in 1525 when Wang was fifty-four, but since it was included in the *Ch'uan-hsi lu* published by Nan Yüan-shan in 1524, the date must have been earlier.

enlightenment out of nothing. Those who hear my views originally have no intention of seeking to become sages and furthermore have not gone into my views thoroughly. It is not strange that they are skeptical. But with your brilliance you should have understood clearly at the very mention of the idea, and yet you say that it is too idealistic and the task involved too abrupt. Why?

132. Your letter says, "You teach us that knowledge and action should proceed simultaneously, that no distinction should be made as to which one should precede the other, and that this is the task of 'honoring the moral nature and following the path of study and inquiry' as taught in the *Doctrine of the Mean*,[2] in which the two nourish and develop each other and the internal and external, the fundamental and the secondary form one thread running through all. Nevertheless, in the performance of a task there must be a distinction between what is to be done first and what later. For example, one knows the food before he eats it, knows the soup before he drinks it, knows the clothes before he wears them, and knows the road before he travels on it. It is not true that one first performs an act without knowing the thing to be acted on. The difference is of course a matter of an instant. I do not mean to say that it is comparable to one's knowing today and then acting tomorrow."

Since you have said that the two nourish and develop each other, and the internal and the external, the fundamental and the secondary form one thread running through all, the idea that knowledge and action proceed simultaneously should no longer be doubted. You also say that in the performance of a task there must[3] be a distinction between what is to be done first and what later. Are you not self-contradictory? This is particularly clear and can easily be seen in your theories that one knows the food before he eats, but your understanding is obscured by recent opinions[4] and you do not realize that it is obscured. A man must have the desire for food before he knows the food. This desire to eat is the will; it is already the beginning of action. Whether the taste of the food is good or

---

[2] Ch. 27.

[3] In the text the word *pu* (not) appears here. It is obviously a misprint and is therefore omitted from the transtation.

[4] Such as Chu Hsi's doctrine that knowledge precedes action.

bad cannot be known until the food enters the mouth. Is there anyone who knows the taste to be good or bad before the food enters his mouth? A man must have the desire to travel before he knows the road. This desire to travel is the will; it is already the beginning of action. Whether the forks of the road are rough or smooth cannot be known until he himself has gone through them. Is there anyone who knows whether the forks of the road are rough or smooth before he has gone through them? The same can be said without a doubt about the theories that one knows the soup before he drinks it and that one knows the clothes before he wears them. The examples you have given are exactly those which show, as you say, that one first performs an act without first knowing the thing to be acted on. You said also that the difference is of course a matter of an instant and that you do not mean to say that it is clearly comparable to one's knowing today and then acting tomorrow. This shows that you have not examined the matter thoroughly. But even as you say, the fact that knowledge and action form a unity and proceed simultaneously is as a matter of course absolutely beyond any doubt.

133. Your letter says, "[You say that] true knowledge is what constitutes action, and unless it is acted on it cannot be called knowledge. This idea is all right as an urgent doctrine for the student, meant to enable him to put his learning into actual practice. But if you really mean that knowledge and action are identical, I am afraid a student will only seek his original mind and consequently neglect the principles of things, and there will be points at which his mind will be closed to the outside world and unable to penetrate it. Is this the established method of the Confucian school for the simultaneous advance of knowledge and action?"

Knowledge in its genuine and earnest aspect is action, and action in its intelligent and discriminating aspect is knowledge. At bottom the task of knowledge and action cannot be separated. Only because later scholars have broken their task into two sections and have lost sight of the original substance of knowledge and action have I advocated the idea of their unity and simultaneous advance. My idea that true knowledge is what constitutes action and that unless it is acted on it cannot be called knowledge can be seen in such ideas as those expressed in your letter that one knows the food before he eats it, and so forth. I have already stated this briefly.

Although my idea arose as an urgent remedial measure, nevertheless the substance of knowledge and action is originally like this. It is not that I have promoted or suppressed either of them according to my own wishes, and purposely propounded such a doctrine carelessly to effect a temporary remedy. He who only seeks his original mind and consequently neglects the principles of things is one who has lost his original mind. For the principles of things are not external to the mind. If one seeks the principles of things outside the mind, there will not be any to be found. And if one neglects the principles of things and only seeks his mind, what sort of a thing would the mind be? The substance of the mind is nature, and nature is identical with principle. Consequently, as there is the mind of filial piety toward parents, there is the principle of filial piety. If there is no mind of filial piety, there will be no principle of filial piety. As there is the mind of loyalty toward the ruler, there is the principle of loyalty. If there is no mind of loyalty, there will be no principle of loyalty. Are principles external to the mind? Hui-an [Chu Hsi] said, "Man's object of learning is simply mind and principles. Although the mind is the master of the body... actually it controls all principles in the world. And although principles are distributed throughout the ten thousand things... actually they are not outside one's mind."[5] These are but the two aspects of concentration and diversification but [the way Chu Hsi put it] has inevitably opened the way to the defect among scholars of regarding the mind and principles as two separate things. This is the reason why later generations have the trouble of only seeking their original minds and consequently neglecting the principles of things. This is precisely because they do not realize that the mind is identical with principle. The idea that if one seeks the principles of things outside the mind there will be points at which the mind is closed to the outside world and cannot penetrate it is the same as Kao Tzu's doctrine that righteousness is external.[6] This is the reason why Mencius said that he did not know the nature of righteousness. The mind is one, that is all. In terms of its total commiseration, it is called humanity. In terms of its attainment of what is proper, it is called righteousness. And in terms of its orderliness, it is called principle. If one should not seek humanity or righteousness outside the mind, should one make an

---

[5] *Ta-hsüeh huo-wen*, p. 60a-b.
[6] See *Book of Mencius*, 6A:4.

exception and seek principles outside the mind? Knowledge and action have been separated because people seek principles outside the mind. The doctrine of the unity of knowledge and action of the Confucian school means seeking principles in the mind. Why do you doubt it?

134. Your letter says, "In explaining the original text of the *Great Learning*, you stressed 'the extension of the knowledge of the original substance [of the mind].'[7] This is of course Mencius' principle of exerting the mind to the utmost. Chu Hsi also regarded 'pure intelligence and consciousness'[8] as the 'test of the mind.'[9] However, exerting the mind to the utmost follows from knowing one's nature, and the extension of knowledge lies in the investigation of things."

You say that exerting the mind to the utmost follows from knowing one's nature and that the extension of knowledge lies in the investigation of things. This is correct. But if I understand your idea correctly, the reason why you have said what you have said is that you are still not clear about something. Chu Hsi considered that exerting the mind to the utmost, knowing one's nature, and knowing Heaven were equivalent to the investigation of things and the extension of knowledge; that preserving the mind, nourishing one's nature, and serving Heaven were equivalent to the sincerity of the will, the rectification of the mind, and the cultivation of the personal life; and that not allowing any double-mindedness regardless of the longevity or brevity of life but cultivating the personal life while waiting for fate to take its own course were the perfection of knowledge and the complete realization of humanity, all of which are matters pertaining to the sage.[10] My humble views, however, are diametrically opposed to those of Chu Hsi. Exerting the mind to the utmost, knowing one's nature, and knowing Heaven are matters known from birth and are practiced naturally and easily. They are matters pertaining to the sage. Preserving the mind, nourishing one's nature, and serving Heaven are matters learned through study and practiced for their advantage. They are matters pertaining to the worthy. Not allowing any double-mindedness regardless of the longevity or

[7] Wang's preface to the original text of the *Great Learning*, in *Wang Wen-ch'eng Kung ch'üan-shu*, 7:25b.
[8] A quotation from the preface to the *Chung-yung chang-chü*.
[9] *Meng Tzu chi-chu*, 13:1, commenting on *Book of Mencius*, 7A:1.
[10] *Ibid*.

brevity of life but cultivating the personal life while waiting for fate to take its own course are learned through hard work and practiced with effort and difficulty. They are matters pertaining to the student.[11] How can one regard as knowledge only the exerting of the mind to the utmost and the knowing of one's nature as knowledge, while regarding the preserving of the mind and the nourishing of one's nature as action? As you suddenly hear this, you are undoubtedly greatly shocked. But actually there is nothing doubtful about it. Let me explain it to you.

The substance of the mind is the nature and the source of the nature is Heaven. This means that one who can exert his mind to the utmost can fully develop his nature. The *Doctrine of the Mean* says, "Only those who are absolutely sincere can fully develop their nature.[12] It also says, "They can know the transforming and nourishing process of Heaven and Earth"[13] and "[their principle] can be laid before spiritual beings without question or fear.... It shows that they know Heaven."[14] Only a sage can do these things. For this reason I say that they are matters known from birth and can be practiced naturally and easily, matters pertaining to the sage.

Those who preserve the mind are those who are not yet able to exert it to the utmost. Therefore they have to make the additional effort of preserving it. As the mind is preserved for a long time, it will be completely preserved without any effort to preserve it, and then one can go a step further and exert it to the utmost. For to know Heaven is the same as "to know the district" or "to know the county," which is what those titles for a prefect and a magistrate mean. If one is the official "to know the district," then all the affairs of the district are his own affairs. If one is the official "to know the county," then all the affairs of the county are his own affairs. This means becoming one with Heaven. To serve Heaven, however, is to act like a son serving his parents or a minister serving his ruler. In so doing, one and Heaven are still separated. My mind and nature are what Heaven has endowed in me. I merely preserve them and dare not lose them, nourish them and dare not injure them, as parents give the son his body in its completeness and the son returns it in its completeness.[15]

[11] See *Doctrine of the Mean*, ch. 20.
[12] *Ibid.*, ch. 22.
[13] *Ibid.*
[14] *Ibid.*, ch. 29.
[15] As described in the *Book of Rites*, "The Meaning of Sacrifices." Cf. trans.

I therefore say that these are matters learned through study and practiced for their advantage, matters of the worthy. As to those who do not allow any double-mindedness regardless of longevity or brevity of life, they are different from those who preserve the mind. Although those who preserve the mind are not yet able to exert the mind to the utmost, they already have single-mindedly determined to do good. When at times the mind has not yet been preserved, they make an effort to preserve it. Even if students do not allow any double-mindedness regardless of longevity or brevity of life, they still allow longevity or brevity of life to divide their minds [since they make a special effort to ignore them], and this means that their determination to do good is not yet single-minded. They are not yet even able to preserve the mind. How can they be said to exert it to the utmost?

Now even if they do not allow longevity or brevity of life to cause any double-mindedness in their desire to do good, but if they believe that life and death, longevity or brevity of life, all are predetermined and that what they should do is to have single-mindedness to do good and cultivate their personal life while waiting for the mandate of Heaven to take its own course, it means that in their daily life they have not realized that the mandate of Heaven already exists. Although those who serve Heaven are separated from Heaven, they truly know where the mandate of Heaven is to be found. They merely accept it with reverence and respect. Those who wait for it, however, evidently do not yet truly know where it is to be found and are still waiting for it to come. For this reason we say "establish destiny [*ming*, mandate]." The word establish means to found, to build up, as in establishing virtue, establishing words, establishing achievement, and establishing fame.[16] Whenever we say "establish," it always means that such and such a thing is not there and is now to be built up from the beginning. This is what Confucius meant when he said, "Without knowing the mandate of Heaven, it is impossible to be a superior man."[17] Therefore I say these things are matters learned through hard work and practiced with effort and difficulty, matters of the student. Now to regard exerting the mind to the

by Legge, *Li Ki*, ch. 21, p. 229. When a son died, it was understood that he was returning his body to his parents.

[16] According to ancient Confucian teaching, these constituted immortality. See *Tso chuan*, Duke Hsiang, 24th year.

[17] *Analects*, 20:3.

utmost, knowing one's nature, and knowing Heaven as the investigation of things and the extension of knowledge is suddenly to compel the beginning student who is not yet able to avoid double-mindedness to practice those things that pertain to the sage who is born to know and can practice naturally and easily. He will be seizing the wind and grasping at shadows, as it were, and will be at a loss and will not know what to do with his mind. How can such a doctrine help resulting in "making the whole empire run about on the road"?[18] Thus you can readily see the defects of present-day theories of the extension of knowledge and the investigation of things. Is not the defect of what you described as devoting oneself to external things and neglecting the internal, being broad but lacking essentials the same as this? This is the most important point in one's learning. If a mistake is made here, then it will be made everywhere. This is the reason I have risked the reproach and ridicule of the world, ignored the personal suffering of punishment, and cannot help but keep on talking.

135. Your letter says, "I have heard that you told students that following the theory of the investigation of the principles of all things that we come into contact with[19] is to trifle with things and to lose one's purpose, and that you have also selected Chu Hsi's doctrines of rejecting the complex and preferring the simple,[20] cultivating the fundamental,[21] and so forth, to show students, labeling them as Chu Hsi's final conclusions arrived at late in life.[22] I am afraid this is also wrong."

What Chu Hsi meant by the investigation of things is "to investigate the principle in things to the utmost as we come in contact with them."[23] To investigate the principles in things to the utmost as we come in contact with them means to look in each individual thing for its so-called definite principles. This means to apply one's mind to each individual thing and look for principle in it. This is to divide the mind and principle into two. To seek for the principle in each individual thing is like looking for the principle

---

[18] A quotation from the *Book of Mencius*, 3A:4.
[19] This is Chu Hsi's theory. See his *Ta-hsüeh chang-chü*, ch. 5.
[20] *Chu Tzu wen-chi*, 35:26b.
[21] *Ibid.*, 47:31a.
[22] See below, pp. 263-67.
[23] *Ta-hsüeh chang-chü*, ch. 5.

of filial piety in parents. If the principle of filial piety is to be sought in parents, then is it actually in my own mind or is it in the person of my parents? If it is actually in the person of my parents, is it true that as soon as the parents pass away the mind will lack the principle of filial piety? When I see a child fall into a well [and have a feeling of commiseration], there must be the principle of commiseration. Is this principle of commiseration actually in the person of the child or is it in the innate knowledge of my mind? Perhaps one cannot follow the child into the well to rescue it. Perhaps one can rescue it by seizing it with the hand. All this involves principle. Is it really in the person of the child or does it emanate from the innate knowledge of my mind? What is true here is true of all things and events. From this we know the mistake of dividing the mind and principle into two.

Such division is the doctrine of Kao Tzu who taught that righteousness is external to the mind, a fallacy which Mencius strongly attacked.[24] You know the defect of devoting oneself to external things and neglecting the internal, and becoming broad but lacking essentials. Why are these defects? Is it not permissible to say that to investigate the principle of all things as we come into contact with them, as Chu Hsi has taught, is trifling with things and losing one's purpose in life? What I mean by the investigation of things and the extension of knowledge is to extend the innate knowledge of my mind to each and every thing. The innate knowledge of my mind is the same as the Principle of Nature. When the Principle of Nature in the innate knowledge of my mind is extended to all things, all things will attain their principle. To extend the innate knowledge of my mind is the matter of the extension of knowledge, and for all things to attain their principle is the matter of the investigation of things. In these the mind and principle are combined into one. As the mind and principle are combined into one, then all my humble opinions which I have just expressed and my theory that Chu Hsi arrived at his final conclusions late in life can be understood without discussion.

136. Your letter says, "The substance of the human mind is completely intelligent and penetrating. But because man's mind is restricted by material force and obscured by external things, few minds

<hr/>

[24] *Book of Mencius*, 6A:4.

are not darkened. Unless one studies extensively, inquires accurately, thinks carefully, and sifts clearly[25] so as to understand the principles of things, he cannot recognize the activating power of good and evil or the distinction between truth and falsehood. He will give free rein to his passions and indulge in his own will, and the harm resulting from them will be beyond words."

This passage in general sounds correct but is wrong. It perpetuates the fallacy of traditional theories. I must refute them.

Study, inquiry, thinking, sifting, and practice are all ways of learning. No one really learns anything without carrying it into action. Take the learning of filial piety. One must relieve his parents of the burden of toil, serve and care for them, and personally put the principle of filial piety into action before one can be said to be learning filial piety. Can merely talking about it in a vacuum be considered as learning? To learn archery, one must hold out the bow, fix the arrow to the string, draw the bow, and take aim. To learn writing, one must lay out the paper, take the brush, hold the inkwell, and dip the brush into the ink. In all the world, nothing can be considered learning that does not involve action. Thus the very beginning of learning is already action. To be earnest in practice means to be genuine and sincere. That is already action. It is to make the action sincere and the effort continuous without stop. In learning, one cannot help having doubts. Therefore one inquires. To inquire is to learn; it is to act. As there is still doubt, one thinks. To think is to learn; it is to act. As there is still doubt, one sifts. To sift is to learn; it is to act. As the sifting is clear, the thinking careful, the inquiry accurate, and the study competent, one goes further and continues his effort without stop. This is what is meant by earnest practice. It does not mean that after study, inquiry, thinking, and sifting one then takes steps to act.

For this reason I hold that in seeking to acquire the ability to do things, we call the seeking study. In seeking to dispel doubts, we call it inquiry. In seeking to understand an idea of a doctrine, we call it thinking. In seeking to examine the idea carefully, we call it sifting. And in seeking to carry the idea out in actual practice, we call it action. Speaking from the point of view of separate efforts, they are five, but speaking from the point of view of a combined

---

[25] *Doctrine of the Mean*, ch. 20.

affair, they are one. This is precisely where my humble views differ from those of later scholars, that in substance mind and principle are a unity and in our effort knowledge and action advance simultaneously.

You have mentioned only study, inquiry, thinking, and sifting as ways to investigate the principles of things to the utmost and have not included earnest action. This means that you regard study, inquiry, thinking, and sifting alone as knowledge and feel that the investigation of the principles of things to the utmost involves no action. Can anyone learn without action? Can anyone be said to have investigated the principles of things to the utmost without having taken any action? Ch'eng Hao said, "By merely investigating the principles of things to the utmost one simultaneously fully develops one's nature to the point of fulfilling one's destiny."[26] Therefore one must extend the humanity in one's action to the ultimate of humanity, and only then can one be said to have investigated the principle of humanity to the utmost. One must extend the righteousness in one's action to the utmost of righteousness. Only then can one be said to have investigated the principle of righteousness to the utmost. When humanity is extended to its ultimate, the nature of humanity will be fully realized. When righteousness is extended to its ultimate, the nature of righteousness will be fully realized. Can there be such a thing as a person whose learning has reached the point of having completely investigated the principles of things to the utmost and yet has not proceeded to action? Therefore if we realize that no learning can be considered learning if it is not carried into action, we know that the investigation of the principles of things to the utmost cannot be so considered if it is not carried into action. If we realize that the investigation of the principles of things to the utmost cannot be so considered if it is not carried into action, we know that knowledge and action are a unity and advance simultaneously, and cannot be separated. For the principle of each and every thing is not external to the mind. To insist on investigating all the principles in the world to the utmost is to regard the innate knowledge of the mind as inadequate and to feel that it is necessary to seek extensively throughout the world in order to supplement and enhance it. This amounts to dividing mind and principle into two.

[26] *I-shu,* 2A:2b; cf. 10:5a.

Although in the task of study, inquiry, thinking, sifting, and earnest practice, those who learn through hard work and practice with effort and difficulty have to exert a hundred times as much effort as others, when the task is fully extended to the point of fully developing one's nature and knowing Heaven, it is no more than extending the innate knowledge of one's mind to the utmost. Is there anything, even an iota, to be added to innate knowledge? Now if we insist on investigating all the principles in the world to the utmost and do not know how to return and seek within our mind, then, aside from the innate knowledge of our mind, what is there to carry out the examination of what you have called the activating power of good and evil and the discrimination of truth and falsehood? The restriction by material force and obscuration by external things that you have mentioned are but the restriction and obscuration of the mind. Now if we wish to get rid of the obscuration of the mind and do not know how to direct our effort to innate knowledge but seek remedy outside, we are comparable to a person whose vision is not clear and who, instead of taking medicine and nourishing his eyes in order to cure them, merely wanders despondently and seeks vision outside. Can vision be attained from the outside? The harm of giving free rein to one's passions and indulging in one's own will is likewise due only to the failure to examine carefully the Principle of Nature in the innate knowledge of our mind. This is a matter in which if an infinitesimal mistake is made in the beginning it will lead to an infinite error at the end, and the statement should not be left unrefuted. Please do not say that I have been too harsh in my words.

137. Your letter says, "You teach people to extend knowledge to the utmost and to manifest clear character, and warn them against investigating the principles of things to the utmost as we come in contact with them. Is it really possible that an unenlightened scholar, living in deep seclusion, sitting erect, and uninformed, can thus be able to achieve the extension of knowledge and the manifestation of clear character? Even if he becomes tranquil and has some realization and to a certain degree intuits his own nature, what he gets is but useless views of calmness and wisdom. Can he really know past and present and understand the change of events, and apply his knowledge to concrete matters of the state and the world? As to your contention that 'knowledge is the substance of the will and things

are functions of the will,'[27] and that the word *ko* in the phrase *ko-wu* (investigation of things) means to rectify, as in the saying, 'It is only the great man who can rectify (*ko*) what is wrong in the ruler's mind,'[28] although your ideas are lofty and stimulating and are distinguished by not conforming to traditional interpretations, I am afraid they are nevertheless not in accord with truth."

My humble views on the extension of knowledge and the investigation of things are precisely for the purpose of investigating the principles of things to the utmost. I have never warned people against investigating the principles of things to the utmost nor urged them to live in deep seclusion, sit erect, and do nothing. My idea is that it is incorrect to interpret the investigation of the principles of things to the utmost as we come into contact with them to mean what I have described before as devoting oneself to external things and neglecting the internal. If an unenlightened student can really carefully examine the Principle of Nature in the mind in connection with things and events as they come, and extend his innate or original knowledge of the good, then though stupid he will surely become intelligent and though weak he will surely become strong.[29] The great foundation will be established and the universal way [in human relations] will be in operation. And the nine standards[30] of ruling a state will be united by one thread that runs through them completely. Why still worry about his having no concrete application? It is precisely people who are characterized by stubborn emptiness and abstract tranquillity who are incapable of carefully examining the Principle of Nature in the mind in connection with things and events as they come, and of extending their innate or original knowledge of the good. Instead they abandon human relations and get used to a life of silence, annihilation, emptiness, and nothingness.[31] Thus essentially speaking their way cannot be used to govern the family, the state, and the world. Who

[27] Possibly a quotation from Wang's *Ku-pen ta-hsüeh p'ang-shih*, which is not included in the *Wang Wen-ch'eng Kung ch'üan-shu*. The original *Ku-pen ta-hsüeh p'ang-shih* has been lost. The present version, included in the *Han-hai* collection, is considered by scholars to be spurious, although the saying itself may well have come from the original. The same idea is expressed above in sec. 6. Cf. above, sec. 78, and below, secs. 174 and 201.

[28] Reference to *Book of Mencius*, 4A:20, in sec. 7, above.

[29] Quoting the *Doctrine of the Mean*, ch. 20.

[30] See above, sec. 128, n. 97, for these nine standards.

[31] Like the Buddhists and Taoists.

will say that the Sage's doctrine of investigating the principles of things to the utmost and fully developing one's nature also has this defect?

The mind is the master of the body, and the pure intelligence and clear consciousness of the mind are the innate or original knowledge. When this innate knowledge which is pure intelligence and clear consciousness is influenced by things and events and responds to them with activity, it is called the will. With knowledge, there will be the will. Without knowledge, there will be no will. Is knowledge not the substance of the will? For the will to function, there must be the thing in which it is to function, and the thing is an event. When the will functions in the service of parents, then serving parents is a thing. When the will functions in governing the people, then governing the people is a thing. When the will functions in study, then study is a thing. When the will functions in hearing a law suit, then hearing a law suit is a thing. Wherever the will is applied, there cannot be nothing. Where this is a particular will, there is a particular thing corresponding to it, and where there is no particular will, there will be no particular thing corresponding to it. Is a thing, then, not the function of the will?

The word *ko* has been interpreted by some as "to reach" (*chih*). It is so interpreted in such sayings as "Emperor Shun reached [*ko*] in the temple of illustrious ancestors"[32] and "The prince of the Miao tribe has come and reached [*ko*]."[33] But in reaching the illustrious ancestors there must first be pure filial piety and sincerity and reverence so that everything between the manifested mundane world and the hidden spiritual world is in accord with principle before the ancestors can be said to have been reached. The Miao tribe was obstinate. It was really after the Great Yü diffused culture and virtue among them that they were reached. In both cases the meaning of rectifying [*cheng*] is also involved and the word "reach" alone does not tell all that it means. In such sayings as "rectifying the evil of his heart"[34] and "A great minister rectifies what is wrong in the ruler's mind" the idea is that of rectifying what is incorrect so it can return to its original correctness, and cannot be interpreted to mean reach.

Furthermore, who knows that the investigation of things in the

---

[32] *Book of History*, "Canon of Yao." Cf. trans. by Legge, *Shoo King*, p. 41.
[33] *Ibid.*, "Counsels of the Great Yü." Cf. trans. by Legge, p. 66.
[34] *Ibid.*, "Charge to Ch'iung." Cf. trans. by Legge, p. 585.

Great Learning[35] should not be interpreted in the sense of rectification but has to be interpreted in the sense of reaching? If it must be interpreted in the sense of reaching, it would be necessary to say "investigating to the utmost until you reach the principle of all things," in order to make sense. In that case, the importance of the task lies completely in investigating to the utmost and the object of the task lies entirely in principles. If now the words "investigate to the utmost" and "principle" were to be omitted and we were really to say, "the extension of knowledge consists of reaching all things," does it make any sense? The accepted teachings of Confucius on the investigation of the principles of things to the utmost and the full development of one's nature are found in the "Appended Remarks" of the *Book of Changes*.[36] If the investigation of things really means the investigation of the principles of things to the utmost, why didn't Confucius directly say that the extension of knowledge consists in the investigation of things to the utmost instead of making such an indirect and incomplete remark to give later scholars trouble? Although the idea of the investigation of things in the *Great Learning* and that of the investigation of the principles of things to the utmost in the "Appended Remarks" are fundamentally in agreement, there are slight differences. By investigating the principles to the utmost is meant that the task includes the investigation of things, the extension of knowledge, the sincerity of the will, and the rectification of the mind. Therefore whenever we talk about the investigation of the principles of things to the utmost, we include in it the task of the investigation of things, the extension of knowledge, the sincerity of the will, and the rectification of the mind; and whenever we talk about the investigation of things, we have to mention the extension of knowledge, the sincerity of the will, and the rectification of the mind at the same time. Only when it includes these can its task be complete and thorough. To mention only the investigation of things and dogmatically to say that that is the investigation of the principles of things to the utmost is to regard the latter as belonging entirely to the sphere of knowledge and the investigation of things as involving no action. This is not only to fail to understand the

[35] In the sentence "The extension of knowledge consists of the investigation of things." The text of the *Great Learning*.

[36] While the "Appended Remarks" of the *Book of Changes* may be said to contain these ideas, the actual terms as quoted here appear in "Remarks on the Trigrams," ch. 1.

idea of the investigation of things but also to fail to grasp the meaning of the investigation of the principles of things to the utmost. This is the reason why later scholars have separated knowledge and action into two sections and have been daily involved in fragmentary and isolated details and broken pieces, and this is really why the doctrine of the Sage has been gradually declining and fading away. After all you are not free from following stereotyped views. It is to be expected that you will consider my views to be out of accord with truth.

138.   Your letter says, "You said that in the task of the extension of knowledge, to know how to care for the comfort of parents in both winter and summer and to know how to serve and support them is itself the sincerity of the will, and that there is no such separate thing as the investigation of things. I am afraid this is also wrong."

You say so because you have projected your own views and suppose they are mine. They are not what I have told you. Does what you have said really make any sense? My view is that when the will desires to care for the comfort of parents in both winter and summer, and to serve and support them, the will exists but not yet the sincerity of the will. Before the will can be said to be sincere, there must be the actual practice of caring for their comfort and of serving and supporting them until one is satisfied and has no self-deception. To know the regular details of caring for the comfort of parents and the proper ways of serving and supporting them is knowledge but not yet the extension of knowledge. The knowledge of the regular details of caring for parents must be extended to become the actual practice of caring, and the knowledge of the proper ways of serving and supporting them must be extended to become the actual practice of serving and supporting before there can be the extension of knowledge. The mere facts of caring for the parents' comfort and serving and supporting them are things and should not be regarded as the investigation of things. Caring for the comfort of parents must be carried out entirely according to what the innate faculty knows to be the regular details of caring for them, without the least bit left undone. Likewise serving and supporting them must be carried out entirely according to what the innate faculty knows to be the proper way of serving and supporting them, without the least bit left undone. Only then can things be said to have been investigated. Only after the things of caring for parents' comfort are investigated can the innate knowledge that knows how to care for them be extended and only after the things of serving and supporting them are investigated can the innate knowledge that knows the proper ways of serving and supporting them be extended. Therefore it is said that "when things are investigated, knowledge is extended."[37] Only after the innate knowledge that knows how to care for the parents' comfort is extended can the will to care for them be sincere, and only after the innate knowledge that knows how to serve and support them is extended can the will to serve and support them be sincere. Therefore it is said that "when knowledge is extended, the will becomes sincere."[38] These are my humble views on the sincerity of the will, the extension of knowledge, and the investigation of things. If you think them over thoroughly, you will no longer have any doubt.

139. Your letter says, "The foundations of truth are easy to understand. As it has been said, 'Innate knowledge of the good and innate ability to do good are possible even in men and women of simple intelligence.'[39] As to the minute details and varying circumstances, in which an infinitesimal mistake in the beginning may lead to an infinite error at the end, they need to be studied before we know them. Who does not know that filial piety involves caring for the comfort of parents in both winter and summer and serving and supporting them? But in such cases as Emperor Shun's getting married without first telling his parents,[40] King Wu's launching a military expedition before burying his father,[41] Tseng Tzu's nourishing the will of his father while his son nourished his mouth and body,[42] Tseng Tzu's bearing his father's heavy beating or light beating without complaint,[43] a filial son's cutting his own thigh to make medicine for his sick parent,[44] and the crown prince of T'eng's

---

[37] The text of the *Great Learning*.   [38] *Ibid.*

[39] Alluding to the *Doctrine of the Mean*, ch. 12.

[40] *Book of Mencius*, 5A:2.

[41] *Shih chi*, 61:7b.

[42] *Book of Mencius*, 4A:19.

[43] *K'ung Tzu chia-yü*, sec. 15, SPTK ed., 4:5a-6a.

[44] *Sung shih*, 155:15a. Most annotators give this general reference. Professors Yang Lien-sheng of Harvard University and Fu Shang-ling of Bennet College have kindly informed me that in the *Hsin T'ang shu*, 195:2a, it is recorded that cases of filial sons' cutting their own thighs to make medicine for their sick parents are based on the words of Ch'en Ts'ang-ch'i (*fl.* 723-33),

building by the grave a shed in which to mourn his father,[45] the question of what to do under normal conditions or under an emergency, and what is too much or not enough, must be deliberated with reference to right and wrong so as to provide a basis for handling affairs in the proper way. Only then can the substance of the mind be free from obscuration and one's will not be at a loss when things happen."

It is quite true, as you have said, that the foundations of truth are easy to understand. However, students of later generations neglect what is easy to understand and do not follow it but seek what is difficult to understand and make it their object of study. This is why "truth lies in what is near and men seek for it in what is remote and the work lies in what is easy and men seek for it in what is difficult."[46] Mencius said, "The way of truth is like a great road. Is it difficult to know? The trouble is that men do not follow it."[47]

In innate knowledge and innate ability, men and women of simple intelligence and the sage are equal. Their difference lies in the fact that the sage alone can extend his innate knowledge while men and women of simple intelligence cannot. It is not that the sage does not know the minute details and varying circumstances. Rather he is not confined to them in his studies. What he studies is precisely the extension of innate knowledge in order carefully to examine the Principle of Nature in the mind. Herein lies the difference between his study [as taught by Confucius] and that taught by later generations. You devote no time to extending innate knowledge but

who in his *Pen-ts'ao shih-i*, which contained notes on medicine, said that human flesh could cure acute illness. Professor Jao Tsung-i of the University of Hong Kong, thanks to Dr. E. Sargent, has also kindly referred me to the *Hsin T'ang shu*, 196:4b, where it is recorded that Wang Yu-chen was commended by the emperor for having cured his mother's illness by feeding her with flesh from his thigh. I have not been able to trace the story to any earlier source than this. Azuma Keiji in his *Denshō-roku kōgi* refers to the case of Chang Mi in the "Biography of a Filial Son" in the *Wei shu* of 554, but there is no such biography there. The name Chang Mi is not found in any biographical dictionary or in the *Index of Personal Names in the Twenty-five Histories*. In the *Chuang Tzu*, ch. 29, SPTK ed., 9:39a (Giles, trans., *Chuang Tzu*, p. 286), there is the story of a minister cutting his own thigh to feed his king. But the moral there is loyalty and not filial piety. Chu Hsi mentioned the act of cutting the thigh in his *Ta-hsüeh huo-wen*, p. 26b, without mentioning the origin of the story.

[45] *Book of Mencius*, 3A:2.
[46] *Ibid.*, 4A:11.
[47] *Ibid.*, 6B:2.

unceasingly worry about details and circumstances. This is exactly the trouble of seeking what is difficult to understand and making it the object of study.

Innate knowledge is to minute details and varying circumstances as compasses and measures are to areas and lengths. Details and circumstances cannot be predetermined, just as areas and lengths are infinite in number and cannot be entirely covered. If compasses and squares are truly set, there cannot be any deception regarding areas, and the possibility of correct areas in the world cannot be exhausted. If measures are well exhibited, there cannot be any deception regarding length, and the possibility of correct lengths in the world cannot be exhausted. If innate knowledge is truly extended, there cannot be any deception regarding minute details and varying circumstances, and the possibility of minute details and varying circumstances in the world cannot be exhausted. If one does not realize that in an instant of thought in his mind of innate knowledge an infinitesimal mistake in the beginning may lead to an infinite error at the end, what is the sense of study? That would amount to hoping to determine squares and circles without compasses and squares, and to cover all lengths without measures. I can see that such a man is unreasonable, absurd, and is working day in and day out without success.

You ask who does not know that filial piety involves caring for the comfort of parents in both winter and summer and serving and supporting them. But those who can extend and apply their knowledge are few. If one who roughly knows the details of caring for parents can be regarded as being able to extend his knowledge, then whoever knows that the ruler should be humane should be regarded as being able to extend his knowledge of humanity and whoever knows that the minister should be loyal should be regarded as being able to extend his knowledge of loyalty. In that case, who in the world does not extend his knowledge? Looking at it this way, we know that the extension of knowledge necessarily consists in action, and it is clear that without action there can be no extension of knowledge. Does not the substance of the unity of knowledge and action stand sharply in focus?

As for Shun's marrying without first telling his parents, was there someone before him who did the same thing and served as an example for him, which he could find out by looking into certain records and asking certain people, after which he did as he did?

Or did he search into the innate knowledge in an instant of thought in his own mind and weigh all factors as to what was proper, after which he could not help doing what he did? Similarly, in the case of King Wu's launching a military expedition before burying his father, was there someone before him who did the same thing and served as an example for him, which he could find out by looking into certain records or asking certain people, after which he did as he did? Or did he search the innate knowledge in an instant of thought in his own mind and weigh all factors as to what was proper, after which he could not help doing what he did? If Emperor Shun's mind was not sincere about having no posterity, and King Wu's mind was not sincere about saving the people, then the former's marrying without first telling his parents and the latter's expedition without first burying his father would be cases of the greatest filial impiety and disloyalty. People of later generations do not devote themselves to the extension of innate knowledge in order carefully to examine the moral principles in the mind's contact with, response to, and dealing with things, but want to discuss these unusual deeds in a vacuum, hold on to them as a basis for handling affairs, and hope not to be at a loss when things happen. They are far off the mark! It can be shown through inference by analogy that the same is true of the other cases you have mentioned. From the above we can know the ancient doctrine of the extension of knowledge.

140.   Your letter says, "To say that the theory of the investigation of things in the *Great Learning* means to seek the original mind may be accepted as an arbitrary combination of the two ideas. But the Six Classics and the Four Books[48] contain sayings that teach 'hearing and seeing much,'[49] 'remembering the words and deeds of former men,'[50] 'love of antiquity and earnestly seeking it there,'[51] 'learning extensively and inquiring accurately,'[52] 'reviewing the old so as to know the new,'[53] 'studying extensively and discussing thoroughly,'[54]

[48] See above, Introduction, n. 1.
[49] *Analects*, 2:18.
[50] *Book of Changes*, commentary on hexagram no. 26. Cf. trans. by Legge, *Yi King*, p. 300.
[51] *Analects*, 7:19.
[52] *Doctrine of the Mean*, ch. 20.
[53] *Analects*, 2:11.
[54] *Book of Mencius*, 4B:15.

and 'taking delight in questioning and examining.'[55] All these clearly show a search within the realm of events and a reliance on deliberation and discussion. It is clear that no confusion should be allowed in the details to which one's effort is devoted."

The meaning of the investigation of things has already been fully explained. I believe your suspicion of arbitrary combination requires no further answer. As to hearing and seeing much [Confucius told Tzu-chang, "Hear much and put aside what is doubtful while you speak cautiously of the rest. Then few will blame you. See much and put aside what seems perilous while you are cautious in carrying the rest into practice. Then you will have few occasions for regret"]. He said so because Tzu-chang sought external things and loved lofty position, wanted to regard merely hearing and seeing much as learning, and was unable to seek within his own mind in order to put aside what is doubtful and what is perilous. For this reason he was in his words and deeds unable to avoid blame by others and regret by himself. What is called hearing and seeing much merely became an aid to his search for external things and his love of lofty position. Thus Confucius meant to remedy Tzu-chang's defect of hearing and seeing much and did not mean to offer what he said as a [regular] way of learning.

Confucius once said, "There are those who act without knowing [what is right]. But I am not one of them."[56] This has the same idea as the saying of Mencius, "The feeling of right and wrong is found in all men."[57] It was intended precisely to show that innate knowledge of our moral nature does not come from hearing and seeing. When Confucius continued to say, "Hear much and select what is good and follow it. See much and remember it," he referred to nothing but seeking solely after the secondary matters of seeing and hearing, thus already falling to the secondary level. This is why Confucius said [in conclusion], "This is secondary knowledge." Since he regarded knowledge from hearing and seeing as secondary, what then is higher knowledge? Here you can have a peep at the place where the Confucian school directs its effort at the extension of knowledge.

Confucius said to Tzu-kung, "Tz'u, do you suppose that I am one who learns a great deal and remembers it?... No, I have a thread that

[55] *Doctrine of the Mean*, ch. 6.
[56] *Analects*, 7:27.
[57] *Book of Mencius*, 6A:6.

runs through it all."[58] If the emphasis really is laid on learning a great deal and remembering it, why did the Grand Master make such a false statement to cheat Tzu-kung? What is the thread that runs through all if it is not the extension of innate knowledge? The *Book of Changes* says, "The superior man remembers many words and deeds of former men in order to nourish his virtue." Since the motive is to nourish virtue, then remembering many words and deeds of former men is the work of nourishing virtue. This is precisely the task of both knowledge and action combined. To love antiquity and earnestly to seek means to love the learning of the ancients and earnestly to seek the principle of the mind. Mind is identical with principle. To learn means to learn this mind. To seek means to seek this mind. Mencius said, "The way of learning is none other than to find the lost mind."[59] This way is different from the learning of later generations who consider the vast memorization and extensive recitation of the words of the ancients to be love of antiquity, and merely devote their unceasing efforts to the search for success, fame, and profit, which are external. I have already commented fully on extensive learning and accurate inquiry. As to reviewing the old so as to know the new, Chu Hsi also regarded reviewing the old as honoring our moral nature.[60] Can moral nature be sought outside the mind? Since knowing the new must necessarily come from reviewing the old and since only through reviewing the old can the new be known, it proves that knowledge and action are not two separate sections. "Study extensively and discuss thoroughly. This is in order to go back and discuss the most restrained."[61] If the words "to go back and discuss the most restrained" are omitted, then what is the objective of studying extensively and discussing thoroughly? The reason Emperor Shun took delight in questioning and examining was to put the mean into application and extend its refinement and singleness to the moral mind. By the moral mind is meant innate knowledge. When has the learning of the superior man departed from practical affairs and discarded discussions? However, whenever he is engaged in practical affairs or discussion, he insists on the task of knowledge and action combined. The aim is precisely to extend the innate knowledge of his original mind. He is unlike those who devote

[58] *Analects*, 15:2. Tz'u was Tzu-kung's private name.
[59] *Book of Mencius*, 6A:11.
[60] *Chu Tzu yü-lei*, 64:26b.
[61] *Book of Mencius*, 4B:15.

themselves to merely talking and hearing as though that were knowledge, and divide knowledge and action into two separate things as though they really could be itemized and take place one after the other.

141. Your letter says, "Yang Chu's [bet. 440 and 360 B.C.] practice of righteousness [in terms of everyone for himself] and Mo Tzu's practice of humanity [in terms of mutual or universal love],[62] the goody-goody's violation of loyalty and faithfulness,[63] the abdication of the sage-emperors Yao and Shun in favor of virtuous ministers,[64] the king of Yen's abdication in favor of the minister Tzu-chih,[65] King T'ang's and King Wu's military expeditions against the wicked rulers,[66] Hsiang Yü's [d. 202 B.C.] killing his king and seating himself on the throne,[67] Duke Chou's assisting King Ch'eng [r.1104-1068 B.C.],[68] Wang Mang's [45 B.C.-A.D.23] and Ts'ao Ts'ao's [A.D. 155-220] assistance in their government,[69] have been loosely judged to be right or wrong without any objective standard. What shall we follow? Furthermore, if we do not investigate to find out about the changing events of past and present, and the names and varieties of ceremonies and music, in case the government wants to construct a Brilliant Hall or palace,[70] build a national university, establish the system of calendar and musical scales, or draft

---

[62] Mencius criticized them as excessive. See *Book of Mencius*, 7A:26.

[63] *Analects*, 17:13.

[64] *Book of Mencius*, 5A:4. Yao abdicated in favor of Shun, and Shun abdicated in favor of the Great Yü. Their deeds have been highly praised.

[65] *Book of Mencius*, 2B:8. The king of Yen abdicated in favor of Tzu-chih and caused great disorder in the state. Consequently the abdication has been condemned.

[66] *Book of Mencius*, 1B:8.

[67] *Shih chi*, 7:20b-21a. See Burton Watson, trans., *Records of the Grand Historian of China* (New York, Columbia University Press, 1961), I, 59. Hsiang Yü has been condemned, while King Wu has been praised.

[68] *Book of History*, "The Great Announcement." Cf. trans. by Legge, *Shoo King*, p. 362.

[69] *Ch'ien-Han shu*, ch. 99B, and *Hou-Han shu*, ch. 9. Duke Chou has been regarded as a sage, whereas Wang and Ts'ao have been regarded as thieves.

[70] *Ming-t'ang*, literally "hall of light," is said by some to be the hall where government was conducted, education propagated, and sacrifices performed. The commentary on ch. 14 of the *Book of Rites* says that it was a place where the king held audiences to receive feudal lords. It was the practice of kings who were touring their kingdoms to build in famous mountains such "Brilliant Halls" for the purpose. The functions of these halls in the Chou times included banquets, education, the selection of officials, etc.

documents to sacrifice to Heaven, mountains, and rivers, how can we proceed? Therefore [a commentator on] the *Analects* said, 'What is known at birth is moral principle only. As to the changing events of past and present and the names and varieties of ceremonies and music, they surely require study before their validity can be verified in practice.'[71] This conclusion seems to be definite and final."

What you said about Yang, Mo, the goody-goody, Yao, Shun, Tzu-chih, T'ang, Wu, Hsiang Yü, Duke Chou, Wang Mang, and Ts'ao Ts'ao may be explained in the same way as I have done above regarding Emperor Shun's marrying without first reporting to his parents and King Wu's military expedition before burying his father. Concerning your doubts about the changing events of past and present, I have already given the analogy of compass, square, and measures when discussing innate knowledge. There should be no need to say any more.

As to matters like the Brilliant Hall and national university, it seems that I should not allow myself to be silent. These matters require a long explanation. But just let me take what you say and correct it, and then your doubt may to some extent be dispelled.

The system of the Brilliant Hall and the national university first appeared in Lü Pu-wei's [d. 235 B.C.] "Monthly Orders"[72] and the textual commentaries on the Confucian Classics by a scholar of the Han period.[73] They are not discussed in the Six Classics or the Four Books in detail. Is the wisdom of Lü and the Han scholar superior to that of the sages and worthies of the Three Dynasties? Some Brilliant Halls were still in existence at the time of King Hsüan [r.342-234 B.C.] of Ch'i.[74] It is clear that those of the Chou dynasty were all intact at the time of wicked Kings Yu [r. 781-771 B.C.] and Li [r. 878-842 B.C.]. Emperors Yao and Shun had palaces of thatched and untrimmed roofs and earthen steps. The system of Brilliant Halls was not necessarily complete. And yet that did not do any harm to their orderly government. The Brilliant Halls of Yu and Li surely followed the tradition of wise kings Wen, Wu, Ch'eng, and

---

[71] A saying by Yin T'un (1061-1132) quoted by Chu Hsi in his *Lun-yü chi-chu*, ch. 4, comment on *Analects* 7:19.

[72] The first section of the twelve chapters on the twelve months in his *Lü-shih ch'un-ch'iu*. These are combined to form the chapter "Yüeh-ling" (monthly orders) of the *Book of Rites*.

[73] Notably Cheng Hsüan (127-200), in his commentary on ch. 14 of the *Book of Rites*.

[74] *Book of Mencius*, 1B:5.

K'ang, and yet they did not help them to prevent disorder. Why? If a government that cannot bear to see the suffering of the people is conducted from a mind that cannot bear to see the suffering of the people[75] even a building with a thatched roof and earthen steps can be a Brilliant Hall, but if a wicked government like those of King Yu and King Li is conducted from a wicked mind like theirs, then even if the place is a Brilliant Hall, it is after all the place where tyrannical government originates. Is this not true? During the Han dynasty [206 B.C.-A.D. 220], Emperor Wu [r. 140-87 B.C.] was the first one to order lectures on the Brilliant Hall [76] and during the T'ang dynasty [618-907] Empress Wu [r.684-705] gloriously built a Brilliant Hall[77] and yet what was the condition in their days, order or disorder?

The national university at the national capital was called *pi-yung* (literally "surrounded jade").[78] The college of feudal lords was called *p'an-kung* (literally "half palace").[79] They were so named to indicate their geographical patterns. However, the education of the Three Dynasties was designed essentially to manifest human relations and its importance did not depend on whether or not the buildings were jade-like or half palaces. Confucius said, "If a man is not humane, what has he to do with ceremonies? If he is not humane, what has he to do with music?"[80] To institute ceremonies and great musical systems, one must possess the moral qualities of equilibrium [before the feeling are aroused] and harmony [after the feelings are aroused] and his voice must be equivalent to the musical notes and his person equivalent to standard measure.[81] Only then can he be qualified. As to the subsidiary matters of articles and numbers, they are the concern of musicians and the duty of priests and clerks. Hence Tseng Tzu said, "There are three principles of conduct which the superior man considers especially important.... As to such matters as attending to the sacrificial vessels, there are the proper officers for them."[82]

---

[75] *Ibid.*, 2A:6.
[76] In 140 B.C., according to Chu Hsi's *T'ung-chien kang-mu*, 4:49a-b.
[77] In A.D. 688, according to *ibid.*, 41:94a.
[78] Alluding to a building surrounded by a moat.
[79] Only one side was surrounded by water.
[80] *Analects*, 3:3.
[81] These are qualities ascribed to the Great Yü in the *Shih chi*, 2:2a.
[82] *Analects*, 8:4.

Emperor Yao commended Hsi and Ho, "In reverent accord with the luminant heaven, calculate and delineate the movements of the sun, the moon, and the stars."[83] The importance here lies in seriously providing the people with definite times to determine the seasons. Emperor Shun depended on gem-inlaid astronomical instruments.[84] The importance here lies in regulating the sun, moon, and five planets. They all unremittingly carried out the governmental measures to nourish the people, with the mind of being humane to all people. Here is the foundation of regulating the calendar and determining the seasons. The learning of Hsi and Ho may not have been matched by Kao and Hsieh or by Yü and Chi[85] or even by Yao and Shun, whose wisdom did not extend to everything.[86] Nevertheless, up to the present time generations have followed the method of Hsi and Ho and practiced their art. Even men with limited knowledge and small wisdom, and shallow astrologers, can make astronomical calendars and foretell weather without error. Shall we say that the people of limited knowledge and small wisdom of later generations are superior to Yü, Chi, Yao, and Shun in virtue and wisdom?

The theories of sacrificing to Heaven, mountains, and rivers are even more absurd. They are the products of later deceitful, flattering scholars who wanted to please their rulers. These scholars exaggerated matters to confuse the rulers' minds and to waste national funds, and as such were outstanding cases of shamelessly cheating Heaven and entrapping the people, unworthy of being mentioned by a superior man. It is for this reason that Ssu-ma Hsiang-ju [179-117 B.C.] was ridiculed by the world and later generations.[87] You consider this [details, such as varieties of ceremonies and music] something a Confucian scholar should study, perhaps due to the fact that you have not seriously thought about it.

A sage is a sage because he is born with knowledge. But a commentator on the *Analects* said, "What is known at birth is moral principle only. As to the changing events of past and present and the names and varieties of ceremonies and music, they surely require

---

[83] *Book of History*, "Canon of Yao." Cf. trans. by Legge, *Shoo King*, p. 18.

[84] *Ibid.*, "Canon of Shun." Cf. trans. by Legge, *Shoo King*, p. 33.

[85] Kao, Hsieh, Yü, and Chi were, respectively, Shun's ministers of justice, education, public works, and agriculture.

[86] So said Mencius, *Book of Mencius*, 7A:46.

[87] *T'ung-chien kang-mu*, 4:173b.

study before their validity can be verified in practice." If the names and varieties of ceremonies and music and the changing events of past and present really had anything to do with the effort to become a sage, and a sage had to depend on study to obtain knowledge, then a sage cannot be said to have been born with knowledge. When a sage is said to be born with knowledge, it means moral principles only and not such things as the names and varieties of ceremonies and music. It is clear that such things as the names and varieties of ceremonies and music have nothing to do with the effort to become a sage. Since by a sage's being born with knowledge is meant his possession of moral principles only and not such things as the names and varieties of ceremonies and music, then to know through study means to study and know these moral principles only, and learning through hard work also means learning through hard work these moral principles only. Nowadays students who study to become sages are not able to study and know what the sage is able to know, but unceasingly seek to know what the sage cannot know, as though it were learning. Don't they thereby lose the means by which they hope to become sages? In what I have said above, I have taken the things you have in doubt and explained them to some extent, but have not touched upon the doctrine of "pulling up the root and stopping up the source."

PULLING UP THE ROOT AND STOPPING UP THE SOURCE (Sections 142-143)

These sections are so important and so outstanding that they have often been singled out as a separate essay. Just as the *Inquiry on the "Great Learning"*[88] represents the essence of Wang's philosophy, so this essay represents the height of his ethics. It centers on his two basic doctrines of the extension of innate knowledge which is "common to the original minds of all men" and of "forming one body with Heaven and Earth and all things." In this latter doctrine, it ranks with China's most celebrated essays on the theme, notably the "Evolution of Rites," which envisages a "great unity" or universal state in which all distinctions disappear,[89] and Chang Tsai's *Western Inscription* in which Heaven and Earth are conceived of as one's parents and all men as brothers.[90]

[88] See below, "Inquiry on the *Great Learning*," pp. 271-80.
[89] *Book of Rites*, "The Evolution of Rites." Cf. trans. by Legge, *Li Ki*, ch. 7.
[90] "Hsi-ming," in the *Chang Heng-ch'ü chi*, ch. 1.

The special importance of the essay lies not only in these teachings themselves but also in their application to society and history. Elsewhere discussions on innate knowledge are by and large inclined to the individual, to the human mind, to what is common to all men, and to ethical problems. Here, however, the emphasis is on its relation to society, to one's talents and ability, to individual differences, and to social and political problems. With innate knowledge as the central theme, Wang vigorously attacks the four tendencies that had dominated the social and political scene for many years, namely, the stress on "hearing and seeing," the habit of "memorization and recitation," "the indulgence in flowery compositions," and the philosophy of "success and profit." He condemns especially the last, for he considers utilitarianism the wicked way of despots, and responsible for China's decline. His analysis of history is of course quite subjective, but there can be no mistake as to where his attention is directed. Wang still looks upon the past as the golden age and is confined to traditional Confucian concepts of value. But his spirit of challenge and his sense of responsibility, together with his powerful, direct, and sincere manner of expression, make the essay an inspiration.

142.   If the doctrine of pulling up the root and stopping up the source does not clearly prevail in the world, people who study to become sages will be increasingly numerous and their task increasingly difficult. They will then degenerate into animals and barbarians and still think this degeneration is the way to study to become a sage. Though my doctrine may perhaps temporarily be made clear and prevail, the situation will ultimately be like that in which the cold abates in the west while the ice freezes in the east, and the fog dissipates in front while clouds rise in the rear. Though I keep on talking until I die in distress, I shall at the end not be the least help to the world.

The mind of a sage regards Heaven, Earth, and all things as one body. He looks upon all people of the world, whether inside or outside his family, or whether far or near, but all with blood and breath, as his brothers and children. He wants to secure, preserve, educate, and nourish all of them, so as to fulfill his desire of forming one body with all things. Now the mind of everybody is at first not different from that of the sage. Only because it is obstructed by selfishness and blocked by material desires, what was originally great becomes small and what was originally penetrating becomes obstructed. Everyone has his own selfish view, to the point where some regard their fathers, sons, and brothers as enemies. The Sage worried over this. He therefore extended his humanity which makes him form one body with Heaven, Earth, and all things, to teach the world, so as to enable the people to overcome their selfishness, remove their obstructions, and recover that which is common to the substance of the minds of all men.

The essentials of this teaching are what was successively transmitted by Yao, Shun, and Yü, and what is summed up in the saying, "The human mind is precarious [liable to make mistakes], the moral mind is subtle [follows the moral law]. Have absolute refinement and single-mindedness and hold fast the mean."[91] Its details were given by Emperor Shun to Hsieh, namely, "between father and son there should be affection, between ruler and minister there should be righteousness, between husband and wife there should be attention to their separate functions, between old and young there should be a proper order, and between friends there should be faithfulness, that is all."[92] At the time of Yao, Shun, and the Three Dynasties, teachers taught and students studied only this. At that time people did not have different opinions, nor did families have different practices. Those who practiced the teaching naturally and easily were called sages, and those who practiced it with effort and difficulty were called worthies, but those who violated it were considered degenerate even though they were as intelligent as Tan-chu.[93] People of low station—those in villages and rural districts, farmers, artisans, and merchants—all received this teaching, which was devoted only to the perfection of virtue and conduct. How could this have been the case? Because there was no pursuit after the knowledge of seeing and hearing to confuse them, no memorization and recitation to hinder them, no writing of flowery compositions to indulge in, and no chasing after success and profit. They were taught only to be filially pious to their parents, brotherly to their elders, and faithful to their friends, so as to recover that which is common to the substance of the minds of all men. All this is inherent in our nature and does not depend on the outside. This being the case, who cannot do it?

The task of the school was solely to perfect virtue. However, people differed in capacity. Some excelled in ceremonies and music; others in government and education; and still others in public works

[91] *Book of History,* "Counsels of the Great Yü." Cf. trans. by Legge, *Shoo King,* p. 61.
[92] *Book of Mencius,* 3A:4.
[93] The son of Yao. See *ibid.,* 5A:6.

and agriculture. Therefore, in accordance with their moral achievement, they were sent to school further to refine their abilities.
When their virtue recommended them to government positions,
they were enabled to serve in their positions throughout life without
change. Those who employed them desired only to be united with
them in one mind and one character to bring peace to the people.
They considered whether the individual's ability was suitable, and
did not regard a high or low position as important or unimportant,
or a busy or leisurely job as good or bad. Those who served also
desired only to be united with their superiors in one mind and one
character to bring peace to the people. If their ability matched their
positions, they served throughout life in busy and heavy work
without regarding it as toilsome, and felt at ease with lowly work
and odd jobs without regarding them as mean. At that time
people were harmonious and contented. They regarded one another
as belonging to one family. Those with inferior ability were contented with their positions as farmers, artisans, or merchants, all
diligent in their various occupations, so as mutually to sustain and
support the life of one another without any desire for exalted
position or strife for external things. Those with special ability like
Kao, K'uei,[94] Chi, and Hsieh, came forward and served with their ability, treating their work as their own family concern, some attending
to the provision of clothing and food, some arranging for mutual
help, and some providing utensils, planning and working together
in order to fulfill their desires of serving their parents above and
supporting their wives and children below. Their only concern was
that those responsible for certain work might not be diligent in it
and become a heavy burden to them. Therefore Chi worked hard in
agriculture and did not feel ashamed that he was not a teacher but
regarded Hsieh's expert teaching as his own. K'uei took charge
of music and was not ashamed that he was not brilliant in ceremonies
but regarded Po-i's understanding of ceremonies as his own.[95] For
the learning of their mind was pure and clear and had what was
requisite to preserve the humanity that makes them and all things
form one body. Consequently their spirit ran through and permeated

[94] *Book of History,* "Canon of Shun." Cf. trans. by Legge, *Shoo King,* pp. 47-48.
K'uei was Emperor Shun's minister in charge of music. For Kao, Hsieh, and Chi,
see above, n.85.
[95] *Book of History,* "Canon of Shun." Cf. Legge, p. 47. By order of Emperor
Shun, Po-i was in charge of ceremonies.

all and their will prevailed and reached everywhere. There was no distinction between the self and the other, or between the self and things. It is like the body of a person. The eyes see, the ears hear, the hands hold, and the feet walk, all fulfilling the function of the body. The eyes are not ashamed of their not being able to hear. When the ears hear something, the eyes will direct their attention to it. The feet are not ashamed that they are not able to grasp. When a hand feels for something, the feet will move forward. For the original material force feels and is present in the entire body, and the blood and veins function smoothly. Therefore in feeling itchy and in breathing, their influence and the speedy response to it possess a mystery that can be understood without words. This is why the doctrine of the Sage is the easiest, the simplest, easy to know and easy to follow. The reason why the learning can easily be achieved and the ability easily perfected is precisely because the fundamentals of the doctrine consist only in recovering that which is common to our original minds, and are not concerned with any specific knowledge or skill.

143. As the Three Dynasties declined, the kingly way was stopped and the techniques of the despot flourished. After the passing of Confucius and Mencius, the doctrine of the Sage became obscure and perverse doctrines ran wild. Teachers no longer taught the doctrine of the Sage and students no longer studied it. Followers of despots stole and appropriated what seemed to be the teaching of ancient kings, and outwardly made a pretense of following it in order inwardly to satisfy their selfish desires. The whole world followed them in fashion. As a result the Way of the Sage was obstructed as though stopped by weeds. People imitated one another and every day searched for theories to acquire national wealth and power, for schemes to destroy and deceive, for plans to attack and invade, and for all sorts of tricks to cheat Heaven and entrap people and to get temporary advantages in order to reap fame or profit. There were numerous such people, like Kuan Chung [d. 645 B.C.], Shang Yang [d. 338 B.C.], Su Ch'in [d. 317 B.C.], and Chang I [d. 309 B.C.].[96] After a long time, the calamity of war and plundering became infinite. Thus people degenerated to the status of animals and barbarians, and even despotism itself could no longer operate.

[96] Economist, legalist, and experts on diplomacy, respectively. All of them stressed success as the central goal and have been condemned by Confucians as immoral.

Confucian scholars of [Han] times were sad and distressed. They searched and collected the literature, documents, laws, and systems of ancient sage-kings and salvaged the remains left from the Burning of the Books[97] and mended them. Their purpose was to restore the way of the ancient kings.

Since Confucian doctrines were discarded and the tradition of the technique of despotism had become strongly entrenched, even the virtuous and wise could not help being influenced by it. The doctrines elucidated and embellished in order to make them clear to the people, make them prevail, and restore them to the world, merely served to fortify the strongholds of despots. As a result, the door of Confucianism was blocked, and it was no longer to be seen. Therefore the learning of textual criticism developed and those perpetuating it were regarded as famous. The practice of memorization and recitation developed and those advocating it were regarded as extensively learned. The writing of flowery compositions developed and those indulging in it were regarded as elegant. Thus with great confusion and tremendous noise they set themselves up and competed with one another, and no one knew how many schools there were. Among tens of thousands of paths and thousands of tracks, none knew which to follow. Students of the world found themselves in a theater where a hundred plays were being presented, as it were. Actors cheered, jeered, hopped, and skipped. They emulated one another in novelty and in ingenuity. They forced smiles to please the audience and competed in appearing beautiful. All this rivalry appeared on all sides. The audience looked to the left and to the right and could not cope with the situation. Their ears and eyes became obscured and dizzy and their spirit dazed and confused. They drifted day and night and remained for a long time in this atmosphere as if they were insane and had lost their minds, and none had the self-realization to return to his family heritage [Confucianism]. Rulers of the time were also fooled and confounded by those doctrines and devoted their whole lives to useless superficialities without knowing what they meant. Occasionally some rulers realized the emptiness, falsehood, fragmentariness, and unnaturalness of their ways, and heroically roused themselves to great effort, which they wished to demonstrate in concrete action. But the most they could do was no more than to achieve national

[97] By the Ch'in in 213 B.C.

wealth, power, success, and profit, such as those of the Five Despots.[98] Consequently the teachings of the Sage became more and more distant and obscured, while the current of success and profit ran deeper and deeper. Some students turned to Buddhism and Taoism and were deceived by them. But at bottom there was nothing in these systems that could overcome their desire for success and profit. Others sought to reconcile the conflicting doctrines within the Confucian school. But in the final analysis there was nothing in these doctrines that could destroy the view of success and profit. For up to the present time it has been several thousand years since the poison of the doctrine of success and profit has infected the innermost recesses of man's mind and has become his second nature. People have mutually boasted of their knowledge, crushed one another with power, rivaled each other for profit, mutually striven for superiority through skill, and attempted success through fame. When they came forward to serve in the government, those in charge of the treasury wanted also to control the departments of military affairs and justice. Those in charge of ceremonies and music wanted also to have one foot in the important office of civil appointments. Magistrates and prefects aspired to the high office of a regional governor. And censors looked forward to the key position of the prime minister. Of course one could not take a concurrent position unless he could do the work and one could not expect any praise unless theories were advanced to justify the practice. Extensive memorization and recitation merely served to increase their pride,[99] substantial and abundant knowledge merely served to help them do evil, enormous information merely served to help them indulge in argumentation, and wealth in flowery compositions merely served to cover up their artificiality. Thus that which Kao, K'uei, Chi, and Hsieh could not manage on the side young students of today want to justify in doctrine and to master in technique. Using slogans and borrowing labels, they say they want to work together with others to complete the work of the empire. In reality their purpose lies in their belief that unless they do so they cannot satisfy their selfishness and fulfill their desires.

Alas! on top of such affectation and such a motive, they preach

[98] See above, sec. 11, n. 46.
[99] Reading *chiao* [education] as *ao* [pride].

such a doctrine! No wonder that when they hear the teachings of our Sage they look upon them as useless and self-contradictory. It is inevitable that they consider innate knowledge as deficient and the doctrine of the Sage as useless. Alas! how can scholars living in this age still seek the doctrine of the Sage? How can they still discuss it? Is it not toilsome and difficult, is it not rugged and hazardous for scholars living in this age to devote themselves to study? Alas! how lamentable!

Fortunately, the Principle of Nature is inherent in the human mind and can never be destroyed and the intelligence of innate knowledge shines through eternity without variation. Therefore when they hear my doctrine of pulling up the root and stopping up the source, surely some will be pitifully distressed and compassionately pained, and will indignantly rise up, like a stream or a river which cannot be stopped, bursting its banks. To whom shall I look if not to heroic scholars who will rise up without further delay?

LETTER TO CHOU TAO-T'UNG[1]

144. The students Wu and Tseng[2] came and told me fully about your keen desire to cultivate the Way. It is most gratifying. A person like you, Tao-t'ung, may be said to be steadfast in belief and strong in the desire to learn. Being in the midst of mourning,[3] I did[4] not talk with them in detail. But they have determination and are willing to make effort. Each time I saw them it seemed they had made some progress. I humbly believe that I have not failed to fulfill the objectives of their long journey and, on their part, they also have not failed in their goal. Now that they are about to leave and have come to me with this folio and, expressing your wishes, have asked me to write a few words in it, I am too distressed and confused to say

---

[1] Chou Heng, literary name Ching-an. He was a disciple of Chan Jo-shui (see below, sec. 201) as well as of Wang. He obtained a "recommended person" degree in 1510, served in various minor official capacities, and died in his forty-seventh year. For an account of him, see *Ming-ju hsüeh-an*, 25:4b-5b. This letter was written from Chekiang in 1524 when Wang was fifty-three.

[2] Nothing is known of them.

[3] Wang's father had died in 1522, two years before this letter was written. The customary mourning period was three years.

[4] Reading *hui* [able] as *ts'eng* [has, did].

anything. In answer to their kind request I shall merely put down a few words in response to questions raised in your letter. Written hurriedly, my words will not be at all thorough. However, I am sure the two students can orally express all that I have in mind.

Your letter says, "The task of daily application consists entirely in making up the mind. Of late I have often realized your teachings through personal experience and have understood them better and better. However, I have not been able to be away from friends for a moment. Only when there are friends around to discuss things with does my mind become strong and broad and full of the spirit of life. If for three or five days there are no friends to discuss things with, it seems to become weak. When things happen it is troubled and it often may forget. On days when there are no friends to talk with, I just sit in meditation or read, or pleasantly walk back and forth in a certain place. I utilize whatever I see or do to nourish my mind, and feel to some extent peaceful and at home. Nevertheless it is not as good as to be together with friends and to talk with them; in which case, the mental energy is more active and the spirit of life greater. What can people living in isolation do to handle the situation?"

This paragraph testifies to your accomplishment in efforts of daily application. This is just about the way the effort should be applied. The main thing is to have no interruption. When the practice has become familiar and smooth one's feeling will be quite different. Generally speaking, the great basis in our task of learning consists only in making up the mind. What you say about its being troubled and forgetful is due purely to its lack of earnestness. People who love sex do not have trouble or forget, because their minds are earnest. One must be able to know his own itch, and to scratch it. One must weigh and consider for himself what the Buddhists call the convenient way. Other people can hardly help. And there is no other way.

145. Your letter says, "Shang-ts'ai [Hsieh Liang-tso, 1050-1103] once asked I-ch'uan [Ch'eng I], 'What is there in the world to think about or to deliberate about?'[5] Ch'eng I answered, "There is such a principle, but you have discovered it too early."[6] The task of a student consists of course in always doing something and

[5] *Book of Changes*, "Appended Remark," pt. 2, ch. 5. Cf. trans. by Legge, *Yi King*, p. 389.   [6] *Wai-shu*, 12:5b.

not forgetting his objectives.[7] Nevertheless he must also recognize and at the same time take into consideration the condition in which there is nothing to think about or to deliberate about. If he does not recognize this situation, he will have the defect of making an artificial effort to help things grow.[8] But if he realizes that there is nothing to think about or to deliberate about and forgets that one must always be doing something, he will be in danger of falling into nothingness. One must not be obstructed by what is and yet not fall into what is not. Is that correct or not?"

What you have said is not far from the truth, except that you have not completely understood the matter. Shang-ts'ai's question and I-ch'uan's answer represent their own opinions. The original purpose of Confucius' saying in the "Appended Remarks" of the *Book of Changes* is somewhat different. The saying in the "Appended Remarks," "What is there to think about or to deliberate about?" means that what is to be thought about or deliberated about is only the Principle of Nature and that outside of it there should be no other thought or deliberation. It does not mean having no thought or deliberation at all. Hence he continues to say, "In the world there are many different roads but the destination is the same. There are a hundred deliberations but the result is one. What is there in the world to think about or to deliberate about?" Since it says "many roads" and "a hundred deliberations," does that mean having no thought or deliberation at all?

The original substance of the mind is the Principle of Nature. The Principle of Nature is single and indivisible. How can it be brought about by thinking or deliberation? In its own nature, it is in the state of absolute quiet and inactivity, and when acted on it immediately penetrates all things.[9] Although in his task a student may engage in a thousand thoughts and ten thousand deliberations, they should be directed at nothing but restoring its original substance and function. This is not to be brought about by pondering or manipulation according to one's personal wishes. Therefore Ming-tao [Ch'eng Hao] said, "For the training of the superior man there is nothing better than to become broad and extremely impartial and to respond

---

[7] *Book of Mencius*, 2A:2.
[8] *Ibid.*
[9] *Book of Changes*, "Appended Remarke," pt. 1, ch. 10. Cf. trans. by Legge, *Yi King*, p. 370.

spontaneously to all things as they come."[10] If one ponders and manipulates according to his personal wishes, that is "the exercise of cunning and selfishness."[11] Having nothing to think about or to deliberate about is precisely the task. It is natural with a sage but requires an effort on the part of a student. However, I-ch'uan took it as an effect of the task and therefore said the discovery was too early. But the fact that he continued to say, "Better make an effort,"[12] shows that he realized what he had said was incomplete. This is also the meaning of Lien-hsi's [Chou Tun-i's] theory of regarding tranquillity as fundamental.[13] What you have just said is not without insight, but you are not entirely free from regarding [thinking about the Principle of Nature and thinking about things] as two different things.

146. Your letter says, "As soon as a student realizes that he should begin his task, he must recognize what the feelings and expressions of a sage are like.[14] For having recognized the feelings and dispositions of the sage and having taken them as his goal, he can proceed in a concrete way. Then he will not make any mistake and the work will be that of becoming a sage. Is this true?"

It has been said, "First of all recognize the feelings and disposition of the sage,"[15] it is true. But the idea misses the basis of the task. The feelings and dispositions of the sage are his own. How can one recognize them? If one does not personally realize truth through one's innate knowledge it would be like weighing things with an unmarked scale or looking at a face in a closed mirror. This is really what is called judging the mind of a superior man by that of an inferior man.[16] How can the feelings and dispositions of a sage be recognized? One's innate knowledge is originally the same as that of the sage. If I personally realize my own innate knowledge with clarity, it means that the feelings and dispositions of the sage are not with the sage but with me. Master Ch'eng I-ch'uan once said, "Merely peep at Emperor Yao and imitate his action! Without his

---

[10] Ch'eng Hao, *Wen-chi*, 3:1a.
[11] *Ibid.*
[12] This is actually a paraphrase.
[13] See his *T'ai-chi t'u-shuo*, in *Chou Lien-hsi chi*, 1:2a.
[14] Quoting the *I-shu*, 22A:5b.
[15] Paraphrasing the preceding quotation.
[16] Quoting the *Shih-shuo hsin-yü*, sec. 6.

quickness of apprehension, intelligence, insight, and wisdom, how can one always act and appear in the proper manner as he did?"[17] He also said, "Only when the mind completely understands the Way can it distinguish right and wrong."[18] Now, let me ask, "Wherein must we understand the Way? Where do quickness of apprehension, intelligence, insight, and wisdom come from?"

147. Your letter says, "[You taught us] to be trained and polished in the actual affairs of life. During the day, whether anything happens or not, one should concentrate on cultivating and nourishing his original mind. If things occur and influence him, or if he himself feels something, we cannot say that nothing happens, since the mind is already conscious of something. However, because the mind is concentrated when things are quiet, one can feel in a large measure that the principles of things are as they are and handle things as though nothing had happened, thus extending his mind to the utmost. But why is the handling sometimes good and sometimes bad? Furthermore, sometimes perhaps many things happen and have to be handled in a certain order. But because of one's deficiency in talent and ability one suddenly gets exhausted. In spite of the greatest effort to rise up to the occasion, the spirit has already seemed weak. In that case one cannot help but withdraw completely to reflect. One would rather leave the work undone but the mind must be cultivated and nourished. What do you think of this?"

For you the effort as described is necessary but it is not entirely correct. Throughout his life, a man's effort to learn aims only at this one thing. From youth to old age and from morning to evening, whether anything happens or not, he works only at this one thing. And that is: "Always be doing something."[19] To say that one would rather leave the work undone but the mind must be cultivated and nourished is to regard [things and the mind] as two different things. Always be doing something. Let the mind not forget its objective but let there be no artificial effort to help it grow.[20] As things come, only extend the innate knowledge of one's mind to respond to them. Then one may be said to be practicing conscientiousness and altruism,

---

[17] *I-shu*, 18:5a. For the four qualities, see *Doctrine of the Mean,* ch. 31.
[18] *Wen-chi*, 5:7b.
[19] *Book of Mencius*, 2A:2.
[20] Quoting *ibid.*

and not far from the Way.[21] Whenever the handling of affairs is sometimes good and sometimes bad, and whenever one has the trouble of getting exhausted or handling things out of order, it is because one is driven by the considerations of praise and criticism or loss and gain and cannot really extend his innate knowledge. If one can really extend his innate knowledge, he will then see that what is ordinarily called good is not necessarily good and what is called bad is, I am afraid, precisely the fact that one is being driven by these considerations to destroy his own innate knowledge.

148. Your letter says, "Regarding the doctrine of the extension of knowledge, last spring I again received instructions from you. I have made further effort and feel that the task is simpler and easier than before. However, in my humble opinion, when we talk to a beginner, we should include the idea of the investigation of things so that he knows where to begin. At bottom the extension of knowledge and the investigation of things are to be done simultaneously. But as for the beginner, he does not know where to begin his effort, and it is necessary to mention the investigation of things so that he understands what the extension of knowledge is."

The investigation of things is the effort to extend knowledge. As one knows how to extend his knowledge, he also knows how to investigate things. If he does not know how to investigate things, it means he does not yet know how to extend his knowledge. Recently I wrote a letter to a friend[22] and discussed this fairly thoroughly. I am now sending you a copy. As you read it carefully, the matter should be self-evident.

149. Your letter says, "At present the debate between those supporting Chu Hsi and those supporting Lu Hsiang-shan has not stopped. I have often said to friends that now that the correct learning has been obscured for a long time, we must not waste our time and energy engaging in the controversy between Chu and Lu,[23] but only enlighten people on the basis of your teaching of making up the mind. If they really understand what this mind is and are

---

[21] A quotation from the *Doctrine of the Mean*, ch. 13.

[22] Probably "Letter in Reply to Ku Tung-ch'iao," above, especially sec. 134, or possibly "Letter in Reply to Lo Cheng-an," below, especially secs. 173-74.

[23] See above, Preface by Ch'ien to secs. 130-43, n. 7.

determined to learn the correct doctrine, then by and large they have already understood the doctrine. Even though the opposite doctrines of Chu and Lu are not debated and made clear, they can find out the truth for themselves. I have noticed that among my friends some are quick to be perturbed when they hear people criticize your theories. The reason why Master Chu and Master Lu aroused criticism in later generations is, I believe, that their own efforts were not entirely thorough and were clearly not free from being perturbed. Ming-tao [Ch'eng Hao], however, was free from such defects. From his discussion with Wu She-li[24] on the doctrine of Wang Chieh-fu [Wang An-shih, 1021-86], saying, 'Tell Chieh-fu all that I said about him. If it does him no good, it will do me good,'[25] we know how much at ease his feelings and dispositions were. I have noticed that you quoted these works in a letter to someone.[26] I hope all my friends are as much at ease as this. What do you think?"

The ideas expressed in this paragraph are very, very sound. I hope you, Tao-t'ung, will tell all our friends to discuss wherein they themselves are right or wrong but not wherein Chu Hsi or Lu Hsiang-shan was right or wrong. To slander people with words is to slander lightly. But if one cannot personnally and sincerely practice their teachings and merely listens to them and talks about them all day without stop, that is to slander them with one's own person and to slander heavily. If I can learn from all those in the world who criticize me and thereby improve myself, they will all be polishing and correcting me. In that case, everywhere is the opportunity for me to be alert, to cultivate and examine myself, and to advance in virtue. An ancient philosopher said, "Those who attack my shortcomings are my teachers."[27] Should we dislike teachers?

150. Your letter says, "Someone quoted Master Ch'eng Hao's saying, 'By nature man is tranquil at birth.[28] The state preceding this cannot be discussed. As soon as we talk about human nature, we already go beyond it.'[29] Asked why it cannot be discussed and

[24] *I-shu*, 1:6a. *Shih* is here mistakenly written in the cursive as *she*.
[25] *Ibid.*
[26] *Wang Wen-ch'eng Kung ch'üan-shu*, 4:6a.
[27] Paraphrasing *Hsün Tzu*, ch. 2, SPTK ed., 1:16a-b. Cf. trans. by Homer H. Dubs, *The Works of Hsüntze* (London, Probsthain, 1928), p. 43.
[28] This first sentence is a quotation from the *Book of Rites*, "Record of Music." Cf. trans. by Legge, *Li Ki*, ch. 17, p. 96.
[29] *I-shu*, 1:7b.

why it is already no longer human nature, Hui-an [Chu Hsi] replied that it cannot be discussed because in the state preceding birth there is no nature to speak of and it is no longer human nature because it is already mixed with physical nature.[30] I do not understand the words of either of them. Whenever I come to this spot in my reading, I have doubts. Please explain."

What is inborn is called the nature.[31] The word "inborn" means physical nature. That is to say, physical nature is the same as the nature. As physical nature is the same as the nature, and since by nature man is tranquil at birth and the state preceding this cannot be discussed, as soon as we say that physical nature is the same as the nature, we fall on one side, and the nature will then cease to be the original nature. When Mencius talked about a man's nature being good, he spoke from the point of view of the original nature. However, the beginnings of goodness of human nature can be seen only in physical nature. Without physical nature the goodness of human nature cannot be revealed. The feelings of commiseration, of shame and dislike, of deference and compliance, and of right and wrong are all physical nature. Master Ch'eng I said, "It would be incomplete to talk about the nature of man and things without including material force, and unintelligible to talk about material force without including the nature."[32] It was because students recognize only one side that he had to say this. If we clearly understand our nature, then we realize that physical nature is the same as the nature and the nature is the same as physical nature, and that at bottom they cannot be separated.

LETTER IN REPLY TO LU YÜAN-CHING[1]

151. Your letter says, "As I engage in the task, I feel that my mind is not at any time peacefully tranquil. An erroneous mind is of course active. But the shining mind is also active. Since the mind is always active, it has not a moment of rest."

[30] Paraphrasing *Chu Tzu wen-chi*, 61:22b.
[31] Quoting the *Book of Mencius*, 6A:3.
[32] *I-shu*, 6:2a. Material force is the element in the nature that makes it physical nature. Both material force and physical nature are *ch'i* in Chinese.

[1] For Lu Yüan-ching, see above, sec. 15, n. 1. This letter was written from Chekiang in 1524 when Wang was fifty-three.

It is because you consciously seek peaceful tranquillity that there is less and less of it. Now an erroneous mind is of course active, but a shining mind is not. If it is always shining, it will always be both active and tranquil. This is the way in which heaven and earth operate forever without cease. The shining mind will of course shine, but the erroneous mind will also shine. "Heaven and earth are without any doubleness [absolutely sincere], and so they produce things without cease."[2] To have a moment of rest would mean to cease. That would not be the learning to achieve the state of absolute sincerity without cease.

152. Your letter says, "Innate knowledge also arises from somewhere...."

Perhaps you did not get exactly what I said. Innate knowledge is the original substance of the mind. It is what I have just referred to as that which is always shining. The original substance of the mind neither rises nor does not rise. Even when erroneous thoughts arise, innate knowledge is present. Only because man does not know how to preserve it is the mind sometimes lost. Even when the mind is most darkened and obstructed, innate knowledge is clear. Only because man does not know how to examine it is the mind sometimes obscured. Although it is perhaps sometimes lost, its substance is always present. The thing to do is to preserve it. And although it is perhaps sometimes obscured, its substance is always clear. The thing to do is to examine it. To say that innate knowledge arises from somewhere is to say that sometimes it is not present. That would not be the original substance of the mind.

153. Your letter says, "Are refinement and singleness which you talked about the other day the task of becoming a sage?"[3]

The word *ching* (refinement) in the phrase "refinement and singleness" refers to the principle of man and things, while the word *ching* in the phrase *ching-shen* (mental energy) refers to material force. Principle is the order according to which material force operates, whereas material force is the functioning of principle. Without order it cannot function, and without functioning there will be nothing to reveal what is called order. Refinement is refinement. If

---

[2] *Doctrine of the Mean*, ch. 26.
[3] This sentence is not found in most editions.

one is refined, he will be intelligent, single-minded, spiritual, and sincere, and if he is single-minded, he will be refined, intelligent, spiritual, and sincere. They are not two different things. However, the doctrine as interpreted by the Confucians of later generations and by [Taoists who advocate] nourishing life has remained one-sided and consequently [refinement as emphasized by the Confucians and singleness as emphasized by the Taoists] do not reinforce each other. Although my discussion of refinement and singleness the other day was in response to your desire to nourish the spirit, nevertheless the task of becoming a sage is none other than this.

154. Your letter says, "The prime spirit, prime force, and prime essence must each have its place of preservation and origination. There are also the essence of the true passive element yin and the force of the true active element yang...."

Now, innate knowledge is one. In terms of its wonderful functioning, it is spirit; in terms of its universal operation, it is force; and in terms of its condensation and concentration, it is essence. How can it be understood in terms of shapes and locations? The essence of true yin is the mother of the force of true yang, and the force of true yang is the father of the essence of true yin. Yin is the root of yang and yang is the root of yin.[4] They are not two different things. If my theory of innate knowledge is clearly understood, then all such matters can be understood without any explanation. Otherwise there will be an infinite number of things in doubt, such as [the Taoist formulas to prolong life] called the "three gates," the "seven returns," and the "nine returns,"[5] mentioned in your letter.

---

[4] According to Chou Tun-i's *T'ai-chi t'u-shuo*, in *Chou Lien-hsi-chi*, 1:2a. His theory is that when the activity of yang reaches its limit, it becomes tranquil. Through tranquillity, yin is generated. When tranquillity reaches its limit, yang begins again. Thus movement and tranquillity alternate and become the root of each other.

[5] The "three gates" were the mouth, hands, and feet, considered as the gates of heaven, man, and earth, respectively; the "seven returns" were the return of the soul after seven periods, and the "nine returns," the return of the soul after a complete cycle.

AGAIN[6]

155. Your letter says, "Innate knowledge is the original substance of the mind. It is what is called the goodness of human nature, the equilibrium before the feelings are aroused, the substance that is absolutely quiet and inactive, and the state of being broad and extremely impartial. When were ordinary people incapable of it, so that they had to learn it? Since equilibrium, absolute quiet, and impartiality are characteristics of the substance of the mind, then it must be innate knowledge. But as I examine the mind, I find that while knowledge is innate and good, it does not really have the characteristics of equilibrium, quiet, and impartiality. Can innate knowledge transcend substance and function?"

There is no human nature that is not good. Therefore there is no innate knowledge that is not good. Innate knowledge is the equilibrium before the feelings are aroused. It is the state of broadness and extreme impartiality. It is the original substance that is absolutely quiet and inactive. And it is possessed by all men. However, people cannot help being darkened and obscured by material desires. Hence they must study in order to get rid of the darkness and obscuration. But to or from the original substance of innate knowledge they cannot add or subtract even an iota. Innate knowledge is good. The reason why equilibrium, absolute quiet, broadness, and impartiality are not complete in it is that darkness and obscuration have not been entirely eliminated and its state of preservation is not yet complete. The substance and function [you refer to] are the substance and function of innate knowledge. How can it transcend them?

156. Your letter says, "Master Chou Tun-i said, 'Regard tranquillity as fundamental.'[7] Master Ch'eng Hao said, 'The nature is calm whether it is in a state of activity or in a state of tranquillity.'[8] And

---

[6] Ordinarily this word means that what follows is a separate letter, but in Ch'ien Te-hung's preface preceding sec. 130 he definitely indicated that there was only one letter to Lu Yüan-ching. Quite correctly in the *Wang Yang-ming chi*, compiled by Wang's descendant Wang I-lo (*fl.* 1680), secs. 151-67 are combined as one letter. Azuma Keiji, in his *Denshō roku kōgi*, argues that secs. 155-67 form a separate letter because in sec. 160 Ku quoted Wang's words, "A shining mind is not active," which appear in sec. 151. However, Ku was probably not quoting any particular letter.

[7] Chou Tun-i, *T'ai-chi t'u-shuo*, in *Chou Lien-hsi chi*, 1:2a.

[8] *Wen-chi*, 3:1a.

you said, 'Calmness is the original substance of the mind.'[9] If so, it is calmness [when the mind is in a state of] tranquillity and is certainly not the state devoid of seeing, hearing, thoughts, and activity. It must mean always to know, always to preserve, and always to regard principle as fundamental. Now, always to know, always to preserve, and always to regard principle as fundamental are clearly activities and the state after the feelings are aroused. Why is it called tranquillity? Why is it called original substance? Can it be that in calmness [when the mind is in the state of] tranquillity there is something that pervades through the activity and tranquillity of the mind?"

Principle involves no activity. Always to know, to preserve, and to regard principle as fundamental means not [deliberately] to see, hear, think, or act. Not to do these things does not mean to be like dry wood or dead ashes. When one sees, hears, thinks, and acts in complete accord with principle and makes no deliberate effort to do so, it means activity and at the same time no activity. This is what is meant by the saying, "The nature is calm whether it is in a state of activity or in a state of tranquillity,"[10] and by the saying, "Substance and function come from the same source."[11]

157. Your letter says, "Does the substance of the mind before the feelings are aroused exist before the state in which feelings are aroused? Or does it exist in the state while the feelings are being aroused and act as its master? Or is it neither before nor after any state and neither internal nor external but one substance without differentiation? When we talk about the activity and tranquillity

[9] See above, sec. 41.
[10] See above, n. 8.
[11] Ch'eng I, in his preface to the *I chuan,* says, "Substance and function come from the same source and there is no gap between the manifest and the hidden." Japanese sources (e.g., *Daikanwa jiten*) maintain that the first half of the saying originated with Ch'eng-kuan in his commentary on *Hua-yen ching* (*Avataṃsaka sūtra*), but as Ōta Kinjō has pointed out (*Gimon roku,* pt. 1, p. 6b), it does not appear there or in any of Ch'eng-kuan's works. It is possible that it was in the portion of his commentary which is now lost, but if so, no one has given any specific source. However, Ch'eng-kuan said virtually the same thing rather extensively, though in slightly different words, in his commentary (*Zokuzōkyō,* 1st. collection, case 88, 3:35a-b). By the eleventh century the saying was common among both Buddhists and Neo-Confucians. As T'ang Shun-chih (1507-60) said, "Both Buddhists and Confucians said the same thing and none could tell whose words they were" (*T'ang Ching-ch'uan chi,* 6:2b). Ōta said that the second half of the saying is Fa-tsang's (643-712) dictum, but he gave no specific reference.

of the mind, are we talking about the former's doing something and the latter's doing nothing, or the former's state of absolute quietness and the latter's being acted upon and penetrating all things, or the former's following principle and the latter's obeying selfish desires? If we regard following principle as tranquillity and obeying desires as activity, then it is absurd to say that 'there is activity in tranquillity and tranquillity in activity,'[12] and to say, 'When activity reaches its limit, it becomes tranquillity, and when tranquillity reaches its limit, it becomes activity.'[13] If we regard the mind's doing something and being acted upon and penetrating things as activity, and its doing nothing but remaining in the state of absolute quietness as tranquillity, then it is absurd to say, 'It is active without activity and tranquil without tranquillity.'[14] If it is said that the state before the feelings are aroused exists before the state in which the feelings are aroused, and that activity is engendered from tranquillity, then absolute sincerity must have moments of rest and the sage [must be one who is not at home with his nature] but has to recover [his lost nature].[15] This, likewise, will not do. If it is said that the state before the feelings are aroused exists in the state in which the feelings have been aroused, then should tranquillity be regarded as fundamental in both states, or should the former state be considered as that of tranquillity and the latter as that of activity, or should both states be regarded as having neither activity nor tranquillity, or having both activity and tranquillity? Please enlighten me on these points."

The equilibrium before the feelings are aroused is innate knowledge. It is neither before nor after any state and is neither internal nor external but is one substance without differentiation. Activity and tranquillity may refer to the mind's engaging in something or nothing, but innate knowledge makes no distinction between doing something and doing nothing. Activity or tranquillity may also refer to the state of being absolutely quiet and that of being acted upon and penetrating things, but innate knowledge does not make any distinction between such states. Activity and tranquillity appertain to the time when the mind comes into contact with things, whereas in the original substance of the mind there is no distinction between activity and tranquillity. Principle involves no activity. When the

[12] Ch'eng I, *I-shu*, 7:2b.
[13] Chou Tun-i, *T'ai-chi t'u-shuo*.
[14] Chou Tun-i, *T'ung-shu*, ch. 16.
[15] *Ibid.*, ch. 3.

mind is active [stirred, perturbed], this means that it has selfish desires. If it follows principle, it is not active [stirred] in spite of countless changes in its dealing with things. On the other hand, if it obeys selfish desires, then even if it is like dry wood and reduced to one single thought, it is not tranquil. Is there any doubt that there is activity in tranquillity and tranquillity in activity?

When the mind engages in something and is thereby acted upon and penetrates things, it can of course be said to be active. But nothing has been added to the state of absolute quietness. When the mind engages in nothing and remains quiet, it can of course be said to be tranquil, but nothing has been subtracted from the state of being acted upon and penetrating. Is there any doubt that the mind is active without activity and tranquil without tranquillity? As the mind is neither before nor after any state, is neither internal nor external, but is one substance without differentiation, the question of absolute sincerity's having any moment of rest requires no answer. The state before the feelings are aroused exists in the state in which feelings have been aroused. But in this state there is not a separate state which is before the feelings are aroused. The state after the feelings are aroused exists in the state before the feelings are aroused. But in this state there is not a separate state in which the feelings have been aroused. Both are not without activity or tranquillity and cannot be separately characterized as active or tranquil.

Whenever we read words of the past, we must try with our thoughts to meet what the writers had in mind and get their main idea. If we are bound by literal meanings, then when the *Book of Odes* says, "[Of the black-haired people of the remnant of the Chou], there is not half a one left,"[16] it would really mean that not any individual of the people of Chou was left![17] Master Chou's theory that when tranquillity reaches its limit activity begins is not free from defects if one does not view it in the right way. His idea is derived from the theory that the Great Ultimate through activity generates the active element yang and through tranquillity generates the passive element yin. The principle of production and reproduction of the Great Ultimate is ceaseless in its wonderful functioning, but its eternal substance does not change. The production and reproduction of the Great Ultimate are the same as those of yin and yang.

---

[16] Ode no. 258.
[17] A comment by Mencius, *Book of Mencius*, 5A:4.

Referring to its processes of production and reproduction and pointing to the ceaselessness of their wonderful functioning, we say that there is activity and that yang is engendered, but do not say that there is first activity and then yang is engendered. Referring to its processes of production and reproduction and pointing to the unchanging aspect of their eternal substance, we say that there is tranquillity and that yin is engendered, but do not say that there is first tranquillity and then yin is engendered. If it is really true that yin is engendered after there is tranquillity and yang is engendered after there is activity, then yin and yang and activity and tranquillity are each a separate and distinct thing. Yin and yang are both the same material force. It becomes yin or yang as it contracts or expands. Activity or tranquillity are the same principle. It becomes activity or tranquillity as it is manifested or remains hidden. Spring and summer can be regarded as cases of yang and activity, but they are not without yin or tranquillity. Autumn and winter may be regarded as cases of yin and tranquillity, but they are not without yang or activity. Spring and summer are ceaseless in their course. So are autumn and winter. In this respect they may both be regarded as cases of yang and activity. The substance of spring and summer is eternal. So is that of autumn and winter. In this respect they may both be regarded as cases of yin and tranquillity. The same may be said of a cycle, an epoch, a revolution, a generation,[18] a year, a month, a day, or a period down to a minute, a second, or an infinitesimal duration. "Activity and tranquillity have no beginning, and yin and yang have no starting point."[19] Those who know the Way will understand this in silence. This idea cannot be completely expressed in words. If one follows words and phrases rigidly, takes them literally, and imitates and copies, then it will be what is called the "mind being turned around by the *Lotus Scripture* and not turning the *Lotus Scripture* around."[20]

158. Your letter says "I have tested my own mind and found that as pleasure, anger, worry, and fear are felt and aroused, although I am much perturbed, nevertheless as soon as the innate knowledge of

---

[18] According to Shao Yung, *Huang-chi ching-shih shu*, ch. 1, pt. 2, 70b, a generation is a period of thirty years, a revolution is a period of twelve generations, an epoch is a period of thirty revolutions, and a cycle is a period of thirty epochs.

[19] Ch'eng I, *Ching-shuo*, 1:2a.

[20] *Liu-tsu t'an-ching*, sec. 7, in *Taishō daizōkyō*, 48:355.

my mind realizes it, then without any resolution on my part the feelings disappear or are stopped. They may be checked at the beginning, or controlled while they are in progress, or changed at the end. It seems that innate knowledge of the good always exists in the condition of leisure and having no activity, serves as the master of the mind, and seems as though not involved in those feelings. Why?"

Since you know this, you know that the equilibrium before the feelings are aroused involves the harmony after the feelings are aroused and each and all attain due measure and degree, and also that the substance that is quiet and inactive involves the wonder of being acted upon and penetrating things. But when you say that it seems that innate knowledge always exists in the condition of leisure and having no activity, your wording is still defective. For although innate knowledge is not impeded in pleasure, anger, worry, and fear, these feelings are after all not outside the realm of innate knowledge.

159. Your letter says, "Sir, lately you have considered innate knowledge as the shining mind. I dare say that innate knowledge is the original substance of the mind, whereas the shining mind is the task of the individual. It is the mind of caution and apprehension, comparable to thought. How is it that caution and apprehension are to be equated with innate knowledge?"

It is innate knowledge that can be cautious and apprehensive.

160. Your letter says, "Sir, you also said, 'A shining mind is not active.'[21] Is it because it follows principle and therefore is considered tranquil? You also said, 'The erroneous mind also shines.' Is it because innate knowledge is always present in it and never ceases to shine in it and therefore all actions like seeing, hearing, speaking, and acting that do not exceed specific principles are all in accord with the Principle of Nature? Furthermore, since you said, 'The erroneous mind [also shines],' then it can be said to shine and the shining mind can also be said to be erroneous. What is the difference between the mind being erroneous and [absolute sincerity] ceasing to function? Now to suppose that the erroneous mind also shines in order to enable the unceasing progress of absolute sincerity to go on is something I do not understand. Kindly enlighten me again."

[21] See above, sec. 151.

The shining mind is not active because it arises from the natural state of the original substance's clear consciousness and there is no effort to be active [to stir it]. To stir it would make the mind erroneous. The erroneous mind also shines, because the natural state of the original substance's clear consciousness is always present in it, but it is in fact stirred. If not stirred, it will shine. To say that the mind is neither erroneous nor shining is not to say that the erroneous mind shines or that the shining mind is erroneous. To say that the shining mind shines [and does nothing else] and that the erroneous mind is erroneous [and is nothing else] is, after all, to separate the erroneous and shining mind. If they are so separated there will be doubleness. And if there is doubleness [absolute sincerity] will cease. If they are not separated as erroneous mind and shining mind, there will not be doubleness, and without doubleness [absolute sincerity] will not cease.

161. Your letter says, "To nourish life it is important to have a pure heart and few desires. In having a pure heart and few desires, the task of becoming a sage is complete. However, if desires are few, the heart is naturally pure. Having a pure mind does not mean to cast aside human affairs, living a secluded life and seeking tranquillity. Rather it means to enable the mind to be completely identified with the Principle of Nature and to be rid of every iota of selfish desire. If, in wanting to accomplish this task, one subdues selfish desires after they have arisen, then the root of the trouble will always be there, and it will be a case of destroying them in the east while they grow in the west. But if one wishes to cut out, pull off, wash out, and dissipate all desires before they have sprouted, there is no way to begin, and one merely causes his heart to be impure. Moreover, if before desires are sprouted one searches and pokes for them in order to get rid of them, it is like leading a dog into the hall and then chasing it away.[22] This is even more unfeasible."

The determination to have the mind completely identified with the Principle of Nature and devoid of even an iota of selfish desire is the task of becoming a sage. But this is not possible unless selfish desires are prevented from sprouting and are subdued at the time of sprouting. To do this is the task of being cautious and apprehensive as taught in the *Doctrine of the Mean*[23] and of the extension of knowl-

[22] *I-shu*, 2B:6b.
[23] *Doctrine of the Mean*, ch. 1.

edge and the investigation of things as taught in the *Great Learning*.[24] There is no other task outside of this.

What is said about desires being destroyed in the east while they grow in the west, or leading a dog into a hall and then chasing it away, is said because of the troubles of selfishness, leaning forward or backward to accommodate things, arbitrariness of opinion, and dogmatism, not because of the difficulty of subduing desires or washing them out and dissipating them. Now you may say that for nourishing life it is important to have a pure heart and few desires. The very idea of nourishing life[25] is the root of selfishness, leaning forward or backward to accommodate things, arbitrariness of opinion, dogmatism. With this root of trouble lying hidden in the mind, no wonder there is the trouble of destroying desires in the east while they grow in the west and of leading a dog into a hall and then chasing it away.

162. Your letter says, "The Buddhists advocate recognizing one's original state at the time when one thinks of neither good nor evil.[26] It is different from our Confucian way of investigating things as they come. If I exert effort to extend knowledge at the time of thinking of neither good nor evil, I would already be involved in thinking of good. The only time when one thinks of neither good nor evil and his mind of innate knowledge is clear, tranquil, and at ease, is the period of transition from sleep to waking. This is precisely Mencius' theory of the restorative power of the night.[27] But this condition does not last long. In an instant thought and deliberation have already arisen. I do not know whether he who has worked at the task for a long time can remain forever in the transition from sleep to waking when thought has not arisen. Now the more I seek peaceful tranquillity, the less I have it, and the more I want thoughts not to arise, the more they come. How can I easily wipe out earlier thoughts and prevent later ones from arising, and have the innate knowledge alone manifest so that I can roam the universe with the Creator?[28]

---

[24] The text of the *Great Learning*.
[25] Advocated by the Taoists.
[26] *Liu-tsu t'an-ching*, sec. 1, in *Taishō daizōkyō*, 48:349.
[27] *Book of Mencius*, 6A:8.
[28] *Chuang Tzu*, ch. 33, SPTK ed., 10:37b. Cf. trans. by Herbert A. Giles, *Chuang Tzu*, p. 321.

To recognize one's original state at the time of thinking of neither good nor evil is the Buddhist expedient or convenient way intended for those who do not yet recognize their original state. The original state is what our Confucian school calls innate knowledge. If we already understand clearly what innate knowledge is, there is no longer any need of recognizing one's original state as the Buddhists have advocated. To investigate things as things come is the task of the extension of knowledge. It is what the Buddhists called "Be always alert,"[29] that is, always preserve one's original state. In broad outline the two methods are about the same. However, the Buddhists are different from us because they have the mind that is motivated by selfishness. Now to wish to think of neither good nor evil and to want the mind of innate knowledge to be clear, tranquil, and at ease, means to have the mind of selfishness, leaning forward or backward, arbitrariness of opinion, and dogmatism. This is why if one exerts effort to extend knowledge at the time of thinking of neither good nor evil, one will have the trouble of already being involved in thinking of good. What Mencius said about the restorative power of the night was merely intended for those who have lost their originally good minds, pointing out where this good mind sprouts so that from here on it may be continually nourished and cultivated. Since you already know clearly what your faculty of innate knowledge is and always exert effort to extend it, there is no need of any restorative power. Otherwise, one is like the man who, having caught the hare [which runs into a tree trunk] and not kept it but instead continuously keeps vigil over the tree trunk [with the hope of another hare running into it],[30] will lose the hare. To seek peaceful tranquillity and to want thoughts not to arise are precisely the trouble of selfishness, leaning forward or backward, arbitrariness of opinion, and dogmatism. Consequently more and more thoughts will arise and there will be less and less peaceful tranquillity. There is but one innate knowledge which by its own nature discriminates between good and evil. What good and evil are there for the mind

---

[29] Derived from a saying of Zen Master Jui-yen (*c*.850-*c*.910). See *Wu-teng hui-yüan*, ch. 7, in *Zokuzōkyō*, 1st collection, pt. 2, B, case 11, p. 120b. The saying is quoted in *Ming-chiao Ch'an-shih yü-lu*, ch. 3, *Taishō daizōkyō*, 47:690. However, it is not found in the section on Jui-yen in *Ching-te ch'üan-teng lu*, 17:17b-18a.

[30] *Han Fei Tzu*, ch. 49, SPTK ed., 19:1a. Cf. trans. by W. K. Liao, *The Complete Works of Han Fei Tzu* (London, Probsthain, 1959), II, 276.

to think about? In its substance innate knowledge is in the state of peaceful tranquillity, and now you want to add the effort to seek peaceful tranquillity. Innate knowledge naturally brings forth thoughts, and now you want to add the wish that thoughts will not arise. Not only is the task of the extension of knowledge practiced in the Confucian school different from this. Even the learning of the Buddhists, I believe, does not go so far in leaning forward or backward, arbitrariness of opinion, and dogmatism. In the functioning of innate knowledge a single thought penetrates all. It has neither beginning nor end. This means that the earlier thoughts cannot be wiped out and later thoughts do not arise. Now to wish earlier thoughts to be easily wiped out and later thoughts not to arise amounts to what the Buddhists call "destroying the seed nature,"[31] and getting into the situation of what is called "dry wood and dead ashes."[32]

163. Your letter says, "The Buddhists also have the saying, 'Constantly bring your thoughts to the fore.'[33] Is this the same as Mencius' saying, 'Always be doing something'[34] and what you called the extension of the innate knowledge to the utmost? Is it the same as constantly being alert, constantly remembering, constantly being aware, and constantly preserving the original state of the mind? If one's thoughts are brought to the fore, when things occur, one can handle them in the proper way. What I am afraid is that more often than not one's thoughts are neglected rather than brought to the fore and one's task will be interrupted. Moreover, thoughts are neglected and lost chiefly because of selfish desires and the stirring of passions caused by external stimuli. As one is suddenly startled and awakened one then brings them to the fore. Between the time when thoughts are neglected and the time when they are brought to the fore, one's mind is confused and disorderly, in most cases without one's realizing it. Now I wish to be more and more refined and clear in thought, always to bring thoughts to the fore and not to neglect them. How can this be accomplished? Does the complete task consist only in thus always bringing them to the fore and not

---

[31] Hsüan-tsang (596-664), *Ch'eng wei-shih lun* (*Vijñatimātratāsiddhi*), ch. 5, in *Taishō daizōkyō*, 31:48.

[32] *Chuang Tzu*, ch. 2, SPTK ed., 1:18a. Cf. trans. by Giles, p. 34.

[33] A Zen saying the origin of which is not known.

[34] *Book of Mencius*, 2A:2.

neglecting them? Or in the midst of this shall I add the further effort of self-examination and self-mastery? Even though I constantly bring thoughts to the fore and do not neglect them, if I do not supplement this with the effort of caution, apprehension, and self-mastery, I am afraid selfish desires cannot be eliminated. But if I supplement it with such effort, then I will be engaging in thinking of good and still keep myself a slight distance from the original state of the mind. What is the way out?"

Caution, apprehension, and self-mastery are the task of constantly bringing thoughts to the fore and not neglecting them. They are the same as always to be doing something. Are they two different things? The first part of what you have asked in this question has already been clearly explained by yourself. In the latter part, however, you have deceived and confused yourself, you have gone into fragmentary and isolated details in your explanation, and you entertain worry about being distant from the original state. All this is because of the defects of selfishness, leaning forward or backward, arbitrariness of opinion, and dogmatism. Get rid of these defects and you will have no such doubts.

164.   Your letter says, " 'One whose physical nature is excellent will be perfectly intelligent, and the impure dregs in him will be completely transformed.'[35] What is meant by being perfectly intelligent? How can the dregs be completely transformed?"

Innate knowledge is by nature intelligent. Those whose physical nature is not excellent have many impure dregs and heavy obscuration and are not easily enlightened. Those whose physical nature is excellent have originally few dregs and not much obscuration. With a little effort at the extension of knowledge, their innate knowledge will of itself become clear and transparent. How can a little dreg, like melting snow in hot water, be an obscuration? This is really not very difficult to understand. You, Yüan-ching, entertain some doubts because, I believe, you do not understand what intelligence means and also because you desire to advance somewhat too rapidly. Previously I discussed with you face to face the meaning of understanding the good. With understanding or intelligence, there will be sincerity. It is not as superficial as what later scholars called the understanding of the good.

[35] Ch'eng Hao, *I-shu*, 11:11b.

165.   Your letter says, "Are quickness of apprehension, intelligence, insight, and wisdom[36] really physical nature;[37] humanity, righteousness, propriety, and wisdom really the nature; and pleasure, anger, sorrow, and joy really the feelings? Are selfish desires and passions caused by external stimuli the same or different? The shining virtue and accomplishments of talented people like Chang Tzu-fang [d. 189 B.C.],[38] Tung Chung-shu [c.179-c.104 B.C.],[39] Huang Shu-tu [fl. A.D. 120],[40] Chu-ko K'ung-ming [181-234],[41] Wen-chung Tzu,[42] Han Ch'i [fl. 1031],[43] and Fan Chung-yen [989-1052][44] all come from innate knowledge. And yet they cannot be characterized as having heard the Way. What is the reason? If it is said that their achievements are merely the results of their excellent physical nature, are not those who are born with knowledge and can practice it naturally and easily superior to those who learn through study and hard work and practice with effort and difficulty? In my humble opinion, it is all right to say that these grand gentlemen understand only part of the Way. But to say that they did not hear the Way at all is, I am afraid. a mistake, resulting from the emphasis of later scholars on recitation and textual criticism. Am I correct or not?"

There is one nature, that is all. Humanity, righteousness, propriety, and wisdom are its basic nature. Quickness of apprehension, intelligence, insight, and wisdom are its physical nature. Pleasure, anger, sorrow, and joy are its feelings, and selfish desires and passions caused by external stimuli are its obscuration. Physical nature may be clear or turbid and therefore feelings are sometimes excessive or insufficient, and the obscuration heavy or light. Selfish desires and passions caused by external stimuli are the same disease with two different kinds of pain, and are not two different things. The grand gentlemen Chang, Huang, Chu-ko, Han, and Fan were

[36] The four qualities of the perfect sage. See *Doctrine of the Mean*, ch. 31.
[37] Chu Hsi, *Chung-yung chang-chü*, ch. 31.
[38] He assisted the founder of Han to establish the empire.
[39] He was instrumental in establishing the supremacy of Confucianism.
[40] He was the son of a veterinarian, and, while neither successful nor known as a writer, was respected and honored by all the famous men throughout the empire.
[41] Chu-ko Liang, the celebrated prime minister who heroically attempted to continue the Han dynasty against great odds.
[42] See above, sec. 11.
[43] A high official who did much to bring about peace in the empire.
[44] Another official who did the same.

all excellent in their natural endowment and were in most cases unnoticeably in accord with the ultimate truth. Although they cannot be said to have completely understood the learning or to have heard the Way fully, nevertheless each had his own learning which did not depart very far from the Way. Had they fully heard the learning and understood the Way completely, they would have been equal to I-yin, Fu Yüeh,[45] Duke Chou, and Duke Chao.[46] As to Wen-chung Tzu, he cannot be said to be ignorant of the teachings of the Sage. Although his books are mostly the products of his pupils and there are many mistakes, their general outline can easily be seen. However, since we are far from his time and have no positive evidence, we cannot arbitrarily conclude from imagination just what he had attained.

Innate knowledge is identical with the Way. That it is present in the mind is true not only in the cases of the sages and worthies but even in that of the common man. When one is free from the driving force and obscurations of material desires, and just follows innate knowledge and leaves it to continue to function and operate, everything will be in accord with the Way. In the case of ordinary men, most of them are driven and obscured by material desires and cannot follow innate knowledge. Since the natural endowment of the several grand gentlemen was by nature pure and clear and they of course were only slightly driven and obscured by material desires, the function and operation of their innate knowledge was naturally abundant, and they naturally did not depart from the Way very far.

To learn simply means to learn to follow innate knowledge. When a person is said to understand the learning, it simply means that he knows how to devote his learning purely to following innate knowledge. Although the several grand gentlemen did not completely devote their effort to innate knowledge, but in some cases drifted into many wrong ways and were confused and deceived by the apparent and therefore sometimes departed from and sometimes were in accord with the Way, so that their minds did not become completely identified with the Principle of Nature, if they had known [how to devote their learning purely to following innate knowledge], they would have been sages. Later scholars have

---

[45] He assisted Kings T'ai-chia (r. 1738-1727 B.C.) and Wu-ting (r.1339-1281 B.C.) in great achievements.

[46] Duke Chao (d. 1056 B.C.) assisted his brother King Wu in his great accomplishments.

regarded them as having behaved on the basis of physical nature and therefore having acted without understanding and habitually without examination.[47] This is not putting it too strongly. However, what later scholars called understanding and examination are, after all, confined to narrow information and obscured by wrong habits of thought. They follow, grope after, and imitate what is apparent or illusory. What they mean by understanding and examination is not what is understood in the Confucian school. How can they expect others to be enlightened by their own darkness?[48]

The words "knowledge" and "practice" in the phrase "born with knowledge and practice it naturally and easily"[49] refer to one's effort. If the original substance of any knowledge and practice were innate knowledge and innate ability, then it would be possible to say that those who learn through hard work and practice their learning with effort and difficulty could practice it naturally and easily. The two words "knowledge" and "practice" should be understood more thoroughly.

166.   Your letter says, "Chou Mao-shu [Chou Tun-i] often asked Po-ch'un [Ch'eng Hao] to find out wherein Confucius and his pupil Yen Hui found their joy.[50] May I ask whether their joy is the same as the joy in the seven feelings.[51] If it is, when any desire of an ordinary man is satisfied, he, like anyone else, can be joyful. Why should it be limited to sages and worthies? If, aside from this, there is a true joy, then is it present when sages and worthies meet with great sorrow, great anger, great terror, and great fear? Furthermore, since the mind of the superior man is constantly occupied with caution and apprehension, he is in sorrow throughout life. How can he have joy? I am often depressed and have not yet experienced true joy. I am eager to find it."

Joy is characteristic of the original substance of the mind. Though it is not identical with the joy of the seven feelings, it is not outside of it. Sages and worthies have another true joy, it is true, but it is shared by ordinary people except that these people do not realize it though they have it. Instead they bring upon themselves a great

---

[47] A quotation from the *Book of Mencius*, 7A:5.
[48] *Ibid.*, 7B:20.
[49] *Doctrine of the Mean*, ch. 20.
[50] *I-shu*, 2A:2b.
[51] Pleasure, anger, sorrow, joy, love, hate, and desire.

deal of sorrow and grief and, in addition, confusion and self-abandonment. Even in the midst of all these, this joy is not absent. As soon as a single thought is enlightened, and one examines himself and becomes sincere, the joy is present right there. I have often discussed with you, Yüan-ching, this same idea and you still ask in what way it can be found. This is a case of obscuration like one's looking for a donkey while riding it.

167.   Your letter says, "According to the *Great Learning*, when the mind is affected by fondness, anger, worries, and fear, it will not be correct.[52] Master Ch'eng Hao also said, 'The feelings of the sage are in accord with all creation and yet he has no feeling of his own.'[53] The *Instructions for Practical Living* compares those who have [the love of sex, wealth, and fame] to people suffering from intermittent fever.[54] The analogy is excellent and exact. According to Master Ch'eng, the feelings of the sage do not originate from his mind but from things. What does this mean? Moreover, when things stimulate the mind and feelings respond, right and wrong can be corrected accordingly. Before things affect the mind, if we say that feelings are present, they are not yet formed, and if we say that they are not, the root of evil is already there. How can I extend my knowledge between their presence and their absence? If learning is to stress having no feelings, though the resulting trouble will be light, nevertheless it will cease to be Confucian and will become Buddhist. Is that all right?"

The sage's effort at extending knowledge is characterized by his absolute sincerity which never ceases. The substance of his innate knowledge is as clear as a bright mirror without any slight obscuration. Whether a beautiful or an ugly object appears, it reflects it as it comes, without anything being left behind on the bright mirror itself. This is what is meant by saying that the feelings of the sage are in accord with all things and yet of himself he has no feelings. The Buddhists have a saying, "One should have no attachment to anything and thus let the mind grow."[55] This is not incorrect. In the

[52] Ch. 7.

[53] *Wen-chi*, 3:1a.

[54] See above, sec. 76, At that time the *Intructions for Practical Living* consisted of only the present Part I.

[55] *The Diamond Scripture*, sec. 10. Cf. trans. by Shao Chang Lee, in *Popular Buddhism in China* (Shanghai, Commercial Press, 1939), p. 35, or by Edward Conze, in *Buddhist Wisdom Books* (London, Allen and Unwin, 1958), p. 47.

bright mirror's response to things, what is beautiful appears beautiful and what is ugly appears ugly. In the same reflection all things are reflected and are true. This is like the mind growing. What is beautiful appears beautiful and what is ugly appears ugly. The things pass along without remaining in the mirror. This is where the mirror has no attachment. Since you have appreciated the excellence and exactness of the analogy of intermittent fever, you should be clear about what you have asked in this section. In the case of people with intermittent fever, although the fever has not yet occurred, the root of the disease is present. Why should the patient neglect medical treatment simply because the fever has not yet occurred? If he insists on waiting for the fever to occur before taking medicine and receiving treatment, it will be too late. The task of the extension of knowledge should not be interrupted whether things happen or not. Has it anything to do with whether or not the disease has occurred? Generally speaking, though the thing about which you are in doubt in this case seems to be different from those earlier cases, they are all caused by the evil influence of selfishness, leaning forward or backward, arbitrariness of opinion, and dogmatism. As soon as this root is removed, all present and earlier doubts will of themselves disappear like ice melting and fog disappearing and there will be no need of asking about them or arguing them out.

Comments by Ch'ien Te-hung, compiler of INSTRUCTIONS FOR PRACTICAL LIVING

When this reply to Lu Yüan-ching was published, readers were all overjoyed at Yüan-ching's skillful questions and the Teacher's skillful answers, and all now have heard what they never heard before. The Teacher said, "Yüan-ching's questions all revolve around book learning and textual understanding. I cannot help answering and explaining to him section by section. If one has faith in innate knowledge and makes effort only along the line of innate knowledge, one will find that the thousands and thousands of classics and canons will all conform to it and all heretical doctrines and narrow learnings will be destroyed when tested against it. What is the need of explaining section by section like this? The Buddhists have the parable of a servant throwing a piece of food [at a dog and a lion. When the lion] sees the stuff but jumps at the man, it gets the man [who is its major objective]. [On the other hand, when the dog] sees the stuff [which does not amount to much], and chases after it, what does the dog really get?"[56] When friends present in the hall heard him they all enjoyed a pleasant awakening. In the task of this learning, the important thing is self-examination, not book learning or textual explanation.

LETTER IN REPLY TO OU-YANG CH'UNG-I[1]

168.   Your letter says, "You said, sir, 'The innate knowledge of our moral nature did not come from hearing and seeing. When Confucius said "Hear much and select what is good and follow it. See much and remember it,"[2] he referred to nothing but seeking solely after the secondary matters of seeing and hearing, thus already falling to the secondary level.'[3] In my humble opinion, although innate knowledge is not derived from hearing and seeing, the knowledge of the student is nevertheless developed from what he hears and sees. To be impeded by hearing and seeing is of course wrong. Yet they are that through which innate knowledge functions. Now you say that it has already fallen to the secondary level. I believe that is said for the benefit of those who regard learning as purely seeing and hearing. If one extends his innate knowledge and seeks knowledge from seeing and hearing, this too would be a united effort of knowledge and action. Is this correct?"

Innate knowledge does not come from hearing and seeing, and yet all seeing and hearing are functions of innate knowledge. Therefore innate knowledge is not impeded by seeing and hearing. Nor is it separated from seeing and hearing. Confucius said, "Have I knowledge? I have not."[4] So outside of innate knowledge there is no other knowledge. Therefore the extension of innate knowledge is the great basis of learning and the first principle of the teaching of the Sage. Now solely to seek in the subsidiary sources of seeing and hearing is to lose that basis, thus clearly falling to the secondary level. Of late, among like-minded friends there is none who does not

---

[56] A parable from the *Mahāprajñāpāramitā śāstra* quoted in the *Tsu-t'ing shih-yüan*, 8:116b.

[1] See above, sec. 104, n.23. According to the *Nien-p'u*, this letter was written from Chekiang in 1526 when Wang was fifty-five, but since it was included in the *Ch'uan-hsi lu* published by Nan Yüan-shan in 1524, the date must have been earlier.

[2] *Analects*, 7:27.

[3] See above, sec. 140.

[4] *Analects*, 9:7.

know the doctrine of the extension of innate knowledge. The reason why it is said that their effort is still very careless and desultory is just because they have neglected to ask the very question you have asked.

Generally speaking, in the task of learning the most important thing is to be sure that the basic idea is correct. If the basic idea is solely to engage in the extension of innate knowledge, then, however much one may hear or see, all belongs to the task of the extension of innate knowledge. For in one's daily life, although there is an infinite variety of experience and dealings with others, there is nothing which is not the functioning and operation of innate knowledge. Without experience and dealings with others, there will be no innate knowledge to be extended. Therefore the task is single. If one speaks of extending innate knowledge and seeking knowledge in seeing and hearing, in his way of putting it he somehow makes them two things. Although this is somewhat different from seeking knowledge solely from the subsidiary seeing and hearing, its lack of refinement and singleness is the same. "Hear much and select what is good and follow it. See much and remember it." Since he says select and remember, innate knowledge is already operating in the process. But the purpose in the saying is solely to select and remember from much hearing and much seeing, thus losing sight of the basis. I believe you, Ch'ung-i, have understood these points clearly. Your question today is precisely for the purpose of elucidating this learning and is extremely beneficial to fellow students. However, the ideas of your statement are not clear. As an infinitesimal mistake in the beginning may lead to an infinite error at the end, they should not be allowed to go without careful examination.

169. Your letter says, "Sir, you said, 'The saying in the "Appended Remarks" of the *Book of Changes*, "What is there to think about or to deliberate about?"[5] means that what is to be thought about or deliberated about is only the Principle of Nature and that outside of it there should be no other thought or deliberation. It does not mean having no thought or deliberation at all…. The original substance of the mind is the Principle of Nature…. How can it be

[5] *Book of Changes*, "Appended Remarks," pt. 2, ch. 5. Cf. trans. by Legge, *Yi King*, p. 389.

brought about by thinking or deliberation?... Although in his task a student may engage in a thousand thoughts and ten thousand deliberations, they should be directed at nothing but restoring its original substance [and function]. This is not to be brought about by pondering or manipulation according to one's personal wishes.... If one ponders and manipulates according to his personal wishes, that is "the exercise of cunning and selfishness." '6 Generally speaking, the trouble with students is either sinking into emptiness and maintaining silence or manipulating and pondering. In the *hsin* and *jen* years [1521-22] I was affected by the former trouble. Recently I have been affected by the latter. But pondering is also a function of innate knowledge. How can it be distinguished from manipulation according to one's personal wishes? I am afraid I am taking a thief to be a son[7] and am deluded without realizing it."

"The virtue of thinking is penetration and profundity.... Penetration and profundity lead to sageness."[8] "The function of the mind is to think. If we think, we will get it."[9] Can thinking be dispensed with? To sink into emptiness and maintain silence and to manipulate and ponder are precisely selfishness and the exercise of cunning. In their loss of innate knowledge, they are the same. Innate knowledge is where the Principle of Nature is clear and intelligent. Therefore innate knowledge is identical with the Principle of Nature. Thinking is the emanation and functioning of innate knowledge. If one's thinking is the emanation and functioning of innate knowledge, whatever he thinks about is the Principle of Nature. Thoughts resulting from the emanation and functioning of innate knowledge are naturally clear, simple, and easy. The faculty of innate knowledge knows them as such. But thoughts issuing from manipulation according to one's personal wishes are naturally troublesome and disturbing, and the innate faculty is naturally able to distinguish them. For whether thoughts are right or wrong, correct or perverse, the faculty of innate knowledge itself knows them all. People take a thief to be their son precisely because they do not understand the learning of the extension of knowledge and do not know how to realize it genuinely and earnestly by means of innate knowledge.

6 See above, sec. 145.
7 See above, sec. 122, n.78.
8 *Book of History*, "Great Norm." Cf. trans. by Legge, *Shoo King*, p. 327.
9 *Book of Mencius*, 6A:15.

170. Your letter also says, "Sir, you said, 'Throughout his life, a man's effort to learn aims only at this one thing…. Whether anything happens or not, he works only at this one thing…. To say that one would rather leave the work undone but the mind must be cultivated and nourished is to regard [things and the mind] as two different things.'10 In my humble opinion, when one's spirit and energy are weak and not sufficient to complete the work, that is a matter of innate knowledge itself. Rather, leaving the work undone but cultivating and nourishing the mind are matters of the extension of knowledge. How is it that [things and the mind] are regarded as two different things? When an unexpected event arises and by circumstance something has to be done but my spirit and energy are weak, if I rouse myself somewhat, I am able to hold on. In that case it is all right to 'hold the will firm and lead the vital force.'11 However, at the end I have no more energy to talk or move. When the work is done, I am completely exhausted. Is not this virtually 'doing violence to the vital force?'12 Innate knowledge surely can weigh a situation—to decide which element is more important and urgent. Nevertheless, one may be forced by circumstances so that he cannot worry about his spirit and energy or he may be exhausted in spirit and energy so that he cannot worry about the circumstances. What can be done?"

The idea that one should rather leave the work undone than neglect cultivating and nourishing the mind is not without merit when told to the beginner. But if [things and the mind] are regarded as two things, it is a defect. Mencius said, "Always be doing something."13 This means that throughout his life the learning of the superior man consists purely of accumulating righteousness.14 What is right means what is proper. When the mind attains what is proper, it is called righteousness. If innate knowledge can be extended, the mind will attain what is proper. Therefore accumulating righteousness is nothing other than the extension of innate knowledge. In the countless changes in his dealings with others, the superior man acts if it is proper to act, stops if it is proper to stop, lives if it is proper to live, and dies if it is proper to die. In all his considerations and

---

10 See above, sec. 147.
11 *Book of Mencius*, 2A:2.
12 *Ibid.*
13 *Ibid.*
14 *Ibid.*

adjustments he does nothing but extend his innate knowledge to the utmost so that he can satisfy himself. Therefore "The superior man does what is proper to his position,"[15] and "in his thought he does not go out of his place."[16] All those who "scheme to get what is beyond their strength and force their intellectual faculty to know what it is incapable of"[17] cannot be considered as extending their innate knowledge. On the other hand, "subjecting one's sinews and bones to hard work, exposing one's body to hunger, putting oneself in poverty, placing obstacles in the path of one's deeds, so as to stimulate one's mind, harden one's nature, and improve oneself wherever one is incompetent"[18] are all ways to extend innate knowledge. If one says that one should rather leave the work undone than neglect to cultivate and nourish the mind, it is first of all to have the idea of success and profit, to weigh matters in terms of success and failure, advantages and disadvantages, to decide to love or hate and to accept or reject. He therefore considers getting the work done as one thing and cultivating and nourishing the mind as quite another. This means he has the desire to consider what is within the mind to be right and what is outside to be wrong. This is selfishness and the exercise of cunning. This is regarding righteousness as external.[19] This is the trouble with "What is not attained in the mind is not to be sought in the vital force [thus separating the mind and the vital force]."[20] And this is not the effort to extend innate knowledge to satisfy yourself. You said that if you rouse yourself you can hold on but that when the work is done you are completely exhausted. You also mentioned being forced by circumstances and being exhausted in spirit and energy. This is the case because you proceed with the idea that [things and the mind] are two different things. In the task of learning, wherever there is singleness, sincerity will prevail, but whenever there is doubleness, there will be falsehood. All the above is due to the fact that in wanting to extend innate knowledge one lacks the true and earnest effort

---

[15] *Doctrine of the Mean*, ch. 14.

[16] *Analects*, 14:28.

[17] Paraphrasing the *Ch'iu-sheng fu* by Ou-yang Hsiu (1007-72), in *Ou-yang Wen-chung Kung wen-chi*, 15:4a.

[18] *Book of Mencius*, 6B:15.

[19] And, consequently, humanity as internal, as Kao Tzu did. See *Book of Mencius*, 6A:4.

[20] Kao Tzu. See *ibid.*, 2A:2.

toward sincerity and single-mindedness. Therefore the *Great Learning* says, "Making the will sincere [is allowing no self-deception] as when we hate a bad odor or love a beautiful color. This is called satisfying oneself."[21] Have you ever seen a person hating a bad odor or loving a beautiful color rouse himself in order to hold on, or getting completely exhausted when the work is done? Or forced by circumstances and exhausted in spirit and energy? From this you can know where the trouble comes from.

171.   Your letter also says, "In human affairs tricks and deceits manifest themselves in a hundred ways. If one handles them without suspicion, one often gets cheated, but if one knows [the intentions behind them] one puts himself in the position of anticipating deceit and predicting being distrusted. To anticipate deceit is itself deceit, and to predict being distrusted is itself distrust. At the same time to be cheated is not to know. Only with the crystal clarity of innate knowledge can one desist from anticipating deceit and predicting being distrusted but always know them readily.[22] However, one often deviates from the norm, in however small degree, betrays one's own knowledge, and falls into deceit."

Confucius told people not to anticipate deceit or to predict being distrusted, but to know readily, because the people of his time wholly devoted their minds to anticipating deceit and predicting being distrusted and thereby fell into the vices of deceit and distrust themselves. There were also others who did not anticipate or predict but, because they did not know the task of extending innate knowledge, were repeatedly cheated and deceived by others. He therefore uttered these words. He did not teach people to harbor these thoughts and to want to know readily other people's deceit and distrust. To harbor such thoughts is the behavior of people of later generations who are suspicious, envious, treacherous, and mean. With this idea of harboring such thoughts alone they will be unable to enter into the Way of the sages, Yao and Shun. He who does not anticipate deceit or predict being distrusted, but is deceived by others, still cannot be said to have failed in doing good, but this is not as worthy as his being able to extend his innate knowledge and naturally know readily. In saying that innate knowledge is

[21] Ch. 6.
[22] That is, to know ahead of others. *Analects,* 14:33.

crystal clear, you, Ch'ung-i, already understand the fundamental point. However, you have arrived at this point probably through your intelligence and [your understanding], I am afraid, is not yet concrete. For the fact that innate knowledge is inherent in the human mind is the same throughout all generations and the entire universe. It is "the knowledge possessed by men without deliberation"[23] which "always operates with ease and thus knows where danger is."[24] It is "the ability possessed by men without having been acquired by learning"[25] which "always operates with simplicity and thus knows what obstructions are."[26] "It may precede Heaven and Heaven does not act in opposition to it.... If even Heaven does not oppose it, how much less will man and how much less will spiritual beings?"[27]

Although what you say about betraying one's own knowledge and falling into deceit is not to anticipate deceit by others, it is, I believe, not free from self-deception. Although it is not to predict being distrusted by others, it is, I believe, not a firm trust in oneself. It is perhaps a case of always having the mind to seek to know readily but not always being able to know by oneself. He who always has the mind to seek to know readily has already drifted into anticipating and predicting sufficiently to obscure his innate knowledge. This is why betraying one's own knowledge and falling into deceit cannot be avoided.

A superior man studies for his own sake.[28] He does not worry about being deceived by others but will not deceive his own innate knowledge at any time. He does not worry about being distrusted by others but will trust in his own innate knowledge at all times. He does not seek to know readily people's deceit and distrust, but always makes an effort to realize himself his innate knowledge. Therefore, if one does not deceive himself, his innate knowledge will have no falsehood but will be sincere. Given sincerity, there will be enlightenment.[29] If one trusts himself, his innate knowledge will

---

[23] *Book of Mencius*, 7A:15.
[24] *Book of Changes*, "Appended Remarks," pt. 2, ch. 12. Cf. trans. by Legge, *Yi King*, p. 404.
[25] *Book of Mencius*, 7A:15.
[26] *Book of Changes*, "Appended Remarks," pt. 2, ch. 12. Cf. trans. by Legge, *Yi King*, p. 404.
[27] *Ibid.*, commentary on hexagram no. 1. Cf. trans. by Legge, *Yi King*, p. 417.
[28] *Analects*, 14:25.
[29] *Doctrine of the Mean*, ch. 21.

have no doubt and will be intelligent. Being intelligent, it will be sincere.[30] Thus intelligence and sincerity produce each other. Consequently, innate knowledge always knows and always shines. Always knowing and shining, it is like a suspended brilliant mirror. As things appear before it, none can conceal its beauty or ugliness. Why? Not deceiving but sincere, it leaves no room for any deception. If there is any deception, it is already known. Trusting itself and being intelligent, it leaves no room for any distrust. If there is any distrust, it is already known. This means that innate knowledge operates easily and knows where danger is, and operates simply and knows what obstructions are. This is what Tzu-ssu meant when he said, "He who has absolute sincerity is like a spirit" and "[It is characteristic of those with absolute sincerity] to be able to fore-know."[31] However, Tzu-ssu said, "*like* a spirit" and "*able to* fore-know." Thus he was still thinking in terms of two levels. These phrases describe by inference the effect of thinking how to be sincere and are meant for those who are not able to know readily. When we come to those with absolute sincerity, the wonderful operation of absolute sincerity itself is called spirit, not just *like* a spirit. Those with absolute sincerity have no knowledge and yet know all, and need not be described as being *able to* foreknow.

LETTER IN REPLY TO VICE-MINISTER LO CHENG-AN[1]

172. I beg respectfully to address you. Yesterday I received your instructive letter regarding the *Great Learning*, but since I was in a

---

[30] *Ibid.*

[31] *Ibid.*, ch. 24.

[1] Lo Ch'in-shun (1465-1547), one of the most outstanding Neo-Confucians of the Ch'eng-Chu school in the Ming dynasty. He was strongly opposed to the idealistic wing of Neo-Confucianism. First in the state civil service examination of 1492, he obtained a "presented scholar" degree the next year. He then held successively a number of high posts, including that of minister of the department of civil personnel. This letter in reply to him was written from Kiangsi in 1520 on Wang's return from the successful suppression of the rebellion there. Wang was then forty-nine. At that time Lo was vice-minister of the department of civil personnel. For an account of Lo, see *Ming-ju hsüeh-an*, ch. 47; and for the complete text of his letter, see *Lo Cheng-an chi*, 1:5b-10b.

hurry, as the boat was leaving, I was not able to answer it. This morning, as the boat proceeds along the Yangtze River, I am somewhat at leisure and so took your letter to read again. Fearing that after arriving at Kan-chou[2] I shall be kept occupied with business, I shall now write briefly to you.

Your letter says, "To see the Way is of course difficult, but personally to demonstrate it is even more so. Truly the Way is not easy to apprehend, but surely its study should not be neglected. I am afraid you should not be satisfied with your own view and without any hesitation regard it as the ultimate principle."

How fortunate am I that I should hear such words! How dare I regard my view as the ultimate principle and how dare I be satisfied with it? I merely wanted to make it clear to those in the world who are in accord with the Way. In the past several years there have been those who heard my theory and ridiculed it. There have been those who cursed it. And there have been those who put it aside as unworthy of deliberation or debate. Would they be willing to instruct me? Would they be willing to instruct me and explain again and again and compassionately feel that it might be too late for them to save and correct me? Therefore among those in the world who regard me deeply, none does so as deeply and as perfectly as Your Honor. How grateful I should be!

Confucius regarded as causes for concern not cultivating virtue and not discussing thoroughly what is learned.[3] But scholars of today all regard themselves as learned as soon as they have acquired some instruction and have reviewed it, or have gained some knowledge of textual criticism, and proceed no further to seek learning. How pitiable! To say that the Way must be personally demonstrated before it can be revealed does not mean that one first sees it and then proceeds to apply the effort of personal demonstration, and to say that the Way must be learned before it can be understood does not mean that outside of pursuing learning there is another undertaking called understanding the Way.

There are two ways to pursue learning. Some pursue it with their bodies and minds and some with their mouths and ears. Those who pursue it with their mouths and ears grope and imagine; they seek after what is apparent. Those who pursue it with their bodies

---

[2] A place in Kiangsi Province.
[3] *Analects*, 7:3.

and minds act with understanding and do so habitually with examination;[4] they sincerely and concretely realize the Way in themselves. He who knows this [the difference of these ways] knows the learning of the Confucian school.

173. Your letter says that I revived the old text of the *Great Learning*[5] because I believe that in the task of learning people should seek learning only from within, whereas according to the doctrine of the investigation of things of Ch'eng I and Chu Hsi, they should seek it in external things, and that I therefore omitted Master Chu's division into chapters and deleted his commentary which was intended to supplement the text. I dare not do so. Is there any distinction between the internal and the external in the matter of learning? The old text of the *Great Learning* is the original text transmitted from generation to generation in the Confucian school. Master Chu, suspecting that parts have been lost and errors have crept in, corrected and mended it. To me, there has been neither loss nor error. I follow the old text entirely, as it originally was, that is all. It is possible that I am wrong in believing too much in Confucius, but I did not purposely omit Master Chu's chapter divisions or delete his commentary.

The important thing in learning is to acquire learning through the exercise of the mind. If words are examined in the mind and found to be wrong, although they have come from the mouth of Confucius, I dare not accept them as correct. How much less those from people inferior to Confucius! If words are examined in the mind and found to be correct, although they have come from the mouth of ordinary people, I dare not regard them as wrong. How much less those of Confucius!

Moreover, the old text has been handed down for several thousand years. As we read its words, we find them to be clear and consistent, and as we view its method of moral cultivation, we find it to be easy, simple, and workable. On what evidence did Chu Hsi decide that this paragraph must be here and that one there, and that this was lost and that must be mended, and forthwith correct it and mend it? Are you not taking my opposition to Chu Hsi too seriously but taking his rebellion against Confucius too lightly?

---

[4] *Book of Mencius*, 7A:5.
[5] See above, introduction to sec. 1, n. 3.

174. Your letter says, "If it is insisted upon that in learning one should not depend on seeking knowledge in external things but should only devote one's effort to introspection and self-examination, then [in the procedure of the investigation of things, the extension of knowledge, the sincerity of the will, the rectification of the mind, and the cultivation of the personal life as prescribed in the text of the *Great Learning*] why is not the work of the rectification of the mind and the sincerity of the will completely sufficient and why is it necessary to burden the student with the investigation of things in the very beginning?"

You are quite right. You are quite right. If we talk about the fundamentals it is even sufficient to mention only the cultivation of the personal life. Why speak in addition of the rectification of the mind? It is even sufficient to mention only the rectification of the mind. Why speak in addition of the sincerity of the will? It is even sufficient to mention only the sincerity of the will. Why speak in addition of the extension of knowledge and also the investigation of things?[6] [All these steps are necessary] so the task will be thorough and careful. Essentially speaking, they are all one and the same. This is what is meant by the learning of refinement and single-mindedness. This should be borne in mind.

Since there is no distinction between the internal and the external in principle and there is no such distinction in human nature, therefore there is no such distinction in learning. Explanation, study, and discussion are also internal, and introspection and self-examination do not neglect the external. To say that learning must depend on the external is to regard one's own nature as having an external aspect, to consider righteousness as external, and to exercise cunning. And to say that introspection and self-examination are seeking learning from within is to regard one's own nature as having an internal aspect, to be egoistic, and to be selfish. In both cases there is evident ignorance of the fact that in the nature there is no distinction between the internal and the external. Therefore it is said, "Investigate the principles of things with care and refinement until we enter into their spirit, for then their application can be extended; and utilize that application and secure personal peace, for then our virtue will be exalted."[7] As it is said, "[Humanity and wisdom]

[6] This is the procedure taught in the text of the *Great Learning*.

[7] *Book of Changes*, "Appended Remarks," pt. 2, ch. 5. Cf. trans. by Legge, *Yi King*, p. 389.

are the character of the nature, and they are the way in which the internal and the external are united."[8] From these we may know the learning of the investigation of things. In the *Great Learning*, the investigation of things is the concrete starting point. From the beginning to the end, from the start of learning to the achievement of sagehood, there is but this one task. It is not a separate section for the beginning of the task. The rectification of the mind, the sincerity of the will, the extension of knowledge, and the investigation of things are all means of cultivating the personal life. But it is in the investigation of things that the effort to cultivate the personal life can be seen in one's daily conduct. Therefore the investigation of things is investigating the things of the mind, the things of the will, and the things of knowledge. To rectify the mind is to rectify the mind of things, to make the will sincere is to make the will of things sincere, and to extend knowledge is to extend the knowledge of things. Is there any distinction between the internal and external or between this or that?

Principle is one and no more. In terms of its condensation and concentration in the individual it is called the nature. In terms of the master of this accumulation it is called mind. In terms of its emanation and operation under the master, it is called the will. In terms of the clear consciousness of the emanation and operation, it is called knowledge. And in terms of the stimuli and responses of this clear consciousness, it is called things. Therefore when it pertains to things it is called investigation, when it pertains to knowledge it is called extension, when it pertains to the will it is called sincerity, and when it pertains to the mind it is called rectification. To rectify is to rectify this [principle], to be sincere is to be sincere about this, to extend is to extend this, and to investigate is to investigate this. These are all means of investigating the principle of things to the utmost so as to develop the nature fully. There is no principle in the world outside nature, and there is no thing outside nature. The reason why the Confucian doctrine is not made clear and does not prevail is because scholars of today consider principle as external and things as external. They do not realize that the doctrine that righteousness is external has been attacked by Mencius[9] and they blindly follow that doctrine and stick to it without

[8] *Doctrine of the Mean*, ch. 25.
[9] *Book of Mencius*, 6A:4.

knowing it. Isn't there something seemingly true and yet difficult to apprehend? We must examine the matter carefully.

175. Your Honor is skeptical about my theory of the investigation of things because you undoubtedly believe that it affirms the internal and rejects the external; that it is entirely devoted to self-examination and introspection and neglects the work of explanation, study, and discussion; that it concentrates on the over-simplified fundamental principles and leaves out the full details; that it submerges itself in the extremes of Buddhist and Taoist lifeless contemplation, emptiness and silence,[10] and fails to take full account of the changing conditions of human affairs and the principles of things. If that were really the case, it would not only be a crime against the Confucian school and Master Chu Hsi; it would be a perverse doctrine to delude the people and a rebellious teaching to violate truth, and I should be punishable by death from all. How much more from a person of your integrity! If that were really the case, anyone who understands textual criticism to a slight degree and has heard the introductory remarks of former wise men would know its incorrectness. How much more such an eminent scholar as Your Honor! Whenever I talk about the investigation of things, I always include all the nine items enumerated by Master Chu.[11] But in their application there is a relative degree of importance, differing, as we say, by a fraction of a fraction. However, an infinitesimal mistake in the beginning may lead to an infinite error at the end. This should be clearly understood.

[10] Especially of Zen Buddhism, popular at Wang's time.

[11] Namely (1) to read books, discuss doctrines, and elucidate principles, to deliberate on people and events of the past and the present and distinguish their right and wrong, to handle affairs and to settle them in the proper way, and to investigate a thing one day and another the next day; (2) to investigate the principles in all things, from one's own person to the ten thousand things; (3) not to investigate extensively all the principles in the world nor to investigate intensively the principle of only one thing but to investigate more and more and thus to accumulate; (4) to investigate either the easy or the difficult according to one's capacity; (5) to realize that every thing has its principle and should be investigated; (6) to know that the investigation of the principle of filial piety means to practice it; (7) to realize that every blade of grass and every tree has its principle and should be investigated; (8) to know where the highest good is to be found; and (9) to examine principle in one's own person. Chu Hsi, *Ta-hsüeh huo-wen*, pp. 46a-52a. Actually these are all quotations or paraphrases of Ch'eng I's sayings.

176. Mencius exposed the fallacies of Yang Chu and Mo Tzu to the point of condemning them for not recognizing the father or the ruler.[12] After all, the two philosophers were worthies of their times. Had they lived at the same time as Mencius, it is quite possible that he would have regarded them as such. Mo Tzu's doctrine of universal love went too far in the practice of humanity, and Yang Chu's doctrine of egoism went too far in the practice of righteousness, that is all. Did these doctrines destroy truth and violate moral standards to such a high degree as to be capable of deceiving the whole world? And yet their harmful effect that had developed was such that Mencius compared these men to beasts and barbarians. It was because they did what is called "destroying later generations by means of learning."[13]

Shall we say that the harmful effect of present-day learning lies in its going too far in teaching humanity or in its going too far in teaching righteousness? Or in its going too far in teaching neither humanity nor righteousness? I do not know how present-day learning compares with a great flood or ferocious beasts. Mencius said, "Do I like to argue? I can't help it."[14] The doctrines of Yang and Mo pervaded the empire. People in Mencius' time who honored and believed them must have been no fewer than those who exalt Chu Hsi's doctrine today. And yet Mencius alone kept on talking against them. Alas, how pitiable!

Han Yü said, "The harm of the Buddhists and Taoists greatly exceeds that of Yang and Mo, and Han Yü's virtue is not equal to that of Mencius. Mencius was not able to save his age before it had been injured, but Han Yü hopes to recover his age after it has been damaged. He fails to realize the limitations of his own duty. It is clear that he will place himself in danger and will perish without anyone's saving him."[15] Alas! I have failed even more to realize the limitation of my ability. It is definitely clear that I shall place myself in danger and shall perish without anyone's saving me. When all people are in the depths of merriment, I alone weep and lament, and when the whole world happily runs [after erroneous doctrines], I alone worry with an aching heart and a knit brow. Either I have lost

---

[12] *Book of Mencius*, 3B:9.
[13] A saying by Lu Hsiang-shan, *Hsiang-shan ch'üan-chi*, 1:3a.
[14] *Book of Mencius*, 3B:9.
[15] *Han Ch'ang-li ch'üan-chi*, 18:9a-b.

my mind or there must surely be a great grief hidden away in the situation. Who except the most humane in the world can understand it?

I wrote "Chu Hsi's Final Conclusions Arrived at Late in Life"[16] because I could not help it. It is true that I have neglected to ascertain whether certain passages were written earlier or later in life. However, although not all of them were written late in his life, most of them were. At any rate, my chief idea was that it was important to compromise as much as possible so as to clarify this doctrine of the investigation of things. All my life Chu Hsi's doctrine has been a revelation to me, as though from the gods. In my heart I cannot bear suddenly to oppose him. Therefore it was because I could not help it that I did it. Those who know me say that my heart is grieved but those who do not know me say that I am after something.[17] The fact is that in my own heart I cannot bear to contradict Master Chu but I cannot help contradicting him because the Way is what it is and the Way will not be fully evident if I do not correct him.[18] As to Your Honor's contention that I purposely differ from Master Chu, do I dare deceive my own mind?

The Way is public and belongs to the whole world, and the doctrine is also public and belongs to the whole world. They are not the private properties of Master Chu or even Confucius. They are open to all and the only proper way to discuss them is to do so openly. If what is said is right, it will be beneficial to one though it may differ from his opinion. If it is wrong, it will be harmful to him even if he may agree with it. One surely rejoices in what is beneficial to him and dislikes what is harmful to him. Thus, even if my present opinion possibly differs from that of Master Chu's, it is not unlikely that he would rejoice in it. The faults of the superior man are like eclipses of the sun and moon. When he corrects them, all men look up to him.[19] But the inferior man is sure to gloss over his faults.[20] Although I am unworthy, I surely dare not treat Chu Hsi with the mind of an inferior man.

[16] See below, pp. 263-67.
[17] Quoting the *Book of Odes*, no. 65.
[18] Quoting the *Book of Mencius*, 3A:5.
[19] *Analects*, 19:21.
[20] *Ibid.*, 19:8.

177. Your Honor has instructed me earnestly in several hundred words all because you have not fully understood my theory of the investigation of things. As soon as my humble theory is understood, these several hundred words will require no explanation and will be clarified without any difficulty. Therefore I do not venture into details to increase your annoyance with trifles. However, unless my humble views are explained face to face, they definitely cannot be fully presented in writing. Ah! the way in which Your Honor enlightens me and directs me may be said to be extremely earnest and thorough. Among those who regard me dearly, who can match Your Honor? Although I am simple-minded, can I fail to be appreciative and thankful? But I cannot cast away the sincerity of my mind and merely accept what you say because I dare not fail in your high esteem of me but instead want to requite it. When I return east at the end of autumn, I shall certainly try to see you so all my requests to you may be fulfilled. Please instruct me to the end under all circumstances.

LETTER IN REPLY TO NIEH WEN-YÜ[1]

178. Last spring[2] you took a long and weary journey to come to see me. Your regard and concern were most earnest and kind. How can I deserve such fond feeling? Originally I had hoped to get you

[1] Nieh Pao (1487-1563), whose literary name was Shuang-chiang. A "presented scholar" of 1517, he eventually became a prefect and in that capacity enabled some 3,000 families to regain employment by carrying out irrigation projects. An honest and outspoken critic of bad government officials, he was imprisoned for over a year and finally dismissed from office. Later, however, he became minister of the department of military affairs and tutor to the crown prince.

He held Wang in great admiration. After Wang died, he deeply regretted that he had not become Wang's disciple. Consequently he formally became one by bowing to Wang's tablet with Ch'ien Te-hung as witness. In his doctrines he differed from Wang and emphasized tranquillity of mind and sitting in meditation, holding that the state of equilibrium before the feelings are aroused is that of innate knowledge. For an account of him, see *Ming-ju hsüeh-an*, 17:8b-17a. According to the *Nien-p'u*, Wang's letter in reply to him was written from Chekiang in 1526 when Wang was fifty-five. On his way to Fukien as censor, Nieh had visited Wang and he wrote to him afterward. But since the letter was included in the *Ch'uan-hsi lu*, which Nan Yüan-shan published in 1524, the date must have been earlier.

[2] According to other editions whieh agree with the *Nien-p'u* it was the summer rather than the spring.

and several other like-minded friends to go to a quiet place and stay for ten days or so so that I might present some of my humble views and reap the benefit of your polishing and refining. Unfortunately both public and private business were so onerous that it was impossible for me to do so. As we separated, I felt dispirited as though I had suffered a loss. Then suddenly your kind letter arrived with an earnest discussion of over a thousand words. As I read it I feel my mind cleansed and my heart comforted. In your letter you praise me exceedingly, no doubt with the generous purpose of encouraging me and leading me forward. Sincerely giving me advice and encouragement, you want to take me into the company of sages and worthies. Moreover, you asked Ch'ung-i[3] to give me your keenest regards. How could you have done so much unless you had deep friendship and great love for me? I am grateful and yet ashamed, and fear that I do not deserve all this. However, how dare I merely engage in expressions of gratitude and compliance and fail to rouse myself to effort?

You said that in me you unexpectedly found Tzu-ssu, Mencius, Chou Tun-i, and Ch'eng I in this late generation, that rather than have the doctrine believed by the whole world, it is better to have it believed truly by one single person, that the Way is self-evident and the Confucian learning is also self-evident, and that they are not augmented because the whole world believes in them nor diminished because only one person believes in them.[4] This is indeed the mind of the superior man who can face disapproval without being troubled.[5] Can people of superficial views understand it? And yet in the way I feel there is something that cannot be helped at all, and I do not mind whether people believe me or not.

179. Man is the mind of the universe. At bottom Heaven and Earth and all things are my body. Is there any suffering or bitterness of the great masses that is not disease or pain in my own body? Those who are not aware of the disease and pain in their own body are people without the sense of right and wrong. The sense of right and wrong is knowledge possessed by men without deliberation and

---

[3] See above, sec. 104, n. 23.

[4] Nieh's letter is not in the *Nieh Shuang-chiang wen-chi*, and this passage does not appear anywhere else in the collection.

[5] A quotation from the *Book of Changes*, commentary on hexagram no. 1. Cf. trans. by Legge, *Yi King*, p. 409.

ability possessed by them without their having acquired it by learning.[6] It is what we call innate knowledge. This knowledge is inherent in the human mind whether that of the sage or of the stupid person, for it is the same for the whole world and for all ages. If gentlemen of the world merely devote their effort to extending their innate knowledge they will naturally share with all a universal sense of right and wrong, share their likes and dislikes, regard other people as their own persons, regard the people of other countries as their own family, and look upon Heaven, Earth, and all things as one body. When this is done, even if we wanted the world to be without order, it would not be possible. When the ancients felt that the good seemed to come from themselves when they saw others do good, when they felt that they had fallen into evil when they saw others do evil, when they regarded other people's hunger and drowning as their own, and when they felt that if one person's condition was not well adjusted it was as if they had pushed him into a ditch,[7] they did not purposely do so in order to seek people's belief in them. They merely devoted their effort to extending their innate knowledge and sought to satisfy themselves. The Sage-emperors Yao and Shun and the Three Kings[8] spoke and all people believed them, because in speaking they extended their innate knowledge. They acted and all people were pleased with them,[9] because in acting they extended their innate knowledge. Therefore their people moved around and were contented. Though these rulers punished the people by death, the people did not complain, and when the rulers benefited the people, the people did not think of the rulers' merit.[10] Their fame extended to all the barbarous tribes and all who had blood and breath honored and loved them.[11] Why? Because all people have the same innate knowledge. Alas, how simple and easy was the way of sages to govern the empire!

180.   In later generations, the doctrine of innate knowledge has not clearly prevailed. People have used their selfishness and cunning

---

[6] A quotation from the *Book of Mencius*, 7A:15.
[7] Quoting the *Book of History*, "The Charge to Yüeh," pt 2. Cf. trans. by Legge, *Shoo King*, p. 262.
[8] T'ang, Wen, and Wu.
[9] A saying from the *Doctrine of the Mean*, ch. 31.
[10] According to the *Book of Mencius*, 7A:13.
[11] According to the *Doctrine of the Mean*, ch. 31.

to compete with and rival one another. Consequently each one has his own opinion, and one-sided, trivial, perverse, and narrow views as well as dishonest, crafty, underhanded, and evil tricks have become innumerable. Outwardly people make pretenses in the name of humanity and righteousness. At heart their real aim is to act for their own benefit. They lie in order to please the vulgar people and affect a certain conduct in order to obtain fame. They cover up other people's good deeds or appropriate them as their own, and they expose other people's selfishness and take advantage of the opportunity to show that they are honest. They overcome one another with anger and yet claim to be seeking ardently for righteousness, and destroy one another with wickedness and yet claim to hate evil. They are jealous of the worthy and envious of the talented, and yet consider themselves to have a universal sense of right and wrong. They indulge in passions and give free rein to selfish desires, and yet regard themselves as sharing the same likes and dislikes with the rest of mankind. They oppose and injure one another. Even among blood relatives, they cannot get rid of the feeling of mutual separation and rivalry or the evidence of mutual antagonism and obstruction. How much more will this be true in regard to the great multitude and the myriad things? How can they regard them as one body? No wonder the world is confused and calamity and disorder endlessly succeed each other.

181.   Thanks to divine guidance I happen to entertain certain views on innate knowledge, believing that only through it can order be brought to the world. Therefore whenever I think of people's degeneration and difficulties I feel pitiful and have a pain in my heart. I overlook the fact that I am unworthy and wish to save them by this doctrine. And I do not know the limits of my ability. When people see me trying to do this, they join one another in criticizing, ridiculing, insulting, and cursing me, regarding me as insane. Alas! Is this to be pitied? Just at the time when I feel the disease and pain in my own body, do I have leisure to pay attention to other people's denunciation and ridicule?

Of course there are cases when people see their fathers, sons, or brothers falling into a deep abyss and getting drowned. They cry, crawl, go naked and barefooted, stumble and fall. They hang onto dangerous cliffs and go down to save them. Some gentlemen who see them behave like this talk, laugh, and bow ceremoniously to one another by their side. They consider them to be insane because they have discarded etiquette and taken off their clothing, and because they cry, stumble, and fall as they do. Now to stand beside those drowing and make no attempt to save them but to bow, talk, and laugh is possible only for strangers who have no feelings natural to blood relatives. Even then, they will be considered to have no sense of pity and to be no longer human beings. In the case of fathers, sons, and brothers, because of love one will surely feel an ache in his head and a pain in his heart, run desperately until he has lost his breath, and crawl to save them. He even ignores the danger of drowning himself. How much more will he ignore being ridiculed as insane! And how much more will he fail to worry about whether people believe him or not! Alas! It is all right if people say that I am insane. The minds of all people are the same as mine. There are people who are insane. How can I not be so? There are people who have lost their minds. How can I not lose mine?

182. When Confucius was alive, some criticized him as a flatterer,[12] some ridiculed him as an insinuating talker, [13] some slandered him as unworthy,[14] some denounced him as ignorant of the rules of propriety,[15] some insulted him by calling him merely "someone" from the east village, [16] some were jealous of him and stopped him from carrying out political reforms,[17] and some hated him and wanted to kill him.[18] People like the gateman and the carrier of a straw basket were virtuous in his time, and even they said that

[12] *Analects*, 3:18.
[13] *Ibid.*, 14:34.
[14] *Ibid.*, 19:24.
[15] *Ibid.*, 3:15.
[16] Dictionaries and commentators (including Miwa Shissai, 1669-1744, in his *Hyōchū denshū roku*) all said that the story came from the *K'ung Tzu chia-yü*. If so, it must have been in the earlier version which has been lost, for it is not found in the existing version. Miwa's pupil, Kawada Kinkyō (1684-1760), noted in his *Denshū roku hikki* that the story is not found in the *K'ung Tzu chia-yü* but comes from the *Shuo-yüan*. But I have not been able to find it there. Professor William Hung of Harvard-Yenching Institute has kindly provided me with several references to the story in later works, for which I am grateful. Of these the earliest is Shen Yüeh (441-513), *Ying Hou chi* 1:83b. It is said here that some of his contemporaries called Confucius "someone from the east village."
[17] *Analects*, 18:4.
[18] *Ibid.*, 7:22.

"he knows that a thing cannot be done and still wants to do it,"[19] and that "he is contemptible and obstinate and should stop seeking public service since people take no notice of him."[20] Even Tzu-lu, who ranked among those who had ascended the hall[21] still was not free from doubts about what he saw[22] and was displeased over his intended visit,[23] and, moreover, regarded him as aiming wide of the mark.[24] This being the case at the time, were there only two or three out of ten who refused to believe in the Grand Master? And yet the Grand Master was extremely busy and anxious, as though he were searching for a lost son on the highways, and never sat down long enough to warm his mat. Was he only trying to get people to know him and believe him? It was rather because his humanity, which regarded Heaven and Earth and all things as one body, was so compassionate, keen, and sincere that he could not stop doing so even if he wanted to. This is why he said, "If I do not associate with mankind, with whom shall I associate?"[25] This is why [Tzu-lu, commenting on the hermit who criticized Confucius,] said, "Wishing to maintain his personal purity he allows the great human relations to come to confusion."[26] And this is why Confucius said, "How determined is the basket carrier! It is not difficult [not to seek public service]."[27] Alas! Aside from those who truly form one body with Heaven and Earth and the myriad things, who can understand the Grand Master's intention? As to those who escape from the world without being troubled and are happy with their nature and know their destiny, they can be at ease with themselves wherever they may be, and see no contradiction between parallel courses of action [those of the hermit and the social reformer].

---

[19] *Ibid.*, 14:41. The gateman was keeper of the Stone Gate through which Confucius once passed.

[20] *Ibid.*, 14:42.

[21] Meaning pupils who learned much.

[22] *Ibid.*, 6:26. Confucius went to see Nan-tzu, consort of a duke, in an effort to sell his political ideas. Tzu-lu thought Confucius should not have gone to see such a woman, whose reputation was not too good.

[23] *Ibid.*, 17:5. An official who was in revolt asked Confucius to go and assist him. Confucius wanted to go, but Tzu-lu objected.

[24] *Ibid.*, 13:3.

[25] *Ibid.*, 18:6.

[26] *Ibid.*, 18:7.

[27] *Ibid.*, 14:42.

183. How dare such an unworthy person as I take the course of Confucius as my own responsibility? However, to some extent I do realize in my mind that the disease and pain are in my own body and therefore desperately search in all directions for those who can be of help to discuss ways and means of removing the disease and pain. Now if I can really find help and assistance from eminent men and like-minded friends and together with them make the doctrine of innate knowledge clearly prevail in the world, so that all people can know how to extend their own innate knowledge, give security and support to one another, eliminate their obscuration and selfishness, wipe out their habits of slander, jealousy, rivalry, and anger, and bring about the world of great unity, then my insanity will be cured in a sudden release and I can finally avoid the disaster of losing my mind. Will that not be a joy!

Alas! If I am truly to look for eminent men and like-minded friends, to whom can I turn if not to people like Wen-yü? Your talents and desire are already sufficient to save those who are drowning. In addition, you know that all that is needed exists sufficiently in the self and does not need to be sought outside. If this desire is followed and carried out to the fullest extent, it will be like a river bursting its banks and flowing to the sea. Who can stop it? You said that even if only one person believes in the doctrine of innate knowledge this is not too few. Can you yield this to someone else?

184. Hui-chi[28] has always been known as an area of beautiful scenery. With every step one takes, one sees thick groves and deep valleys. It is just right at all times, whether in winter or summer, and whether in morning or evening. One lives comfortably and eats fully, and is not bothered by bustle or dust. As good friends gather from all directions, one's moral life is daily renewed. What a free and easy life! Can one be happier anywhere else in the world? Confucius said, "I do not complain against Heaven. I do not blame men. I study things on the lower level but my understanding penetrates the higher level."[29] Two or three like-minded friends and I are about to try to put this saying into practice. Where do I have time to seek external glory? It is only because the pain is very personal to me that

---

[28] A place in Chekiang Province, where Wang Yang-ming founded an academy.

[29] *Analects*, 14:37.

I cannot ignore it. That is why I have continued to express myself as I have done. As my cough is very severe, I have been extremely lazy in writing. Your honorable messenger came from afar. I have detained him for a month. As he departs and I pick up my pen, I do not realize that page after page has been written. Since we know each other well, though I have gone into details to this extent, I feel especially that I have not said what I wanted to say.

ANOTHER LETTER IN REPLY TO NIEH WEN-YÜ[1]

185. Having received your letter, I know of the recent rapid progress in your study. I am happy and gratified beyond words. I have carefully read your letter several times. That there are nevertheless one or two points not crystal clear to you is because you are not yet completely at home with the task of extending innate knowledge. When you have become familiar with it, the lack of clarity will vanish of itself. It may be compared to driving a vehicle. You are driving it on a broad highway. But sometimes it goes obliquely or zigzags, because the horse is not yet well trained and the bit and bridle are not even. However, you are already on the broad highway itself and will certainly not mistakenly go into sidetracks or crooked paths. Of late, only a few of our like-minded friends in the country have reached this stage of progress. I am happy and gratified beyond words that you have. This is good fortune for the Confucian doctrine.

Previously my humble body was afflicted with a cough and the fear of heat. Since my recent arrival in this hot region,[2] these have suddenly reoccurred to a high degree. His Majesty, possessing sagely intelligence and great understanding, has given me great responsibility which I dare not abruptly decline. Local military affairs have been heavy and busy. I have handled all of them while going about in carriages in spite of illness. Fortunately the region is now pacified. I have presented a memorial seeking permission to return home for treatment of my disease. If I can rest in a grove and

[1] This letter was written in 1528 from Kwangsi, to which Wang had gone to suppress a rebellion, a month before Wang died. Nieh's letter to which this is a reply is found in the *Shuang-chiang wen-chi*, 8:1a-6b.

[2] Kwangsi.

enjoy to some extent the clear and cool air, perhaps I can recover. As your messenger is about to return, I have hastily written while resting on my pillow, but I cannot fully express my regard for you. In addition I am sending a letter to Wei-chün.[3] Please deliver it to him.

186. Let me roughly answer one or two questions you put forth in your letter. In the last year or two, those who came to the mountains to study with me have repeatedly said that the task of not forgetting one's objective and not making any artificial effort to help the mind grow[4] is most difficult. When asked for an explanation, they said, "As soon as one fixes his attention, he is helping, and as soon as he pays no attention, he forgets. Therefore it is most difficult." I then asked them, "What is it that you forget and what is it that you help?" They remained silent and made no reply, and then asked me for my opinion. Whereupon I explained to them as follows:

In my discussions here I talk only about the point that "One must always be doing something"[5] and not about forgetting or not helping. "One must always be doing something" means that one should accumulate righteous deeds at all times. If one devotes all his time to the task of seeing to it that he must always be doing something and yet he is interrupted at times, it means he forgets. The immediate task here is not to forget. If one devotes all his time to the task of always doing something and is impatient and seeks quick results, it means he helps. The immediate task here is not to help. The task lies wholly in the practice of the teaching that one must always be doing something. In this situation the injunctions not to forget and not to help are meant only to hold the individual's attention and make him alert. If from the start the task is not interrupted, there is no further need of talking about not forgetting, and if from the start one is not impatient and does not seek quick results, there is no further need of talking about not helping. How clear, simple, and easy is this task, and how free and natural!

Now if one does not devote himself to the task of always doing something and clings in a vacuum to not forgetting or helping, it is just like heating the skillet to cook rice without first putting in

---

[3] See below, sec. 201, n. 1. This letter, dated 1527, is found in the *Wang Wen-ch'eng Kung ch'üan-shu*, 6:31b-33a.

[4] *Book of Mencius*, 2A:2.

[5] *Ibid.*

water and rice but only adding fuel and starting the fire. I don't know what stuff can in the end be cooked by this. I am afraid that before the intensity of the fire can be adjusted the skillet will already be cracked. Nowadays, the trouble of those who devote their efforts only to not forgetting and not helping is precisely like this. All day long they attempt to practice not forgetting in a vacuum and also attempt to practice not helping in a vacuum. Pushing and rushing, they completely lack a concrete starting point. In the end their task will result only in their sinking into emptiness and maintaining quietness[6] and learning to be stupid fools. As soon as anything happens to them, they are handicapped and confused and cannot manage or control it. These are all gentlemen with ambition, and now they must toil, be bound, and waste all their lives. It is all because of the fact that an over-emphasis on intellectual learning spoils them. What a great pity!

187. "One must always be doing something" means merely the accumulation of righteous deeds, and the accumulation of righteous deeds means merely the extension of innate knowledge. To talk about accumulating righteous deeds does not immediately reveal the basis, but as soon as we talk about the extension of innate knowledge there is right away a concrete basis on which to engage in the task. I therefore advocate solely the extension of innate knowledge. To extend innate knowledge in daily affairs as they occur is to investigate things. To extend innate knowledge in a genuine and earnest way is to make the will sincere. To extend innate knowledge in a genuine and earnest way without the least arbitrariness of opinion, dogmatism, obstinacy, or egotism[7] is to rectify the mind. If one extends innate knowledge genuinely and earnestly, there will naturally be no defect of forgetting, and if one has not the least arbitrariness of opinion, dogmatism, obstinacy, or egotism, there will naturally be no defect of helping. Therefore if we advocate the investigation of things, the extension of knowledge, the sincerity of the will, and the rectification of the mind, there will be no need of any further talk of forgetting or helping. Mencius talked of them in order to prescribe a formula for remedying the defects of Kao Tzu. Kao Tzu's control of the mind is the defect of helping the mind to grow. Therefore

[6] Like the Buddhists and Taoists.
[7] *Analects*, 9:4.

Mencius only talked about the harm of helping. Kao Tzu advocated helping the mind to grow because he regarded righteousness as external to the mind and failed to realize that righteousness should be accumulated in and through one's own mind and that one should devote his effort to the task of always doing something. This is why he had this defect. If one accumulates righteousness in and through his own mind every hour and every minute, the substance of innate knowledge will be absolutely clear and it will spontaneously see right as right and wrong as wrong, neither of which can escape from it in the least. How, then, can there be the trouble that "What is not attained in words is not to be sought in the mind, and what is not attained in the mind is not to be sought in the vital force"?[8] Mencius' doctrine of accumulating righteousness and nourishing the vital force is of course a great help to students. Nevertheless, it is but a prescription for a particular ailment expounded at length. It is not as good as the task of the investigation of things, the extension of knowledge, the sincerity of the will, and the rectification of the mind taught in the *Great Learning*, which is much more refined, unified, simple, and easy. It penetrates both the higher and the lower levels and is good for ten thousand generations.

188. In discussing learning, sages and worthies mostly do so in accordance with the times and with events. They seem to differ from one another in what they say, but essentially they are in complete harmony on the basis of the task. The reason for this is that in the universe there is only this one nature, this one principle, this one innate knowledge, and this one endeavor. Therefore, whenever we discuss our task on the basis of the doctrines of the ancients, we should not force extraneous ideas upon them or mix them with such ideas. Then they will naturally blend together and penetrate one another. As soon as one feels the necessity of forcing extraneous ideas upon them or mixing them with such ideas, it is apparent that one's own task is not yet clearly understood.

In recent days it is said that the task of accumulating righteousness must be combined with the extension of innate knowledge before it can be complete. Such a contention shows that the task of accumulating righteousness is not yet thoroughly understood. If the task of accumulating righteousness is not thoroughly understood, the exten-

---

[8] Kao Tzu, in *Book of Mencius*, 2A:2.

sion of innate knowledge will suffer. To say that the task of the extension of innate knowledge must be combined with the effort not to forget or to help before it becomes clear means that the task of the extension of innate knowledge is not yet thoroughly understood. If the task of the extension of innate knowledge is not yet thoroughly understood, the effort not to forget or help will suffer. All such contentions are the results of literal interpretations and far-fetched explanations for the purpose of combining together or mixing various elements and not the results of personal realization obtained in one's own concrete task. Consequently, the more refined one's discussion becomes, the farther he is away from the truth. In your deliberation, Wen-yü, it is abundantly clear that you are free from doubt so far as the great foundation and universal way of virtue are concerned. As to the doctrines of the extension of knowledge and the investigation of the principles of things to the utmost, not forgetting, not helping, and so forth, at times you have forced extraneous ideas upon them or mixed them with other elements. This is why I have said that in riding along the broad highway one sometimes goes obliquely or zigzags, and that after one masters the task everything will be clear to him.

189.   You said, Wen-yü, that when the doctrine of the extension of knowledge is sought in serving one's parents and obeying one's elder brother, it will be felt that there is something concrete to grasp and to follow. This section shows best the result of your recent genuine and concrete effort. However, if from this you think that if you follow this procedure yourself, it will be effective, and forthwith teach it to others as an established doctrine, you will not be free from the defect of incurring disease because of the application of medicine. This matter should not be passed over without comment.

Innate knowledge is nothing other than the Principle of Nature where the natural clear consciousness reveals itself. Its original substance is merely true sincerity and commiseration. Therefore, when the true sincerity and commiseration of this innate knowledge is extended to serve one's parents, it becomes filial piety. When the true sincerity and commiseration of this innate knowledge is extended to obey one's elder brother, it becomes brotherly respect. And when the true sincerity and commiseration of this innate knowledge is extended to serve one's ruler, it becomes loyalty. There is but one innate knowledge, one true sincerity and commiseration. If in obeying one's elder brother the true sincerity and commiseration of innate knowledge cannot be extended, they cannot be extended in serving one's parents. If they cannot be extended in serving one's ruler, they cannot be extended in obeying one's elder brother. Therefore, to have extended the innate knowledge that serves the ruler is to have extended the innate knowledge that obeys one's elder brother. To have extended the innate knowledge that obeys one's elder brother is to have extended the innate knowledge that serves one's parents. This does not mean that if the innate knowledge that serves one's ruler cannot be extended one has to develop the innate knowledge that serves one's parents. That would be departing from the root and looking for it in twigs and branches. There is only one innate knowledge. In its manifestation and universal operation, it is then and there self-sufficient. It comes from nowhere and goes nowhere. It depends on nothing. However, in its manifestation and universal operation, there are degrees of importance and intensity to and from which not the slightest amount can be added or subtracted. This is what is called "the equilibrium that is self-existent in everything."[9] Although there are degrees of importance and intensity to and from which not the slightest amount can be added or substracted, at bottom it is only one. And although it is only one, its degrees of importance and intensity cannot be altered in the least. If it can be altered or if it depends on anything, it will no longer be the original substance of true sincerity and commiseration. This is why the wonderful functioning of innate knowledge has neither spatial restriction nor physical form and is unlimited. If one speaks of its greatness, nothing in the world can contain it, and if one speaks of its smallness, nothing in the world can split it.[10]

190. Mencius said, "The Way of Yao and Shun was simply that of filial piety and brotherly respect."[11] He said so because he wanted to call people's attention to the point where the manifestation of innate knowledge is the most genuine and earnest and in which no obscuration can be allowed, so that in their serving the ruler, living with friends, being humane to all people and kind to creatures, and in all their activities and tranquillity, and speech and silence,

---

[9] Ch'eng I, quoted by Chu Hsi in his *Ta-hsüeh huo-wen*, p. 56b.
[10] *Doctrine of the Mean*, ch. 12.
[11] *Book of Mencius*, 6B:2.

they will only extend the truly sincere and commiserate innate knowledge which is expressed in the single desire to serve one's parents and obey one's elder brother. Then everything will naturally be in accord with the Way.

Although there is an infinite amount of change and variety in the world, so much so that it is impossible to investigate all of them, if one responds to them by merely extending this truly sincere and commiserate innate knowledge expressed in the single desire to serve one's parents and obey one's elder brother, nothing will be left out of its operation. This is because there is only one innate knowledge. Outside of this innate knowledge expressed in the single desire to serve one's parents and to obey one's elder brother, there is no other innate knowledge that can be extended. Therefore Mencius said, "The Way of Yao and Shun was simply that of filial piety and brotherly respect." This is why it is the learning of refinement and single-mindedness, and will be correct when expanding in all four directions and timeless when applied to later generations.[12]

You say that you desire to seek the learning of innate knowledge in serving your parents and obeying your elder brother. From the point of view of efficiency in your own effort, it is not wrong to say so. It is also all right if you say that one extends the true sincerity and commiseration of innate knowledge in order to practice the way of serving one's parents and obeying one's elder brother to the fullest. Ch'eng Ming-tao [Ch'eng Hao] said, "The practice of humanity begins with filial piety and brotherly respect. Filial piety and brotherly respect are items in the practice of humanity. It is all right to say that they are the root of the practice of humanity but not all right to say that they are the root of humanity itself."[13] What is said is correct.

191.   Regarding anticipating someone's attempt to deceive and predicting someone's distrust and knowing them readily,[14] you say that if one is sincere, then taking special means and doing the best thing under the circumstances in order to protect oneself is also an application of innate knowledge. This is very, very well said. As I have said before, you are not entirely free from forcing extraneous

---

[12] Paraphrasing the *Book of Rites*, "The Meaning of Sacrifices." Cf. trans. by Legge, *Li Ki*, ch. 21, p. 227.

[13] *I-shu*, 18:1b. Actually this is not a saying of Ch'eng Hao but one of Ch'eng I.

[14] *Analects*, 14:33.

ideas upon things or mixing them with other elements. What Wei-chün said is not wrong.[15] On your part, you need to take in his words before yours can be fully stated, and on his part he needs to take in your words before his can be made clear. Otherwise, each of you will have the defect of relying on and clinging to your own viewpoint. Emperor Shun examined the simple words of others[16] and asked questions of grass and reed cutters.[17] He did not do so because simple words should be examined and grass and reed cutters should be questioned. Rather, his behavior was the manifestation and universal operation of his innate knowledge which was clear and perfect, without any obstruction or obscuration. This is why it is called great knowledge. As soon as there is any clinging to arbitrariness of opinion or dogmatism, knowledge becomes small. Naturally, in the course of discussion, distinctions and adjustments will be made. However, for the mind to be engaged in a genuine and earnest task, one must proceed in this manner.

192.   With reference to the three sections on exerting one's mind to the utmost [preserving one's mind, and not allowing any double-mindedness], I have elaborated on the ideas that some people are born with knowledge [and can exert their minds to the utmost], some learn through study [and can preserve their minds], and some learn through hard work [and can allow no double-mindedness].[18] My exposition was quite clear and should not be questioned. For one who exerts his mind to the utmost, knows his nature, and knows Heaven, there is no need to talk about preserving the mind, nourishing the nature, and serving Heaven, or about not allowing any double-mindedness regardless of longevity or brevity of life and about cultivating one's personal life while waiting for the mandate of Heaven to take its own course,[19] for what he does already involves these efforts. Although he who preserves his mind, nourishes his nature, and serves Heaven has not attained the position of exerting the mind to the utmost and knowing Heaven, yet in so doing he has already found the task of exerting the mind to the utmost and of knowing Heaven. There is no need to talk about having no double-

---

[15] See below, sec. 201, n. 1. What he said is no longer known.
[16] *Doctrine of the Mean*, ch. 6.
[17] *Book of Odes*, no. 254.
[18] *Doctrine of the Mean*, ch. 20. See above, sec. 6.
[19] *Book of Mencius*, 7A:1.

mindedness regardless of longevity or brevity of life and about cultivating the personal life while waiting for the mandate of Heaven to take its own course, for what he does already involves these efforts.

This may be compared to walking. He who exerts his mind to the utmost and knows Heaven is like a strong adult who is able to run back and forth for thousands of *li*.[20] He who preserves his mind and serves Heaven is like a child who is being taught to walk and stride in the vestibule. He who does not allow any double-mindedness regardless of longevity or brevity of life, but cultivates his personal life while waiting for the mandate of Heaven to take its own course, is like an infant who has just been allowed to support himself against the wall and gradually is learning to stand and to take a step. Since an individual is already able to run back and forth for several thousand *li*, it is unnecessary to have him learn to walk or stride in the vestibule, for he is already able to do so. If he is able to walk and stride in the vestibule, there is no need to have him support himself against the wall and learn to stand or to take a step, for he is already able to do so. But learning to stand and to take a step is the beginning of learning to walk and to stride in the vestibule, and learning to walk and stride in the vestibule is the foundation of running back and forth for several thousand *li*. They are surely not two different things, but the difference in the difficulty or easiness in the task is very, very wide.

Mind, the nature, and Heaven are one. Therefore when people finally come to know this, their success is the same. But for the three types of people there are naturally different steps according to their capability or ability, which should not be skipped over. In carefully examining your ideas, Wen-yü, it seems to me that you are afraid that he who exerts his mind to the utmost and knows Heaven neglects the effort of preserving the mind and cultivating the personal life, and thus creates trouble for the task of exerting the mind and knowing Heaven. This is to worry for the sage lest his task might be interrupted without knowing how to worry for yourself lest your effort is not yet genuine and concrete. In making efforts, we should have a concentrated mind and a fixed purpose and devote ourselves to the task of not allowing any double-mindedness but cultivating our personal lives while waiting for the mandate to

[20] A *li* is about one third of a mile.

take its own course. This is the beginning of the effort to exert the mind and to know Heaven, just as learning to stand and to take a step is the beginning of learning to run for a thousand *li*. We should worry lest we cannot stand or take a step. Why should we worry about not being able to run a thousand *li* ? How much less should we worry for those who can run for a thousand *li* lest perchance they forget how to stand or to take a step!

Wen-yü, basically your knowledge is advancing vigorously. The way you deliberate, however, shows that you have not been able to rid yourself of the old habit of textual explanation and literal interpretation. Thus you have written these three sections, separating, analyzing, comparing, and combining [the three different steps of exerting the mind, preserving the mind, and not allowing any double-mindedness] with the hope of blending the steps together and harmonizing them. However, you have added many complicating ideas of your own which prevent you from concentrating your effort. This is precisely the defect of the view of recent scholars who try in a vacuum not to forget their objective or to help their mind grow. It is a most serious handicap and most harmful and should be gotten rid of.

193. In the section on honoring the moral nature and following the path of study and inquiry,[21] what you said is without any doubt all perfectly correct and reverts to one truth. You can say what you have said only because you have made genuine and sincere effort. Basically this is not an obscure truth or difficult to understand. People hold on to their different opinions because there is still some little obscuration latent in their innate knowledge. If this little obscuration is removed, it will be perfectly clear.

194. After I had finished my letter to you, my bed was moved under the eaves of the house. Since I do not happen to have anything to do, I have written here some more in answer to your letter. In your learning you have already grasped the fundamentals. The points bothering you should of themselves be clear to you in time, and it should not have been necessary for me to examine them one by one like this. But your regard for me is profound so that you have sent a man a thousand *li* to me and have made most earnest inquiry. Should I disappoint you in your kind intention? I therefore cannot

[21] *Doctrine of the Mean*, ch. 27.

help expressing myself. However, I have spoken too frankly and have bored you with too many details. Counting on your trust and affection for me, I hope you will excuse me. Please make copies and send one each to Wei-chün, Ch'ien-chih,[22] and Ch'ung-i.[23] I shall then be all the more benefited by the good will of all you gentlemen.
The above letters were recorded by Nan Ta-chi.[24]

INSTRUCTIONS FOR LIU PO-SUNG AND OTHERS ON FUNDAMENTAL IDEAS ON ELEMENTARY EDUCATION (Sections 195-200)

In April, 1518, after the rebellion in southern Kiangsi was subdued, Wang established community schools and issued the following instructions and school regulations to teachers. Instead of makeshift measures for expedient rehabilitation, he insisted on the fundamentals of moral training. This is of course entirely consonant with his own philosophy of training the will and emphasizing the essentials. What is more significant in his instructions, however, is the spirit of revolt against the formalistic education prevalent at his time, which consisted of memorization, recitation, and the writing of flowery compositions on the side of learning, and restraint, suppression, and formality on the side of discipline. The spirit of freedom and spontaneity must have been shocking in the early sixteenth century, especially to the orthodox Confucians of the Chu Hsi school. Because of this, the following two short pieces are not included in the sections of official documents (chs.16-18 of the *Wang Wen-ch'eng Kung ch'üan-shu*) but here in the *Instructions for Practical Living*.

195.   In education the ancients taught the fundamental principles of human relations. As the habits of memorization, recitation, and the writing of flowery compositions of later generations arose, the teachings of ancient kings disappeared. In educating young boys today, the sole task should be to teach filial piety, brotherly respect, loyalty, faithfulness, propriety, righteousness, integrity, and the sense of shame. The ways to raise and cultivate them are to lure them

---

[22] See below, sec. 314, n. 99.
[23] See above, sec. 104, n. 23.
[24] The second letter to Nieh Wen-yü (secs. 185 ff.) was recorded by Ch'ien Te-hung, not by Nan Ta-chi. This attribution was intended as an expression of respect.

to singing so their will will be roused, to direct them to practice etiquette so their demeanor will be dignified, and to urge them to read so their intellectual horizon will be widened. Today singing songs and practicing etiquette are often regarded as unrelated to present needs. This is the view of small and vulgar people of this degenerate modern age. How can they know the purpose of the ancients in instituting education?

Generally speaking, it is the nature of young boys to love to play and to dislike restriction. Like plants beginning to sprout, if they are allowed to grow freely, they will develop smoothly. If twisted and interfered with, they will wither and decline. In teaching young boys today, we must make them lean toward rousing themselves so that they will be happy and cheerful at heart, and then nothing can check their development. As in the case of plants, if nourished by timely rain and spring wind, they will all sprout, shoot up, and flourish, and will naturally grow by sunlight and develop under the moon. If ice and frost strip them of leaves, their spirit of life will be dissipated and they will gradually dry up. Therefore, to teach young boys to sing is not merely to rouse their will. It is also to release through singing their [energy as expressed in] jumping around and shouting, and to free them through rhythm from depression and repression. To lead them to practice etiquette is not only to make their demeanor dignified. It is also to exhilarate their blood circulation through such activities as bowing and walking politely, and to strengthen their tendons and bones through kneeling, rising, and extending and contracting their limbs. To urge them to read is not only to widen their intellectual horizon. It is also to preserve their minds through absorption in repeating passages and to express their will through recitation, now loudly and now softly. All this is smoothly to direct their will, adjust and regulate their nature and feelings, quietly to get rid of their meanness and stinginess, and silently to transform their crudeness and mischievousness, so that they will gradually approach propriety and righteousness without feeling that it is difficult to do so and will steep themselves in equilibrium and harmony without knowing why. This is the subtle purpose of the ancient kings in instituting education.

However, in recent generations the teachers of youngsters merely supervise them every day as they recite phrases and sentences and imitate civil service examination papers. They stress restraint and discipline instead of directing their pupils in the practice of propriety.

They emphasize intelligence instead of nourishing goodness. They beat the pupils with a whip and tie them with ropes, treating them like prisoners. The youngsters look upon their school as a prison and refuse to enter. They regard their teachers as enemies and do not want to see them. They avoid this and conceal that in order to satisfy their desire for play and fun. They pretend, deceive, and cheat in order to indulge in mischief and meanness. They become negligent and inferior, and daily degenerate. Such education drives them to do evil. How can they be expected to do good?

In truth the following is my idea of education. I fear that ordinary folk do not understand it and look upon it as being wide of the mark, and moreover, since I am about to leave, I therefore earnestly say to all you teachers: Please understand and follow my idea and forever take it as a counsel to you. Never alter or give up your standard just because ordinary folk may say something against it. Then your effort to cultivate correctness in youngsters will succeed. Please bear this in mind.

School Regulations

196. Every day, early in the morning, after the pupils have assembled and bowed, the teachers should ask all of them one by one whether at home they have been negligent and lacked sincerity and earnestness in their desire to love their parents and to respect their elders, whether they have overlooked or failed to carry out any details in caring for their parents in the summer or the winter, whether in walking along the streets their movements and etiquette have been disorderly or careless, and whether in all their words, acts, and thoughts they have been deceitful or depraved, and not loyal, faithful, sincere, and respectful. All boys must answer honestly. If they have made any mistake, they should correct it. If not, they should devote themselves to greater effort. In addition, the teachers should at all times, and in connection with anything that may occur, use special means to explain and teach them. After that, each pupil should withdraw to his seat and attend to his lessons.

197. In singing, let the pupils be tidy in appearance and calm in expression. Let their voices be clear and distinct. Let their rhythm be even and exact. Let them not be hasty or hurried. Let them not be reckless or disorderly. And let them not sound feeble or timid. In

time their spirits will be free and their minds will be peaceful. Depending on the number of pupils, each school should be divided into four classes. In rotation each class sings on one day, while the others sit down to listen respectfully with a serious expression. Every five days all the four classes will sing one after another in their own school assembly. On the first and the fifteenth day of every month the several schools will assemble to sing together in the academy.

198. In the practice of etiquette, let the pupils be clear in their minds and serious in their thoughts. Let them be careful with details and correct in demeanor. Let them not be negligent or lazy. Let them not be low-spirited or disconcerted. And let them not be uncontrolled or rough. Let them be leisurely but not to the point of being dilatory and be serious but not to the point of being rigid. In time their appearance and behavior will be natural and their moral nature will be firmly established. The order for the pupils to follow should be the same as that in singing. Every other day it will be the turn of one class to practice etiquette, while others are seated to observe respectfully with a serious expression. On the day of etiquette practice, the pupils will be excused from composition. Every ten days all four classes will assemble in their own schools and practice in rotation. On the first and fifteenth day of every month, all schools will assemble and jointly practice in the academy.

199. In reading, the value does not lie in the amount but in learning the material well. Reckoning the pupils' natural endowments, if one can handle two hundred words, teach him only one hundred so that he always has surplus energy and strength and then he will not suffer or feel tired but will have the beauty of being at ease with himself. While reciting the pupils must be concentrated in mind and united in purpose. As they recite with their mouths, let them ponder with their minds. Every word and every phrase should be investigated and gone over again and again. The voice and rhythm should go up and down and their thoughts should be relaxed and empty. In time they will be in harmony with propriety and righteousness and their intelligence will gradually unfold.

200. In the daily work first examine the pupils' moral conduct. Next let them repeat their old lessons and recite new ones. Then

comes the practice of etiquette or composition, then repeating and recitation again, and finally singing. The practice of etiquette, singing, and so forth is intended to preserve the boys' minds so that they enjoy their study without getting tired and have no time for bad conduct. If teachers know this principle, they will know what to do. However, these are the essentials. "To see the spirit [of changes and transformations] and manifest them depends on the proper men."[1]

[1] *Book of Changes*, "Appended Remarks," pt. 1, ch. 12. Cf. trans. by Legge, *Yi King*, p. 378.

Instructions for Practical Living, Part III

201. In the tenth year of Cheng-te [1515] I first saw our Teacher in Lung-chiang.² He was then discussing with Master Kan-ch'üan³ the doctrine of the investigation of things. Kan-ch'üan held the old theory.⁴ The Teacher said, "That is to seek principles in external things."

Kan-ch'üan said, "If you consider the investigation of the principles of things as external, you are belittling your mind."

I was much delighted to hear that the old theory was correct. Then our Teacher discoursed on the chapter on exerting the mind to the utmost.⁵ As soon as I heard that, I no longer doubted that the old theory was wrong.

Later, when I was staying home, I further inquired of our Teacher by letter on the doctrine of the investigation of things. He replied,

---

¹ Ch'en Chiu-ch'uan (1495-1562), whose courtesy name was Wei-chün and literary name Ming-shui. A "presented scholar" of 1514, he was appointed erudite scholar in the board of imperial sacrifices. Because he urged the emperor to cancel a projected pleasure-seeking tour, he was beaten with fifty strokes and was dismissed. Later he became a division chief of the department of rites. Because he opposed waste in expenditure, he was hated by wicked officials who brought about his imprisonment. However, eventually he was reinstated. For an account of him, see Ming-ju hsüeh-an, 19:15b-19b.

² Now Nanking.

³ The literary name of Chan Jo-shui (1471-1555), a native of Kwangtung. Holder of a "presented scholar" degree of 1505, he rose to be minister of the departments of rites, civil personnel, and military affairs successively. As an outstanding Neo-Confucian of his time, he had followers from all parts of China. He advocated the doctrine that "the Principle of Nature should be genuinely and earnestly realized wherever one may be." Wang criticized this doctrine as seeking principles externally. Chan replied that to realize the principle wherever one may be means to do so whether in connection with the self, the family, or the state and in the condition either before or after the feelings are aroused, and charged that Wang taught investigating things in the mind. For an account of him, see Ming-ju hsüeh-an, ch. 37.

⁴ That of Chu Hsi that principles are to be sought in things and not in the mind.

⁵ Book of Mencius, 7A:1.

"If you can only make earnest and sincere effort, in time you will understand."[6] There in the mountains I myself copied the old text of the *Great Learning* and studied it. I felt that Chu Hsi's doctrine of the investigation of things was wrong. However, I also felt that our Teacher's theory that wherever the will is directed it is a thing[7] did not make clear what a thing was.

In the fourteenth year of Cheng-te [1519], I was returning from the capital and saw our Teacher again in Hung-tu.[8] He was extremely busy with military affairs. Whenever he had a moment of leisure, he discussed things with me and instructed me. First of all he asked about my efforts in recent years. I said, "In recent years I have realized through personal experience that the task of manifesting the clear character consists only in making the will sincere. I believed that if one pushed step by step from manifesting the clear character to the world back to the source, then one would arrive at the task of making the will sincere. One cannot go any further. I wondered why it was that before making the will sincere there had to be the two further steps of extending knowledge and investigating things. Later I again personally realized that one must first be aware whether his will is sincere or not. I used as proof the fact that whenever Yen Hui [Confucius' most virtuous pupil] did anything wrong, he never failed to realize it and, having realized it, never did it again.[9] I felt completely clear as though without a doubt. However, I still felt the task of the investigation of things (*ko-wu*) to be superfluous. Then upon further thinking, I realized that the human mind is intelligent and cannot fail to know whether one's will is good or evil. However, because it is obscured by material (*wu*) desires [selfish desires for external things, it sometimes does not function freely]. Therefore it is necessary to purge (*ko*) the mind of material (*wu*) desire before one can resemble Yen Hui in never failing to realize the wrong things one does. But then I suspected that [in thus making efforts to investigate things and extend knowledge before making the will sincere] the procedure was upside down and that these efforts did not form

[6] This correspondence is no longer extant.

[7] See above, sec. 6.

[8] Now Nan-ch'ang.

[9] According to the *Book of Changes*, "Appended Remarks," pt. 2, ch. 5. Cf. trans. by Legge, *Yi King*, p. 392.

a unity with making the will sincere. Later I asked Hsi-yen[10] about it. He said, 'According to our Teacher, the investigation of things and the extension of knowledge are tasks to make the will sincere. This teaching is excellent.' I said, 'What is the task of making the will sincere?' He told me to think again and personally realize and then see. But to the end I did not understand. Please explain to me."

The Teacher said, "How pitiable! This can be understood in one utterance, namely, the story you told about Yen Hui. The important thing to know is that the personal life, the mind, the will, knowledge, and things are one."

I was doubtful and said, "A thing is external. How can it be the same as the personal life, the mind, the will, and knowledge?"

The Teacher said, "The ears, the eyes, the mouth, the nose, and the four limbs are parts of the body. But how can they see, hear, speak, or act without the mind? On the other hand, without the ears, the eyes, the mouth, the nose, and the four limbs, the mind cannot see, hear, speak, or act when it wants to. Therefore if there is no mind, there will be no body, and if there is no body, there will be no mind. As something occupying space, it is called the body. As the master, it is called the mind. As the operation of the mind, it is called the will. As the intelligence and clear consciousness of the will, it is called knowledge. And as the object to which the will is attached, it is called a thing. They are all one piece. The will never exists in a vacuum. It is always connected with some thing or event. Therefore if one wants to make his will sincere, he should rectify (*ko*) it right in the thing or event to which the will is directed, get rid of selfish human desires, and return to the Principle of Nature. Then in connection with this thing or event the innate knowledge will be free from obscuration and can be fully extended. This is the task of making the will sincere." Thereupon my doubts of several years were completely dispelled.

I inquired further and said, "Recently Kan-ch'üan also accepted the old text of the *Great Learning*. He declares that the investigation of things is like arriving at a road. He also declares that the investigation of the principles of things to the utmost is like going to the innermost part of a den. It means that one must arrive at the destination personally. Therefore he contends that the investigation of things is

[10] Nothing is known of him.

nothing but 'personally realizing the Principle of Nature wherever one may be.' It seems that his theory is getting to be like yours."

The Teacher said, "Kan-ch'üan has made some effort and therefore has been able to change his position. At the time when I remarked to him that the word *ch'in* need not be changed,[11] he would not believe me. His present view on the investigation of things is, generally speaking, nearer to the truth, but it is not necessary for him to substitute the word 'principle' for the word 'thing'. Let the word 'thing' be restored and his doctrine will be correct."

Later someone asked me, "Why is no question raised on the word 'thing'?"

I said, "In the *Doctrine of the Mean* it is said, 'Without sincerity there will be nothing.'[12] Master Ch'eng Hao said, 'Respond spontaneously to all things as they come.'[13] Also 'Leave things as they are,'[14] 'Harbor nothing in the mind,'[15] and so forth. The word 'thing' has often been used by scholars of the past." On another day, the Teacher also agreed.

202. I said, "In recent years I have gotten tired of extensive but cursory learning and have often wanted to sit quietly and stop all thoughts and deliberations. Not only was I unable to do so; I was troubled all the more. Why?"

The Teacher said, "How can thoughts be stopped? They should only be corrected."

"Should there be times when thoughts are absent?"

The Teacher said, "There is really no time when thoughts are absent."

"In that case, how can one speak of tranquillity?"

"Tranquillity is not without activity and activity is not without tranquillity. Caution and apprehension are all thoughts. Is there any distinction between activity and tranquillity in them?"

"Why did Master Chou Tun-i say, 'The sage settles (*ting*, calms)

---

[11] See above, sec. 1. Ch'eng I and Chu Hsi had advocated that the word *ch'in*, in the sentence from the *Great Learning*, "The way to manifest the clear character consists in loving the people (*ch'in-min*)" should be changed to *hsin* [to renovate the people].

[12] Ch. 25.

[13] *Wen-chi*, 3:1a.

[14] Ch'eng I, *I-shu*, 18:15b.

[15] This is a general paraphrase, rather than a quotation of any definite saying.

human affairs by the principles of the mean, correctness, humanity, and righteousness, and regards tranquillity as fundamental'?"[16]

"One is tranquil because one has no desires.[17] The word *ting* is the same one used in Ch'eng Hao's saying that 'the nature is calm whether it is in a state of activity or in a state of tranquillity.'[18] To regard it as fundamental means to regard one's original substance as fundamental. The thoughts of caution and apprehension are lively ones. This is where the secret way of nature never ceases. 'The mandate of Heaven is profound and unceasing.'[19] If the thoughts stop for a single moment, they will be dead. They will not be the thoughts of one's original substance but selfish thoughts."

203. I further said, "When in devoting oneself to one's task one gathers his mind and there are music and women in front of him, if he notices them as usual, I am afraid his mind is not concentrated."

"How can one expect not to hear or see them unless he is dry wood or dead ashes, or deaf and blind? The right thing to do is to hear and see them but not to be driven by them."

"Formerly someone was engaged in sitting in meditation. His son was studying in the next room and he did not know whether the boy was diligent or lazy. Master Ch'eng I praised him as being very serious and reverential.[20] What do you think?"

"I-ch'uan [Ch'eng I] was probably ridiculing him."

204. I further said, "In devoting myself to sitting in meditation, I feel to some extent that my mind is collected and concentrated. As some affair occurs, however, the concentration is interrupted. Then I make up my mind to examine [principles] in that affair. When that is over, I return to the former task of sitting in meditation. Still I feel that the internal and external aspects of the mind are not blended into one."

The Teacher said, "This shows you have not thoroughly understood the doctrine of the investigation of things. The mind has neither internal nor external aspects. For instance, you are now having a discussion with me. Is there a mind within you to take care

[16] *Chou Lien-hsi chi*, 1:2a.
[17] *Ibid.*
[18] *Wen-chi*, 3:1a.
[19] *Book of Odes*, no. 267.
[20] *I-shu*, 3:5a.

of this discussion? When you are talking and your mind concentrates on being serious, it is the same mind as when you are engaged in sitting in meditation. The task is a continuous and unified one. What is the need of making up the mind on top of it? One must be trained and polished in the actual affairs of life. Only when the effort is made that way will it be beneficial. If one merely likes tranquillity, he will get confused whenever anything happens and will never progress. The effort made during sitting in meditation will also be ineffective. The mind will seem to be collected and concentrated but in reality will be scattered and lost."

Later in Hung-tu I again discussed the theory of the internal and the external with Wang Yü-chung[21] and Shu Kuo-shang.[22] Both of them said that things naturally have their internal and external aspects, but that one's effort should be directed to both of them without making any distinction between them. I asked the Teacher about this and he said, "The task should never depart from the original substance, and the original substance from the beginning makes no distinction between the internal and the external. Only because in their devotion to the task people of later generations make such a distinction do they lose their original substance. It is now necessary to explain that only that kind of task which makes no distinction between the internal and the external can be the task devoted to the original substance." On that day all of us realized some new truth.

205.   I further asked, "What do you think of the teachings of Master Lu Hsiang-shan?"

The Teacher said, "Since the time of Lien-hsi [Chou Tun-i] and Ming-tao [Ch'eng Hao], there has been only Lu Hsiang-shan. But he was still somewhat crude."

I said, "In his elucidations, every chapter reveals the innermost

---

[21] We have no more information about him.

[22] Shu Fen (1484-1527), holder of a "presented scholar" degree of 1517. He was appointed an official historian. Because he urged the emperor not to make a proposed pleasure-seeking tour, he was punished by being made to kneel for three days and being beaten thirty strokes and then banished to an inferior position in Fukien. Reinstated later, he was imprisoned because he opposed the emperor's plan to confer on the emperor's father the posthumous title "August Ancestor" which Shu Fen felt should go to the emperor's uncle. For an account of him, see *Ming-ju hsüeh-an*, 53:13b-16a.

fundamentals [of what is right] and every sentence seems to attack the underlying causes [of what is wrong]. He does not seem to be crude."

The Teacher said, "He had made some effort in his mind and was of course different from those who imitated others, depended on others, or sought only literal meanings. However, if you scrutinize his doctrines carefully, you will find there are crude spots. You will see if you continue your effort long enough."

206. In the fifteenth year of Cheng-te [1520], I went to Ch'ien-chou[23] and saw our Teacher again. I said, "In my recent efforts, although I seem to know the basis somewhat, I have found it difficult to have any sense of security or joy."

The Teacher said, "But you go to your mind to seek the Principle of Nature. This is what the Buddhists call 'obscuration by principle.'[24] There is a secret in this matter."

"What is it, please?"

"It is nothing but the extension of knowledge."

"How does one extend knowledge?"

"Your innate knowledge is your own standard. When you direct your thought your innate knowledge knows that it is right if it is right and wrong if it is wrong. You cannot keep anything from it. Just don't try to deceive it but sincerely and truly follow it in whatever you do. Then the good will be preserved and evil will be removed. What security and joy there is in this! This is the true secret of the investigation of things and the real effort of the extension of knowledge. If you do not rely on this true secret, how can you proceed to investigate things? I have only in recent years realized this through personal experience and become so clear about it. At first I was still suspicious that relying on it alone would not be sufficient. But after I had examined it carefully I found nothing wanting in it."

207. Wang Yü-chung, Tsou Ch'ien-chih,[25] and I were in attendance together in Ch'ien-chou. The Teacher said, "There is the sage in

[23] In southern Kiangsi.

[24] That is, not knowing that the mind itself is principle but seeking it in the mind so that principle itself becomes an obstacle. *Yüan-chiao ching*, in the *Taishō daizōkyō*, 17:16.

[25] See below, sec. 314, n. 99.

everyone. Only one has not enough self-confidence and buries his own chance." Thereupon he looked at Yü-chung and said, "From the beginning there is the sage in you." Yü-chung rose and said that he did not deserve it.

The Teacher said, "This potentiality originally belongs to you. Why decline?"

Yü-chung said again, "I do not deserve it."

The Teacher said, "Everyone has this potentiality. How much more is that true of you, Yü-chung! Why be so modest? It won't do even if you are modest." Whereupon Yü-chung smiled and accepted the compliment.

The Teacher further discoursed, "No matter what man does, innate knowledge is in him and cannot be destroyed. Even a thief realizes in himself that he should not be a thief. If you call him a thief, he will still blush."

Yü-chung said, "One's innate knowledge can only be obscured by material desires. It is within him and can never be lost. Similarly clouds may of course obscure the sun but the sun is never lost."

The Teacher said, "How brilliant is Yü-chung! Others do not see it so clearly."

208.   The Teacher said, "If you see this little thing [innate knowledge] clearly, no matter how much and how eloquently one may talk, all right and wrong, sincerity and insincerity in what he says are manifested right in front of it. What is in accord with it is right and what is not in accord with it is wrong. It is like what the Buddhists call the 'spiritual seal.'[26] It is truly a gold-testing stone and a compass."

209.   The Teacher said, "If people know the true secret of this innate knowledge, no matter how many evil thoughts and wrong desires there may be, as soon as it realizes them they will all disappear of themselves. It is truly a highly effective medicine, one touch of which will turn iron into gold."[27]

210.   Ou-yang Ch'ung-i[28] said, "Sir, your principle of the extension of knowledge expresses all that is excellent and deep. As we see it, one cannot go any further."

---

[26] The Buddha-mind in all men which can seal or assure the truth, or the intuitive mind independent of any spoken or written word.

[27] A Taoist expression.

[28] See above, sec. 104, n. 23.

The Teacher said, "Why speak of it so lightly? Make a further effort for another half year and see how it is. Then make an effort for another year and see how it is. The longer one makes an effort, the more different it will become. This is something difficult to explain in words."

211. The Teacher asked me about my progress in personally realizing the doctrine of the extension of knowledge. I said, "I feel that there has been a difference. Formerly when I tried to practice moral principles, I was never able to do just as I wanted. Now I can do so."

The Teacher said, "From this we can know that knowledge acquired through personal realization is different from that acquired through listening to discussions. When I first lectured on the subject, I knew you took it lightly and were not interested. However, when one goes further and realizes this essential and wonderful thing personally to its very depth, he will see that it becomes different every day and is inexhaustible." He further said, "This phrase, 'the extension of knowledge,' is truly a secret transmitted from the sages of thousands of years ago. If we realize this, [we know that] it can wait a hundred generations for a sage to confirm it without a doubt."[29]

212. I asked, "When I-ch'uan [Ch'eng I] reached the point of saying that 'substance and function come from the same source' and 'there is no gap between the manifest and the hidden,'[30] his students said that he divulged the secret of nature.[31] Doesn't your doctrine of the extension of knowledge, sir, also go too far in divulging the secret of nature?"

The Teacher said, "The Sage has already shown it to people. Only it has been hidden by later generations and I now bring it to light. Why speak of divulging any secret? This [innate knowledge] is everybody's natural possession. When one realizes it it seems to be nothing extraordinary. If one talks about it with those who do not exert any real and genuine effort, they will take it most lightly, and, to our regret, it will do neither party any good. But to talk to those

---

[29] Quoting the *Doctrine of the Mean*, ch. 29.
[30] Preface to the *I chuan*. See above, sec. 156, n. 11.
[31] *Wai-shu*, 12:8a

who have made real and genuine effort but have not found the essentials, and to help them bring themselves forward, is vastly effective."

213. The Teacher further said, "In reality knowledge and realization come without our knowing or realizing. However, if we don't know this, we will be lost."[32]

214. The Teacher said, "In general, among friends there should be little admonishing and fault-finding, but much directing and encouraging." Later he further cautioned me, saying, "In discussing learning with friends, one should be accommodating, be humble, and dwell broad-mindedly in what one has learned."[33]

215. I was sick in bed in Ch'ien-chou. The Teacher said, "This thing, sickness, is also difficult to rectify (*ko*). How do you feel?"
I replied, "The task is very difficult."
The Teacher said, "Always be cheerful. That is the task."

216. I said, "In my self-examination and deliberations, I sometimes drift into depraved and erroneous thoughts and sometimes imagine various ways and means of managing the affairs of the world. When these thoughts reach the highest point, they come in orderly succession and are most absorbing, and then I am bound by them and cannot get rid of them. If I realize the situation early, it is easy to dispel them, but if I realize it late, it is difficult. The more I apply my strength to overcoming them, the greater the obstacles seem to be. But to some extent if I shift my thoughts to other things, then both [those erroneous thoughts and my effort to overcome them] will be forgotten. It seems to me that to purge my mind completely in this way will do no harm."
The Teacher said, "What is the necessity for this? You need only direct your effort to innate knowledge."
I said, "The trouble is that just at those moments I fail to know how to direct the effort."
The Teacher said, "If one makes effort in his own mind, how can

[32] That is, one should be spontaneous in knowledge but not unconscious like the Buddhists.
[33] Quoting the *Book of Changes*, commentary on hexagram no. 1. Cf. trans. by Legge, *Yi King*, p. 416.

that happen? It is only because your effort is interrupted that innate knowledge is obscured. If the effort is interrupted, the thing to do is to continue the former effort [to extend innate knowledge]. What is the necessity for this [trying to overcome erroneous thoughts or shifting to other things]?"

I said, "It is simply difficult to fight them. Although I know they should be discarded, I can't do it."

The Teacher said, "It is necessary to have courage. If you exert effort long enough, you will have it. It is therefore said, 'The vital force is produced by the accumulation of righteous deeds.'[34] Those who succeed easily are men of great virtue."

217. I said, "This task can be clearly understood in my mind through personal realization, but it does not make sense according to books."

The Teacher said, "It is only necessary for it to make sense to the mind. If the mind understands it, books will surely come along. If it does not make sense to the mind but only does so according to a literal interpretation of books, then one will have all kinds of subjective ideas."

218. A certain subordinate official, having heard for a long time our Teacher's exposition on learning, said, "This learning is very good. Unfortunately, my duties of keeping records and presiding over litigations are so heavy that I cannot pursue it."

When the Teacher heard this he said, "When did I teach you to drop your work of keeping records and presiding over litigations and then to pursue learning in a vacuum? Since you have your official duties, you should pursue learning right in those official duties. Only then will you be truly investigating things. For instance, when you interrogate a litigant, do not become angry because his replies are impolite or become glad because his words are smooth; do not purposely punish him because you hate his effort to solicit help from your superiors; do not bend your will and yield to him because of his pleading; do not decide the case carelessly on the spur of the moment because you are too busy with your own trifling affairs; and do not settle it according to the opinions of others because people on the side praise you, criticize you, or are building

---

[34] *Book of Mencius*, 2A:2.

up a case against you. To do any of these is selfish. You need only follow what you know yourself. You must carefully examine yourself and control yourself, lest your mind become in the least prejudiced and destroy the truth as to who is right and who is wrong. This is the investigation of things and the extension of knowledge. Among the duties of keeping records and presiding over litigations, there is none that is not concrete learning. If learning has to be done outside of things and events, it will be something in a vacuum."

219. As I was leaving Ch'ien-chou to go home, I wrote a poem to bid our Teacher farewell, which read:

Innate knowledge has nothing to do with hearing much.
At the time of mysterious union [of the active element
      yang and the passive element yin and the five agents
      of metal, wood, water, fire, and earth] the root was
      already planted.
If we follow it in our likes and dislikes, that is the
      learning of the Sage.
When we do not lean forward or backward to accommodate things,
      there is the Principle of Heaven [foundation of truth].

The Teacher said, "Before you came here to discuss this learning [innate knowledge], I don't know what you might have meant if you said, 'Follow it in our likes and dislikes.' "

Fu-ying,[35] who was in attendance, said, "How true! I used to read your preface to the old text of the *Great Learning*,[36] sir, and did not know what you were talking about. After I came to listen to your lectures for some time, I began to have some general idea."

220. Wang Yü-chung and Shu Kuo-shang were accompanying the Teacher at dinner. He said, "The use of all food is solely to nourish the body. After it is eaten, it must be digested. If it accumulates in the stomach, it will cause constipation. How can it build up muscles? Scholars of later generations acquire extensive information and much knowledge, and keep them in their stomachs undigested. All this is a disease resulting from harmful eating."

[35] We have no more information on this man.
[36] This preface is found in *Wang Wen-ch'eng Kung ch'üan-shu*, 7:25a-26a.

221. The Teacher said, "The sage also learns through study. Ordinary people are also born with knowledge."

I asked, "How is that?"

He said, "All people have this innate knowledge. Only the sage preserves it completely and keeps it free from the least obscuration. He is cautious, careful, tirelessly diligent, and of course never stops in these efforts. This is already study. Only because with him the product of inborn knowledge is greater, he is therefore said to be born with knowledge and to practice it naturally and easily. Ordinary people possess this innate knowledge in total from infancy, except that it is much obscured. But the knowledge of the original substance [of the mind] cannot be obliterated. Even study and self-control depend on it. Because with ordinary people the proportion of knowledge acquired through study is greater, they are therefore said to learn through study and to practice it for its advantage."[37]

CONVERSATIONS RECORDED BY HUANG I-FANG[1] (Sections 222-236)

222. I asked, "Sir, according to your doctrine of the investigation of things and the extension of knowledge, one should investigate things at any time in order to extend knowledge. If so, the knowledge extended is only a part and not the entirety. How can it reach the state described as 'all embracing and extensive as heaven and deep and unceasingly springing as an abyss'?"[2]

The Teacher said, "The human mind is heaven and it is the abyss. The original substance of the mind contains everything. In reality it is the whole heaven. Only because it is hidden by selfish desires is the original substance of heaven lost. The principle of the mind is infinite. In reality it is the whole abyss. Only because it is obstructed by selfish desires is the original substance of the abyss lost. Now if

---

[37] See *Doctrine of the Mean*, ch. 20.

[1] His private name was Chih. Otherwise, nothing is known of him. The general practice was to use one's private name instead of saying "I." In sec. 222, however, his courtesy name is used, contrary to general practice. Most probably the courtesy name was substituted for the private name when Ch'ien Te-hung edited the book.

[2] As described in the *Doctrine of the Mean*, ch. 31.

one extends the innate knowledge in every thought and removes all these hindrances and obstacles, its original substance will be recovered and right then it will become both heaven and abyss." Thereupon he pointed to heaven, saying, "For instance, we see heaven in front of us. It is bright and clear heaven. If we see heaven outside the house, it is the same bright and clear heaven. Only because it is obscured by these many walls of the building do we not see heaven in its entirety. If we tear down the walls, we will see only one heaven. We should not say that what is in front of us is the bright and clear heaven but what is outside the house is not. From this we know that the knowledge of a part is the same as the knowledge of the whole, and the knowledge of the whole is the same as the knowledge of a part. All is but one original substance."

223. The Teacher said, "Sages and worthies are not without achievements or moral integrity. But since they are in accord with the Principle of Nature, they represent the Way itself. Therefore their fame does not rest merely in achievements or moral integrity."

224. [The Teacher said,] "Confucius 'forgot his food when engaged in vigorous pursuit of something' because his purpose was like this and he really had no time to lose. He was so 'happy as to forget his worries,'[3] because his Way was like this and he was really without a moment of sorrow. It is not necessary to say whether he succeeded or not."[4]

225. The Teacher said, "In the extension of knowledge, we should do so according to our capacity. Here is our innate knowledge today. We should extend it to the utmost according to what we know today. As our innate knowledge is further developed tomorrow, we should extend it to the utmost according to what we know then. Only this can be said to be the task of refinement and single-mindedness. In discussing learning with others we should also do so according to their capacity. For instance, when the tree has sprouted only a little, give it a little water. As the sprout grows, give it more water. From the time that the tree stem can be encircled by the fingers

[3] *Analects*, 7:18.
[4] Chu Hsi had contended that the Sage made vigorous pursuit before success was achieved and was happy afterwards. *Lun-yü chi-chu*, ch. 4, comment on *Analects*, 7:18.

of one hand and then by those of two hands to the time when it can be encircled by both arms, the watering should be done according to its capacity to absorb. Suppose there is but a small sprout and here is a pail of water. If all the water is poured over it, it will be drenched to death."

226. I asked about the unity of knowledge and action. The Teacher said, "You need to understand the basic purpose of my doctrine.In their learning people of today separate knowledge and action into two different things. Therefore when a thought is aroused, although it is evil, they do not stop it because it has not been translated into action. I advocate the unity of knowledge and action precisely because I want people to understand that when a thought is aroused it is already action. If there is anything evil when the thought is aroused, one must overcome the evil thought. One must go to the root and go to the bottom and not allow that evil thought to lie latent in his mind. This is the basic purpose of my doctrine."

227. [The Teacher said,] "That the sage is omniscient merely means that he knows the Principle of Nature and that he is omnipotent merely means that he is able to practice the Principle of Nature. The original substance of the mind of the sage is clear and therefore in all things he knows where the Principle of Nature lies and forthwith carries it out to the utmost. It is not that after the original substance of his mind becomes clear he then knows all the things in the world and is able to carry all of them out. Things in the world, such as the names, varieties, and systems, and plants and animals, are innumerable. Although the original substance of the sage is very clear, how can he know everything?[5] What is not necessary to know, he does not have to seek to know. What he should know, he naturally asks others, like Confucius, who, when he entered the grand temple, asked about everything.[6] A former scholar said that the fact that although Confucius knew he still asked shows he was perfectly serious and careful.[7] Such an interpretation is absurd. A sage does not have to know all the names and varieties of ceremonies and music. But since he knows the

[5] Reading *hsü* [must] as *sui* [although].
[6] *Analects*, 3:15.
[7] Yin T'un (1061-1132,) quoted by Chu Hsi in his *Lun-yü chi-chu*, ch. 2, comment on *Analects*, 3:15.

Principle of Nature, all measures, regulations, and details can be deduced from it. The fact that when he did not know he asked shows how the measure and pattern of the Principle of Nature operates."

228. I asked, "Sir, you once said that good and evil are one thing.[8] But good and evil are opposed to each other like ice and burning coals. How can they be said to be only one?"

The Teacher said, "The highest good is the original substance of the mind. When one deviates a little from this original substance, there is evil. It is not that there is a good and there is also an evil to oppose it. Therefore good and evil are one thing."

Having heard our Teacher's explanation, I know that we can no longer doubt Master Ch'eng Hao's sayings, "Man's nature is of course good, but it cannot be said that evil is not his nature"[9] and "Good and evil in the world are both the Principle of Nature. What is called evil is not originally evil. It becomes evil only because of deviation from the mean."[10]

229. The Teacher once said that to be a sage one simply has to love good as he loves beautiful colors and hate evil as he hates a bad smell.[11] When I first heard it, I felt it was very easy. But as I proceeded to realize it through personal experience, I found this task to be really difficult. For instance, although in an instant of thought I know that I should love good and hate evil, yet unconsciously the thought gets mixed and impure. As soon as it is mixed and impure, the mind is no longer that which loves good as it loves beautiful colors and hates evil as it hates a bad smell. If one really and earnestly loves good, then all his thoughts will be good, and if one really and earnestly hates evil, then none of his thoughts will approach evil. Why should such a man not be be a sage? Therefore to learn to become a sage requires sincerity and sincerity only.

230. I said, "Sir, in your 'Essay on Cultivating the Way'[12] you say in effect that 'To follow our nature is called the Way' refers to the

[8] Cf. above, sec. 101.
[9] *I-shu*, 1:7b.
[10] *Ibid.*, 2A:1b.
[11] Cf. above, sec. 5.
[12] "Hsiu-tao lun," in *Wang Wen-ch'eng Kung ch'üan-shu*, 7:60a-b.

function of the sage, while the saying 'Cultivating the Way is called education'[13] refers to the function of the worthy. [Please explain.]"

The Teacher said, "Ordinary people also fulfill their nature. But fulfilling nature is more the function of a sage. Therefore 'To fulfill our nature is called the Way' refers to the function of the sage. The sage also cultivates the Way. But cultivating the Way is more the function of the worthy. Therefore 'The cultivation of the Way is called education' refers to the function of the worthy." He further said, "Generally speaking, the entire *Doctrine of the Mean* talks about the cultivation of the Way. Therefore when it later talks about the superior man, about Yen Hui, and about Tzu-lu, it deals with those who could cultivate the Way. When it talks about the inferior man, about those who are wise or stupid, worthy or unworthy, and about the common folk, it deals with those who are unable to cultivate the Way. And aside from these, when it talks about Emperor Shun, King Wen, Duke Chou, Confucius, and those who are perfectly sincere and perfectly sagely, it deals with sages who can naturally cultivate the Way."

231. I asked, "When midnight comes and a Confucian wipes out all thoughts and deliberations from his mind, there will be only emptiness and tranquillity, which is no different from the tranquillity of the Buddhists. If at this moment he entertains neither thoughts and deliberations nor emptiness and tranquillity, what is the difference between the Confucian and the Buddhist?"

The Teacher said, "Activity and tranquillity are one. If it is in accord with the Principle of Nature, the mind that is empty and tranquil at midnight will be the same mind that responds to events and deals with affairs now. If it is in accord with the Principle of Nature, the mind that responds to events and deals with affairs now is the same mind that is empty and tranquil at midnight. Therefore activity and tranquillity are one and cannot be separated. If we know that activity and tranquillity form a unity, the fact that the Buddhist's infinitesimal mistake at the beginning leads to an infinite error in the end cannot be concealed."

232. Among the followers in attendance one was exceedingly serious in his disposition. The Teacher said, "If one goes too far in

[13] *Doctrine of the Mean*, ch. 1.

being serious, it will be a defect in the end." I said, "Why is excessive seriousness a defect?"

The Teacher said, "Man's mental energy is limited. If one is devoted solely to his appearance, there will be many occasions when he neglects his mind."

One follower was too straightforward. The Teacher said, "As we are engaged in this discussion on learning, you are not attentive to your appearance at all. Thus you have separated the mind and events."

233. A student wrote an essay to bid farewell to a friend. He said to the Teacher, "Composition requires much thought. After it is finished, it lingers in the memory for a day or two."

The Teacher said, "It does no harm to think when writing. But if after it is finished it is always kept in mind, then writing will be a hindrance to you. There will be something in your mind and that won't do."

The student further wrote a poem of farewell. After reading the poem, the Teacher said, "Whenever one writes, one should do so within the limit of his capacity. If one is too excessive in expression, then one will not be carefully employing his words or establishing his sincerity."[14]

234. [The Teacher said,] "In his doctrine of the investigation of things, Wen Kung [Chu Hsi] lacked a basis. For instance, he said [that among the methods of investigating things] is 'the examination of one's subtle thoughts and deliberations.' [Being the most fundamental,] this should not be grouped together with 'searching for the principles of things in books,' 'testing them in one's conspicuous activities,' and 'finding them out in discussion.'[15] He lacked a sense of relative importance."

235. I asked about the statement, "Whenever one is affected by wrath to any extent [his mind will not be correct]."[16]

The Teacher said, "How can the human mind be free from anger,

---

[14] Quoting the *Book of Changes*, commentary on hexagram no. 1. Cf. trans. by Legge, *Yi King*, p. 410.

[15] *Ta-hsüeh huo-wen*, pp. 58b-59a.

[16] *Great Learning*, ch. 7.

and so forth? But it should not have them. When one shows even a little bit of feeling of wrath, his anger is excessive and his mind is no longer the original substance that is broad and extremely impartial.[17] Therefore, whenever one is affected by wrath to any extent, his mind will not be correct. Now with regard to wrath and so forth, if one can only respond to all things spontaneously as they come[18] and show not a bit of subjective feeling, the nature of his mind will be broad and extremely impartial and will naturally attain the correctness characteristic of its original substance. Suppose we go outside and find some people fighting. We all feel angry in our minds at the party who is wrong. However, although we are angry, our minds are broad and our vital force is not perturbed in the least. This is the way to be angry at people. Only in this way can we be correct."

236. The Teacher once said, "Buddhism claims to be free from attachment to phenomenal things but actually the opposite is the case. We Confucians seem to be attached to phenomenal things but in reality the opposite is true." I asked him for an explanation. He said, "The Buddhists are afraid of the burden in the relationship between father and son and therefore escape from it. They are afraid of the burden in the relationship between ruler and minister and therefore escape from it. They are afraid of the burden in the relationship between husband and wife and therefore escape from it. In all cases, because the relationships between ruler and minister, father and son, and husband and wife involve attachment to phenomena, they have to escape from them. We Confucians accept the relationship between father and son and fulfill it with the humanity it deserves. We accept the relationship between ruler and minister and fulfill it with the righteousness it deserves. We accept the relationship between husband and wife and fulfill it with the attention to their separate functions it deserves. When have we been attached to these relations?"

[17] Quoting Ch'eng Hao, *Wen-chi*, 3:1a.
[18] *Ibid.*

CONVERSATIONS RECORDED BY HUANG MIEN-SHU[1] (Sections 237-247)

237. I asked, "When the mind is free from evil thoughts, it is empty and vast. Should we then harbor a good thought?"

The Teacher said, "As evil thoughts are eliminated, the good thought is already there and the original substance of the mind is already restored. It is like the sunlight which is obscured by clouds. When the clouds are gone, the sunlight appears again. If after evil thoughts are gone one then harbors a good thought, it would be like adding a lamp to sunlight."

238. I said, "In my recent efforts, I seem to feel that erroneous thoughts no longer arise. But within me there is still something pitch-dark. What can be done to turn it into light?"

The Teacher said, "In the first stage of the task how can one expect to be clear within? Take for example some turbid water from a rapid current. When it has just been stored in a jar, although at this beginning state it is settled, it is still murky and turbid. We must wait till it has been still for a long time and then the dregs will naturally all be gone and the water will be all clear once more. You have only to exert effort in your innate knowledge. As innate knowledge is preserved for a long time, the pitch-darkness will naturally become clear. If you demanded results right away, you would be making an artificial effort to help it grow.[2] And the task would be no good."

239. The Teacher said, "I teach people to devote their efforts to the investigation of things in extending their innate knowledge. It is learning with a foundation. The longer one engages in the task, advancing every day, the more intelligent he will be. Famous but mediocre scholars, on the other hand, teach people to search for the principles of each and every thing. Their learning is entirely without foundation. When one is young one can temporarily put up a good front and does not seem to be mistaken. But when he gets old his mental energy will decline and he will ultimately collapse. It is like a tree without a root. When it is transplanted to a place near water,

---

[1] His courtesy name was Hsiu-i. Otherwise, nothing is known of him.
[2] Quoting the *Book of Mencius*, 2A:2.

although temporarily it looks fresh and beautiful, in time it will finally wither."

240. I inquired about the chapter in the *Analects* on "Setting your will on the Way."[3]

The Teacher said, "This expression alone involves the forms of efforts that follow in the chapter.[4] One cannot just stop here.

"Take for instance building this house. Setting your will on the Way means setting the mind constantly on selecting the plot, collecting the material, planning and completing this small house. Having a firm grasp on virtue means that the completed plan can firmly be grasped. Relying on humanity means always to live in this small house without leaving, and finding recreation in the arts means to add decorations to the house to beautify it. By arts (*i*) is meant righteousness (*i,*), what is proper according to principle. Activities like reciting poems, reading books, playing the lute, and practicing archery are all intended to regulate the mind so that it will be at home with the Way. If one finds recreation in the arts without first setting the will on the Way, he will be like a worthless fellow who does not first build a house but attends only to buying pictures to hang up for show. I don't know where he is going to hang them."

241. I said, "Reading is indispensable to the recuperation and refreshment of the mind. However, while I read, certain ideas associated with questions in civil service examinations keep on coming up. How can I avoid that?"

The Teacher said, "So long as your innate knowledge is genuine and earnest, even if you engage in preparing for civil service examinations, it will not be a source of trouble for your mind. Or, even if it is, it will be easy to realize and overcome it. Take this matter of reading. Innate knowledge knows that it is wrong to try to force oneself to memorize, and when there is such an intention it immediately overcomes it and gets rid of it. It knows that impatience is wrong, and if there is such an intention it immediately overcomes it and gets rid of it. It knows that to strive for plenty and to boast about excess is wrong, and if there is such an intention

[3] *Analects*, 7:6.
[4] Namely, having a firm grasp on virtue, relying on humanity, and finding recreation in the arts.

it immediately overcomes it and gets rid of it. Thus one is in perfect accord with sages and worthies at all times, and his mind becomes completely identified with the Principle of Nature. Let him read, and he will be doing nothing but giving recuperation and refreshment to his mind. What trouble is there?"

I said, "Although you have enlightened me, unfortunately my capacity is low and I really can hardly avoid such trouble. I have heard that prominence in public life or obscurity depend on fate. People with the highest intelligence probably do not care for civil service examinations. But I, unworthy one, am a slave to fame and profit and am willing to do this. I only bring sorrow to myself. I wish to abandon the attempt but cannot give up because I am bound by my duty to support my parents. What can I do?"

The Teacher said, "In this matter many have made their parents the excuse. Actually the reason is the lack of a purpose. If one's purpose is established, so far as innate knowledge is concerned, one's thousand acts and tens of thousands of deeds are only one. How can reading and writing be a trouble to a person? The person only gives himself trouble in worrying about success and failure." Thereupon he sighed and said, "This doctrine of innate knowledge is not well understood. I do not know how many brilliant people have been hindered at this point."

242. I asked, "In saying that 'what is inborn is called the nature,'[5] Kao Tzu was, after all, right. Why did Mencius criticize him?"

The Teacher said, "What is inborn is of course nature. But Kao Tzu recognized only one side and failed to understand the basis. If he had understood the basis, what he said would have been correct. Mencius also said, 'Form and color [our body] are nature endowed by Heaven.'[6] This also refers to material force."

The Teacher further said, "Whenever people talk at random and act by impulse, they always say that they do so according to their mind and their nature. This is what is meant by 'what is inborn is called the nature.' But doing thus necessarily involves mistakes. If, however, one understands the basis and follows innate knowledge, then whatever he says or does is naturally all right. But innate knowledge speaks through the same mouth and acts through the

[5] *Book of Mencius*, 6A:3.
[6] *Ibid.*, 7A:38.

same body. How can it get outside material force and have another organ with which to speak or act? Therefore it has been said, 'It would be incomplete to talk about the nature of man and things without including material force and unintelligible to talk about material force without including the nature.'[7] Material force is also nature and nature is also material force. If we realize the basis, it will be all right."

243. The Teacher further said, "Gentlemen, in your task the worst thing to do is to make an artificial effort to help the mind grow.[8] There are extremely few people of the highest intelligence. A student cannot jump into the rank of a sage. Rising, falling, advancing, and receding are the natural order of the task. If one had some success in his effort yesterday but fails today, he should not pretend that nothing has gone wrong. That would be making an artificial effort to help the mind grow, and any success previously achieved would be spoiled. This is not a small mistake. For example, when a person who walks on the road happens to stumble, he should get up and keep on walking, and should not deceive others by acting as though he had not fallen. You gentlemen should always cherish the mind that can retreat from the world without being troubled and can face disapproval without being troubled.[9] Follow the dictate of innate knowledge and proceed patiently and pay no attention to people's ridicule, slander, praise, or humiliation. Whether the task advances or recedes, remain the master that extends the innate knowledge. Act like this without cease, and in time the effort will be effective and no external things can disturb you."

He again said, "If one is genuinely and earnestly devoted to his task, let people slander him and let them insult him. He will gain in everything and everything will become for him material for the advancement of virtue. If he does not exert effort, everything will have an evil effect on him and he will ultimately be ruined."

244. One day the Teacher went to visit Yü-hsüeh.[10] He looked at the rice in the field and said, "How long has it been that it has grown

---

[7] *I-shu*, 6:2a.

[8] Quoting the *Book of Mencius*, 2A:2.

[9] As described in the *Book of Changes*, commentary on hexagram no. 1. Cf. trans. by Legge, *Yi King*, p. 409.

[10] A peak in Chekiang, not a cave where Emperor Yü was buried, as is sometimes believed. The word *yü* has nothing to do with the legendary emperor.

like this!" Fan Chao-ch'i,[11] who was beside him, said, "This is because it has roots. If in our learning we can grow roots, we don't have to worry about its growth either."

The Teacher said, "Who has no roots? Innate knowledge is man's root which is intelligent and is grown by nature. It naturally grows and grows without cease. It is only because some people are afflicted by the trouble of selfishness and injure and obstruct it that it cannot grow."

245. A friend of ours very often became angry easily and proceeded to criticize other people. The Teacher admonished him, saying, "In the matter of learning, one must examine oneself. If one merely criticizes others, one sees only their faults and not his own. If he can examine himself he will see that there are many places where he is wrong. Where has he the leisure to criticize others? Emperor Shun was able to change his brother Hsiang's arrogance. His secret merely lay in not noticing Hsiang's mistakes. If Shun had only wished to correct Hsiang's wickedness, he would have seen his mistakes. Since Hsiang was arrogant and would not yield, how could he have influenced him?"[12]

The friend was moved and repented. The Teacher said, "From now on, never talk about the right or wrong of others. Whenever someone should be criticized or refuted, you should immediately take that situation as your selfish desire to become a big fellow and overcome it."

246. The Teacher said, "When friends question or challenge you, even if sometimes they are shallow and rude or boasting and showing off, it is because their disease is growing. You should prescribe medicine according to the disease. Do not just for that reason harbor any feeling of spite. If you do, your mind will not be that of a superior man who helps others to do good."

247. I asked, "Chu Hsi considers divination by means of tortoise shells and stalks of plants as fundamental,[13] while Ch'eng I, in his commentary, considers principle as fundamental.[14] What do you think?"

---

[11] We know nothing about him.
[12] See below, sec. 296.
[13] In interpreting the *Book of Changes*. *Chu Tzu yü-lei*, 66:1a ff.
[14] Preface to the *I chuan*, and also the *Wen-chi*, 5:16a.

The Teacher said, "Divination involves principle and principle is [a form of] divination. Among the principles in the world, is there any greater than that of divination? Because later generations regard divination as fundamentally fortune telling, they look upon it as a petty craft. They don't know that questions and answers between teachers and friends, such as we are engaging in today, and studying extensively, inquiring accurately, thinking carefully, sifting clearly, practicing earnestly,[15] and the like are all forms of divination. Divination is no more than to remove doubt and to give the mind divine intelligence. The *Book of Changes* seeks answers from Heaven. Man has doubts and does not have sufficient self-confidence. He therefore seeks answers from Heaven by use of the *Book of Changes*. The idea is that the human mind involves some [selfish desires]. Heaven alone leaves no room for falsehood."

CONVERSATIONS RECORDED BY HUANG MIEN-CHIH[1] (Sections 248-316)

248. I asked, "[Confucius said, 'A superior man, in dealing with the world,] is not for or against anything. He follows righteousness, as the standard.'[2] Should one act like this in everything?"

The Teacher said, "Of course one must act like this in everything. Nevertheless, one needs to know the basis. Righteousness is identical with innate knowledge. Only when one realizes that innate knowledge is the basis can one be free from bias. Take the acceptance of gifts. Some should be accepted now but declined at other times.

---

[15] Steps outlined in the *Doctrine of the Mean*, ch. 20.

[1] This disciple's name was Hsing-tseng. A literary and carefree man, he had no distinguished public career. According to Huang Tsung-hsi, he did not quite grasp the true meaning of the Master's teachings. See *Ming-ju hsüeh-an*, 25:4b.

Although the text indicates that secs. 248-316 were recorded by Huang Mien-chih, secs. 260, 297, 313, 315, 338, 339, and 343 were almost surely recorded by Ch'ien Te-hung. Here Huang does not seem to be involved and Ch'ien's personal name is used, a practice followed only by the person doing the writing. And Ch'ien definitely said in the *Postscript* that he had incorporated some of his own records. It is most probable that secs. 260-316 were recorded by Ch'ien. For this reason, in certain Japanese editions Ch'ien's *Postscript* is put at the end of sec. 316 instead of at the end of sec. 343.

[2] *Analects*, 4:10.

Others should be declined now but accepted at other times.[3] If you are biased toward what you should accept now and go right on to accept everything or if you are biased against what you decline now and go right on to decline everything, this is setting the mind for or against things. That is not the original substance of innate knowledge. How can it be called righteousness?"

249.   I asked, "How can the one sentence, 'Have no depraved thought,'[4] cover the meaning of three hundred poems in the *Book of Odes*?"

The Teacher said, "It covers and runs through not only the three hundred odes but also the Six Classics[5] and all the sayings of sages and worthies of the whole world, past and present. What more can be said? This is the type of thing that, once it is done, settles everything."

250.   I asked about the human mind [which is precarious and liable to make mistakes] and the moral mind [which is subtle and follows moral principles].[6] The Teacher said, " 'To follow our nature is called the Way.'[7] This refers to the moral mind. Because it involves some selfish ideas, it becomes the human mind. The moral mind in its true nature has neither sound nor smell. Therefore it is described as subtle. When it obeys the human mind in its action, there will be many places where it is insecure. Therefore it is described as precarious."

251.   I asked, " 'One may not talk of the higher things to those who are below average.'[8] Even when we talk of the higher things to the stupid person, he will not advance. How much less will he do so if we do not talk to him!"

The Teacher said, "It is not that the Sage did not want to talk to him at all. The Sage was anxious to have everyone become a sage. But people vary in endowment. In giving them education, there

---

[3] A matter discussed in the *Book of Mencius*, 2B:3.

[4] *Analects*, 2:2.

[5] See above, Introduction, n. 1.

[6] So described in the *Book of History*, "Counsels of the Great Yü." Cf. trans. by Legge, *Shoo King*, p. 61.

[7] A quotation from the *Doctrine of the Mean*, ch. 1.

[8] Confucius, *Analects*, 6:19.

should be an order. If you talk of the nature and destiny of man and things to people below average, they do not understand. It is necessary to polish them slowly."

252. A friend asked, "Why is it that I do not remember the words I read?"

The Teacher said, "You need only understand the meaning of the words. Why should you need to remember the words? Even understanding the meaning of the words is to fall down to the level of subsidiary things. The important thing is to realize clearly the original substance of one's own mind. If one merely remembers, he will not understand. And if he merely understands what he reads, he will not clearly realize his own original substance."

253. I asked, "[When Confucius stood by the stream and said,] 'It passes on like this'[9] was he talking about his own mind and nature as being extremely lively and dynamic?"

The Teacher said, "Yes. However, one must exert the effort to extend innate knowledge at all times before one can be extremely lively and dynamic like that stream of water. If there is a moment of interruption, one will not be as extremely lively as Heaven and Earth. This is the height of learning. Even a sage can do no more."

254. I asked about the chapter "A resolute scholar and a man of humanity will never seek to live at the expense of injuring humanity."[10]

The Teacher said, "[Confucius said this] because people of the world all think too highly of their bodies and lives. They do not ask whether they should die or not but resort to any special means or accommodation to preserve their lives. For this reason they cast aside the Principle of Nature, harden their conscience and destroy principle, and will do anything conceivable. Since they have violated the Principle of Nature, they are no different from beasts. Even if they could cheat their fate so as to live in the world for a hundred or a thousand years, they would be existing as beasts for a hundred or a thousand years. The student should have a clear

[9] *Ibid.*, 9:16.
[10] *Ibid.*, 15:8.

understanding in these matters. Because Pi-kan and Lung-p'eng saw clearly, they could fulfill their humanity."[11]

255. I asked, "Shu-sun Wu-shu slandered Confucius.[12] Why is it that even a great sage cannot avoid being slandered?"

The Teacher said, "Slander comes from the outside. Even a sage cannot avoid it. The important thing is for a man to cultivate his own virtue. If one is truly and definitely a sage or a worthy, even if people slander him, it will not affect him. It is like floating clouds obscuring the sun. How can they hurt its brilliance? If one is respectful only on the surface, is serious only in appearance, and is neither firm nor resolute, even though no one speaks unfavorably of him, his concealed wickedness will inevitably be exposed one day. Therefore Mencius said, 'There are cases of reproach by perfectionists and of unexpected praise.'[13] Praise and condemnation come from the outside. How can one escape from them? The important thing is how he cultivates himself."

256. Liu Chün-liang[14] wanted to engage in sitting in meditation in the mountains. The Teacher said, "If you seek tranquillity because you feel disgusted with external things, you will only build up an air of arrogance and laziness. But if you are not disgusted with external things, it will be good for you to cultivate yourself in a quiet place."

257. Wang Ju-chung[15] and I were in attendance. The Teacher

---

[11] By sacrificing their lives to admonish their wicked rulers, King Chieh and King Chou, respectively. Reading *jen* [man] as *jen* [humanity].

[12] *Analects*, 19:23.

[13] *Book of Mencius*, 4A:21.

[14] His courtesy name was Yüan-tao. See Wang's letter to him in *Wang Wen-ch'eng Kung ch'üan-shu*, 5:19a-b. He was not the Liu Chün-liang of the Wang school to whom part of the *Ming-ju hsüeh-an*, 19:5a-7b, is devoted.

[15] Wang Chi (1498-1583). His literary name was Lung-hsi. When he failed in the civil service examination in 1523 he became a follower of Wang, although he was still a very young man and in spite of the fact that Wang's radical doctrine of the extension of innate knowledge frightened scholars away from him. Later Wang Chi and Ch'ien Te-hung were urged to take and pass the examinations, which they did primarily to gain an advantageous position from which to defend the Master's doctrine. Although he served as a division chief in the department of military personnel, his life was primarily private, and for forty

held a fan and commanded us, saying, "You use it." I rose and replied, "I dare not."

The Teacher said, "The teachings of the Sage are not so restrictive or difficult to endure, and do not mean that people should assume the appearance of a rigid, strict schoolman."

Ju-chung commented, "This can be seen somewhat in the chapter about Confucius and Tseng Tien telling their wishes."[16]

The Teacher said, "Right. From this chapter we can see how broad, great, and all-embracing the disposition of the Sage was. Furthermore, when the Master asked his pupils about their wishes, the other three answered seriously. Tseng Tien, however, was quite carefree, ignored the other three, and went so far as to play the lute! What an unrestrained attitude! When it came to telling his wishes, Tseng Tien did not answer the Master's particular question. What he said were words of unrestraint. I-ch'uan[17] would have scolded Tseng Tien. But instead the Sage praised him. What a disposition! In the Sage's way of teaching people, he did not restrict them or treat them all alike. If a pupil was unrestrained, he brought him to perfection through his unrestraint. If he was restrained, he brought him to perfection through his restraint. How can people's abilities be the same?"

258.   The Teacher said to Lu Yüan-ching,[18] "When you were young, Yüan-ching, you also wanted to understand the Five Classics.[19] You also had the ambition for extensive learning. But in teaching people the Sage only worried about their not following what is simple and easy. All that he said establishes the standard for simplicity and easiness. From the point of view of people today who are fond of extensive learning, it would seem that the Sage had taught in the wrong way."

years he taught and elucidated the doctrine. Lecture halls were established in the two capitals as well as in south and central China, especially in Kiangsi and Chekiang. For other important facts about him, see preface by Ch'ien Te-hung preceding sec. 130 above, and for an account of him, see *Ming-ju hsüeh-an*, ch. 12.

[16] *Analects*, 11:25. See above, secs. 27 and 29.
[17] Ch'eng I, who was well known for his strictness.
[18] See above, sec. 15, n.1.
[19] See above, Introduction, n. 1.

259. The Teacher said, "Confucius never acted without knowing why[20] and whenever Yen Hui did anything wrong he never failed to realize it.[21] This is the real essence of the doctrine of the Sage."

260. Ho T'ing-jen,[22] Huang Cheng-chih,[23] Li Hou-pi,[24] Wang Ju-chuang,[25] and I [Ch'ien Te-hung][26] were in attendance. The Teacher turned to us and said, "You have not made progress in your learning because you have not made up your minds." Hou-pi rose and responded, "Like others I also want to make up my mind."

The Teacher said, "Shall I say that you have not made up your mind? I say only that it is not the mind determined to become a sage."

Hou-pi replied, "I want my mind to be determined to become a sage."

The Teacher said, "If you really have the mind to become a sage, your innate knowledge should be extended to the utmost in everything. If in your innate knowledge you retain the least trace of alien thought, that is not the mind determined to become a sage."

When I first heard the conversation, I was not satisfied. At this point, however, I was frightened and sweated.

261. The Teacher said, "Innate knowledge is the spirit of creation. This spirit produces heaven and earth, spiritual beings, and the Lord. They all come from it. Truly nothing can be equal to this.[27] If people can recover it in its totality without the least deficiency, they will surely be gesticulating with hands and feet. I don't know if there is anything in the world happier than this."

262. A friend who was engaging in sitting in meditation attained some insight. He ran to make an inquiry of the Teacher. The

---

[20] According to *Analects*, 7:27.

[21] According to the *Book of Changes*, "Appended Remarks," pt. 2, ch. 5. Cf. trans. by Legge, *Yi King*, p. 392.

[22] His courtesy name was Shan-shan (1486-1551). He was an assistant to a division chief in the department of public works, and one of the most outstanding of Wang's disciples. For an account of him, see *Ming-ju hsüeh-an*, 19:13a-15b.

[23] See above, sec. 120, n. 65.

[24] Nothing is known of him except that his name was Kung.

[25] See above, n. 15.

[26] See above, preface to sec. 130, n. 1; also see above, sec. 248, n. 1.

[27] Quoting Ch'eng Hao, *I-shu*, 2A:3b.

Teacher said, "Formerly, when I stayed in Ch'u-chou,[28] seeing that students were mostly occupied with intellectual explanations and debates on similarities and differences, which did them no good, I therefore taught them sitting in meditation. For a time they realized the situation a little bit [they saw the true Way] and achieved some immediate results. In time, however, they gradually developed the defect of fondness for tranquillity and disgust with activity and degenerated into lifelessness like dry wood. Others purposely advocated abstruse and subtle theories to startle people. For this reason I have recently expounded only the doctrine of the extension of innate knowledge. If one's innate knowledge is clear, it will be all right either to try to obtain truth through personal realization in a quiet place or to discover it through training and polishing in the actual affairs of life. The original substance of innate knowledge is neither tranquil nor active. Recognition of this fact is the basis of learning. From the time of Ch'u-chou until now, I have tested what I said several times. The point is that the phrase 'the extension of innate knowledge' is free from any defect. Only a physician who has broken his own arm can understand the causes of human disease."[29]

263. A friend asked, "In our task, if we want to have this innate knowledge continue at all times, we shall not be able to deal with all the influences of external things and respond to them. On the other hand, if we go to things and deal with them, innate knowledge seems to disappear. What is the solution?"

The Teacher said, "This is simply because your recognition of innate knowledge is not yet genuine, and you still separate the internal and the external. In this task of mine, impatience won't do. If you realize that innate knowledge is the foundation and is correct, and go ahead to make a real and concrete effort, you will understand it thoroughly. When this point is reached, the separation of the internal and the external will be forgotten. Wherein can the mind and things fail to be united as one?"

264. The Teacher further said, "If in the task one does not penetrate the true secret, how can innate knowledge be abundant and brilliantly displayed? If you want to penetrate it, you cannot do so

---

[28] In modern Anhui Province, near Nan-ch'ang. Wang was there in 1510 when he was thrity-nine.
[29] Quoting the *Tso chuan*, Duke Ting, 13th year.

through intelligence or intellectual understanding. You must transform all the impurities in the mind so that not the slightest selfish attachment will be retained."

265. I asked, "You said that the sentence 'What Heaven imparts to man (*ming*, destiny) is called his nature' means that man's destiny is identical with his nature, that the sentence 'To fulfill our nature is called the Way' means that man's nature is identical with the Way, and that the sentence 'Cultivating the Way is called education' means that the Way is identical with education.[30] Why is the Way identical with education?"

"The Way is innate knowledge. From the beginning it is perfect. It regards what is right as right and what is wrong as wrong. If we only rely on it with regard to what is right and what is wrong, everything will be correct. This innate knowledge is, after all, your wise teacher."

266. I asked, " 'What is not seen' and 'what is not heard' refer to original substance, and 'cautions' and 'apprehensions'[31] refer to effort. Is this correct?"

The Teacher said, "Here you must believe that while original substance is neither seen nor heard, it is also cautious and apprehensive. Caution and apprehension are not anything to be added to what is not seen or heard. If original substance is truly understood, it will be all right to say that caution and apprehension refer to original substance and that what is not seen or what is not heard refer to effort."

267. I asked about the sentence about 'penetrating to a knowledge of the course of the day and night.'[32] The Teacher said, "From the beginning innate knowledge knows the course of day and night."

I said, "When a person sleeps soundly, even innate knowledge is unconscious."

"If it is unconscious, how is it that as soon as he is called he answers?"

[30] Quotations from the *Doctrine of the Mean*, ch. 1. For Wang's comments, see above, sec. 127.
[31] *Doctrine of the Mean*, ch. 1.
[32] *Book of Changes*, "Appended Remarks," pt. 1, ch. 1, ch. 4. Cf. trans. by Legge, *Yi King*, p. 354.

"If innate knowledge is always conscious, why is there the state of sound sleep?"

"It is a general law in the universe that when it gets dark, things rest. As night falls, heaven and earth become an undifferentiated state. Forms and colors all disappear. With man also, the ears hear nothing, the eyes see nothing, and all the apertures are closed. This is the time when innate knowledge is collected and concentrated. As heaven and earth open up again, all the myriad things reveal themselves and grow. With man also, the ears and eyes now see and hear, and all apertures are open. This is the time when the wonderful functioning of innate knowledge starts. From this we can see that the human mind and heaven and earth form one body. Therefore 'It forms the same current above and below with that of heaven and earth.'[33] People today do not know how to rest. At night, if they are not in dull slumber, they are occupied with erroneous thoughts and nightmares."

"How can we exert effort during sleep?"

"To know day is to know night. In the daytime, innate knowledge responds smoothly without any impediment. Although at night, innate knowledge is collected and concentrated, when there is a dream, it already shows some sign of things to come."

268. The Teacher further said, "Only when innate knowledge operates with the restorative power of the night[34] is it in its original substance, because then it is free from the impurity of material desires. The student must see to it that when he is busy with or disturbed by things, he always remains as if he is under the restorative power of the night. If so, then he penetrates to a knowledge of the course of day and night."

269. The Teacher said, "Taoist seekers of immortality have reached the conclusion of the vacuity [of the mind]. Is the sage able to add an iota of reality to that vacuity? The Buddhists have reached the conclusion of non-being [of the mind]. Is the sage able to add an iota of being to that non-being? But the Taoist talk about vacuity is motivated by a desire for nourishing everlasting life, and the Buddhist talk about non-being is motivated by the desire to escape

---

[33] *Book of Mencius*, 7A:13.
[34] Mencius' phrase, *ibid.*, 6A:8.

from the sorrowful sea of life and death. In both cases, certain selfish ideas have been added to the original substance [of the mind], which thereby loses the true character of vacuity and is obstructed. The sage merely returns to the true condition of innate knowledge and does not attach to it any selfish idea. The vacuity of innate knowledge is the Great Vacuity[35] of nature. The non-being of innate knowledge is the formlessness of the Great Vacuity. Sun, moon, wind, thunder, mountains, rivers, people, and things, and all things that have figure, form, or color, all function and operate within this formlessness of the Great Vacuity. None of them has become an obstacle to nature. The sage merely follows the functioning of his innate knowledge and Heaven, Earth, and all things are contained in its functioning and operation. How can there be anything to transcend innate knowledge and become its obstacle?"

270.   Someone said, "The Buddhists also devote themselves to the nourishing of the mind, but fundamentally they are incapable of governing the world. Why?"

The Teacher said, "In nourishing the mind, we Confucians have never departed from things and events. By merely following the natural principles of things we accomplish our task. On the other hand, the Buddhists insist on getting away from things and events completely and viewing the mind as an illusion, gradually entering into a life of emptiness and silence, and seeming to have nothing to do with the world at all. This is why they are incapable of governing the world."

271.   Someone asked about heresy. The Teacher said, "What can be understood and practiced by men and women of simple intelligence is called universal virtue. What cannot be understood and practiced by men and women of simple intelligence is called a heresy."

272.   The Teacher said, "The difference between Mencius' idea of the unperturbed mind and that of Kao Tzu is exceedingly small.[36] Kao Tzu directed his effort only to keeping the mind from being perturbed. Mencius, on the other hand, went right on to the under-

---

[35] This concept is expounded in Chang Tsai, *Cheng-meng*, ch. 1.
[36] *Book of Mencius*, 2A:2.

standing that the mind is originally not perturbed. The mind is not perturbed in its original substance. It is perturbed only because one's action is not in accord with righteousness. Mencius did not discuss whether the mind is perturbed or not. He talked only about the accumulation of righteous deeds. If every action is right, there will naturally be nothing to perturb the mind. As Kao Tzu only wanted the mind not to be perturbed, his effort amounts to holding on to the mind and bending and breaking its root that by nature grows and grows without cease. This not only does no good; it is harmful. Mencius' task of accumulating righteous deeds, on the other hand, can naturally be cultivated to the full without any deficiency. It is naturally free and at ease, and is extremely lively and dynamic. This is 'strong moving power.' "[37]

273. The Teacher further said, "The source of Kao Tzu's trouble can be seen in his doctrine that the nature is neither good nor evil. Since the nature is neither good nor evil, it is not a great mistake to say so. But Kao Tzu looked at the matter too rigidly. Therefore to him internally there is the nature which is neither good nor evil. He saw good and evil in things and the stimulation they give. Therefore externally there is the thing. In this way he looked at the nature from two sides and hence he was mistaken. The nature in its original state is neither good nor evil. If we understand it adequately this one sentence covers all, and there is no separation of the internal and the external. Kao Tzu saw the nature as internal and things as external. From this we can see that he had not understood the nature thoroughly."

274. Chu Pen-ssu[38] asked, "Man has innate knowledge because he possesses pure intelligence. Have such things as plants and trees, tiles and stones innate knowledge also?"

The Teacher said, "The innate knowledge of man is the same as that of plants and trees, tiles and stones. Without the innate knowledge inherent in man, there cannot be plants and trees, tiles and stones. This is not true of them only. Even Heaven and Earth cannot exist without the innate knowledge that is inherent in man. For at bottom Heaven, Earth, the myriad things, and man form one

[37] *Ibid.*
[38] His name was Te-chih. He was a minor official and was inclined to Buddhism and Taoism. See *Ming-ju hsüeh-an,* 25:5b-8b.

body. The point at which this unity is manifested in its most refined and excellent form is the clear intelligence of the human mind. Wind, rain, dew, thunder, sun and moon, stars, animals and plants, mountains and rivers, earth and stones are essentially of one body with man. It is for this reason that such things as the grains and animals can nourish man and that such things as medicine and minerals can heal diseases. Since they share the same material force, they enter into one another."

275.   The Teacher was roaming in Nan-chen.[39] A friend pointed to flowering trees on a cliff and said, "[You say] there is nothing under heaven external to the mind.[40] These flowering trees on the high mountain blossom and drop their blossoms of themselves. What have they to do with my mind?"

The Teacher said, "Before you look at these flowers, they and your mind are in the state of silent vacancy. As you come to look at them, their colors at once show up clearly. From this you can know that these flowers are not external to your mind."

276.   I said, "The great man and things form one body. Why does the *Great Learning* say that there is a relative importance among things?"[41]

The Teacher said, "It is because of principles that there necessarily is relative importance. Take for example the body, which is one. If we use the hands and the feet to protect the head, does that mean that we especially treat them as less important? Because of their principles this is what should be done. We love both plants and animals, and yet we can tolerate feeding animals with plants. We love both animals and men, and yet we can tolerate butchering animals to feed our parents, provide for religious sacrifices, and entertain guests. We love both parents and strangers. But suppose here are a small basket of rice and a platter of soup. With them one will survive and without them one will die. Since not both our parents and the stranger can be saved by this meager food, we will prefer to save our parents instead of the stranger. This we can tolerate. We can tolerate all these because by principle these should be done. As to the relationship between ourselves and our parents

[39] The Hui-chi Mountain in present Chekiang.
[40] See above, sec. 6.
[41] The text of the *Great Learning*.

there cannot be any distinction of this or that or of greater or lesser importance. For being humane to all people and feeling love for all comes from this affection toward parents.[42] If in this relationship we can tolerate any relative importance, then anything can be tolerated. What the *Great Learning* calls relative importance means that according to innate knowledge there is a natural order which should not be skipped over. This is called righteousness. To follow this order is called propriety. To understand this order is called wisdom. And to follow this order from beginning to end is called faithfulness."

277. The Teacher said, "The eye has no substance of its own. Its substance consists of the colors of all things. The ear has no substance of its own. Its substance consists of the sounds of all things. The nose has no substance of its own. Its substance consists of the smells of all things. The mouth has no substance of its own. Its substance consists of the tastes of all things. The mind has no substance of its own. Its substance consists of the right or wrong of the influences and responses of Heaven, Earth, and all things."

278. I asked about "not allowing any double-mindedness regardless of longevity or brevity of life."[43]
The Teacher said, "In the task of learning, if one is able to get rid of all desires for fame and profit and other interests but still has the least bit of concern over life and death, it means that his mind in its totality is not harmonious or at ease. Ideas of life and death come with life itself and cannot easily be gotten rid of. If one sees through life and death, then the mind in its totality will be able to operate everywhere without obstacle. Only then can learning become the full development of one's nature and the fulfillment of one's destiny."

279. A friend asked, "If during meditation one searches one by one for the roots of the love for fame, sex, profit, and so forth, and wipes them out completely, is that not comparable to cutting out flesh to patch up a sore?"
The Teacher looked very serious and said, "This is my formula to cure people. It can surely remove the cause of diseases. Is there

---

[42] *Book of Mencius*, 7A:45. On meager food, see *ibid.*, 6A: 10.
[43] *Ibid.*, 7A:1.

anything better? Even after a decade or more people still find it useful. If you do not use it, leave it alone, but don't spoil this formula of mine."

The friend was very much ashamed.

A little later, the Teacher added, "I believe this is not your doing. It must be someone within our school who knows my formula only superficially and expressed such an opinion to give you trouble." All those present were so deeply affected as to be frightened.

280.   A friend asked why one's effort is not earnest. The Teacher said, "I have already covered everything about the task of learning in one sentence. How is it that the more you talk about it, the more you are off the mark, and none of what you say touches the root of the matter?"

The friend replied, "I have heard your instructions on the extension of innate knowledge. But it requires elucidation."

The Teacher said, "If you already know what the extension of innate knowledge is, how can it be elucidated? From the beginning innate knowledge is clear. The thing to do is to exert effort earnestly and concretely. Otherwise, the more one talks about it, the more muddled it will become."

"My request is precisely on the elucidation of the effort to extend innate knowledge."

The Teacher said, "You have to find the way yourself. I have no other method to offer. Once there was a Zen master. When someone came to him to ask about the Law of the Buddha, he merely raised a dust whisk. One day his followers hid his dust whisk to see what other schemes he would resort to. [When someone asked him about the Law] he looked for the dust whisk but could not find it, and merely raised his empty hand.[44] This innate knowledge of mine is the dust whisk of my scheme. Aside from it, what can I raise?"

A little later, another friend asked about essentials of the task. The Teacher looked to the side and asked, "Where is my dust whisk?"

Those present were excited and happy.

281.   Someone asked about the idea that absolute sincerity is able to foreknow.[45]

[44] A well-known Buddhist story, the source of which is unidentified.
[45] *Doctrine of the Mean*, ch. 24.

The Teacher said, "Sincerity is a true principle. It is only innate knowledge. The true principle in its wonderful functioning and universal operation is spirit. The point at which it emerges and begins to act is incipient activating force. The sage is the one who is in the state of sincerity, spirit, and incipient activating force.[46] The sage does not value foreknowledge. When blessings and calamities come, even a sage cannot avoid them. He only knows the incipient activating force of things and handles it in accordance with the circumstance. To innate knowledge there is neither the past nor the future. It knows only the incipient activating force of the present moment, and once this succeeds everything else will succeed. If one has the desire to foreknow, it means selfishness and the intention to go after advantage and avoid disadvantage. Master Shao Yung insisted on foreknowledge.[47] In the final analysis, he was not entirely free from the consideration of advantages and disadvantages."

282. The Teacher said, "The original substance [of the mind] knows nothing and yet knows everything. From the beginning it is like this. For example, the sun does not purposely shine on anything and yet there is nothing it does not shine on. Not [purposely to] shine and yet shining on everything is characteristic of the original substance of the sun. Innate knowledge originally knows nothing and now we want it to know. Originally it knows everything and now we suspect that there is something it does not know. This is because we have not sufficient confidence in it."

283. The Teacher said, "Only the perfect sage in the world has quickness of apprehension, intelligence, insight, and wisdom.[48] How deep and mysterious this formerly seemed! But as we look at it today, we realize that these qualities are common to all men. Man's ears are by nature quick of apprehension, his eyes intelligent, and his mind and thought have insight and wisdom. The sage is the only one who can demonstrate them with one effort. What enables him to do so is his innate knowledge, and the reason ordinary people cannot

---

[46] According to Chou Tun-i, *T'ung-shu*, ch. 4.
[47] This is merely a general characterization of Shao Yung's philosophy, not a specific reference.
[48] As described in the *Doctrine of the Mean*, ch. 31.

do so is that they do not extend their knowledge. How clear! How simple! And how easy!"

284.   I asked, "What Confucius called 'thinking far ahead'[49] and Duke Chou's thinking about a thing from daytime into the night[50] are different from leaning forward or backward to accommodate things. Why?"

The Teacher said, "To think far ahead does not mean to think and deliberate vaguely and recklessly. It means only to preserve this Principle of Nature. The Principle of Nature is present in the human mind at all times, past and present, and has neither beginning nor end. It is identical with innate knowledge. In our thousands of thoughts and tens of thousands of deliberations, we must only extend innate knowledge. The more innate knowledge thinks, the more refined and clear it becomes. If it does not think carefully but vaguely responds to things as they come, it will become crude. If, in connection with a thing, one merely thinks vaguely and recklessly, and considers that to be thinking far ahead, then concern about praise or criticism and about gain or loss and other selfish human desires will inevitably enter into his mind and become mixed with it. This is leaning forward or backward to accommodate things. Duke Chou's thinking about a thing from daytime into the night merely means the effort to be cautious with what is not seen and apprehensive of what is not heard.[51] If we understand this, we will realize that his disposition is quite different from leaning forward or backward."

285.   I said, " 'If a man can for one day master himself and return to propriety, all under heaven will return to humanity.'[52] In his commentary, Chu Hsi interpreted it from the point of effect.[53] What do you think of that?"

The Teacher said, "The learning of the sage and the worthy is for themselves. Its emphasis is on effort and not on effect. The man of humanity regards all things as one body. If one fails to achieve

[49] *Analects*, 15:11.
[50] *Book of Mencius*, 4B:20.
[51] Quoting the *Doctrine of the Mean*, ch. 1.
[52] *Analects*, 12:1.
[53] That its effect is so great that all people in the world will share his humanity. *Lun-yü chi-chu*, ch. 6, comment on *Analects*, 12:1.

this unity, it is because his selfishness has not been eliminated. If the true nature of humanity is preserved, then all under heaven will come under this humanity, or 'The whole universe is inside my room!'⁵⁴ [What Chu Hsi understood as] the entire world sharing one's humanity is included in it. Take for instance [the Confucian saying, 'Behave in such a way that] there will be no complaint against you in the state or in the family.⁵⁵ This means that one does not complain himself, that is, does not complain against Heaven or blame man.⁵⁶ Nevertheless the idea that none in the country or the family will complain against him is included in it. But the emphasis does not lie here."

286. I said, "Mencius [considered Po-i as a sage who is pure, I-yin as a sage who has a great sense of responsibility, Liu-hsia Hui as a sage who was in harmony with all, and Confucius as a sage who acted according to the need of the time, that is, he could be pure, responsible, harmonious, and so forth. Mencius also] said that wisdom is comparable to skill and sageness to strength.⁵⁷ Chu Hsi said that the first three gentlemen were excessive in strength and deficient in skill [and that only Confucius possessed all wisdom, skill, sageness, and strength].⁵⁸ Is he correct?"

The Teacher said, "The three gentlemen, of course, had strength. But they also had skill. Strength and skill are not two different things. Skill is found only in the application of strength and strength without skill will be in vain. The three gentlemen may be compared to archers. One can shoot while walking, one on horseback, and one from a great distance. If they all reach the mark, they may be said to have strength, and if they hit the mark, they may be said to have skill. But the one able to shoot while walking may not be able to do so on horseback and the one able to do so on horseback may not be able to do so from a great distance. Each has his own proficiency. This is where they differ in the amount and limit of their ability. Confucius, on the other hand, was expert in all three. However, Confucius' harmony with all only reached the maximum attained

⁵⁴ A quotation from Lü Ta-lin (1044-90), *K'o-chi ming*. See *Sung-Yüan hsüeh-an*, 31:8a; also *Hsing-li ta-ch'üan*, 70:56b-57a.

⁵⁵ *Analects*, 12:2.

⁵⁶ *Ibid.*, 14:37.

⁵⁷ *Book of Mencius*, 5B:1.

⁵⁸ *Meng Tzu chi-chu*, ch. 10, comment on *Book of Mencius*, 5B:1.

by Liu-hsia Hui, his purity only reached the maximum attained by Po-i, and his great sense of responsibility only reached the maximum attained by I-yin. When did he add an iota to them? If we say that the three gentlemen were excessive in strength but deficient in skill, it would mean that they surpassed Confucius in strength. Skill and strength are useful only in making clear the meaning of sageness and wisdom. If we understand what the original substance of sageness and wisdom is, the meaning will be quite clear."[59]

287.   The Teacher said, "The statement, 'The superior man may precede Heaven and Heaven will not act in opposition to him,' means that Heaven is the same as innate knowledge. The statement, 'He may follow Heaven but will act only as Heaven at the time would do,'[60] means that innate knowledge is the same as Heaven."

288.   [The Teacher said,] "Innate knowledge is nothing but the sense of right and wrong, and the sense of right and wrong is nothing but to love [the right] and to hate [the wrong]. To love [the right] and to hate [the wrong] cover all senses of right and wrong and the sense of right and wrong covers all affairs and their variations."

He further said, "The two words 'right' and 'wrong' are general standards. How to deal with them skillfully depends on the man."

289.   [The Teacher said,] "The knowledge of the sage is comparable to the sun in the clear sky, that of the worthy to the sun in the sky with floating clouds, and that of the stupid person to the sun on a dark, dismal day. Although the three kinds of knowledge differ in darkness or clearness, they are the same in the fact that they can distinguish between black and white. Even in a dark night one can tell black and white in a hazy way, which shows that sunlight has not entirely disappeared. The task of learning through study or hard work is nothing other than examining things carefully with this trace of light as the starting point."

290.   I said "Knowledge may be compared to the sun and desire to the clouds. Though the clouds can obscure the sun, they are

---

[59] Cf. above, sec. 99.

[60] Statements from the *Book of Changes*, commentary on hexagram no. 1. Cf. trans. by Legge, *Yi King*, p. 417.

natural to heaven as part of the same atmosphere. Are desires also natural to the human mind?"

The Teacher said, "Pleasure, anger, sorrow, fear,[61] love, hate, and desire are the seven feelings. These seven are also natural to the mind. But you should understand innate knowledge clearly. Take, for example, sunlight. We cannot pin it down to any definite direction or place. When even a small crack is penetrated by the brightness of the sun, sunlight is located there. Although clouds and fog fill all space, color and form in the Great Vacuity can still be distinguished. This also shows that sunlight cannot be obliterated. Simply because clouds can obscure the sun, we should not on that account tell heaven not to produce any cloud. When the seven feelings follow their natural courses of operation, they are all functions of innate knowledge, and cannot be distinguished as good or evil. However, we should not have any selfish attachment to them. When there is such an attachment, they become selfish desires and obscurations to innate knowledge. Nevertheless, as soon as there is any attachment, innate knowledge is naturally aware of it. As it is aware of it, the obscuration will be gone and its substance will be restored. It is only when one can penetrate this point that his task becomes simple, easy, and thorough."

291.   I asked, "It is by nature that the sage is born with knowledge and can practice it naturally and easily.[62] What is the need of any effort?"

The Teacher said, "Knowledge and action are effort. The difference lies in whether it is thorough or shallow and hard or easy. Innate knowledge is by nature refined and clear. In the wish to be filial toward parents, for example, those born with the knowledge of filial piety can practice filial piety naturally and easily, merely follow the innate knowledge, and sincerely and earnestly practice filial piety to the utmost. Those who learn filial piety through study and practice it for its advantage must merely be alert at all times and be determined to follow the innate knowledge and practice filial piety to the utmost, that is all. As to those who learn filial piety through hard work and practice it with effort and difficulty, their obscuration and impediments are already quite great. Although they

---

[61] Ordinarily joy is mentioned instead of fear.

[62] The references in this section to learning and practice are to the *Doctrine of the Mean*, ch. 20.

are determined to follow this innate knowledge and practice filial piety, they cannot do so because they are hindered by selfish desires. They must apply a hundred efforts where others can succeed by only one, and a thousand efforts where others can succeed by ten. Only then can they follow this innate knowledge and practice filial piety to the utmost. Although the sage is born with knowledge and can practice his learning naturally and easily, he is not overly self-confident and is willing to make the same effort as those who learn through hard work and practice their learning with effort and difficulty. But when those who learn through hard work and practice their learning with effort and difficulty try to do the same as those who are born with knowledge and practice naturally and easily, how can they succeed?"

292. I said, "You said that 'joy is characteristic of the original substance of the mind.'[63] When one's parent dies and one cries sorrowfully, is this joy still present?"

The Teacher said, "There is real joy only if the son has cried bitterly. If not, there won't be any joy. Joy means that in spite of crying, one's mind is at peace. The original substance of the mind has not been perturbed."

293. I said, "Innate knowledge is one. King Wen wrote the explanations of hexagrams in the *Book of Changes*, Duke Chou wrote the explanation of the lines of the hexagrams, and Confucius wrote the commentaries and 'Appended Remarks.' Why did each view principle differently?"

The Teacher said, "How could these sages be confined to a rigid pattern? So long as they all sincerely proceeded from innate knowledge, what harm is there in each one's explaining in his own way? Take for example a garden of bamboos. So long as they all have branches and joints, they are similar in general. If it were rigidly insisted upon that each and every branch or joint had to be of the same size or height, that would not be the wonderful handiwork of creation. You people should just go ahead and cultivate innate knowledge. If all have the same innate knowledge, there is no harm in their being different here and there. But if you are not willing to exert effort, you don't even sprout. What branches or joints are there to talk about?"

[63] See above, sec. 166.

294. Among the village people a father and son engaged in litigation, and each asked to plead his case before our Teacher. His attendant wanted to stop them but the Teacher heard them. Before he had finished talking, father and son, having been greatly moved, embraced each other and left weeping.[64] Ch'ai Ming-chih[65] entered and asked, "What did you say, sir, that affected them and caused them to repent so quickly?"

The Teacher said, "I said that Emperor Shun was the most unfilial son in the world and Ku-sou the most affectionate father in the world."

Ming-chih was startled and asked for an explanation. The Teacher said, "Shun always viewed himself as most unfilial and therefore he was able to be filial. Ku-sou always viewed himself as most affectionate and therefore he was unable to be affectionate. He only remembered that Shun was a child he had reared, and wondered why Shun had not appeared delighted to please him.[66] He did not realize that his own mind had been changed by the influence of his second wife, and he still claimed to be affectionate. This is why he was all the more unable to be affectionate. On the other hand, Shun only thought of how his father had loved him when he reared him and felt that his father did not love him now only because he himself had failed to practice filial piety to the utmost. Therefore every day he thought of where and how he had failed in filial piety. For this reason he was all the more able to be filial. When finally Ku-sou was delighted in his son, he did no more than recover the affection which was native to the original substance of his mind. For this reason, later generations have praised Shun as the most filial son of all time, and Ku-sou also became an affectionate father."

295. The Teacher said, "When a simple and rustic person came to ask Confucius a question, he did not have the answer ready for him. His mind was wide open. He merely asked the man about the two sides of right and wrong which the man had already known himself, and made a decision with him, and the mind of the simple and rustic man would become perfectly clear. The right and wrong that the simple and rustic person had already known himself was the

---

[64] This instance occurred in 1510 when Wang was magistrate of Lu-ling County in modern Kiangsi. He was then thirty-nine.

[65] Nothing is known of him.

[66] *Book of Mencius*, 5A:5, 4A:28.

natural standard original with him. Even a sage, who is quick of apprehension and intelligent, could not add or subtract the least bit to or from it. That man merely lacked self-confidence. As soon as the Grand Master made the decision with him, [his innate knowledge was extended] to the utmost without any reservation. If while talking to him the Grand Master had withheld anything he knew, he would not have been able to help him to extend his innate knowledge to the utmost, and then there would have been two substances of the Way."[67]

296. The Teacher said, "[According to the *Book of History*, a high official of Emperor Yao's said of Shun that] he led [his parents and brother] gradually to self-discipline, so that they no longer proceeded to great mischiefs.[68] A commentary said that Hsiang, Shun's brother, had already been gradually approaching righteousness and could not have been liable to commit great mischiefs.[69] After Shun was appointed to office by Emperor Yao, Hsiang still sought daily to kill him.[70] What greater evil can there be? Shun merely improved himself in self-discipline so that this discipline would influence his brother instead of trying to correct his brother's evil. It is the normal behavior of a wicked person to gloss over his mistakes and conceal his shame. If one insisted on criticizing his mistakes, it would aggravate his evil nature. At first Shun brought about the condition in which Hsiang desired to kill him because he was too anxious for Hsiang to become good. This was where he was mistaken. After some experience he then realized that the task merely consisted of disciplining himself and not of admonishing others. Consequently harmony was achieved. This was where Shun could stimulate his mind, harden his nature, and improve his incompetence.[71] The words of the ancients are all the results of personal experience. Therefore they uttered them intimately and to the point, and have transmitted them to later generations so that human feelings can be fully satisfied. Unless they had gone through much, how could they have taken so much pains to say so?"

[67] That is, one to be realized through innate knowledge and the other through ordinary knowledge.
[68] *Book of History*, "Canon of Yao." Cf. trans. by Legge, *Shoo King*, p. 26.
[69] Ts'ai Ch'en (1167-1230), *Shu chi-chuan*, ch. 1.
[70] According to the *Book of Mencius*, 5A:2.
[71] *Ibid.*, 6B:15.

297. The Teacher said, "Ancient music has not been played for a long time. However, present-day theatrical music is still close to it." I [Ch'ien Te-hung][72] did not understand and asked for an explanation.

The Teacher said, "The nine movements of *shao* were a piece of Emperor Shun's theatrical music and the nine variations of *wu* were a piece of King Wu's theatrical music. The actual facts in the lives of these sages were brilliantly exhibited in the music. Therefore when a person of virtue [Confucius] heard it, he knew wherein *shao* was perfectly good and perfectly beautiful and wherein *wu* was perfectly beautiful but not perfectly good.[73] However, when later generations composed music they merely wrote some verses for certain tunes without any relation to social mores or customs at all. How could they influence people and improve customs? If we want to return people's customs to simplicity and purity, we must take the theatrical music of today, eliminate all the depraved and licentious words and tunes, and keep only the stories about loyal ministers and filial sons, so that everyone among the simple folk can easily understand, and their innate knowledge can unconsciously be stimulated into operation. Then it will do some good to mores and ancient music can gradually be restored."

I said, "I cannot even find the pure original tones. I am afraid it is difficult to restore ancient music."

The Teacher said, "Tell me. Where do you look for the pure original tones?"

I replied, "The ancients made pitch pipes[74] and waited for the response of material force to the weather. Perhaps this was the way to find the pure original tones."

The Teacher said, "To seek the pure original tones in reed ashes or millet grains is like dredging up the moon from the bottom of the water. How can that be possible? The pure original tones can be sought only in your own mind."

"How can one seek them in the mind?"

The Teacher said, "In government, the ancients first nourished

---

[72] See above, preface to secs. 130 ff., n. 1.

[73] *Analects*, 3:25.

[74] There were twelve pipes, one for each of the twelve semi-tones, which were filled with reed ashes and buried, with one end exposed, in the ground, in an enclosed room. If the ashes in the tube flew off at the proper time of the corresponding month, this indicated that the material force responded to the proper weather, and therefore the pitch would be correct. See above, sec. 61.

the people's minds to the point of peace and harmony and then instituted musical systems. Suppose we sing songs in this place. If your mind and disposition are harmonious and peaceful, the listeners are naturally pleased, happy, and aroused. This is the beginning of the pure original tones. The *Book of History* says, 'Poetry is the expression of the will.' The will is the foundation of music. It further says, 'Singing is the prolongation of that expression.' Singing is the foundation of instituting musical systems. And it goes on to say, 'The notes accompany that prolongation and they are harmonized by the pitch pipes.'[75] The purpose of pitch pipes is simply to harmonize the notes. To harmonize the notes is the foundation of making pitch pipes. When did the ancients seek [the pure original notes] outside?"

"What was the purpose of the ancients in devising the method of waiting for material force to respond to weather?"

The Teacher said, "In instituting musical systems, the ancients possessed in themselves the substance of equilibrium and harmony. In reality one's equilibrium and harmony correspond to the material force of heaven and earth. To wait for the response of material force to weather or to harmonize tones with those uttered by the male and female phoenix is no more than to test whether one's material force is harmonious or not. This is done after the pitch pipes are made; we do not test first and then make them. Now if we have to wait for the ashes in the tubes for the fundamental notes to respond, we must first determine the time of the winter solstice. But the first two-hour period of the solstice may not be exact. Where, then, can exactness be found?"

298. The Teacher said, "In learning it is necessary to have teachers and friends to point out and explain things. But it is not as good as to find out and understand them oneself, for then if one succeeds in one case, one will succeed in all cases. Otherwise, there will be no end to other people's helping."

299. [The Teacher said,] "Confucius' spiritual energy and ability to handle things were extremely great. He understood the principles of all the undertakings and achievements of ancient emperors and kings. This all comes from the mind. For example, a big tree has

---

[75] *Book of History*, "Canon of Shun." Cf. trans. by Legge, *Shoo King*, p. 48.

many branches and leaves. This is so because the root has been effectively nourished and cultivated. It is not that the effort is first directed to the branches and leaves and that then the root grows. If a student who wants to model himself after Confucius does not devote his efforts to the mind but anxiously tries to imitate Confucius' spiritual energy and ability, he is putting the cart before the horse."

300. [The Teacher said,] "People who have faults generally try to do something about them. This is like mending a cracked boiler. The upshot will be an effort to cover up the faults."

301. [The Teacher said,] "While the people of today are eating, their minds are always occupied and are not in repose, although nothing is happening before them. Purely because their minds are used to being busy, they cannot be collected and firmly controlled."

302. [The Teacher said,] "The student should not ignore music and books. If he occupies his sphere of activity [with sincerity],[76] his mind will not be lost."

303. The Teacher said with a sigh, "People who know how to pursue learning have only this little trouble which they cannot remove, and that is that they do not share the good with others."
Ou-yang Ch'ung-i[77] said, "This trouble is primarily the love for exalted positions and the inability to forget oneself."

304. I asked, "Innate knowledge is in fact characterized by equilibrium and harmony. Why does it have excess or deficiency?"
The Teacher said, "To realize wherein one is excessive or deficient means equilibrium and harmony."

305. [The Teacher said,] " 'What a man dislikes in his superior let him not display in his own dealings with his inferior.'[78] The first part of the sentence refers to innate knowledge and the second part to the extension of knowledge."

[76] A quotation from the *Book of Changes*, commentary on hexagram no. 1. Cf. trans. by Legge, *Yi King*, p. 410.
[77] See above, sec. 104, n. 23.
[78] *Great Learning*, ch. 10.

306. The Teacher said, "The wisdom possessed by Su Ch'in and Chang I[79] can also [be used as] an aid to a sage. In later generations many eminent men of literature and famous men of accomplishments merely followed the old wisdom of Su and Chang. In their learning Su and Chang were skillful in estimating and gauging the feelings of people and therefore they never failed to hit the central spot. Consequently, their doctrines are always effective. They can be said to have understood to a small extent the wonderful functioning of innate knowledge, but they did not use it in the right way."

307. Someone asked about the states before and after the feelings are aroused. The Teacher said, "[These are considered as two contrasting states] purely because later scholars talked about them separately. The thing to do is to say from the very start that there are no such contrasting states, so that people can think for themselves and arrive at the truth. If we say that there are states before and after the feelings are aroused, the listener will still be bound by the views of these later scholars. However, if one really understands that there are no such contrasting states, there is indeed no harm in saying that there are these states, for in fact there are."

"[According to the *Doctrine of the Mean*,[80] the state before the feelings are aroused is characterized by equilibrium and the state after the feelings are aroused is characterized by harmony.] But the state before is not devoid of harmony and the state after is not devoid of equilibrium. Take the sound of the bell. We cannot say that there is no sound before the bell is struck or that there is sound after it is struck. Nevertheless there is the difference between its having been struck and not having been struck. How do you explain it?"

The Teacher said, "Before the bell is struck [the sound], essentially speaking, startles the universe. [Reality is then as active as it has always been.] After the bell is struck, it only keeps the universe silent. [Reality is then as tranquil as it ever was before.]"

308. I asked, "In the discussion on the nature of man and things, the ancients agreed in certain respects but differed in others. Which is the final and accepted conclusion?"

The Teacher said, "One's nature has no definite form. The discus-

[79] Famous experts on diplomacy, who died in 317 and 309 B.C., respectively.
[80] See ch. 1.

sion of nature also has no definite form. Some discussed it from the point of view of its original substance, some from the point of view of its emanation and functioning, some from the point of view of its source, and some from the point of view of the defects that may develop in the course of its operation. Collectively, they all talked about this one nature, but their depth of understanding it varied, that is all. If one held rigidly to one aspect as they did it would be a mistake. In its original substance, nature is in fact neither good nor evil. In its function it can indeed be made to be good or evil, and in its defects it is indeed definitely good or evil. It may be compared to the eyes. There are eyes when one is joyous and there are eyes when one is angry. When one looks straight ahead, the eyes see openly. When one looks stealthily, the eyes peep. Collectively speaking, they are all eyes. If one sees a person with angry eyes and forthwith declares that he has no joyous eyes, or if one sees a person with peeping eyes and forthwith declares that he has no openly seeing eyes, one is holding onto a fixed viewpoint and from this we know that one is making a mistake. When Mencius talked about nature, he discussed it directly from the point of view of its source and said only that generally speaking [nature is originally good].[81] Hsün Tzu's doctrine that nature is originally evil[82] was arrived at from the point of view of its defects and we should not say that he was entirely wrong, only that he did not understand the matter perfectly. As to ordinary people, they have lost the original substance of the mind."

"In discussing nature from the point of view of its source, Mencius wanted people to achieve in their task a thorough understanding at the source. In discussing nature from the point of view of its defects, Hsün Tzu merely wanted people to save and correct themselves in their task at the last stage. This would be a waste of effort."

The Teacher said, "You are right."

309. The Teacher said, "As one's effort reaches the point of greatest refinement, it will be increasingly difficult to express it in words or to discuss it. If one attaches any personal ideas to what is refined and subtle, the entire effort will be obstructed."

[81] *Book of Mencius*, 2A:6.
[82] *Hsün Tzu*, ch. 17. See trans. by Homer H. Dubs, *The Works of Hsüntze* (London, Probsthain, 1928).

310. [The Teacher said,] "Yang Tz'u-hu[83] was not without insight. But his insight was derived from an attachment to that which is without sound or smell."

311. [The Teacher said,] "In a single day a person experiences the entire course of history. Only he does not realize it. At night when the air is pure and clear, with nothing to be seen or heard, and without any thought or activity, one's spirit is calm and his heart at peace. This is the world of Fu-hsi.[84] At dawn one's spirit is bright and his vital power clear, and he is in harmony and at peace. This is the world of Emperors Yao and Shun. In the morning one meets people according to ceremonies, and one's disposition is in proper order. This is the world of the Three Dynasties.[85] In the afternoon one's spirit and power gradually become dull and one is confused and troubled by things coming and going. This is the world of the Spring and Autumn and the Warring States periods.[86] As it gradually gets dark, all things go to rest and sleep. The atmosphere becomes silent and desolate. This is the world in which all people disappear and all things come to an end. If a student has confidence in his innate knowledge and is not disturbed by the vital force, he can always remain a person in the world of Fu-hsi or even better."

312. Hsüeh Shang-ch'ien,[87] Tsou Ch'ien-chih,[88] Ma Tzu-hsin,[89] and Wang Ju-chih[90] were in attendance.[91] In the course of the con-

---

[83] Yang Chien (1140-1226), a disciple of Lu Hsiang-shan, whose idealistic Neo-Confucianism was even more influenced than Lu's by Zen Buddhism. For an account of him, see Sung-Yüan hsüeh-an, ch. 74.

[84] Legendary emperor of great antiquity.

[85] Hsia, 2183-1752 B.C.; Shang, 1751-1112 B.C.; and Western Chou, 1111-770 B.C.

[86] 722-222 B.C.

[87] See above, sec. 81, n. 85.

[88] See below, sec. 314, n. 99.

[89] See above, sec. 40, n. 28.

[90] Wang Ken, whose literary name was Hsin-chai (1483-1540). Born in a poor family, he did business and practiced medicine but did not do so for long. At twenty-five, when he passed by the native place of Confucius, he made up his mind to study the Confucian Classics. Eventually he developed his own doctrine of the realization of one's own nature and returning to the self. Wang Yang-ming had been lecturing on innate knowledge and was well known, but Ken, living in an interior area, did not hear of him. When he finally did, he was surprised at the similarity of his and Wang's beliefs. He went to visit Wang

versation, they sighed over the fact that since our Teacher had subdued the rebellion of Prince Ning he had been slandered and criticized by more and more people. Each asked the others to give their versions of the reason. One said that as the Teacher's achievements, power, and position became more prominent, more and more people became jealous of him. One said that as the Teacher's doctrines became more manifest, there have been more and more scholars to defend the Sung Neo-Confucianism. And one said that since our Teacher was at Nanking the number of like-minded friends who believe him and follow him has increased every day and those in all parts of the country who attack them and prevent them from coming have become more vigorous every day.

The Teacher said, "What you have said, gentlemen, is all true. However, there is one point I have realized myself, which you gentlemen have not mentioned."

The several friends asked him what it was. The Teacher said, "Before I went to Nanking I still harbored a few ideas of the goody-goody villager.[92] Now I believe in innate knowledge. To me what is right is right and what is wrong is wrong. I act freely without any effort to cover up or to conceal. Only now have I come to have the mind of the unrestrained.[93] Let all the people in the world say that my deeds do not fulfill my words. It is all right with me."

Shang-ch'ien went out and said, "Only such a belief can be the true essence of being a sage."

313. The way our Teacher trains and disciplines people is one in which a single word often influences people most deeply. One day Wang Ju-chih returned from a leisurely walk. The Teacher asked him, "What did you see in your walk?" Ju-chih answered, "I saw that the people filling the street were all sages."

Yang-ming, debated with him, and finally, at thirty-eight, became his disciple. He was, however, much inclined to Buddhism and Taoism, and was an eccentric. Wang Yang-ming once refused to see him for three days. In spite of the fact that he was never a government official, his fame spread far and wide. He and Wang Chi (see above, sec. 257, n. 15) were known as the Two Wangs of the Wang Yang-ming school. See below, sec. 313. For an account of him, see *Ming-ju hsüeh-an*, 32:6a-11b.

[91] In the second month of the second year of Chia-ching (1523).

[92] Who is pleasant but not always honest. See *Analects*, 17:12; *Book of Mencius*, 7B:37.

[93] *Book of Mencius*, 7B:37.

The Teacher said, "In your view the people filling the street are all sages, but in their view, you are a sage."

On another day, Tung Lo-shih[94] returned from a leisurely walk, and went to the Teacher, and told him, "I saw a strange thing today."

The Teacher said, "What is strange?"

"I saw that all the people filling the street were sages."

The Teacher said, "This is after all a common thing. Why should it be strange?"

Because Ju-chih was not quite adjusted to the ordinary people [and deep in his mind did not consider them sages] and because Lo-shih's realization [that sagehood for all was a surprise] was dim, the Teacher responded differently to the same statement, but in each case he took the opposite position in order to help them advance.

Huang Cheng-chih,[95] Chang Shu-ch'ien,[96] Wang Ju-chung,[97] and I [Ch'ien Te-hung][98] returned from the civil service examinations in the fifth year of Chia-ching [1526]. We told our Teacher that as we lectured on the doctrine in our travels some believed in us and others did not. The Teacher said, "You assumed the bearing of a sage to lecture to people on learning. When they saw a sage coming they were all scared away. How could you succeed in lecturing to them? You must become one of the people of simple intelligence and then you can discuss learning with them."

To which I added, "If one wishes to see the level of anyone's character today, it is very easy."

The Teacher said, "How do you know that?"

I replied, "You, sir, are comparable to Mount T'ai standing right before us. He who does not look up with respect must be blind."

The Teacher said, "Mount T'ai is not as large as the level ground. What is there to look up to on the level ground?"

A single word of our Teacher's cuts off and wipes out our perennial defects of desiring exalted positions and striving for external

---

[94] His name was Yün (1457-1533). A poet without any civil service examination degree or any official position, he heard Wang's lectures at sixty-eight and became his disciple.

[95] See above, sec. 120, n. 65.

[96] His name was Yüan-ch'ung, and he was known for his courage in giving unpleasant advice to the emperor. For an account of him, see *Ming-ju hsüeh-an*, 14:5b-6a.

[97] See above, sec. 257, n. 15.

[98] See above, preface to secs. 130 ff., n. 1.

things. All present in the hall were struck with fear and were trembling.

314. In the spring of the second year of Chia-ching [1523] Tsou Ch'ien-chih[99] came to Yüeh[100] to make an inquiry about learning of our Teacher. He stayed for several days. Our Teacher saw him off at Fou-feng. That evening he, Ts'ai Hsi-yüan,[101] and other friends sailed to spend the night in the Yen-shou Temple. At night, as we were holding candles in our hands and sitting down, the Teacher remained melancholy. He said, "Over the waves of the river and through the fog that hid the willows, in an instant an old friend has gone for over one hundred *li*."[102]

A friend asked, "Sir, why do you think of Ch'ien-chih so much?"

The Teacher said, "Tseng-tzu said, 'Gifted with ability and yet asking those without ability; possessing much and yet asking those who possess little; having and yet seeming not to have; full, and yet seeming vacuous; offended, and yet not contesting.'[103] A person like Ch'ien-chih is truly near to this description."

THE DOCTRINE IN FOUR AXIOMS

Few conversations have led to such divergent viewpoints and have aroused such bitter criticisms as the famous "doctrine in four axioms"

[99] Courtesy name of Tsou Shou-i, whose literary name was Tung-kuo (1491-1562). A "presented scholar" of 1511, he was appointed official historian. Because he criticized a proposed title for the emperor's father, he was banished to be a prefect. As a prefect he abolished excessive temples, established schools, promoted learning, and improved morals. His influence was such that people built a temple to honor him during his lifetime. Eventually he was promoted to be junior lord of the board of religious rites and later director of education at the national university, but was ultimately dismissed because of his admonition to the emperor. For the next twenty years he lectured on the doctrine of innate knowledge and attracted a large number of followers. Among Wang's disciples he probably best understood the essential meanings of the Master's doctrines. He also assisted Wang in his military operations. In so doing he exemplified more than any other disciple the traditional Confucian ideal of both ability and scholarship. For an account of him, see *Ming-ju hsüeh-an*, ch. 16.

[100] In what is now Chekiang Province.

[101] See above, sec. 99, n. 5.

[102] A *li* is about a third of a mile.

[103] *Analects*, 8:5.

recorded in this section. Wang's two star disciples differed radically in their views concerning the way to become a sage. To Wang Chi[104] the mind in its original state transcends good and evil and consequently any distinction of good and evil also disappears in the will, in knowledge, and in things which emanate from it. He believes that reality is to be intuited directly and totally through the spontaneous awakening of the mind itself. (This is called the doctrine of "four non-beings.") Ch'ien Te-hung,[105] on the other hand, held that while the original mind is above good and evil, the human mind is dominated by habits and is therefore not free from such distinctions and consequently the will, knowledge, and things are all characterized by the distinction between good and evil. He believed that sagehood is to be achieved through the concrete and earnest effort of moral cultivation. (This is called the doctrine of "four beings.") As Wang Chi noted, his own view may be compared to the sudden enlightenment of Buddhism.[106] Actually Wang Yang-ming approved of both. This is clearly recorded in both the following section and the account given in the *Nien-p'u*.[107] Wang Chi in his own account, however, added that the Teacher held the doctrine of four non-beings as a secret and was reluctant to tell people about it, thus implying that it was his final doctrine.[108] Wang Chi's account, which presents the Teacher's doctrine as one of nondistinction between good and evil, is of course a distortion. Unfortunately, this distortion came to be accepted as the Teacher's correct teaching and as such was attacked vigorously for a hundred years.[109] Critics attacked Wang the Teacher for falling into Buddhism. Such a criticism may justifiably be applied to Wang the pupil, whose ideas approximate those of Buddhism very closely, but not to Wang the Teacher. The Teacher definitely stated, "The original substance of the mind is characterized by the highest good."[110] This idea underlies

---

[104] See above, sec. 257, n. 15.

[105] See above, preface to secs. 130 ff., n. 1.

[106] *Wang Lung-hsi Hsien-sheng ch'üan-chi*, 1:1a-3a.

[107] *Wang Wen-ch'eng Kung ch'üan-shu*, 34:39a-41b. There is an important variation in the account by Tsou Tung-kuo, in the *Tsou Tung-kuo chi*, 3:47a, where Ch'ien is quoted as saying, "The mind is characterized by perfect goodness but not evil." But Tsou's record is a secondary source, whereas Ch'ien recorded or at least edited this section and compiled the *Nien-p'u*.

[108] *Wang Lung-hsi Hsien-sheng ch'üan-chi*. For discussions of the doctrine among Wang's followers, see *Ming-ju hsüeh-an*, chs. 12, 18, 32, and 62.

[109] The most severe criticisms are found in Ku Hsien-ch'eng (1550-1612), *Hsiao-hsin-chai cha-chi*, 11:7b-8a, 16:8a-b, 18:1b-3b; and in Kao P'an-lung (1562-1626), *Kao Tzu i-shu*, 1:15a-b. Criticisms in Liu Tsung-chou (1578-1645), *Liu Tzu ch'üan-shu*, 8:24a-26a, and in Huang Tsung-hsi, *Shih-shuo*, in *Ming-ju hsüeh-an*, p. 5a-b, are more correctly directed against Wang Chi.

[110] See below, sec. 318. See also above, secs. 3, 4, 91, and 92.

practically all of his teachings. When he said that "in the original substance of the mind there is no distinction of good and evil," he did not mean there is no moral distinction but that the mind does not make a special effort to desire good or evil. This has been pointed out by Huang Tsung-hsi, who presented a strong defense and counterattack.[111] It was unfortunate that the Teacher passed away in the year following the conversation before he had an opportunity to clarify his position. The whole critical reception of his doctrine in four axioms was really part of a violent reaction against the entire Wang school rather than against this particular teaching. Unfair as the attack was, however, it did check what the Confucians considered to be a possible deterioration into Buddhist neutralization of good and evil.

315. In the ninth month of the sixth year of Chia-ching [1527] our Teacher had been called from retirement and appointed to subdue once more the rebellion in Ssu-en and T'ien-chou[112] [when the earlier expedition under another official had failed]. As he was about to start, Ju-chung [Wang Chi] and I [Ch'ien Te-hung] discussed learning. He repeated the words of the Teacher's instructions as follows:

"In the original substance of the mind there is no distinction of good and evil.
When the will becomes active, however, such distinction exists.
The faculty of innate knowledge is to know good and evil.
The investigation of things is to do good and remove evil."

I asked, "What do you think this means?"
Ju-chung said, "This is perhaps not the final conclusion. If we say that in the original substance of the mind there is no distinction between good and evil, then there must be no such distinction in the will, in knowledge, and in things. If we say that there is a distinction between good and evil in the will, then in the final analysis there must also be such a distinction in the substance of the mind."
I said, "The substance of the mind is the nature endowed in us by Heaven, and is originally neither good nor evil. But because we have a mind dominated by habits, we see in our thoughts a distinction between good and evil. The work of the investigation of things, the extension of knowledge, the sincerity of the will, the rectification of the mind, and the cultivation of the personal life is aimed precisely at recovering that original nature and substance. If

[111] *Ming-ju hsüeh-an*, 10:1b, 16:4a.
[112] Both were counties in Kwangsi.

there were no good or evil to start with, what would be the necessity of such effort?"

That evening we sat down beside the Teacher at the T'ien-ch'üan Bridge. Each stated his view and asked to be corrected. The Teacher said, "I am going to leave now. I wanted to have you come and talk this matter through. You two gentlemen complement each other very well, and should not hold on to one side. Here I deal with two types of people. The man of sharp intelligence apprehends straight from the source. The original substance of the human mind is in fact crystal-clear without any impediment and is the equilibrium before the feelings are aroused. The man of sharp intelligence has accomplished his task as soon as he has apprehended the original substance, penetrating the self, other people, and things internal and things external all at the same time. On the other hand, there are inevitably those whose minds are dominated by habits so that the original substance of the mind is obstructed. I therefore teach them definitely and sincerely to do good and remove evil in their will and thoughts. When they become expert at the task and the impurities of the mind are completely eliminated, the original substance of the mind will become wholly clear. Ju-chung's view is the one I use in dealing with the man of sharp intelligence. Te-hung's view is for the second type. If you two gentlemen use your views interchangeably, you will be able to lead all people—of the highest, average, and lowest intelligence—to the truth. If each of you holds on to one side, right here you will err in handling properly the different types of man and each in his own way will fail to understand fully the substance of the Way."

After a while he said again, "From now on whenever you discuss learning with friends be sure not to lose sight of my basic purpose.

In the original substance of the mind there is no distinction of good and evil.
When the will becomes active, however, such distinction exists.
The faculty of innate knowledge is to know good and evil.
The investigation of things is to do good and remove evil.

Just keep to these words of mine and instruct people according to their types, and there will not be any defect. This is indeed a task that penetrates both the higher and the lower levels. It is not easy to find people of sharp intelligence in the world. Even Yen Hui and Ming-tao [Ch'eng Hao] dared not assume that they could fully realize the original substance of the mind as soon as they apprehended the task. How can we lightly expect this from people? People's minds are dominated by habits. If we do not teach them concretely and sincerely to devote themselves to the task of doing good and removing evil right in their innate knowledge rather than merely imagining an original substance in a vacuum, all that they do will not be genuine and they will do no more than cultivate a mind of vacuity and quietness.[113] This defect is not a small matter and must be exposed as early as possible." On that day both Ju-chung and I attained some enlightenment.

316. When the Teacher first returned to Yüeh,[114] very few friends came to visit him. Later more and more came from all parts of the country. From the second year of Chia-ching [1523] the people who surrounded him were so many that they sat shoulder to shoulder. Take Buddhist temples like the Kuang-hsiang and the T'ien-fei in the city. Often several tens of people were housed in one room where they ate together. At night there was no room for them to sleep. They took turns at sitting, and the singing lasted until dawn. Temples far and near in mountains like Nan-chen, Yü-hsüeh, and Yang-ming-tung[115] were all places where like-minded friends visited and stayed. Whenever our Teacher took his chair to lecture, there were always several hundred people sitting around him to listen. There was not a single day in any month in which we did not send off ot welcome someone. The point was reached when there were some who attended the Teacher for over a year and yet their names were not known. Whenever some left, the Teacher always sighed and said, "Although you gentlemen are leaving, you do not go outside heaven and earth. So long as you share this feeling of mine I can forget my own seeming physical existence." When the students left the room after listening to his lectures, all leaped for joy. I have heard seniors of the school say that, although before the Nanking days [1514-16] the followers were many, they had never been as numerous as in Yüeh. Although this was because the more he lectured the more extensive

---

[113] Like that of the Taoists and Buddhists.

[114] Wang returned to Yüeh from the successful suppression of Prince Ning's revolt in 1521.

[115] Neither Yü-hsüeh nor Yang-ming-tung was a cave, as the words *hsüeh* and *tung* have misled many people into believing. See Mao Ch'i-ling (1623-1716), *Wang Wen-ch'eng chuan-pen*, pp. 1b-2a.

the belief and confidence in him became, essentially it was because our Teacher's learning increasingly advanced so that the subtlety of his influence and attraction was like ever-changing spirit[116] that cannot be localized in any particular place or direction. It was this, of course, that made the difference.

CONVERSATIONS RECORDED BY HUANG I-FANG[1] (Sections 317-343)

317. "According to you,[2] 'Extensive study of literature,'[3] means that in whatever thing one may be doing, one should learn to preserve this Principle of Nature. If this is so, it does not seem to agree with the Confucian saying, 'When a student has any energy to spare after the performance of moral duties, he should use it to study literature and the arts.' "[4]

The Teacher said, "The Six Arts, like the *Book of Odes* and the *Book of History*,[5] are manifestations of the Principle of Nature. Literature is included in them. Investigation shows that the Six Arts, like the *Book of Odes* and the *Book of History*, are all ways of learning to preserve this Principle of Nature. Literature is not restricted to what has taken place in human affairs. To devote extra energy to studying literature means merely to study extensively the human affairs recorded in literature."

Someone asked about the saying, "He who learns but does not think [is lost. He who thinks but does not learn is in danger]."[6]

The Teacher said, "This was also said for a particular reason. Actually thinking is no different from learning. When doubt arises in one's learning, he must think it over. There are, of course, the kind of people who think but do not learn. They only think in a vacuum, hoping to evolve truth through imagination. They do not definitely and concretely devote their efforts to their bodies and

---

[116] Reading *shen* [to expand] as *shen* [spirit].

[1] See above, sec. 222, n. 1.
[2] See above, sec. 9.
[3] *Analects*, 6:25.
[4] *Ibid.*, 1:6.
[5] Another interpretation: "The two Classics and the Six Arts [of ceremonies, music, archery, carriage-driving, writing, and mathematics"]. Since the topic under discussion is literature, the interpretation adopted is more appropriate.
[6] *Analects*, 2:15.

minds so as to learn to preserve the Principle of Nature. They look
upon thinking and learning as two different things and therefore
have the troubles of being lost and being in danger. Actually thinking
is thinking about one's learning. Thinking and learning are in fact
not two different things."

318. The Teacher said, "Former scholars[7] interpreted the investigation of things as investigating all the things in the world. How can
all things in the world be investigated? [Ch'eng I] even said 'Every
blade of grass and every tree possesses principle.'[8] How can we
investigate? Even if we could succeed in investigating every blade of
grass and every tree, how can we return to ourselves and make the
will sincere? I interpret the word *ko*[9] to mean rectifying and *wu* to
mean affairs or events. By personal life the *Great Learning* means the
ears, the eyes, the mouth, the nose, and the four limbs. To cultivate
the personal life means for the eyes not to see what is contrary to
propriety, the ears not to hear what is contrary to propriety, the
mouth not to say what is contrary to propriety, and the four limbs
not to do what is contrary to propriety. But if we want to cultivate
the personal life, how can we do so by applying the effort to the
body? The mind is the master of the body. Although the eye sees,
what makes it see is the mind. Although the ear hears, what makes it
hear is the mind. And although the mouth and the four limbs speak
and move, what makes them speak and move is the mind. Therefore
to cultivate the personal life lies in realizing through personal
experience the true substance of one's mind and always making it
broad and extremely impartial without the slightest incorrectness.
Once the master is correct, then, as it operates through the channel
of the eye, it will naturally see nothing which is contrary to propriety. As it operates through the channel of the ear, it will naturally
hear nothing which is contrary to propriety. And as it operates
through the channels of the mouth and the four limbs, it will
naturally say or do nothing which is contrary to propriety. This
means that the cultivation of the personal life consists in rectifying
the mind.[10]

[7] Like Ch'eng I and Chu Hsi.
[8] *I-shu*, 18:9a.
[9] In the phrase *ko-wu* [investigation of things].
[10] The text of the *Great Learning*.

"But the original substance of the mind is characterized by the highest good. Is there anything in the original substance of the mind that is not good? Now that we want to rectify the mind, where in this original substance must we direct our effort? We must direct it where the mind operates and then the effort can be earnest and concrete. In the mind's operation, it is impossible for it to be entirely free from evil. Therefore it must be here that we make earnest and concrete effort. This means to make the will sincere. For instance, when a thought to love the good arises, right then and there make an earnest and concrete effort to love the good. When a thought to hate evil arises, right then and there make an earnest and concrete effort to hate evil. If whenever the will operates it is sincere, how can the original substance of the mind help being correct? Therefore if one wishes to rectify the mind, he must first make his will sincere. Only when the effort reaches this point of sincerity of the will will it find a solution.

"However, the foundation of the sincerity of the will lies in the extension of knowledge. What has been described as 'what people do not know but I alone know'[11] is exactly the innate knowledge in our mind. If one knows what good is but does not do it right then and there according to this innate knowledge, or knows what evil is but does not get rid of it according to this innate knowledge, this innate knowledge will be obscured. This means that knowledge cannot be extended. If the innate knowledge of our mind cannot be extended to the utmost, then although we know that we should love the good, we cannot earnestly and concretely love it and although we know that we should hate evil, we cannot earnestly and concretely hate it. How can the will be sincere? Therefore the extension of knowledge is the foundation of the sincerity of the will. But this extension of knowledge is not something to be done in a vacuum. It is to rectify [what is wrong in the mind] in whatever actual things one is doing. For instance, if one has the will to do good, then he should do it right in the things he happens to be doing. If one has the will to get rid of evil, he should resist evil right in the things he is doing. Getting rid of evil is, of course, to rectify what is incorrect in the mind and return to the original state of correctness. When good is done, evil is corrected. Hence, doing good is also to rectify what is incorrect in the mind and return to the original state of

[11] Chu Hsi, *Ta-hsüeh chang-chü*, ch. 6, and *Ta-hsüeh huo-wen*, pt. 2, p. 28b.

correctness. In this way the innate knowledge of our mind will not be obscured by selfish desires and can then be extended to the utmost, and whenever the will operates, its desire to love good and to get rid of evil will always be sincere. Thus the concrete starting point of the effort to make the will sincere lies in the investigation of things. If the investigation of things is to be done in this way, everyone can do it. This is why 'Every man can become Yao and Shun.' "[12]

319.   The Teacher said, "People merely say that in the investigation of things we must follow Chu Hsi, but when have they carried it out in practice? I have carried it out earnestly and definitely. In my earlier years[13] my friend Ch'ien[14] and I discussed the idea that to become a sage or a worthy one must investigate all the things in the world. But how can a person have such tremendous energy? I therefore pointed to the bamboos in front of the pavilion and told him to investigate them and see. Day and night Mr. Ch'ien went ahead trying to investigate to the utmost the principles in the bamboos. He exhausted his mind and thoughts and on the third day he was tired out and took sick. At first I said that it was because his energy and strength were insufficient. Therefore I myself went to try to investigate to the utmost. From morning till night, I was unable to find the principles of the bamboos. On the seventh day I also became sick because I thought too hard. In consequence we sighed to each other and said that it was impossible to be a sage or a worthy, for we do not have the tremendous energy to investigate things that they have. After I had lived among the barbarians for [almost] three years,[15] I understood what all this meant and realized that there is really nothing in the things in the world to investigate, that the effort to investigate things is only to be carried out in and with reference to one's body and mind, and that if one firmly believes that everyone can become a sage, one will naturally be able to take up the task of investigating things. This idea, gentlemen, I must convey to you."

[12] *Book of Mencius*, 6B:2.
[13] According to the *Nien-p'u*, the following incident took place in 1492.
[14] This friend was not Ch'ien Te-hung (see above, preface to secs. 130 ff.), since he did not meet Wang until 1521.
[15] When he was banished to become an official in Kuei-chou between 1506 and 1508.

320. One of the disciples said that Shao Tuan-feng[16] maintained that boys are not able to investigate things and therefore they should only be taught to sprinkle and sweep the floor and to answer questions.

The Teacher said, "Sprinkling and sweeping the floor and answering questions are also things. Since the innate knowledge of a boy can only reach this level, to teach him to sprinkle and sweep the floor and to answer questions is to extend his innate knowledge. Again, if a boy knows enough to stand in awe of a teacher or an elder, this is also due to his innate knowledge. Therefore, although he may be playing, if he sees a teacher or an elder, he will bow and show his respect right away. This shows that he is able to investigate things and extend his innate knowledge of revering teachers and elders. A boy naturally has a boy's way of investigating things and extending knowledge."

He further said, "In this investigation of things that I am talking about here, from the boy to the sage, all require the same kind of effort, with the exception that the sage is more expert in investigating things and therefore does not need to spend any energy. Even a vendor of fuel wood can investigate things in this way. From nobilities and high officials to the emperor, all investigate in this way."

321. Someone suspected that knowledge and action do not form a unity and asked about the saying, "It is not difficult to know."[17] The Teacher said, "The innate faculty naturally knows, which is in fact quite easy. But often one cannot extend his innate knowledge to the utmost. This shows that it is not difficult to know but difficult to act."

322. A disciple asked, "How can knowledge and action form a unity? The *Doctrine of the Mean*, for example, talks about learning extensively and also practicing earnestly.[18] This would clearly distinguish knowledge and action as two different things."

The Teacher said, "To study extensively is nothing but to learn to preserve the Principle of Nature in everything one does, and to practice earnestly is nothing but to study incessantly."

[16] Nothing is known of him.
[17] But difficult to act. *Book of History*, "Charge to Yü," pt. 2. Cf. trans. by Legge, *Shoo King*, p. 258.
[18] *Doctrine of the Mean*, ch. 20.

The disciple again asked, "The *Book of Changes* says, '[The superior man] studies to accumulate it' and then also says, 'He practices it with humanity.'[19] How is this?"

The Teacher said, "It is the same. If in everything one learns to preserve this Principle of Nature, then the mind will never be lost. Hence it is said, '[The superior man] studies to accumulate it.' If one learns always to preserve this Principle of Nature without allowing any selfish desire to interrupt the effort, it means that this mind never ceases working. Hence it is said, 'He practices it with humanity.' "

The disciple again asked, "Confucius said, 'When a man's knowledge is sufficient to attain but his humanity is not sufficient for him to hold [what he may have gained, he will lose it again].'[20] Here knowledge and action are two."

The Teacher said, "To say 'sufficient to attain' already implies action. Because one cannot practice all the time and his effort is already interrupted by selfish desires, his humanity is not sufficient for him to hold it."

The disciple further asked about the theory that the mind is identical with principle and said, "Master Ch'eng I said, 'What is inherent in a thing is principle.'[21] How can it be said that the mind is identical with principle?"

The Teacher said, "The word 'mind' should be added to the saying to mean that when the mind is engaged in a thing, there is principle. For example, when the mind is engaged in serving one's father, there is the principle of filial piety, and when the mind is engaged in serving the ruler, there is the principle of loyalty, and so forth."

Thereupon the Teacher said to the disciples, "You gentlemen must understand the basic purpose of my founding this doctrine. Why should I now declare that the mind is identical with principle? Simply because people of the world divide the mind and principle into two, thus giving rise to many defects and evils. For instance, the five powerful despots[22] drove out the barbarians and honored the House of Chou all because of their selfishness, and therefore they were not in accord with principle. Some people say that they

---

[19] *Book of Changes*, commentary on hexagram no. 1. Cf. trans. by Legge, *Yi King*, p. 416.

[20] *Analects*, 15:32.

[21] *I chuan*, 4:20b. Cf. *I-shu* 18:17a.

[22] See above, sec. 11, n. 46.

acted in accord with principle, but their minds did not completely become identified with the Principle of Nature. These people always admire the deeds of the powerful despots. They just want their deeds to look good on the outside and completely ignore the relationship to the mind. They divide the mind and principle into two and unwittingly drift into the insincerity which is characteristic of the way of despots. Therefore I talk about the identification of the mind and principle so people will know that mind and principle are one and devote their efforts to the mind instead of accumulating individual acts of righteousness externally.[23] This is the essence of the kingly way of moral principles. This is the basic purpose of my founding the doctrine."

The disciple asked, "There are many sayings of sages and worthies. Why should they be lumped together as one?"

The Teacher said, "I do not lump them together as one. It has been said, 'The Way is one and only one.'[24] It is also said, '[Heaven and earth] are without any doubleness and so they produce things in an unfathomable way.'[25] Heaven, Earth, and the sage are all one. How can they be separated?"

323. [The Teacher said,] "The mind is not a piece of flesh with blood. It is wherever consciousness is. For example, the ears and the eyes know to see and hear and the hands and feet know the feeling of itches and pain. All this consciousness is the mind."

324. I said, "According to your doctrine of the investigation of things, when the *Doctrine of the Mean* teaches people to be watchful over themselves when alone,[26] when [Mencius taught people to] accumulate righteous deeds,[27] and when [Confucius taught] the extensive study of literature and restraining oneself with the rules of propriety,[28] they are each teaching different ways of investigating things."

The Teacher said, "This is not true. The investigation of things is the same as being watchful over oneself when alone. It is the same

[23] Reading *i* [righteousness] as *wai* [external].
[24] *Book of Mencius*, 3A:1.
[25] *Doctrine of the Mean*, ch. 26.
[26] *Ibid.*, ch. 1.
[27] *Book of Mencius*, 2A:2.
[28] *Analects*, 6:25.

as being cautious and apprehensive.[29] From these efforts to the accumulation of righteous deeds, the extensive study of literature, and restraining oneself with the rules of propriety, the task is the same. They are not to be considered as several and separate ways of investigating things."

325. I asked about the saying in the *Doctrine of the Mean*, "The superior man honors the moral nature [and follows the path of study and inquiry]."[30] The Teacher said, "To follow the path of study and inquiry is the way to honor one's moral nature. Hui-weng [Chu Hsi] said that Tzu-ching [Lu Hsiang-shan] had taught people about honoring the moral nature but that he himself emphasized more strongly following the path of study and inquiry.[31] This is to separate honoring the moral nature from following the path of study and inquiry. Take our studies and discussions now. We devote much work to them for no other reason than to preserve this mind and not to lose its moral nature. Is there such a thing as honoring the moral nature in a vacuum without also pursuing study and inquiry or pursuing study and inquiry in a vacuum without any relation to the moral nature? If so, I don't know what there is to learn in all our present studies and discussions."

I asked about the next two sentences: "He achieves breadth and greatness and pursues the refined and subtle to the limit. He seeks to reach the greatest height and brilliancy and follows the path of the mean."[32]

The Teacher said, "Pursuing the refined and subtle to the limit is the way to achieve breadth and greatness, and following the path of the mean is the way to reach the greatest height and brilliancy. For the original substance of the mind is broad and great. If one cannot pursue the refined and subtle to the limit, his mind will be obscured by selfish desires and it will become exceedingly small. If he scrutinizes even the most minute points or angles in every possible way, selfish desires will not be able to obscure his mind, and thus naturally there will not be many opportunities for these

[29] *Doctrine of the Mean*, ch. 1.

[30] *Ibid.*, ch. 27.

[31] *Chu Tzu wen-chi*, 54:5b. Hui-weng was Chu Hsi's literary name and Tzu-ching was Lu Hsiang-shan's courtesy name.

[32] *Doctrine of the Mean*, ch. 27.

obscurations and obstructions. How can he then fail to extend to the height of breadth and greatness?"

I further asked, "Do the refined and subtle refer to thoughts or to principle?"

The Teacher said, "The refinement and subtlety of thought are the same as the refinement and subtlety of the principles of things."

326. The Teacher said, "People who discuss the nature of man and things today agree and differ in many ways. But they are all talking about nature and not realizing it. Among those who realize nature, there is neither similarity nor difference to talk about."

327. I asked, "I am afraid innate knowledge cannot be free from the desires for music, sex, wealth, or profit."

The Teacher said, "Of course not. But in his effort the beginner must wipe the desires all out and clean them up and not allow any to stay or accumulate. Then as they occur and as he encounters them, they will not be a cause for trouble, and he will naturally respond to them and handle them smoothly. Innate knowledge operates only in [human experience with things such as] music, sex, wealth, and profit. If one can extend his innate knowledge in a most refined and clear way without the least obscuration, then all his dealings with music, sex, wealth, and profit will be instances of the operation of the natural principle."

328. The Teacher said, "You gentlemen and I have been discussing the extension of knowledge and the investigation of things every day. For one or two decades it has been the same. If after hearing what I say you gentlemen earnestly and definitely proceed to devote yourselves to the task, you will realize that with each talk of mine you will have made some progress. Otherwise, each session will be just so much talk. What is the use even if you listen to it?"

329. The Teacher said, "The original substance of the human mind is always in the state of absolute quiet and inactivity, and when acted on will immediately penetrate all things.[33] The state before there is any response to it is not an earlier one, and the state after there has been response to it is not a later one."[34]

---

[33] Quoting the *Book of Changes,* "Appended Remarks," pt. 1, ch. 10. Cf. trans. by Legge, *Yi King,* p. 370.
[34] A quotation from Ch'eng I, *I-shu,* 15:8a.

330. A friend related a Buddhist story saying, "A Buddhist pointed his finger and asked, 'Have you seen this?' 'Yes,' replied the monks. He then put his finger in his sleeve and asked, 'Do you still see it?' The monks said, 'No.'[35] According to the Buddhist interpretation, this means that they had not seen the Buddha-nature. I do not understand this."

The Teacher said, "Fingers may or may not be seen. Your way of seeing nature is always directed to the human mind, only to its active occupation with what can be seen or heard and not to its concrete effort concerning what is not seen or heard. But the original substance of innate knowledge consists in what is not seen or heard and the effort to extend innate knowledge consists in the mind's being cautious [over things one does not see] and apprehensive [over things one does not hear]. The student must at all times and at every moment see what he does not see and hear what he does not hear and then his effort can be concrete and sincere. When after a long time he has mastered the task, he does not need to exert energy, and without any caution or control the true nature will naturally operate without cease. How can seeing or hearing external things be any trouble?"

331. I said, "A former scholar said that the flying of the hawk, the leaping of fishes,[36] and the feeling that one must always be doing something[37] are all very lively and dynamic in the same way."[38]

The Teacher said, "Correct. The whole universe is very lively and dynamic because of the same principle. It is the unceasing universal operation of one's innate knowledge. To extend innate knowledge is the task of always doing something. Not only should this principle not be departed from, in reality it cannot be. The Way is everywhere, and so is our task."

332. The Teacher said, "Here, gentlemen, all of you must have your minds determined to become sages. At all times and at every moment, your effort must be so earnest and strong that 'Every beating on the body will leave a scar and every slap on the face will fill the palm with blood.[39] Only then can every sentence of mine be

[35] The origin of this story is not known.
[36] Ch'eng Hao, quoting *Book of Odes*, ode no. 239.
[37] Mencius' saying, in *Book of Mencius*, 2A:2.
[38] Ch'eng Hao, *I-shu*, 3:1a.
[39] A tenth-century saying often quoted by the Zen Buddhists.

effective as you listen to me. If you while away your time aimlessly, you will be like a piece of dead flesh which feels no pain even if it struck. In this way you will never amount to anything. When you go home, you will find only your old cunning way of doing things. Will that not be a pity?"

333. I said, "Recently I seem to have few erroneous thoughts and not any attachment in my thoughts as to any particular way of making an effort. Is this the right way to pursue the task?"

The Teacher said, "Go ahead and make earnest and sincere effort. It will do no harm even if you have little bit of attachment in your thoughts. In time you will naturally be at ease and calm. If, on the other hand, after you have made only a little effort, you think there is already a result, how can that be reliable?"

334. A friend sighed and said, "When a selfish desire begins to emerge, one clearly knows it in his own mind but cannot immediately get rid of it."

The Teacher said, "As the desire emerges, your knowledge of it is your very life. Right then and there go ahead and erase the desire. That is the task of establishing one's destiny."

335. [The Teacher said,] "Confucius' doctrine, 'By nature men are alike [but through practice they have become far apart],'[40] is the same as Mencius' doctrine that human nature is originally good,[41] and should not be understood solely in terms of physical nature. If we speak in terms of physical nature, then the strong and the weak are opposed to each other, for instance. How can they be alike? Only in their original goodness are people the same. When people are born, they are the same in original goodness. When those who are strong practice the good, they become strength that is good, and when they practice evil, they become strength that is evil. When those who are weak practice good, they become weakness that is good, and when they practice evil, they become weakness that is evil.[42] Consequently, they become farther and farther apart."

336. The Teacher once told the students, "Not a single idea should be allowed to attach to the original substance of the mind, just

---

[40] *Analects*, 17:2.
[41] *Book of Mencius*, 2A:6, 6A:1-6.
[42] These ideas are derived from Chou Tun-i, *T'ung-shu*, ch. 7.

as not the least dirt should be allowed to stick to the eye. It does not take much dirt for the whole eye to see nothing but complete darkness."

He further said, "This idea need not be a selfish idea. Even if it is good, it should not be attached to the mind. If you put some gold or jade dust in the eye, just the same it cannot open."

337. I said, "The human mind and things form the same body.[43] In the case of one's body, blood and the vital force in fact circulate through it and therefore we can say they form the same body. In the case of men, their bodies are different and differ even more from those of animals and plants. How can they be said to form the same body?"

The Teacher said, "Just look at the matter from the point of view of the subtle incipient activating force of their mutual influence and response. Not only animals and plants, but heaven and earth also, form the same body with me. Spiritual beings also form the same body with me."

I asked the Teacher kindly to explain.

The Teacher said, "Among the things under heaven and on earth, which do you consider to be the mind of Heaven and Earth?"

"I have heard that 'Man is the mind of Heaven and Earth.' "[44]

"How does man become mind?"

"Clear intelligence and clear intelligence alone."

"We know, then, in all that fills heaven and earth there is but this clear intelligence. It is only because of their physical forms and bodies that men are separated. My clear intelligence is the master of heaven and earth and spiritual beings. If heaven is deprived of my clear intelligence, who is going to look into its height? If earth is deprived of my clear intelligence, who is going to look into its depth? If spiritual beings are deprived of my clear intelligence, who is going to distinguish their good and evil fortune or the calamities and blessings that they will bring? Separated from my clear intelligence, there will be no heaven, earth, spiritual beings, or myriad things, and separated from these, there will not be my clear intelligence. Thus

---

[43] Undoubtedly a quotation of Wang's, although it cannot be located. The idea is quite obvious in sec. 267.

[44] *Book of Rites*, "The Evolution of Rites." Cf. trans. by Legge, *Li Ki*, ch. 7, p. 382.

they are all permeated with one material force. How can they be separated?"

I asked further, "Heaven, earth, spiritual beings, and the myriad things have existed from great antiquity. Why should it be that if my clear intelligence is gone, they will all cease to exist?"

"Consider the dead man. His spirit has drifted away and dispersed. Where are his heaven and earth and myriad things?"

338.   Our Teacher began his journey to Ssu-en and T'ien-chou[45] to subdue the rebellion. Wang Ju-chung[46] and I [Ch'ien Te-hung][47] followed after him and saw him off at Yen-t'an.[48] Ju-chung raised the question of the Buddhist doctrine of the true state of dharmas [elements of existence] and illusory state of dharmas.[49]

The Teacher said, "Wherever the [original] mind is, there is the true state. Wherever the [original] mind is not, there is the illusory state. At the same time, wherever the [subjective] mind is not, there is the true state, and wherever the [subjective] mind is, there is the illusory state."

Ju-chung said, "When you say 'Wherever the mind is, there is the true state and wherever the mind is not, there is the illusory state,' you are talking about the task from the point of view of the original substance of the mind, and when you say, 'Wherever the mind is not, there is the true state, and wherever the mind is, there is the illusory state,' you are talking about the original substance from the point of view of the task."

The Teacher approved his interpretation. At that time I was not quite clear. After several years of effort, I began to believe that the original substance and the task are one. Our Teacher uttered those words at that time incidentally in answer to a question. In teaching others we Confucians should not rely on Buddhist ideas to formulate our doctrines.

339.   I once saw our Teacher bid farewell to two or three elderly gentlemen at the gate. He withdrew and sat in the vestibule and

---

[45] In 1527.

[46] See above, sec. 257, n. 15.

[47] See above, preface to secs. 130 ff., n. 1.

[48] In modern Chekiang Province.

[49] The doctrine that the elements of existence are real is taught in the *Lotus Scripture*, ch. 1; the doctrine that the elements of existence are illusory is taught in the *Pārinirvāṇa Scripture*, chs. 2 and 12.

appeared to be sad. I[50] walked quickly forward to ask what the matter was.

The Teacher said, "I have just discussed learning with these elders. Like trying to put a square into a circle, I got nowhere with them. This Way of ours is like a level road. Unfortunately, famous but mediocre scholars often block their own way and consequently fall into a field of obstacles for their whole lives without repentance. I don't know what they are talking about."

I withdrew and told friends, "In teaching people our Teacher does not prefer others to the senile. His is the mind of a humane man with compassion toward things."

340. The Teacher said, "A great defect in life is pride. The proud son is sure not to be filial, nor the proud minister loyal, nor the proud father affectionate, nor the proud friend faithful. Thus Hsiang and Tan-chu,[51] both being unworthy, wasted their whole lives simply because of their pride. You gentlemen should always realize this personally: the human mind is in fact the natural principle. It is refined and clear without an iota of defilement or selfish attachment. It is just a non-ego. One must not harbor any egoism in the mind. To do so means to have pride. The many good points about ancient sages are but selflessness. Being selfless, one is naturally humble. Humility is the foundation of all virtues, while pride is the chief of all vices."

341. The Teacher further said, "The Way is most simple and easy. It is also most refined and subtle. Confucius said, 'It is as easy as to look at one's palm.'[52] Who does not see his palm every day? But when you ask him how the various lines and patterns in his palm look, he does not know. It is the same with the innate knowledge that I am talking about. It is immediately clear as soon as it is mentioned. Who does not know it? But if one purposely wants to see it, who can do so?"

I said, "This innate knowledge probably has neither spatial restriction nor physical form.[53] It is most difficult to grasp."

[50] See above, preface to secs. 130 ff., n. 1.
[51] See above, secs. 142, 245, 296, and see *Book of Mencius*, 5A:2.
[52] *Doctrine of the Mean*, ch. 19.
[53] *Book of Changes*, "Appended Remarks," pt. 1, ch. 4. Cf. trans. by Legge, *Yi King*, p. 354.

The Teacher said, "Innate knowledge is the same as changes. 'As the Way, it changes frequently. It changes and moves without staying in one place, flowing about into any one of the six places of the hexagram. It ascends and descends without any constancy, and its elements of strength (yang) and weakness (yin) interchange. It cannot be considered as an invariable standard. It changes to suit the circumstances.'[54] How can this innate knowledge be grasped? When one understands it thoroughly, he is a sage."

342. I asked, "Confucius said, 'Hui is not any assistance to me. [Nothing that I say does not please him].'[55] Does this mean that the Sage really expected assistance from his disciples?"

The Teacher said, "This is also true. The Way is indeed inexhaustible. The more people ask and argue about it, the more manifest will its refinement and subtlety become. The words of the Sage naturally cover all. But some questioners are obstructed in their minds. As they pressed a question on the Sage, he expounded all the more energetically. But when Yen Hui heard one part, he knew all. He was very clear in his mind. Why did he need to ask or argue? Consequently, the Sage remained in the state of absolute quiet and inactivity and did not expound anything. Hence Yen Hui was no assistance to him."

343. Tsou Ch'ien-chih[56] once told me [Ch'ien Te-hung],[57] "Shu Kuo-shang[58] once took a sheet of paper and asked the Teacher to write the following passage: 'Anybody who wishes to cultivate the *t'ung* and *tzu* trees, which may be grasped by one or both hands, knows how to nourish them. In the case of their own persons, men do not know how to nourish them.'[59] The Teacher wrote, suspending the brush in his hand. When he came to the last sentence, he looked around and said smilingly, 'Kuo-shang studied and succeeded in obtaining the highest degree in civil service examination. Can it really be that he does not know to nourish the person[60] and still

---

[54] *Ibid.*, "Appended Remarks," pt. 2, ch. 8. Cf. Legge, p. 399.

[55] *Analects*, 11:3.

[56] See above, sec. 314, n. 99.

[57] See above, preface to secs. 130 ff., n. 1.

[58] See above, sec. 204, n. 22.

[59] *Book of Mencius*, 6A:13.

[60] Through civil service degrees and official positions according to the general philosophy of life at the time.

needs to recite this passage in order to warn himself?' For a time all friends in attendance were awed."

Postscript by Ch'ien Te-hung[1]

In the winter of the seventh year of Chia-ching [1528-29], Wang Ju-chung[2] and I were rushing to the funeral of our Teacher. When we reached Kuang-hsin[3] we sent obituary notices to all fellow disciples and invited them to collect and record within three years our Teacher's sayings. Subsequently some fellow disciples sent me individually what they could remember.[4] I selected those that had to do with questions presented to our Teacher for correction, and combined them with what I had recorded, and got a certain number of items. When I stayed at Wu [in 1535],[5] I was about to publish them together with the *Wen-lu* (Literary works).[6] I left Wu because of a death in the family and therefore did not succeed in publishing them.

At that time more and more followers lectured on our Teacher's doctrines in all parts of the country, the fundamental doctrines of our school had been clarified, and it appeared that any publication would be superfluous. I therefore no longer thought of it. Last year a fellow disciple, Mr. Tseng Ts'ai-han,[7] got hold of my manuscript, collected more sayings on the side, and published it in Ching-chou[8] under the title *I-yen* (Surviving words). I read it and felt that the selection was not refined. I therefore eliminated the repetitions and discarded the unimportant, kept a third of it, and published it at the Shui-hsi Academy in Ning-kuo[9] under the title *Ch'uan-hsi hsü-lu* (Supplement to the instructions on practical living).[10] In the summer

[1] See above, preface to secs. 130 ff., n. 1.
[2] See above, sec. 257, n. 15.
[3] A prefecture in modern Kiangsi.
[4] These are not to be confused with secs. 1-129, which had been published in 1518.
[5] In Kiangsu Province.
[6] See above, preface to secs. 130 ff., n. 8.
[7] Nothing is known of him.
[8] In modern Hupei Province.
[9] Capital of a prefecture in modern Anhui Province.
[10] Meaning the supplement to the present Parts I and II.

of this year I came here to Ch'i-chou.[11] Mr. Shen Ssu-wei[12] said to me, "The teachings of our Teacher's school have for a long time prevailed in all parts of the country except in Ch'i-chou. Those scholars of Ch'i-chou who have been able to read the *I-yen* of the Teacher felt as if they had received instructions from him personally, which pointed the way to them and led them to see innate knowledge as though seeing the light of the sun and moon once more. However, I am afraid that the transmission and practice of the doctrine have not been extensive, and I do not believe it is troublesome to republish them. Why not collect the missing sayings and publish an enlarged edition?"

I said, "You are right." The tenets of the extension of knowledge and the investigation of things of our school were to enlighten those who came to learn. Students practiced personally and came to realize silently. They dared not seek understanding through intellection but only tried to attain concrete, personal realization. This was why our Teacher spoke all day without feeling troubled and the students listened all day without getting tired of the repetition. For as his instructions were concentrated, the students' personal realization became increasingly refined. Before he spoke we understood his subtle meaning. After he spoke the spirit manifested itself far beyond his words. This was all due to the sincerity of our gratitude for his influence. Now it has not been three decades since the death of our Teacher and it seems that his wise sayings and profound tenets are gradually fading away. Has this bad effect not come about because our group has not practiced them personally with sufficient effort but has talked too much instead? As the tendencies of followers have become diverse, the doctrines of our school have not spread. I therefore took the unpublished material, selected those sayings that are not contradictory, and succeeded in putting them together as one part. Those remaining that do not reflect the true teachings of our Teacher and those already contained in the *Wen-lu* are all omitted. I also changed the middle part [of the *I-Yen*] into question and answer form.[13] I sent them to Mr. Chang, magistrate of Huang-mei,[14] to be published in an enlarged version so that the reader will

[11] A county in present Hupei.
[12] Disciple of Ou-yang Ch'ung-i (see above, sec. 104) and Wang Chi (see above, sec. 257).
[13] Referring to secs. 260-317.
[14] A county in present Hupei.

not seek understanding through intellection but only through concrete, personal realization and that he will have no more doubt about what is contained in this work.

> Respectfully written by disciple Ch'ien Te-hung
> at the Ch'ung-cheng Institute, Ch'i-chou, in the
> fourth month of the thirty-fifth year of Chia-ching [1556]

PREFACE TO CHU HSI'S FINAL CONCLU-SIONS ARRIVED AT LATE IN LIFE

The following "Preface" was written in 1515 when Wang was forty-four, three years before the "Final Conclusions" was published. Ever since he had gone to Nanking in 1514, he had aroused tremendous criticism because of his own critical spirit and because of his opposition to the Chu Hsi philosophy which had controlled the civil service examinations for over a century. Wang's situation must have been very desperate. Partly to lessen the animosity and partly to put his own theories into the mouth of Chu Hsi with the hope of wider acceptance of his own views, he selected a passage each from thirty-four letters written by Chu to twenty-four people, as well as a passage from Wu Ch'eng (1249-1333),[1] and published them under the above title in 1518 in an attempt to show that Chu Hsi had changed his position in late life and adopted the views now advocated by Wang. These selections are arbitrary and mostly out of context. In the end Wang had to confess to Lo Ch'in-shun (1465-1547)[2] that his "chief idea was that it was important to accommodate and compromise." The matter created one of the most violent intellectual storms in Chinese history. Throughout the Ming and Ch'ing dynasties, Wang was severely criticized for intellectual dishonesty and for trying to deceive students by utilizing Chu Hsi's name and influence to promote his own doctrine.[3] These are harsh criticisms, mostly made by Chu Hsi's followers. Others tended to sympathize with Wang and said that he did no more than early Confucians who put their doctrines into the mouths of ancient sages. One thing is certain: Wang's intent was not to compromise but to

[1] He was honored as Master Ts'ao-lu. The greatest Neo-Confucian of the Yüan dynasty, he attempted to synthesize the rationalistic Neo-Confucianism of Chu Hsi and the idealistic Neo-Confucianism of Lu Hsiang-shan.

[2] His literary name was Cheng-an. See above, sec. 176.

[3] The most severe criticisms are found in: *Lo Cheng-an chi*, ch. 1; Ch'en Chien (Ch'en Ch'ing-lan, 1497-1567), *Hsüeh-pu t'ung-pien*, I, B; Feng K'o (fl. 1562), *Ch'iu-shih pien*, ch. 4; Lu Lung-ch'i (1630-92), *San-yü-t'ang wen-chi*, ch. 2; and Juan Yüan (1764-1849), *Yen-ching-shih hsü-chi*, ch. 3.

apply the Taoist tactics of withdrawing in order to advance. It is not necessary to include here the passages selected by Wang. The significance of the whole episode is sufficiently clear from the following "Introduction" by Ch'ien Te-hung and Wang's own "Preface."

Introduction by Ch'ien Te-hung: The "Final Conclusions" was at first published in southern Kiangsi [in 1518].[4] During his long period of rest because of an eye ailment, Master Chu suddenly realized the depth and subtlety of the doctrine of the Sage. Consequently, he regretted that his commentaries and writings during middle age had done damage to himself as well as others. He wrote to many of his like-minded friends about it.

In reading these letters, our Teacher was glad that his own convictions agreed with those of Chu Hsi. He personally copied passages from them to make up an article. His pupil published and circulated it. From then on few people engaged any further in the controversy on the question of whether our Teacher differed from or agreed with Master Chu. Our Teacher said, "This is an unexpected help I get."

In the sixth year of Lung-ch'ing [1572], Mr. Hsieh T'ing-chieh published our Teacher's *Complete Works.* He told me to include this article at the end of the recorded sayings [*Instructions on Practical Living*] so as to show that our Teacher's teachings and those of Master Chu do not conflict and that all correct doctrines throughout the ages have come from the same source. This article consists of a number of items, including our Teacher's own "Preface" and the "Postscript" by Yüan Ch'ing-lin.[5] Violating modesty, I have written this introduction.

The Preface

As an introduction, Wang Yang-ming says: The transmission of the teachings of Confucius terminated with Mencius. It was not until one thousand and five hundred years later that Lien-hsi [Chou Tun-i] and Ming-tao [Ch'eng Hao] began to search again for its clues. From then on the system was developed [by Chu Hsi and his followers] and

---

[4] According to the *Nien-p'u.*

[5] He followed Chu Hsi's doctrines for some thirty years. Finally he heard Wang's teachings and found them to be very simple and easy and turned away from Chu in favor of Wang. The "Postscript" was written in 1518.

branched off more and more, at the same time gradually tending to become fragmented and torn apart, and finally was altogether dissipated. I have gone deeply into the reasons for this, and believe that for the most part the whole situation has been confused by the fact that famous but mediocre scholars talk too much.

Since in my youth I was devoted to preparation for obtaining a civil service degree, my ambition was completely submerged in writing flowery compositions. Later I knew to a small extent how to engage in correct learning. However, I faced the difficulty that the various theories and interpretations were confusing and worrisome, and I was at a loss and did not know where to begin. Consequently, I sought answers in Taoism and Buddhism. I was happy to find something after my heart and felt that here lay the teachings of the Sage. But their teachings are sometimes at odds with those of Confucius, and when applied to the ordinary affairs of life they were often inadequate and had no solution to offer. I half followed them and half rejected them. I half tended toward them and half tended away from them. I believed in them and yet I doubted them.

Later when I was banished to become an official in Lung-ch'ang,[6] I lived among the barbarians [1508-9] and in the midst of great difficulties. As a consequence of stimulating my mind and hardening my nature, I seemed to have rapidly awakened. I searched and made an effort at personal realization for another year, and looked for confirmation in the Five Classics[7] and the Four Masters.[8] It was like a torrent bursting the river bank and rushing to the sea. Then I realized, alas, that the path of the Sage is as level as a broad way. But scholars of today have erroneously opened a hole here and a crack there, have trod over obstacles and have fallen into ditches. In the final analysis their doctrines are inferior even to those of Buddhism and Taoism. No wonder the best scholars of the world have gotten tired of Confucianism and rushed to the other two systems. Shall we blame Buddhism and Taoism for this?

I have occasionally talked to like-minded friends about this. However, those who heard me lost no time in disapproving and criticizing me. They considered me as setting up strange doctrines and looking for novelty. Although I earnestly searched within myself

[6] In modern Kuei-chou.
[7] See above, Introduction, n. 1.
[8] Meaning the Four Books. See above, Introduction, n. 1.

and tried hard to be humble and made sure to detect and remove any flaw there might be, my thoughts turned out to be more refined, clearer, and surer, and there was absolutely no more doubt left in my mind. Only in Master Chu's doctrines did I find some disagreement, for which I felt sorry for a long time. I was wondering whether, with his wisdom and virtue, Master Chu could still have failed to understand. When I was an official in Nanking [1514] I got hold of his works and searched through them. Only then did I find that in his later years he clearly realized the mistakes of his earlier doctrines. He regretted them so deeply as to say that he "cannot be redeemed from the sin of having deceived others as well as himself."⁹ His *Chi-chu* (Collected commentaries)¹⁰ and *Huo-wen* (Questions and answers)¹¹ that have been transmitted from generation to generation represent the tentative conclusions of his middle age. He blamed himself for not having been able to correct the mistakes of the old text of the *Great Learning*, much as he had wanted to. As to his *Yü-lei* (Classified conversations)¹² and the like, since his disciples, each with the spirit of rivalry, had injected into them their subjective viewpoints, they contradict even more his usual doctrines. Because of their limited information, scholars of today have followed and studied only these works. They have heard nothing about Chu Hsi's ideas after his awakening. Is it any wonder, then, that my words are not accepted and that what Master Chu had in mind has not been able to reveal itself to later generations?

As I feel fortunate that my ideas are not in conflict with those of Master Chu, and also am happy that he apprehended before me what our minds have in common, and furthermore, as I am sorry that scholars of today have only adhered to the tentative doctrine of Master Chu's middle age and do not know how to find what he taught after his awakening late in life, but compete with one another in making endless noise to confuse the correct learning without realizing that they themselves have joined the camps of heretics, I have selected and gathered passages privately to show like-minded

⁹ A quotation from one of Chu Hsi's letters in *Chu Tzu wen-chi*, 40:27a.

¹⁰ These are the *Ta-hsüeh chang-chü*, the *Chung-yung chang-chü*, the *Lun-yü chi-chu*, and the *Meng Tzu chi-chu*.

¹¹ These are the *Ta-hsüeh huo-wen*, the *Chung-yung huo-wen*, the *Lun-yü huo-wen*, and the *Meng Tzu huo-wen*.

¹² *Chu Tzu yü-lei*.

friends so that they will no longer doubt my position and that we may hope that the doctrine of the Sage will be made clear to the world.

> Written by humble student Wang Shou-jen
> of Yü-yao[13] on the first day of the
> eleventh month in the winter of the
> tenth year of Cheng-te

---

[13] Wang's native place in what is now Chekiang.

Inquiry on the *Great Learning*

Inquiry on the *Great Learning*

(*Wang Wen-ch'eng Kung ch'üan-shu*, 26:1b-5a)

This is Wang Yang-ming's most important writing, for it embodies his basic teachings and represents his final conclusions. As his outstanding disciple Ch'ien Te-hung noted, Wang always discussed with the beginners the first chapter of the *Great Learning* and that of the *Doctrine of the Mean*, which he believed taught the complete task of Confucian learning.[1] When his disciples requested him to write down his ideas, he refused, for he distrusted the written word and preferred oral transmission, and, furthermore, he did not want to aggravate with his unorthodox ideas the already bitter controversy between his school and its opponents. It was not until 1527, a little over a year before he died, when he was about to leave on a campaign to suppress a rebellion in South China, that he finally wrote this down.[2]

Of greater significance is the fact that this essay contains all of Wang's fundamental doctrines: that the man of humanity forms one body with all things and extends his love to all, that the mind is principle, that the highest good is inherent in the mind, that to investigate things is to rectify the mind, and that the extension of the innate knowledge of the good is the beginning and end of a moral life. The theory of the unity of knowledge and action is not explicitly stated but is implied throughout, for in insisting that manifesting the clear character and loving the people are identical, he refused to separate the internal and the external life. Indeed he stressed the point that, from the investigation of things to bringing peace to the world, all steps form one single task. In this he clearly departed from the *Great Learning*, which definitely says there is an order of first and last. Actually Wang merely used the *Great Learning* as a vehicle to express his own ideas. In this sense he was quite different from Chu Hsi, who only elaborated the teachings of the *Great Learning*. However, he still adhered to this ancient Classic and followed its old text.[3] In spite of his direct opposition to Chu Hsi in the interpretation of the *Great Learning*, he did not, after all, go beyond Chu Hsi's position, that the *Great Learning* is the "gate to virtue."[4]

---

[1] *Wang Wen-ch'eng Kung ch'üan-shu*, 26:2a.
[2] *Ibid.*, 26:10b.
[3] See above, secs. 1, 2, 129, and 173.
[4] Chu Hsi's introduction to the *Great Learning*. Chu here is quoting Ch'eng I, *Ts'ui-yen*, 1:25a.

Question: The *Great Learning* was considered by a former scholar as the learning of the great man.[5] I venture to ask why the learning of the great man should consist in "manifesting the clear character."[6]

Master Wang said: The great man regards Heaven, Earth, and the myriad things as one body. He regards the world as one family and the country as one person. As to those who make a cleavage between objects and distinguish between the self and others, they are small men. That the great man can regard Heaven, Earth, and the myriad things as one body is not because he deliberately wants to do so, but because it is natural to the humane nature of his mind that he do so. Forming one body with Heaven, Earth, and the myriad things is not only true of the great man. Even the mind of the small man is no different. Only he himself makes it small. Therefore when he sees a child about to fall into a well, he cannot help a feeling of alarm and commiseration.[7] This shows that his humanity forms one body with the child. It may be objected that the child belongs to the same species. Again, when he observes the pitiful cries and frightened appearance of birds and animals about to be slaughtered, he cannot help feeling an "inability to bear" their suffering.[8] This shows that his humanity forms one body with birds and animals. It may be objected that birds and animals are sentient beings as he is. But when he sees plants broken and destroyed, he cannot help a feeling of pity. This shows that his humanity forms one body with plants. It may be said that plants are living things as he is. Yet, even when he sees tiles and stones shattered and crushed, he cannot help a feeling of regret. This shows that his humanity forms one body with tiles and stones. This means that even the mind of the small man necessarily has the humanity that forms one body with all. Such a mind is rooted in his Heaven-endowed nature, and is naturally intelligent, clear, and not beclouded. For this reason it is called the "clear character." Although the mind of the small man is divided and narrow, yet his humanity that forms one body can remain free from darkness to this degree. This is due to the fact that

---

[5] Chu Hsi, *Ta-hsüeh chang-chü,* commentary on the text. Actually, by "great learning" (*ta-hsüeh*) Chu Hsi meant "education for the adult," but the Chinese phrase can also mean the learning of the great man. Wang used the latter interpretation.

[6] The text of the *Great Learning.*

[7] *Book of Mencius,* 2A:6.

[8] *Ibid.*

his mind has not yet been aroused by desires and obscured by selfishness. When it is aroused by desires and obscured by selfishness, compelled by greed for gain and fear of harm, and stirred by anger, he will destroy things, kill members of his own species, and will do everything. In extreme cases he will even slaughter his own brothers, and the humanity that forms one body will disappear completely. Hence, if it is not obscured by selfish desires, even the mind of the small man has the humanity that forms one body with all as does the mind of the great man. As soon as it is obscured by selfish desires, even the mind of the great man will be divided and narrow like that of the small man. Thus the learning of the great man consists entirely in getting rid of the obscuration of selfish desires in order by his own efforts to make manifest his clear character, so as to restore the condition of forming one body with Heaven, Earth, and the myriad things, a condition that is originally so, that is all. It is not that outside of the original substance something can be added.

Question: Why, then, does the learning of the great man consist in loving the people?

Answer: To manifest the clear character is to bring about the substance of the state of forming one body with Heaven, Earth, and the myriad things, whereas loving the people is to put into universal operation the function of the state of forming one body. Hence manifesting the clear character consists in loving the people, and loving the people is the way to manifest the clear character. There- fore, only when I love my father, the fathers of others, and the fathers of all men can my humanity really form one body with my father, the fathers of others, and the fathers of all men. When it truly forms one body with them, then the clear character of filial piety will be manifested. Only when I love my brother, the brothers of others, and the brothers of all men can my humanity really form one body with my brother, the brothers of others, and the brothers of all men. When it truly forms one body with them, then the clear character of brotherly respect will be manifested. Everything from ruler, minister, husband, wife, and friends to mountains, rivers, spiritual beings, birds, animals, and plants should be truly loved in order to realize my humanity that forms one body with them, and then my clear character will be completely manifested, and I will really form one body with Heaven, Earth, and the myriad things. This is what is meant by "manifesting the clear character throughout the world."[9] This is what is meant by "regulation of the family," "ordering the state," and "bringing peace to the world."[10] This is what is meant by "full development of one's nature."[11]

Question: Then why does the learning of the great man consist in "abiding in the highest good"?[12]

Answer: The highest good is the ultimate principle of manifesting character and loving people. The nature endowed in us by Heaven is pure and perfect. The fact that it is intelligent, clear, and not beclouded is evidence of the emanation and revelation of the highest good. It is the original substance of the clear character which is called innate knowledge of the good. As the highest good emanates and reveals itself, we will consider right as right and wrong as wrong. Things of greater or less importance and situations of grave or light character will be responded to as they act upon us. In all our changes and movements, we will stick to no particular point, but possess in ourselves the mean that is perfectly natural. This is the ultimate of the normal nature of man and the principle of things. There can be no consideration of adding or subtracting anything to or from it. Such a suggestion reveals selfish ideas and shallow cunning, and cannot be said to be the highest good. Naturally, how can anyone who does not watch over himself carefully when alone, and who has no refinement and singleness of mind, attain to such a state of perfection? Later generations fail to realize that the highest good is inherent in their own minds, but exercise their selfish ideas and cunning and grope for it outside their minds, believing that every event and every object has its own peculiar definite principle. For this reason the law of right and wrong is obscured; the mind becomes concerned with fragmentary and isolated details and broken pieces; the selfish desires of man become rampant and the Principle of Nature is at an end. And thus the learning of manifesting character and loving people is everywhere thrown into confusion. In the past there have, of course, been people who wanted to manifest their clear character. But simply because they did not know how to abide in the highest good, but instead drove their own minds toward something too lofty, they thereby lost them in illusions, emptiness, and quietness, having

[9] The text of the *Great Learning*.
[10] *Ibid.*
[11] *Doctrine of the Mean*, ch. 22.
[12] The text of the *Great Learning*.

nothing to do with the work of the family, the state, and the world. Such are the followers of Buddhism and Taoism. There have, of course, been those who wanted to love their people. Yet simply because they did not know how to abide in the highest good, but instead sank their own minds in base and trifling things, they thereby lost them in scheming strategy and cunning techniques, having neither the sincerity of humanity nor that of commiseration. Such are the followers of the Five Despots[13] and the pursuers of success and profit. All of these defects are due to a failure to know how to abide in the highest good. Therefore abiding in the highest good is to manifesting character and loving people as the carpenter's square and compass are to the square and the circle, or rule and measure to length, or balances and scales to weight. If the square and the circle do not abide by the compass and the carpenter's square, their standard will be wrong; if length does not abide by the rule and measure, its adjustment will be lost; if weight does not abide by the balances, its exactness will be gone; and if manifesting clear character and loving people do not abide by the highest good, their foundation will disappear. Therefore, abiding in the highest good so as to love people and manifest the clear character is what is meant by the learning of the great man.

Question: "Only after knowing what to abide in can one be calm. Only after having been calm can one be tranquil. Only after having achieved tranquillity can one have peaceful repose. Only after having peaceful repose can one begin to deliberate. Only after deliberation can the end be attained."[14] How do you explain this?

Answer: People fail to realize that the highest good is in their minds and seek it outside. As they believe that everything or every event has its own definite principle, they search for the highest good in individual things. Consequently, the mind becomes fragmentary, isolated, broken into pieces; mixed and confused, it has no definite direction. Once it is realized that the highest good is in the mind and does not depend on any search outside, then the mind will have definite direction and there will be no danger of its becoming fragmentary, isolated, broken into pieces, mixed, or confused. When there is no such danger, the mind will not be erroneously perturbed but will be tranquil. Not being erroneously perturbed but being

[13] See above, sec. 11, n. 46.
[14] The text of the *Great Learning*.

tranquil, it will be leisurely and at ease in its daily functioning and will attain peaceful repose. Being in peaceful repose, whenever a thought arises or an event acts upon it, the mind with its innate knowledge will thoroughly sift and carefully examine whether or not the thought or event is in accord with the highest good, and thus the mind can deliberate. With deliberation, every decision will be excellent and every act will be proper, and in this way the highest good will be attained.

Question: "Things have their roots and their branches."[15] A former scholar considered manifesting the clear character as the root (or fundamental) and renovating the people as the branch (or secondary), and thought that they are two things opposing each other as internal and external.[16] "Affairs have their beginnings and their ends."[17] The former scholar considered knowing what to abide in as the beginning and the attainment of the highest good as the end, both being one thing in harmonious continuity. According to you, "renovating the people" (*hsin-min*) should be read as "loving the people" (*ch'in-min*). If so, isn't the theory of root and branches in some respect incorrect?

Answer: The theory of beginnings and ends is in general right. Even if we read "renovating the people" as "loving the people" and say that manifesting the character is the root and loving the people is the branches, it is not incorrect. The main thing is that root and branches should not be distinguished as two different things. The trunk of the tree is called the root, and the twigs are called the branches. It is precisely because the tree is one that its parts can be called root and branches. If they are said to be two different things, then since they are two distinct objects, how can we speak of them as root and branches of the same thing? Since the idea of renovating the people is different from that of loving the people, obviously the task of manifesting the character and that of loving the people are two different things. If it is realized that manifesting the clear character is to love the people and loving the people is to manifest the clear character, how can they be split in two? What the former scholar said is due to his failure to realize that manifesting the character and loving the people are basically one thing. Instead, he believed them to be two different things and

[15] *Ibid.*
[16] Chu Hsi, *Ta-hsüeh chang-chü*, commentary on the text.
[17] The text of the *Great Learning*.

consequently, although he knew that root and branches should be one, yet he could not help splitting them in two.

Question: The passage from the phrase, "The ancients who wished to manifest their clear character throughout the world" to the clause, "first [order their state... regulate their families...] cultivate their personal lives,"[18] can be understood by your theory of manifesting the character and loving the people. May I ask what task, what procedure, and what effort are involved in the passage from "Those who wished to cultivate their personal lives would [first rectify their minds... make their will sincere... extend their knowledge]" to the clause, "the extension of knowledge consists in the investigation of things"?[19]

Answer: This passage fully explains the task of manifesting the character, loving the people, and abiding in the highest good. The person, the mind, the will, knowledge, and things constitute the order followed in the task. While each of them has its own place, they are really one thing. Investigating, extending, being sincere, rectifying, and cultivating are the task performed in the procedure. Although each has its own name, they are really one affair. What is it that is called the person? It is the physical functioning of the mind. What is it that is called the mind? It is the clear and intelligent master of the person. What is meant by cultivating the personal life? It means to do good and get rid of evil. Can the body by itself do good and get rid of evil? The clear and intelligent master must desire to do good and get rid of evil before the body that functions physically can do so. Therefore he who wishes to cultivate his personal life must first rectify his mind.

Now the original substance of the mind is man's nature. Human nature being universally good, the original substance of the mind is correct. How is it that any effort is required to rectify the mind? The reason is that, while the original substance of the mind is originally correct, incorrectness enters when one's thoughts and will are in operation. Therefore he who wishes to rectify his mind must rectify it in connection with the operation of his thoughts and will. If, whenever a good thought arises, he really loves it as he loves beautiful colors, and whenever an evil thought arises, he really hates it as he hates bad odors, then his will will always be sincere and his mind can be rectified.

[18] *Ibid.*
[19] *Ibid.*

However, what arises from the will may be good or evil, and unless there is a way to make clear the distinction between good and evil, there will be a confusion of truth and untruth. In that case, even if one wants to make his will sincere, he cannot do so. Therefore he who wishes to make his will sincere must extend his knowledge. By extension is meant to reach the limit. The word "extension" is the same as that used in the saying, "Mourning is to be carried to the utmost degree of grief."[20] In the *Book of Changes* it is said: "Knowing the utmost, one should reach it."[21] "Knowing the utmost" means knowledge and "reaching it" means extension. The extension of knowledge is not what later scholars understand as enriching and widening knowledge.[22] It is simply extending one's innate knowledge of the good to the utmost. This innate knowledge of the good is what Mencius meant when he said, "The sense of right and wrong is common to all men."[23] The sense of right and wrong requires no deliberation to know, nor does it depend on learning to function.[24] This is why it is called innate knowledge. It is my nature endowed by Heaven, the original substance of my mind, naturally intelligent, shining, clear, and understanding.

Whenever a thought or a wish arises, my mind's faculty of innate knowledge itself is always conscious of it. Whether it is good or evil, my mind's innate knowing faculty itself also knows it. It has nothing to do with others. Therefore, although an inferior man may have done all manner of evil, when he sees a superior man he will surely try to disguise this fact, concealing what is evil and displaying what is good in himself.[25] This shows that innate knowledge of the good does not permit any self-deception. Now the only way to distinguish good and evil in order to make the will sincere is to extend to the utmost the knowledge of the innate faculty. Why is this? When [a good] thought or wish arises, the innate faculty of my mind already knows it to be good. Suppose I do not sincerely love it but instead turn away from it. I would then be regarding good as evil and obscuring my innate faculty which knows the good. When

[20] *Analects*, 19:14.
[21] Commentary on hexagram no. 1. Cf. trans. by Legge, *Yi King*, p. 410.
[22] Chu Hsi, *Ta-hsüeh chang-chü*, commentary on the text.
[23] *Book of Mencius*, 2A:6, 6A:6.
[24] Quoting *Book of Mencius*, 7A:15.
[25] Paraphrasing the *Great Learning*, ch. 6.

[an evil] thought or wish arises, the innate faculty of my mind already knows it to be evil. If I did not sincerely hate it but instead carried it out, I would be regarding evil as good and obscuring my innate faculty which knows evil. In such cases what is supposed to be knowledge is really ignorance. How then can the will be made sincere? If what the innate faculty knows to be good or evil is sincerely loved or hated, one's innate knowing faculty is not deceived and the will can be made sincere.

Now, when one sets out to extend his innate knowledge to the utmost, does this mean something illusory, hazy, in a vacuum, and unreal? No, it means something real. Therefore, the extension of knowledge must consist in the investigation of things. A thing is an event. For every emanation of the will there must be an event corresponding to it. The event to which the will is directed is a thing. To investigate is to rectify. It is to rectify that which is incorrect so it can return to its original correctness. To rectify that which is not correct is to get rid of evil, and to return to correctness is to do good. This is what is meant by investigation. The *Book of History* says, "He [Emperor Yao] investigated (*ko*) heaven above and earth below";[26] "[Emperor Shun] investigated (*ko*) in the temple of illustrious ancestors";[27] and "[The ruler] rectifies (*ko*) the evil of his heart."[28] The word "investigation" (*ko*) in the phrase "the investigation of things" combines the two meanings.

If one sincerely loves the good known by the innate faculty but does not in reality do the good as he comes into contact with the thing to which the will is directed, it means that the thing has not been investigated and that the will to love the good is not yet sincere. If one sincerely hates the evil known by the innate faculty but does not in reality get rid of the evil as he comes into contact with the thing to which the will is directed, it means that the thing has not been investigated and that the will to hate evil is not sincere. If as we come into contact with the thing to which the will is directed, we really do the good and get rid of the evil to the utmost which is known by the innate faculty, then everything will be investigated and what is known by our innate faculty will not be

---

[26] *Book of History*, "Canon of Yao." Cf. trans. by Legge, *Shoo King*, p. 15.
[27] *Ibid.*, "Canon of Shun." Cf. Legge, *Shoo King*, p. 41.
[28] *Ibid.*, "The Charge to Ch'iung." Cf. Legge, *Shoo King* p. 585.

deficient or obscured but will be extended to the utmost. Then the mind will be joyous in itself, happy and without regret, the functioning of the will will carry with it no self-deception, and sincerity may be said to have been attained. Therefore it is said, "When things are investigated, knowledge is extended; when knowledge is extended, the will becomes sincere; when the will is sincere, the mind is rectified; and when the mind is rectified, the personal life is cultivated."[29] While the order of the tasks involves a sequence of first and last, in substance they are one and cannot be so separated. At the same time, while the order and the tasks cannot be separated into first and last, their function must be so refined as not to be wanting in the slightest degree. This is why the doctrine of investigation, extension, being sincere, and rectification is a correct exposition of the true heritage of Sage-Emperors Yao and Shun and why it coincides with Confucius' own ideas.

[29] The text of the *Great Learning*.

Some Social and Political Measures

Some Social and Political Measures

In both his career and his teachings, Wang aimed at concrete and earnest practice rather than words. Consequently, although he gave attention to social and political matters, he did not discuss them systematically in writing, Rather, he believed that once the fundamentals are realized and adhered to, details will naturally follow. What he had to say on these matters is found only in incidental remarks or short passages in his letters, official documents, and the like. It is therefore not easy to select from his works passages that will represent his over-all social and political views.

Several documents that do suggest some of his fundamental beliefs are translated below. They happen to represent his programs for both external security (no. 1) and internal peace (nos. 2-7). It is true that they deal with specific and abnormal situations of an emergency nature, since his policies for the frontier (no. 1) were intended to resist foreign invasion in the northwest and his domestic measures (nos. 2-7) were designed to pacify areas in southern Kiangsi and Fukien where banditry and rebellions had just been suppressed. It is also true that these documents deal with the years 1499 and 1517-20 and therefore antedate his doctrine of the extension of innate knowledge in 1521. Nevertheless one can see how comprehensive his programs were and how even under emergency conditions he insisted on the ethical essentials.

The memorial on policies for the frontier (no. 1) covers military, economic, personnel, and psychological matters. As a youth he visited frontiers. Two years before the memorial he had studied military techniques and earlier in the year he had earned his "presented scholar" degree in the national civil service examination. His loyalty was therefore solidly supported with knowledge. Although his recommendations for frontier policy were not accepted and enforced, his fame rose as a result of them. In the case of southern Kiangsi and Fukien where he had suppressed several large groups of bandits and rebels, some of whom declared themselves kings, instead of showing bitterness toward the former outlaws and advocating revenge or punishment, he stressed the need for "new citizens" to reform (no. 4), an adequate food supply, the dual application of the power of law and the kindness of the government, security (no. 5), and the institution of schools and moral training (nos. 3 and 6). In all these his earnestness and sincerity are obvious and are undoubtedly the natural expression of his own philosophy that the man of humanity forms one body with all things. Even in the joint system of family responsibility he proposes (nos. 2 and 7), the idea of moral persuasion is a central one.

Actually none of the measures recommended or applied was new. Both the joint responsibility system and the community compact had a long tradition behind them. And the moral and social ideals advocated in these documents are no more than orthodox Confucian values. So far as Wang's own teachings are concerned, these documents are not nearly as important as his essay "Pulling Up the Root and Stopping Up the Source," "The Doctrine in Four Axioms," or the "Inquiry on the *Great Learning*."[1] However, they are significant because they express the spirit of "forming one body with all things" even under emergency conditions. The appeal to moral sense and "innate knowledge" is unmistakable. It was under such critical situations as the ones that produced these documents that Wang "polished and trained" himself; out of such situations he eventually developed his central doctrine of "the extension of innate knowledge."

1. *Memorial Outlining Policies for the Frontier* (1499)

(*Wang Wen-ch'eng Kung ch'üan-shu*, 9:2a-10a)

Wang was serving in the department of public works in Peking in the fall of 1499 when the imperial government made a public request for recommendations concerning the alleviation of the critical condition of the state. The following memorial was Wang's response. Although his recommendations were not implemented, his fame spread as a result of them.

I respectfully submit eight emergency measures for your consideration, namely: building up a reservoir of personnel for emergency use, overlooking defects and utilizing excellences, reducing the army to save expenses, carrying on military farming to provide sufficient food, enforcing the law to inspire awe toward the government, showing imperial kindness to arouse indignation against the enemy, sacrificing the small in order to preserve the great, and using a strong defense in order to take advantage of the enemy's defects.

What is meant by building up a reservoir of personnel for emergency use? In my opinion, the operation of an army depends on this. If it has the proper personnel, it will overcome the enemy and win. If it does not have the proper personnel, it will be defeated and perish. Should we not build up a reservoir? At present the insignificant bandits along the frontier are not even capable of humiliating a lieutenant general, and yet in its discussions and recommendations

---

[1] See above, pp. 117-24, 241-45, and 272-80, respectively.

the court is already disturbed and does not know what to do. Reluctantly it thinks of people of secondary quality, but even here, outside of one or two people, there is none to continue the leadership. How can this be relied upon to overcome the enemy and win victory?...[2] In my stupid opinion, the military examinations of today can merely produce horsemen, archers, and boxers, but are not capable of attracting the talents of policy-making and leadership. At present, although noble families have schools to educate their children, these merely fulfill the need of old customs and have in reality not done any good. Let the sons of nobles be ordered to gather in one place, and select a man with the ability to handle both civil and military affairs, in a position like that of the present superintendent of education, to teach them. Let them practice writing, history, horse riding, and archery, and instruct them in military strategy and planning. In addition, among military students promote the outstanding ones every year and send them to join this group so that they can refine and polish one another and study and investigate at all times. Distinguish the superior and inferior in ability, examine them every year, and award degrees every three years. As to the department of military affairs, let officials from the minister down to the two vice-ministers take turns in inspecting the frontier every year, and select two or three persons from the personnel of the department who are adaptable and outstanding to accompany them so that these persons may be enabled to know the geography of the areas, the important and strategic points of passes on the frontier, the real strength of the enemy, and whether the situation is critical or not. As they would already have gone deeply into these matters and understood them well, in case an emergency arose, there would be no fear of lacking a qualified person to send from a great distance to handle them. Mencius said, 'If a thing has not been kept in store, one may not get it all his life.'[3] I hope from now on we can build up a reservoir.

What is meant by overlooking defects and utilizing excellences? In my opinion, in abilities and capacities we are not all sages or worthies. As we have certain excellences, so we necessarily have certain defects. As we are enlightened in certain things, so we are

---

[2] These and the following ellipses are mine. In all cases the omissions are historical incidents which Wang cited to support his views.

[3] *Book of Mencius*, 4A:9.

necessarily beclouded in others. And it is a common characteristic of man to have learned a lesson only after he has been punished.... I have heard the rumor that in the past officers of passes on the frontier who were known to be brave, daring, and fierce, have been in many cases dismissed and cast aside under the charge of having made certain mistakes, so that now they are idle. Of course in times of peace people who have been punished for mistakes certainly should not be placed in the position of command. However, in times of many troubles, like today, those who are brave, daring, and fierce can surely be utilized. Furthermore, people who have been cast aside for a long time surely repent their former mistakes and wish to show their enthusiasm and effort. Now if a few thousand troops are entrusted to their leadership so that they may establish their merits to redeem themselves, since they are very familiar with the affairs of the frontiers and are used to [fighting], their achievements should be far, far above those of men who are not familiar with the various favorable geographical factors and who aim only at defense. The ancients had a saying, "To utilize people's merits is not as good as to utilize their mistakes." What I have suggested is to utilize people's mistakes.

What is meant by reducing the army to save expenses? I have heard that the *Art of War* says that "it costs a thousand pieces of silver a day to operate an army of ten thousand men."[4] Ancient experts in army operation "acquired weapons in their own countries but depended on obtaining food supplies in the enemy states."[5] But even they had to spend a thousand pieces of silver every day. Now, in defending China against the barbarian enemies, there can be no food without a system of transportation, and there can be no money without a system of taxation. Consequently, it should not be said that the enemy can be depended on to supply food. This being the case, should an expedition be undertaken lightly today? I was away because of public duties and returned home only about ten days ago. When I heard while away that an expedition had been undertaken, I humbly considered that to be a mistake. Why? It is very cold in the north.[6] Now the severe heat is increasingly intense. By nature the enemy cannot endure it, whereas the climate is

---

[4] Sun Tzu (*fl.* 513-494 B.C.?), *Sun Tzu ping-fa*, ch. 2. Cf. trans. by Cheng Lin, *The Art of War: A Military Manual* (Shanghai, World Book Co., 1946).
[5] *Ibid.*
[6] Where the invaders came form.

agreeable to us. This is the first reason. The enemy depends on bows and arrows. Now is the season for frequent heavy rains, which will make the bow strings sticky and loose. This is the second reason. The enemy are nomads whose habitation follows rivers and swamps and who depend on hunting for food. Now they have already been stationed on the frontier for two months. The vegetation along the frontier is almost entirely exhausted and there are no more animals for them to hunt. This is the third reason. As I figure it, they will flee as soon as our army approaches. Of course, in conducting a campaign, there are cases where an onslaught on nerves must precede real strength. Now that our imperial army has already been dispatched, it is too late to stop it. The only thing to do is to reduce it, which can still save unnecessary expenses and achieve concrete results. The value of an army is its excellence and not its large size. I beg you to issue an edict immediately and order the generals secretly to select and retain a third of the ten thousand men who are excellent and strong and can be relied on, and send the rest back to the capital. Since the news of the dispatch of ten thousand men has already spread, the secret return of the troops to the capital will not be known on the frontier. The effect of the force of ten thousand men still exists. At the same time, an infinite amount of expense can in fact be saved. Are these not double advantages? Furthermore, when the imperial troops get to the frontier, in case of a reverse, they will retreat to the rear, but in case of any success, they will compete for the first place. This will not please the officers of the frontier troops. They asked for reinforcement simply so that in case the situation cannot be saved someone will share their responsibility. Now if these frontier troops are truly to be fed as the imperial troops are fed and rewarded as they are rewarded, several tens of thousands of recruits can be found locally and gathered to the tents in ten days or so. What is the need of sending imperial troops from the capital?

What is meant by using military farming to provide sufficient food? In my opinion, food is fundamental to an army. Without food there will be no army. Transportation by water or over land to passes on the frontier extends to a thousand *li*.[7] Ten percent of the items transported goes to waste. Therefore the *Art of War* says, "An army causes a country to be poor when it transports things

[7] About a third of a mile.

over a long distance, for such distant transportation makes the people poor. As an army gets to a place, its proximity causes prices to rise, and the rise of prices exhausts the people's financial resources."[8] This is what I mean. Now since the imperial troops are not capable of fighting and, in addition, are permitted to sit idle and consume food and thus to aggravate the economic difficulties of the frontier, this is tantamount to helping the enemy. Because of fighting and defense, the frontier guards have no time to farm. Let the imperial troops be separately stationed and divided into units and let them farm their land and supply them with seeds and implements. Wait till the autumn harvest and let them obtain their food from their own labor. When the enemy comes, give them military weapons and let them return to their army posts to stage a show of power at a distance and to form two wings. When the enemy withdraws, let them return to their farming once more. Taking advantage of their leisure, let them repair those parts of the Great Wall and its towers that have been destroyed by the enemy, to prevent his sudden penetration. In this way, although they cannot supply all the people in the military outposts, they can relieve to some extent the pressure on the local population to pay taxes and to make contributions. This is truly the way to hold on and to wait for opportunity, and is the long range policy for the imperial army's safety.

What is meant by enforcing the law to inspire awe toward the government?... At present officials on the frontier who have blundered in their strategy have often escaped from punishment by resorting to tricks. In the morning they lost their armies on the eastern frontier. In the evening they were transferred to the western border. Because punishment had not been meted out to them, their soldiers became uncontrolled. This being the case, Your Majesty has not only committed the sin of ignoring their crimes but has, in addition, gone to great lengths to accommodate them. What do they fear and why should they fight until death? Laws cannot be enforced because those on high violate them. At present there are at any time one or two hundred military officers. Had they been selected honestly for their strength and courage, what would be wrong with it? However, they are either younger members of powerful families or their favorites recommended by them, and in

[8] *Sun Tzu ping-fa*, ch. 2.

all cases their appointments have been forced upon the government because of their power. Their concern is to demand and squeeze, to disturb the communities on their routes, grasp other people's merits as their own on the strength of their power, and accept rewards through forgery without having done the work. They discourage soldiers and arouse the hatred of the frontier people. Generals commanding them depend on their power to help each other. Do they dare decline whatever these officers send them as bribes? Do they dare expose whatever they themselves have given the officers? If these officers violate any law, do they dare execute them to warn the rest? Thus the prestige and power of the generals are lost because of the officers. How can the generals handle the troops and satisfy the people? I beg Your Majesty to issue an edict written in your own hand to the provincial commander in chief to the effect that, beginning with the date of the order, those who are the first to lose their armies will be executed at the gate of the headquarters so that military discipline can be rectified. The so-called headmen and the like shall all be forbidden to commit further crimes and returned to the interior so they will no longer disturb or oppress the people and usurp the authority of the generals. Then all fighting men will be roused to effort and the prestige of the army will become prominent and be respected. This is the foundation on which to overcome the enemy and to achieve victory. Otherwise, even if we have a million troops, they will only deplete the country and over-work the people, and will be of no use.

What is meant by showing imperial kindness to arouse indignation against the enemy? I have heard that "the thing that kills the enemy is indignation."[9] At present our armies are losing advantageous positions. Soldiers' morale is low. With regard to frontier guards, many people who have been killed were their fellow clansmen or relatives, if not their parents or sons or younger brothers. If Your Majesty can soothe their pains, inquire into their suffering, give relief to the orphaned and the widowed, and lift up the destitute and the poor, then the dead will have nothing to complain of and the living will naturally be moved. Then select the healthy and the strong, show them imperial kindness, explain to them the enmity of the invaders, make them understand the natural principle of human relations, and rouse them with the great principle of right-

[9] *Ibid.*

eousness. Also post awards to promote their courage, and expose the evils of the enemy so as to heighten their indignation. Let them have a pain in their hearts and an ache in their heads and train and polish themselves day and night so as to make sure that together they will kill the enemy of their fathers and elder brothers and requite the kindness of the court. As a result, the power of our army will gradually expand, the morale of the soldiers will gradually be strengthened, and it will be nothing to destroy the little enemy.

What is meant by sacrificing the small in order to preserve the great? I have heard that the *Art of War* says, "In order to take a thing away, it is necessary first to give it."[10] It also says, "Do not pursue the enemy who simulate retreat. Do not swallow the bait offered by the enemy."[11] All these are instances of sacrificing the small in order to preserve the great. Now that the strength of the enemy is increasing, if we hold back our army and do not advance, the enemy will dispatch his crack troops to challenge us. Not only that, he will set traps to entice our army, perhaps by deserting oxen and horses and feigning retreat, perhaps by hiding his excellent and ruthless fighters to suggest weakness, perhaps by staging a mock defeat and preparing for an ambush, and perhaps by hiding his troops and suing for peace. All these are tricks to entice us. If we believe him and act accordingly, we will fall into his traps. At present commanders guarding passes on the frontier all have their own ideas. Furthermore, it is difficult to decide whether the enemy is weak or strong. If he challenges and entices them and the imperial troops hold back and do not respond, it is not impossible that they will be crushed. One general believes that efforts should be made to save them. Another believes that the enemy can be intercepted. To believe the generals will surely place the army in a fatal position. Not to believe them, it is feared, may result in punishment by death for sitting down and merely looking on. This is the reason why the imperial troops have been tired out by being rushed here and rushed there, why their losses have been severe and heavy, and why the ugly enemy has been able to fulfill his wishes. If now the control over them is relaxed and permission is given them to act according to circumstances, and if they are not accused of sitting down and

[10] This saying, with slight variations, is found in several ancient classics, including *Lao Tzu*, ch. 36. It is not found in the *Sun Tzu ping-fa*, however, though the latter expresses the same spirit.

[11] *Sun Tzu ping-fa*, ch. 8.

looking on when they allow the enemy the chance to play his trick and not regarded as having made a strategic mistake when they give up a chance to fight, and if we nourish their power and turn it into indignation against the enemy, and if we only expect them to achieve great success, whereas small setbacks will be ignored, then our imperial troops will always be rested and the prestige of the army will not suffer any loss. This is truly the critical turning point that will determine whether we shall win or lose, and whether we shall live or perish.

What is meant by a strong defense in order to take advantage of the enemy's defects? I have heard that "the ancient expert of war would first of all secure himself against defeat in order to wait for the opportunity to defeat his enemy."[12] For China is skillful in self-defense, whereas the barbarian enemy is superior in irregular, open fighting. Now that the frontier troops have just been broken up and the enemy's position of power is extremely strong, if we engage him in fighting again, it will be to submit to his superiority and present him with victory. The policy now should be to close the city for a strong defense, send scouts far out to prevent the enemy from playing any tricks on us, dispatch spies with all diligence to plot against the enemy, train troops well so as to utilize their best ability, and be strict with orders in order to eliminate any laxity in effort. In addition, feast the men often so they can all nourish their strength and cultivate their ardent spirit. It is like accumulating water. Wait till the water reaches the spilling point and then let it break loose, utilizing, in the case of troops, their anger at the enemy. Their power will then be doubled and their strength violent, and they will not stop at crashing mountains and sending rocks rolling.... Now that our food supply is adequate, our power great, our indignation deep, our armies rested, our defense strong, and our spirit ardent, our safety is perfect, and it is entirely within our power to be undefeated. The result will be that as our food is adequate, that of the enemy will gradually be deficient; as our power is great, that of the enemy will gradually be weak; as our indignation is deep, the enemy will feel more and more guilty; as we are rested, the enemy will be more and more fatigued; as we are strong, the enemy will be more and more depleted; and as our morale is high, the enemy will be more and more dispirited. As he compares the situations and

[12] *Ibid.*, ch. 4.

calculates the relative strengths, he will realize that he is exhausted and will retreat at high speed. We shall then use novel tactics and lay an ambush. We shall mobilize the entire army. We shall go to places to which he does not go and rush to places where he does not expect us to go. We shall move forward and backward and attack him from the front and from behind. We shall approach him from this and that direction and attack him from the sides. This is to face deficiency with adequacy, to oppose weakness with strength, to increase the sense of guilt with indignation, to hit exhaustion with ease, to destroy depletion with strength, and to attack dispiritedness with high morale. This is what is called victory resulting from complete safety. "Stand in the position where defeat is impossible and do not miss any opportunity to defeat the enemy."[13]

What I have presented above is nothing unusual or different from the viewpoints of other people. These recommendations are common sayings among military specialists and common viewpoints of generals today. However, although generals and commanders at the passes on the frontier know these recommendations, they may not be able to follow them. They all regard them as merely common sayings and do not examine their validity at all. When they suffer losses, they blame it on what they consider to be an inevitable outcome. If there are complications, they dally and muddle through. This is why discipline has broken down and the habit of carelessness has been carried to its present length. If Your Majesty does not overlook the subtle situation, I beg you to order the department of military affairs to discuss thoroughly the recommendations of this memorial and see if they are acceptable. If so, let them in turn order the provincial commanders and other officials concerned immediately to consider the recommendations carefully and to carry them out; let them not look upon the orders as routine and conventional documents, but instead demand of the officials concrete results. Then I am sure their efforts will be of some help to our military strategy.

I submit this with unlimited loyalty and devotion to the country.

[13] *Ibid.*

2. *Instruction to the Old and the Young in the Several Prefectures Concerning the System of the Ten-Family Joint Registration Board* (1517)

(*Wang Wen-ch'eng Kung ch'üan-shu,* 16:6a-8a)

When Wang arrived at Kan-chou in southern Kiangsi in the first month of 1517 to suppress rebels and bandits, he found that the natives provided information to the outlaws and often hid them in their homes. Wang therefore instituted the ten-family joint registration system first in the city and later in the prefecture. His campaign succeeded in several months; however, it is difficult to determine how far the system contributed to its success. Wang used the system again in Kiangsi in 1519 and 1520 and in Kwangsi in 1528.

In touring and comforting this area by imperial order, I simply hope to eliminate bandits and to give security and a livelihood to the citizens. I regret that my abilities are limited and my wisdom deficient. Although I have the mind to love the people I do not as yet have the governmental measures to implement it. If any of you, old or young, has measures to help me in my shortcomings and to be of benefit to the people, please let me know. I shall consider their feasibility and carry them out one after another.

This registration board seems to be a burden. There are many in your midst who belong to families with a tradition of classical literature and social and moral principles. How can I bear to treat you good citizens with cunning and deceit? But in order to prevent wickedness and to correct defects so that you good citizens can have security and peace, it is impossible not to have the registration. I hope all of you, both old and young, will appreciate this motive. From now on in every family the father should be affectionate; the son, filial; the elder brother, loving; the younger brother, respectful; the husband, obliging; the wife, obedient; the old, kind; and the young, compliant. All of you shall be meticulous in following the laws of the government and be diligent and serious in paying national taxes. You should be respectful and thrifty in maintaining your family heritage, and humble and peaceful in dealing with fellow villagers. Your minds should be fair and forgiving and you should not lightly show wrath or engage in a fight. In handling affairs, you should be tolerant and patient, and should not readily engage in litigation. When you see a good deed, you should exhort and encourage one another to do it, and when you see an evil deed, you should warn and restrain one another. Devote your efforts to promoting the custom of propriety and compliance so as to produce the custom of honesty and generous earnestness. I regret that I have not extended any benevolent governmental measures and that I merely instruct you with words. But I hope you, both old and young, will make a special effort to understand my intention. Do not forget.

Each day the one in charge of the registration board should explain these instructions to every family.

The form of the registration board:

Name of the country:	Name of the village:
Name of person:	Native of:
Name of person:	Native of:
Name of person:	Native of:
Name of person:	Native of:
Name of person:	Native of:
Name of person:	Native of:
Name of person:	Native of:
Name of person:	Native of:
Name of person:	Native of:
Name of person:	Native of:
Name of the head of the first family :	
Name of the head of the last family :	

The above board is to be circulated daily among the ten families for whom this board is issued. The family in charge of the board for the day shall go to each family with the board from 5 to 7 P.M. and investigate according to the standard board and record that in such and such family so-and-so is absent, that he has gone to such and such place for such and such business, and that he will return on such and such day, or that in such and such family there is such and such additional person whose name is so-and-so and who has come from such and such place for such and such business. The inquiry must be accurate and the findings will then be made known to all families of the tithing so they will be informed. If there is anything suspicious, it must be reported to the government immediately. If anything is concealed, upon exposure all the ten families will be jointly punished....[14]

---

[14] What follows is the form of registration for the individual family. It is omitted from the translation.

3. Instruction to Both the Old and the Young in the Several Prefectures (1517)

(*Wang Wen-ch'eng Kung ch'üan-shu*, 16:10b-11a)

After southern Kiangsi had been pacified in the spring of 1517, the following positive and encouraging announcement was made in Kan-chou.

This is to instruct both the old and the young. Now, in the aftermath of the devastation of war, suffering and difficulties have certainly reached a very high degree. All of you must recuperate and be rehabilitated, and you should exhort one another to do good. The father should be affectionate; the son, filial; the elder brother, friendly; the younger brother, respectful; the husband, obliging; the wife, obedient; the elder person, kind; and the younger person, compliant. Be diligent and thrifty so as to maintain the family heritage, and be humble and peaceful in dealing with fellow members of your community. In your heart you should be impartial and forgiving, and never harbor any treacherous or deceptive thoughts. In your handling of affairs, you should be patient and never quarrel lightly. Have you, both the old and the young, ever seen any person who is amiable and complaisant, honoring others and humbling himself, not loved and respected by others? Have you seen any person who is violent, greedy, aggressive, and who encroaches upon others for his own selfish benefit, not detested and hated by others? The aim of those who stupidly resort to litigation is to struggle for benefits, but they do not necessarily obtain them. They aim to expose justice but justice is not necessarily exposed. Externally they arouse the hatred of government officials and internally they destroy their own family heritage. They bring disgrace to their ancestors above and give trouble to their offspring below. Why take so much trouble to engage in litigation? Because it is a common practice in this part of the country to struggle for benefits and vigorously to pursue litigation, I have therefore sincerely and earnestly spoken as I have. I am ashamed that I am unable to rule by virtue and merely instruct you with words. Elders, please make a special effort to follow my words and each and all admonish the young. Don't forget.

4. *Instructions to New Citizens*[15] (1517)

(*Wang Wen-ch'eng Kung ch'üan-shu*, 16:20a-21a)

Like the preceding document, this proclamation was issued in the spring of 1517 in Kiangsi after Wang had subdued the rebels and bandits. Similar instructions were given out in Kiangsi in 1518 and in Kwangsi in 1520.

All of you should feel secure and contented in your occupations. All elders should teach the young. Leaders on all levels should bring those below them into peace. And every one of you should be diligent in your farm duties, protect your home, value your own life, provide security for your family, be filial and obedient to your parents, and tenderly rear your offspring. There has been none who has done good and has not been blessed with happiness. And there has been none who has done evil and has not been visited by misfortune. Do not be aggressive to the few because you are many, and do not oppress the weak because you are strong. You must promote the customs of propriety and righteousness and forever be good citizens. In case some among the young people disobey your instructions and set out to create trouble and do wrong, elders and leaders must immediately apprehend them and deliver them to the government so that the law can be openly and correctly applied to them. On the one hand, this is to display your sincerity to do good and to remove evil. On the other, it is to eliminate undesirable elements so that they will not spread and cause trouble to those of you who are good. I am now touring and comforting this area by imperial order. I only hope all of you are secure in your homes and happy in your work, and enjoy peace together. I regret that my ability and knowledge are limited and that although I have the mind to love the people I do not as yet have the governmental measures to implement it. Because after my personal supervision of the attacks on the bandit strongholds in Hsiang-hu, K'o-t'ang,[16] and other places, the bandits have been totally wiped out through capture or killing, my troops are now stationed here. At this time of spring farming, I want very much to come personally to the villages where you live, and inquire face to face about your suffering. However, I am afraid my many attendants may disturb you. I am therefore sending this instruction

[15] Former outlaws now pardoned.
[16] In modern southern Kiangsi.

through government officials and village elders and am also sending rolls of cloth as gifts to elders and leaders to show my earnest desire to pacify and comfort you. I am sorry I cannot send gifts to everyone, as there are so many of you. However, I hope all of you will understand the purpose for which this instruction is issued.

5. *Memorial Petitioning for the Additional Establishment of Ho-p'ing County* (1518)

(*Wang Wen-ch'eng Kung ch'üan-shu*, 11:25b-31b)

Having eliminated the bandits and rebels on the Kiangsi-Kuangtung border early in 1518, Wang petitioned on the first day of the fifth month for the establishment of a new county as a means of furthering rapid economic reconstruction and effective military control. The request was granted.

The southeastern territory has been the stronghold of bandits. It is an area of great mountains and deep valleys as isolated as they are dangerous. Consequently, after the expedition to exterminate the bandits, the citizens there all want the place to be made a county so that it will be possible to control the strategic points, to propagate education and carry out governmental measures, and gradually to influence and transform the former bandits. Therefore, to stop banditry in the southeast and to give the people security, it is a good policy to establish a county....[17] As to where cities and moats are to be built, where additional patrol units should be set up, what subdivisions from what neighboring counties can be appropriated, what population from which adjacent villages can be shifted, what patrol headquarters can be transferred, what male members from what community can be grouped together, what population can be moved to suit the land, what groups of soldiers can be transferred to defend a strategic post—all the labor necessary and the areas involved have to be investigated, and records have to be looked into, and elders have to be consulted, so that all that is correct will revert to one truth....

As to the land, aside from the properties of good citizens which have been seized by bandits to farm and which should be returned

---

[17] Long passages on various official actions taken and the transmission of various official documents are omitted here and below, since they add little to Wang's ideas and policies.

to their owners in exact amount, there are among them some lands that have been leased to new citizens. Half the amount of the lease money must be turned over to the government and the land returned to the owners. As to the rest, all land belonging to the chief bandits of the area shall be confiscated and sold, with the proceeds to be used for the construction or repair of cities, moats, and government buildings... .

The administrative personnel should be few in order to save expenses; the land should be evenly distributed in order to make conscript labor service fair. Patrols should be shifted to control dangerous and important points, and taxation and conscript labor should be liberalized in order to relieve the distress of the masses. If this is done, danger will be transformed into security and bandits will be made into good citizens, and the result can be achieved in a matter of days.

6. The Community Compact for Southern Kan-chou (1518)

(Wang Wen-ch'eng Kung ch'üan-shu, 17:42b-49b)

Among the reconstructionary measures Wang introduced following the pacification of the southern Kiangsi area in 1518, the most famous is the Community Compact, said by some to be Wang's own invention. Although the specific organization here is new, the idea of a community pact for moral and social advancement is old.[18]

Ah, you citizens! There is an ancient saying that "when raspberry grows in the midst of hemp, it is straight without the need of any support, and when white sand is in the midst of mud, it becomes black without the need of any dyeing."[19] Have not the customs of the people become good or bad because of accumulated behavior which makes them so? In the past, new citizens have often deserted their own clans, rebelled against their own community, and gone in all directions to do violence. Was this merely because their nature was different and they were criminals? It was also because, on our part, the government did not govern them properly or teach them in the

[18] The only mention in the Nien-p'u of a community compact is in the entry for the tenth month of 1518. Most scholars have dated the Community Compact in this year. However, the document is included in the Wang Wen-ch'eng Kung ch'üan-shu, ch. 17, as a document of the first month of 1520. The first and most renowned community pact is that of Lü Ta-lin (1044-90) and his brothers, revised by Chu Hsi, which consists of a series of moral injunctions.

[19] A saying quoted in several ancient works, including the Hsün Tzu, ch. 1, SPTK ed., 1:8b-9a, and the Ta-Tai li chi, sec. 54, SPTK ed., 5:2a.

right way, and on your part, all of you, both old and young, did not teach and regulate your families early enough or exert good influence on your fellow villagers regularly enough. You did not put inducement and encouragement into practice and had no sufficient arrangements for cooperation and coordination. In addition, perhaps you roused the resentment of the new citizens or harmed one another with deceit and insincerity. Consequently new citizens have been allowed gradually to degenerate into wickedness as though following a fashion. The responsibility for all this should be shared by us government officials and all of you, old and young.

Alas! Nothing can be done to change what has already gone by, but something can still be done in the future. Therefore a community compact is now specially prepared to unite and harmonize all of you. From now on, all of you who enter into this compact should be filial to your parents and respectful to your elders, teach your children, live in harmony with your fellow villagers, help one another when there is death in the family and assist one another in times of difficulty, encourage one another to do good and warn one another not to do evil, stop litigations and rivalry, cultivate faithfulness and promote harmony, and be sure to be good citizens so that together you may establish the custom of humanity and kindness. Alas! although a man is most stupid, when it comes to criticizing others his mind is quite clear, and although a person is intelligent, when it comes to criticizing himself his mind is beclouded. All of you, both old and young, do not remember the former evil deeds of the new citizens and ignore their good deeds. As long as they have a single thought to do good, they are already good people. Do not be proud that you are good citizens and neglect to cultivate your personal life. As long as you have a single thought to do evil, you are already evil people. Whether people are good or evil depends on a single instant of thought. You should think over my words carefully. Don't forget.

Item : Elect from the compact membership an elderly and virtuous person respected by all to be the compact chief and two persons to be assistant chiefs, four persons who are impartial, just, and firm in judgment to be compact directors, four persons who are understanding and discriminating to be compact recorders, four persons who are energetic and scrupulous to be compact executives, and two persons who are well versed in ceremonies to be compact masters of ceremonies. Have three record books. One of these is to record the names of compact members and their daily movements and activities, and is to be in charge of the compact executives. Of the remaining record books, one is for the purpose of displaying good deeds and the other for the purpose of reporting evil deeds, both to be in charge of the compact chief.

Item: Each member shall contribute three *fen*[20] at each banquet meeting to the compact executives who will provide the food. Do not be extravagant. The point is that there shall be no thirst or hunger, that is all.

Item: The time of meeting shall be the fifteenth of each month. Those who because of illness or other business are unable to attend may send a messenger to inform a compact executive ahead of time. Those who fail to attend without reason will be recorded as having committed an evil deed and, in addition, fined one *liang*[21] for the use of the group.

Item: Build a compact hall on level ground. Choose a spacious temple compound and build it there.

Item: To display good deeds, the language used must be clear and decisive, but in reporting mistakes, the language must be obscure and gentle. This is after all the way of liberality and loyalty. If someone has been disrespectful toward his elder brother, do not say so directly, but say that you have heard that he has not done his best in observing the etiquette of serving the elder brother and respecting the elders, that you dare not believe in the report, but that you will tentatively record it and see. This should be the example for all cases of reporting mistakes. In case of an evil deed that is difficult to correct, do not report it and make the situation unbearable for the guilty person, for it may rouse him and cause him finally to give free rein to his wickedness. The chief, assistant chiefs, etc. should talk to him privately beforehand and advise him to confess, and members should together induce him, encourage him, and rouse his desire to do good. Record the case tentatively and let him reform. If he does not reform, then report it and record it. If he still does not reform, report it to the government. If he still fails to reform, then members of the compact should seize him and deliver him to the government so that he may be openly punished. If the situation is such that it is impossible to seize him, make a special effort and cooperate with the government to send troops to destroy him.

[20] A small unit of money.
[21] 100 *fens*.

Item: In case of anything dangerous, doubtful, or difficult to settle, members of the compact must ask the chief, together with compact members, to deliberate and make arrangements and not to stop until a solution is found which is in accord with moral principles and is effective. You must not sit idle, pass the responsibility to others, or make excuses, and thus cause people to fall into evil deeds and crime and get the compact chief, compact directors, etc. into trouble.

Item: Many nonnative residents have sneaked back to their native places when taxes or military conscription are due and have often gotten their fellow members of the tithing into trouble. Hereafter the compact chief, etc. should admonish them to pay their full tax on time and to answer conscription. If they repeat their former delinquencies, report them to the government for punishment and cancel their nonnative resident status.

Item: People of prominent local families who are doing business in a distant place and loan money for interest[22] must follow the usual practice and cannot compound the interest. In case the debtor is too poor to repay, he should be treated liberally according to what is right. There have been inhumane people who would immediately seize the debtor, put him in chains, and demand the accumulated amount or force him to mortgage his land, so that the poor people have no way out but to run away to become bandits. Hereafter, if there is any such case, inform the compact chief, etc. so they can explain to the creditor. In case the payment is insufficient, they will urge the creditor to forgive it, and if he is overpaid, they will force him to return the excessive amount. If he refuses to listen, thinking that he can rely on his own power, let them lead members of the compact to report to the government.

Item: Among relatives and neighbors, there have often been cases where, because of some minor resentment, people would join bandits in order to get revenge, thus doing great harm to good people and causing great calamity. From now on all cases of injustice or quarrels must be reported to the compact chief, etc. so that they can hold a public discussion on who is right and who is wrong. Or in case the compact chief hears about any injustice or quarrel, he should immediately enlighten and explain to the parties concerned.

[22] And are therefore not present to collect debts when they are due.

If they still act erroneously as before, let him lead members of the compact to petition the government for their punishment.

Item: If any soldier or civilian outwardly behaves well but secretly is in communication with bandits, sells animals to them, or speedily provides them with information, in order to benefit himself and harm tens of thousands of citizens, let the compact chief, etc., lead members of the compact to point out the concrete evidence and admonish him. If he does not reform, they should petition the government to investigate and punish him.

Item: If any government clerk, bad official,[23] warden of a tithing, village elder, captain of troops, bowman, or shooter induces any government servant to descend on the community to demand gifts, the compact chief shall lead the members of the compact to petition the government to investigate and punish him.

Item: New citizens used to do a great deal of harm to residents of various military outposts, which we really cannot bear to describe. Now that they are permitted to reform, they have been ordered to return the properties which they have appropriated. Former owners must no longer harbor any old grievances which would create disturbances in the locality. The compact chief, etc. should frequently instruct the people and tell them to abide by their own stations and attend to their own duties. If anyone disobeys, petition the government to punish him for his crime.

Item: New citizens who have answered the call! Because you had a single thought to do good, you have been pardoned. You should take special pains to master yourselves and reform, correct your mistakes and become new persons. Farm and weave diligently. Buy and sell reasonably. Aspire to be the same as the good citizens. Do not be satisfied with being in a low class because of your former label and invite your own destruction. You, the compact chief, etc. should teach and instruct new citizens at all times. If they repeat their former mistakes, petition the government to punish them.

Item: When boys and girls are grown up, they should be married at the proper age. Often the girl's family has complained that the money presented by the boy's family at betrothal was insufficient and the boy's family has complained that the dowry was not rich

---

[23] The term *i-min* ordinarily means a righteous citizen, but here means a depraved person, more especially a bad official.

enough, with the consequence that the marriage was postponed. The compact chief, etc. should teach and explain to these people. From now on, marriage should take place at the proper age and the provision of the betrothal gifts or dowry should be in accord with the economic conditions of the families.

Item : In the case of a parent's funeral, the clothing and the inner and outer coffins should be in accord with the economic condition of the family, the purpose being merely to exert filial piety and sincerity to the utmost. Aside from these, things like elaborate Buddhist rites or extravagant feasts merely waste money and lead to bankruptcy and do no good to the dead at all. The compact chief, etc. should teach members of the compact to follow the correct system of ceremonies. If they still fall into former mistakes, they should be recorded as unfilial in the book devoted to reporting evil deeds.

Item : The day before the compact meeting, the compact executive shall clean up the compact hall and arrange proper furniture in the central room. He shall set up an announcement board and incense stands, facing south. On the day of the meeting, all members shall come. As the compact master of ceremonies strikes the drum three times, all shall stand in front of the incense stands, then kneel down, facing north, and listen to the instructions of a compact director. Then the compact chief and members shall all say out loud, "From now on, all of us compact members will reverently obey warnings and instructions. We will unite as one mind and join together in virtue, and will arrive at goodness together. If anyone should have any double-mindedness, outwardly doing good but secretly doing evil, let the gods and spirits destroy him." All members shall say again, "If anyone should have any double-mindedness, outwardly doing good but secretly doing evil, let the gods and spirits destroy him." After bowing twice, all shall rise and go to the meeting room and line up on the east and the west. A compact director then reads the community compact. Having done so, he shall say with a loud voice, "All of us in this alliance must follow the community compact." The members shall say, "Yes." Then people standing in the east and west shall bow to each other, and according to proper order, move to take their seats. Junior members shall pour wine three times for senior members.

The compact executive shall now rise to set up seats for displaying good deeds in the central hall, facing south. On the table shall be laid writing brushes and ink, and the record to display good deeds shall be displayed there. After the compact master of ceremonies has struck the drum three times, all shall rise. The compact master of ceremonies shall then request the members in a chanting voice to announce the good deeds. All members shall say, "This is the function of the compact recorder." The compact recorder shall then take a seat for displaying good deeds, and say out loud, "So-and-so has done such and such good deed and so-and-so has been able to correct such and such mistake. May I request that they be recorded in order to encourage all of us." The compact director shall ask all members, "What do you think?" All shall answer, "The compact recorder's announcement is quite right." The compact director shall then bow and invite all doers of good deeds to come before the seats for displaying good deeds, standing in the east and in the west. The compact recorder shall again say to the members, "I have only announced these. Please announce any others that you know." If the members know of any, they should announce them right away. If not, they should say, "What is announced by the compact recorder is correct." Thereupon, the compact chief, assistant chiefs, and directors all take their seats for displaying good deeds. When the compact recorder finishes his recording, the compact chief shall raise his cup and say loudly, "So-and-so has done such and such good deed and so-and-so has been able to correct such and such mistake. This means that they can cultivate their personal lives. So-and-so has enabled his fellow clansmen to do such and such good deed or correct such and such mistake. This means they can regulate their families. If everyone does this, how can our customs not be sound? All of us in this compact should take them as models." Thereupon, he shall offer the cups to those doers of good deeds. In return they shall also offer wine to the compact chief, saying, "Ours is not worthy of being called good. And yet you, venerable sir, have taken the trouble to overpraise us. We truly feel alarmed and ashamed. How can we not make further effort so that we may not fail your instructions?" All now shall drink and bow twice to thank the compact chief. The compact chief shall bow and rise. Everyone now shall return to his seat, and the compact executive shall remove the seats for displaying good deeds.

After three rounds of wine, the compact executive shall rise and set up seats for reporting evil deeds at the bottom of the steps, facing north. On the table shall be laid writing brushes and ink, and the record to report evil deeds shall be displayed there. After the compact master of ceremonies has struck the drum three times, all shall rise. The compact master of ceremonies shall then request the members in a chanting voice to report the evil deeds. All members shall say, "This is the function of the compact recorder." The compact recorder shall then take a seat for reporting evil deeds, and say out loud, "I have heard that so-and-so has done such and such evil deed, but I am not sure. How about recording it and waiting until later to decide what to do?" The compact director shall ask all members, "What do you think?" All shall answer, "The compact recorder must have some evidence." The compact director shall then bow and ask all doers of evil deeds to come before the seat for reporting evil deeds, standing and facing north. The compact recorder shall again say to the members, "I have heard only this much. Please say what you have heard." If the members have heard anything, they should say so right away. If not, they should say, "What has been heard by the compact recorder is correct." Thereupon, the compact chief, assistant chiefs, and directors all come before the seat for reporting evil deeds, standing in the east and in the west. When the compact recorder finishes his recording, the compact chief shall say to the guilty, "However, we are not interested in punishment but in your early reform." The guilty one shall kneel down and plead, "How dare I not yield to punishment?" Having said so, he shall rise, pour wine, kneel down again and drink, and shall say, "How dare I not reform quickly but instead cause my elders to worry for me again?" The compact chief, assistant chiefs, and compact recorder all shall say, "We have not been able to advise and instruct you in time so that you have fallen into this trouble. How can we be free from guilt?" They shall now all drink to punish themselves. The guilty one shall kneel again to plead, "As I already know my own guilt and as you, venerable sirs, take this to be your own guilt, how dare I not submit to the most severe punishment right away? If you permit me to reform, please do not drink and that would be my good fortune." He shall then quickly withdraw to the rear and drink to punish himself. The compact chief and assistant chiefs shall all say, "As you are so courageous as to accept punishment like this, it means you can reform to do good, and we may be free from guilt." Having said so, they shall all lay down their wine cups. The guilty party shall now bow twice and the compact chief shall bend down in response. They shall all rise and return to their seats. The compact executive shall remove the seats for reporting evil deeds. After two rounds of wine, rice shall be served.

After the meal, the compact master of ceremonies shall sound the drum three times, and in a chanting voice announce the issuance of warning. All shall rise. The compact directors shall stand in the middle of the hall and say in a loud voice, "Alas! All members of the compact please listen distinctly to this warning. Who among men has no good in him, and who has no evil in him? Although our good deeds are not known to others, as they accumulate, in time this accumulation of good will no longer remain hidden. If we do evil deeds and do not reform, in time they will accumulate and reach the point where they can no longer be pardoned. Now we have done some good deeds and they have been displayed by others. This is of course a joyful thing. However, if just because of this we feel that we are good people and become proud, we shall gradually degenerate into evil. We have done some evil deeds and they have been reported by others. This is of course a shameful thing. But if we can repent and change our ways, we shall gradually advance to be good. Therefore, those who are good today should not be proud and be satisfied and consider themselves as good. And who can be sure that those who are evil today will finally end up in evil? All members of this compact must encourage each other in their effort." All members shall then say, "How dare we not make the effort?" Thereupon all shall leave their tables, line up in the east and west, bow to each other, arise, and withdraw.

7. *Instruction on the Ten-Family Joint Registration System* (1520)

(*Wang Wen-ch'eng Kung ch'üan-shu*, 17:56b-58b)

Having put down the rebellion of Prince Ning, Wang returned to Kiangsi toward the end of 1519 as governor. He reached Kan-chou in the middle of 1520. The following order for a ten-family joint registration system, which was issued at this time, suggests that the system set up two years before had not been very effective. This time Wang emphasized reform and persuasion rather than restriction and control.

With regard to the order concerning the ten-family joint registration regulations enacted by this censorate, recently it has been found that officials in various localities have all looked upon it as a routine and conventional document and are unwilling to carry the investigation out definitely and concretely. According to law, this violation should be punished immediately. However, for fear that the idea behind the regulations adopted by this censorate is not yet clearly understood, the reasons for it are now especially recited and instructions are given once more.

Whenever a ten-family joint registration board is set up, first of all the data contained in the individual boards in front of each household must be examined for their accuracy. For example, if according to the data there are so many males in the household, it must be investigated whether such and such male member is such and such government official, or is a first-degree licentiate, or is serving as a servant of officials, or is practcing such and such craft or is doing such and such business, or has been taken into such and such clan as a son-in-law, or has such and such disease or deformity. All these and the population record under which the household is registered, the amount of land tax the household has been paying, and so forth, must be carefully investigated item by item as to fact. When the data from all the ten families have been arranged systematically, make a copy of the record and leave it with the county office for reference. In cases of absence from home on official business or transfer and so forth, the data should be revised according to the record. Nothing can be concealed or overlooked, and then the affairs of the whole county can be looked up as easily as one looks at his palm. Every one of the ten families is required to report according to order the names of those in the tithing who have such habits as stealing, swindling, or blackmailing, and together they will sign a bond pledging not to hide any such crime, omit it from the record, or repeat it. The government will provide facilities to keep these new and old records where their names are recorded. Former evil deeds will be forgotten, and the culprits will be given the opportunity to reform from now on. If one can really change his ways, his name will be taken off the record. In case there are thieves within the territory, these reformed people will be ordered to search their houses and seize them. If there is any evasion or omission in the tithing report, all families of the tithing will be jointly punished as usual.

Furthermore, according to the order in the registration board one family each day will take turns to explain to the other families and investigate. In this way no wicked persons can be concealed and thieves and bandits can be stopped. If there is anything like litigation among the ten families, fellow families of the tithing should explain and arbitrate immediately. If anyone refuses to listen but oppresses the weak on account of his strength or falsely accuses others, members of the tithing should join together and report him to the government, and government officials should immediately consider the case, mete out punishment, and dispatch him to the place where the sentence is to be carried out; they need not retain him in jail and slow up the case. If in the process of interrogation or examining a written charge it is discovered that there is a false accusation, it is still necessary to investigate and punish fellow members of the tithing for having failed to exhort the parties to make peace or to report the false accusation. Also, according to the order in the registration board, one family each day will exhort and instruct the others, and urge them to cherish faithfulness and cultivate harmony, stop litigation and quarrels, and gradually be enlightened. In this way, citizens will increasingly realize the mistake of quarrels, and litigation can be reduced.

The system of the ten-family joint registration is very simple and its ability to bring order is very great. If officials can really carry it out concretely and definitely, not only can thieves and bandits be stopped and litigation be reduced. If this system is put into practice, whatever imbalance or defect there may be in the taxation and conscription for government service will be corrected and those requirements will become equalized. If this system is put into practice, small groups will be lined up and large groups will be coordinated, and aggression from outside can be checked. If this system is put into practice, members will be warned against the nonessential and exhorted to make effort toward the essential, and social customs will become pure. If this system is put into practice, members will be led to virtue and instructed in learning and the instructions of propriety and music will flourish. For those officials with great ability and extensive knowledge, there is no need to make any further regulations. When they find any imperfection in local customs or in people's sentiment, they can just follow this system and embellish or modify it. Then order and peace in the county can really be achieved without effort.

I am now taking the special opportunity to explain briefly once more the purpose of this regulation. Where my words cannot express everything, please think carefully and consider thoroughly on my behalf and earnestly put these instructions into practice. Do not consider this instruction as empty words, obstruct it, or let it be a conventional piece of writing to be hung on the wall. If you follow this instruction, everything will be all right.

Bibliographical and Historical Notes
on the *Ch'uan-hsi lu*

There are only two books and a booklet in Western languages which are completely devoted to Wang Yang-ming. The first book is Tch'ang-tche Wang's *La philosophie morale de Wang Yang-ming* (Shanghai, T'ou-Sè-Wè Press, 1936), which concentrates on Wang's doctrine of innate knowledge. It is fairly thorough but there is neither a comparison of this doctrine with earlier or later theories nor an explanation of what the doctrine has meant to Chinese philosophy and to Chinese and Japanese history. The second is a translation by Frederick Goodrich Henke, *The Philosophy of Wang Yang-Ming* (Chicago, Open Court, 1916). In addition to a slightly abridged translation of the *Ch'uan-hsi lu*, there is a sizable selection from Wang's letters. The selection of material is not bad but the translation is very faulty and lacks the support of modern critical scholarship. (See above, Introduction, n. 2, on Henke's work.) The best studies in English are: Fung Yu-lan, *A History of Chinese Philosophy*, translated by Derk Bodde (Princeton, Princeton University Press, 1953), II, 596-620; his *A Short History of Chinese Philosophy* (New York, Macmillan, 1948), pp.308-18; Carsun Chang, "Wang Yang-Ming's Philosophy," in *Philosophy East and West*, V (1955), 3-18, and the booklet referred to above, *Wang Yang-ming: Idealist Philosopher of Sixteenth-Century China* (New York, St. John's University Press, 1962), an elaboration of the article just cited, with some new material on Wang's position in Neo-Confucianism and on Chinese intuitionism. Wing-tsit Chan's article "Wang Yang-ming", in the *Encyclopaedia Britannica* (1960), his "How Buddhistic Is Wang Yang-ming?", in *Philosophy East and West*, XII (1962), 203-16, and Hiroyuki Iki's "Wang Yang-ming's Doctrine of Innate Knowledge," in *Philosophy East and West*, XI (1961-62), 27-44, may be helpful. Selections with an introduction may be found in Chan's *A Source Book in Chinese Philosophy* (Princeton, Princeton University Press, 1963) chapter 35, and in Wm. Theodore de Bary, Wing-tsit Chan, and Burton Watson, eds., *Sources of Chinese Tradition* (New York, Columbia University Press, 1960), pp. 569-81. For short accounts and general surveys, see Chan's *An Outline and An Annotated Bibliography of Chinese Philosophy* (New Haven, Far Eastern Publications, 1961), pp. 55-57.

The most authentic edition of Wang's complete works is the *Wang Wen-ch'eng Kung ch'üan-shu* (Complete works of Wang Yang-ming), *Ssu-pu ts'ung-k'an* (Four Libraries series) edition. It is a photographic reproduction of the edition of 1572 compiled by Hsieh T'ing-chieh. The

Ssu-pu pei-yao (Essentials of the Four Libraries) edition, entitled *Yang-ming ch'üan-shu* (Complete works of Wang Yang-ming), is collated but contains many misprints. Well-known selections from the *Ch'uan-hsi lu* (Records of instructions for practical living) are found in Chou Ju-teng (1547-1629), *Wang-men tsung-chih* (Fundamental doctrines of the Wang Yang-ming school) (1609), ch. 1; Ch'en Lung-cheng (1585- ?), *Yang-ming Hsien-sheng yao-shu* (Important works of Master Wang Yang-ming) (1632), ch. 1; Shih Pang-yao (1585-1644), *Yang-ming Hsien-sheng chi-yao* (Collection of important works by Master Wang Yang-ming), published *c.* 1636, *passim*. All of these works were of the Ming period, appearing not long after Wang's death. Chou Ju-teng also has a selection in his *Sheng-hsüeh tsung-ch'uan* (Orthodox transmission of the doctrine of the Sage) (1606), ch. 13, which was made from the point of view of the idealistic wing of Neo-Confucianism. On the other hand, the selection by Sun Ch'i-feng (1584-1675), in his *Li-hsüeh tsung-ch'uan* (Orthodox transmission of Neo-Confucianism) (1666), ch. 9, is from the point of view of the rationalistic wing of Neo-Confucianism. This work is far superior to Chou's and contains a lengthy biography of Wang, although Chou's has a long dissertation on Wang's philosophy. By far the best selection not only from the *Ch'uan-hsi lu* but from Wang's work in general is Liu Tsung-chou's (1578-1645) *Yang-ming ch'uan-hsin lu* (Records of Wang Yang-ming's transmission of truth), which constitutes chs. 11-13 of the *Liu Tzu ch'üan-shu i-pien* (Supplement to the complete works of Master Liu) (1850). Ch. 13, which consists of selections from the *Ch'uan-hsi lu*, has been reproduced with minor omissions in Huang Tsung-hsi's (1610-95) *Ming-ju hsüeh-an* (Anthology and critical accounts of Neo-Confucians of the Ming dynasty) (1693), ch. 10, which also contains Huang's own excellent account of Wang's life and thought. It is indispensable to any study of Wang. For commentaries, the most extensive, though not the most outstanding, is Wang Ying-ch'ang (*fl.* 1573), *Wang Yang-ming Hsien-sheng ch'uan-hsi lu lun* (On Master Wang Yang-ming's *Instructions for Practical Living*) (1646). It includes comments by T'ang Chiu-ching, which are often expressed in Buddhist terminology. Sun Ch'iang's *Ch'uan-hsi lu chi-p'ing* (Collected comments on the *Instructions for Practical Living*) (Shanghai, 1915), conveniently puts in one place remarks from six works, including those of Shih, Sun, and Huang. A recent commentary is Tan Heng-chin's *Wang Yang-ming ch'uan-hsi lu cha-chi* (Notes on Wang Yang-ming's *Instructions for Practical Living*) (Taipei, 1957), which has philosophical comments on about half of the book.

For critical studies of Wang's philosophy, the standard works are: Chan Jo-shui (1471-1555), *Chan Kan-ch'üan wen-chi* (Collection of literary works of Chan Jo-shui) (1579), ch. 7; Lo Ch'in-shun (1465-1547), *Lo cheng-an chi* (Collected works of Lo Ch'in-shun) (1534), I, B; Ch'en Chien (1497-1567), *Hsüeh-pu t'ung-pien* (General critique of obscurations of learning) (1548), bk. 4, pt. 3; Feng K'o (*fl.* 1562), *Ch'iu-shih pien* (An essay in search of the right), ch. 4; Lu Lung-ch'i (1630-92), *San-yü-t'ang wen-chi* (Collection of literary works of the hall dedicated to three fish) (1701), ch. 2; and Chang Lieh (1622-85), *Wang-hsüeh chih-i* (Questions on Wang Yang-ming's philosophy) (1681), *passim*. The latter work is entirely devoted to a vehement and reckless attack and does not recommend itself. For critical studies on the "Doctrine in Four Axioms," see above, introduction to sec. 315, n. 109.

As to modern studies, the best are: Ch'ien Mu, *Yang-ming hsüeh shu-yao* (Essentials of Wang Yang-ming's philosophy) (1955); Fung Yu-lan (referred to above); and Jung Chao-tsu, *Ming-tai ssu-hsiang shih* (History of thought during the Ming dynasty) (1941), pp. 71-109. They are all first-rate studies. Two in Japanese are highly recommended. They are: Yamada Jun, *Yōmeigaku seigi* (Essentials of Wang Yang-ming's philosophy) (Tokyo, 1926), and Mishima Fuku, *Ōyōmei no tetsugaku* (Philosophy of Wang Yang-ming) (Tokyo, 1934).

For sources on Wang's biography, see Ch'ien Te-hung, *Nien-p'u* (Chronological biography), in the *Complete Works*, ch. 23; Huang Wan, *Hsing-chuang* (Biography), in *ibid.*, ch. 37; Chang T'ing-yü (1672-1755) *et al.*, *Ming shih* (History of the Ming dynasty) (1739), ch. 195; Wang Hung-hsü (1645-1723), *Ming shih kao* (Draft history of the Ming dynasty) (1714), biography 80; Huang Tsung-hsi *et al.*, *Ming-ju hsüeh-an*, ch. 10; Mao Ch'i-ling (1623-1716), *Wang Wen-ch'eng chuan-pen* (Basic materials for the biography of Wang Yang-ming); Yü Ch'ung-yao, *Yang-ming Hsien-sheng chuan-tsuan* (Collated biography of Master Wang Yang-ming) (Shanghai, 1923); Takase Takejirō, *Ōyōmei shōden* (Detailed biography of Wang Yang-ming) (Tokyo, 1915); Frederick Goodrich Henke, *The Philosophy of Wang Yang-ming*, pp. 3-44. For comments on these works, see above, Introduction, n. 2.

The best annotations on the *Ch'uan-hsi lu* are in Japanese, notably: Miwa Shissai (1669-1744), *Hyōchū denshū roku* (The *Instructions for Practical Living* punctuated and annotated) (1712); Kawada Kinkyō (1684-1760), *Denshū roku hikki* (Notes on [Shissai's edition of] the *Instructions for Practical Living*) (undated manuscript); Satō Issai (1772-1859), *Denshū roku rangai sho* (Notes and comments on the *Instructions for Practical Living*) (1830); Azuma Keiji, *Denshū roku kōgi* (Elucidations on the *Instructions for Practical Living*) (Tokyo, 1907); Yamada Jun and Suzuki Naoji, *Denshū roku* (*Instructions for Practical Living*) (Tokyo, 1936). Of the two Chinese annotations, Yeh Shao-chün, *Ch'uan-hsi lu tien-chu* (The *Instructions for Practical Living* punctuated and annotated) (Shanghai, 1927), leaves much work undone, and Ni Hsi-en, *Hsiang-chu Wang Yang-ming ch'üan-chi* (Complete works of Wang Yang-ming fully annotated) (Shanghai, 1928), is practically useless.

Turning to the history of the *Ch'uan-hsi lu* itself, we find that it goes back to Wang's lifetime. According to Wang's pupil Hsü Ai, when Wang heard that some of his disciples privately recorded his sayings, he disapproved, saying that he taught as a physician prescribed medicine, varying from time to time according to the case, and that his sayings were not to be followed rigidly. But Hsü had recorded some himself, and in spite of his teacher's injunctions he wrote a preface to the collection (which is included among the prefaces in the *Complete Works*, pp. 1a-2a) and justified his collection by saying that the sayings would serve as excellent guidance while followers were away from the teacher.

Hsü died in 1518. In August of that year (when Wang was forty-seven), another pupil, Hsüeh K'an, collected what was left of Hsü Ai's records (secs. 1-14), conversations recorded by Lu Ch'eng (secs. 15-94), and those recorded by himself (secs. 95-129) and published them in Ch'ien-chou, Kiangsi, under the title *Ch'uan-hsi lu*, in three chapters, later known as the *Ch'u-k'o ch'uan-hsi lu* (Original edition of the *Instructions for Practical Living*). This is Part I (secs. 1-129) of the present *Ch'uan-hsi lu*.

In 1524, when Wang was fifty-three, Wang's pupil Nan Ta-chi supplemented the *Original Edition* with eight of Wang's letters and published them in Yüeh (in modern Chekiang) under the title *Ch'uan-hsi lu*, in two volumes, vol. 1 consisting of the *Original Edition* in three chapters and vol. 2 consisting of the letters in five chapters. In his preface to the anthology his brother Nan Feng-chi noted that some of Hsü Ai's records had been lost. This work later came to be known as the *Hsü-k'o ch'uan-hsi lu* (Supplementary edition of the *Instructions for Practical Living*). Vol. 2 is now Part II (secs. 130-200) of the present *Ch'uan-hsi lu*.

In 1535, when Wang's pupil Ch'ien Te-hung published Wang's *Wen-lu* (Literary works), he took Wang's two letters to Hsü Ch'eng-chih out of the *Supplementary Edition* and put them in the "Additional Works" section of the *Wen-lu* (in present *Complete Works*, 21:9a-17b) and added Wang's second letter to Nieh Wen-yü (secs. 185-94). Ch'ien's reason for doing so is given in his introduction to Part II preceding sec. 130. He also added the two short pieces on education (secs. 195-200).

In 1556 Ch'ien edited the additional sayings that others had collected, specifically, secs. 201-21 by Ch'en Chiu-ch'uan, 222-36 by Huang I-fang, 237-47 by Huang Mien-shu, 248-316 by Huang Mien-chih, and 317-43 by Huang I-fang. (For details see his *Postscript* following sec. 343.) Ch'ien incorporated into them some sayings recorded by himself, notably secs. 260, 297, 313, 315, 338, 339, and 343. Probably secs. 260-316 had all been recorded by himself. He published these sayings in Ch'i-chou in present Hupeh under the title *Ch'uan-hsi hsü-lu* (Supplement to the *Instructions for Practical Living*). In 1572, when Hsieh T'ing-chieh compiled the *Complete Works* of Wang, he asked Ch'ien to add Wang's "Chu Hsi's Final Conclusions Arrived at Late in Life." This is the present Part III (secs. 201-343).

These three parts, collectively called the *Ch'uan-hsi lu*, were placed by Hsieh at the head of the *Complete Works* as chs. 1-3 under the heading *Yü-lu* (Recorded sayings). Hsieh's is the oldest and best edition of Wang's complete works and has remained standard ever since its publication. It is included in both the Ssu-pu ts'ung-k'an series where it is entitled *Wang Wen-ch'eng Kung ch'üan-shu*, and in the Ssu-pu pei-yao series where it is entitled *Yang-ming ch'üan-shu*.

There have been many editions of the *Ch'uan-hsi lu*, including some in Japan, issued either independently or as part of a collection of works. Some of these editions have included one or more additional essays, notably those on making up the mind (*Complete Works*, 7:51a-54b) and on cultivating the Way (*ibid.*, 7:59b-60b), following the recorded sayings in Part II. These essays add little to Wang's fundamental philosophy.

The number of conversations varies with different editions. Sec. 95 is omitted from Nan's *Ch'u-k'o ch'uan-hsi lu* and from Sung I-wang (*fl.* 1547), *Yang-ming wen-ts'ui* (Collection of literary works of Wang Yang-ming) (1553). Shih Pang-yao, *Yang-ming Hsien-sheng chi-yao*, Nan, and Yü Lin (1814-73), *Wang Yang-ming Hsien-sheng ch'üan-chi* (Complete works of Master Wang Yang-ming) (1673), have added one conversation after sec. 24. It is the same conversation in all three works. In Yü, secs. 209, 216, 262, and 300 are put at the end. Following sec. 241, the Lü-tung edition of the *Original Edition* has added two conversations. Following sec. 312, Yü and Wang I-lo (*fl.* 1680), *Wang Yang-ming chi* (Collected works of Wang Yang-ming) (1680), have added one conversation, which is the same in the two works. Following sec. 316, the Lü-tung edition has added one and following sec. 336, Chang Wen-ta (*fl.* 1621), *Yang-ming wen-ch'ao* (Selections from Wang Yang-ming's works) (1689), has added two. After sec. 343, Shih and Yü have added six conversations, which are the same in both, Wang six different conversations, and Chang twenty-eight conversations, six of which are the same as in Wang, two the same as in Shih and Yü, and one the same as the first conversation added in the Lü-tung edition after sec. 241, thus making nineteen additional and different conversations in Chang. All these additions are found in Satō Issai's *Denshū roku rangai sho*, already cited. Their sources and authenticity are not clear, except for the one added after sec. 312, which is recorded in the *Chronological Biography*, Chia-ching, second year, as part of the same conversation as sec. 312. None of these additional sections alters Wang's teachings in any significant way.

Variations of individual words or short phrases appear in various editions. They are noted in several Japanese annotated editions, especially in Satō Issai, *Denshū roku rangai sho*, and in Miwa Shissai, *Hyōchū denshū roku*, cited above. These variations are minor or obvious misprints and present no problem of textual or philosophical interpretation of Hsieh's edition.

A List of Chinese and Japanese Works

Works generally referred to by their titles are listed under title with cross reference to author. Editions indicated are those used in this book.

Azuma Keiji. *Denshū roku kōgi* (Elucidations on the *Instructions for Practical Living*).

Bodhidharma, *see under Liu-men chi*.

Chan Jo-shui (1471-1555). *Chan Kan-ch'üan wen-chi* (Collection of literary works of Chan Jo-shui).

Chang Lieh (1622-85). *Wang-hsüeh chih-i* (Questions on Wang Yang-ming's philosophy).

Chang Po-hsing, *see under Cheng-i-t'ang ch'üan-shu*.

Chang T'ing-yü, *see under Ming shih*.

Chang Tsai (1020-77). *Chang Heng-ch'ü chi* (Collected works of Chang Tsai), *Cheng-i-t'ang ch'üan-shu* edition.

——— *Cheng-meng* (Correcting youthful ignorance). In *Chang Heng-ch'ü chi*.

——— *Hsi-ming* (Western inscription). In *Chang Heng-ch'ü chi*.

Chang Wen-ta, *see under* Wang Yang-ming.

Chen-chiao (d. 712). *Cheng-tao ko* (Ode to the understanding of the way). In *Ching-te ch'uan-teng lu*.

Ch'en Chien (1497-1567). *Hsüeh-pu t'ung-pien* (General critique of obscurations of learning).

Ch'en Lung-cheng, *see under* Wang Yang-ming.

Ch'en Ts'ang-ch'i (*fl.* 723-33). *Pen-ts'ao shih-i* (Supplementary notes on medicine).

Cheng-i-t'ang ch'üan-shu (Complete library of the hall of rectifying the way), comp. by Chang Po-hsing (1651-1725).

Ch'eng Hao (1032-85). *Wen-chi* (Collection of literary works). In *Erh-Ch'eng ch'üan-shu*.

———, and Ch'eng I (1035-1107). *Erh-Ch'eng ch'üan-shu* (Complete works of the two Ch'engs), SPPY edition.

——— *I-shu* (Surviving works). In *Erh-Ch'eng ch'üan-shu*.

——— *Ts'ui-yen* (Pure words). In *Erh-Ch'eng ch'üan-shu*.

——— *Wai-shu* (Additional works). In *Erh-Ch'eng ch'üan-shu*.

Ch'eng I. *Ching-shuo* (Explanations of the Classics). In *Erh-Ch'eng ch'üan-shu.*

—— *I chuan* (Commentary on the *Book of Changes*). In *Erh-Ch'eng ch'üan-shu.*

Chi Chün, *see under Ssu-k'u ch'üan-shu tsung-mu t'i-yao.*

Ch'ien-Han shu (History of the Former Han dynasty), by Pan Ku (32-92), PNP edition.

Ch'ien Mu. *Yang-ming hsüeh shu-yao* (Essentials of Wang Yang-ming's philosophy).

Ch'ien Te-hung (1496-1574). *Nien-p'u* (Chronological biography). In *Wang Wen-ch'eng Kung ch'üan-shu. See under* Wang Yang-ming.

Ching-te ch'uan-teng lu (Records of the transmission of the lamp compiled during the Ching-te period), by Tao-yüan (*fl.* 1004), SPTK edition.

Chiu-ch'iu (Nine mounts).

Chou Ju-teng (1547-1629). *Sheng-hsüeh tsung-ch'uan* (Orthodox transmission of the doctrine of the Sage).

—— *Wang-men tsung-chih* (Fundamental doctrines of the Wang Yang-ming school).

Chou-li (The rites of Chou).

Chou Tun-i (1017-73). *Chou Lien-hsi chi* (Collected works of Chou Tun-i), *Cheng-i-t'ang ch'üan-shu* edition.

—— *T'ai-chi-t'u shuo* (Explanation of the diagram of the Great Ultimate). In *Chou Lien-hsi chi.*

—— *T'ung-shu* (Penetrating the *Book of Changes*).

Chu Hsi (1130-1200). *Chu Tzu ch'üan-shu* (Complete works of Chu Hsi), comp. by Li Kuang-ti (1642-1718) *et al.,* 1713 edition.

—— *Chu tzu wen-chi* (Collection of literary works of Chu Hsi), also called *Chu Tzu ta-ch'üan* (Complete literary works of Chu Hsi), SPPY edition.

—— *Chu Tzu yü-lei* (Classified conversations of Chu Hsi), comp. by Li Ching-te (*fl.* 1263), 1880 edition.

—— *Chung-yung chang-chü* (Commentary on the *Doctrine of the Mean*).

—— *Chung-yung huo-wen* (Questions and answers on the *Doctrine of the Mean*).

—— *Lun-yü chi-chu* (Collected commentaries on the *Analects*).

—— *Lun-yü huo-wen* (Questions and answers on the *Analects*).

—— *Meng Tzu chi-chu* (Collected commentaries on the *Book of Mencius*).

—— *Meng Tzu huo-wen* (Questions and answers on the *Book of Mencius*).

—— *Ta-hsüeh chang-chü* (Commentary on the *Great Learning*).

—— *Ta-hsüeh huo-wen* (Questions and answers on the *Great Learning*).

———— *T'ung-chien kang-mu* (Outline of the *Comprehensive Mirror for the Aid of Government*), 1804 edition.

Ch'u-shih (1290-1370). *Ch'u-shih Fan-ch'i Ch'an-shih yü-lu* (Recorded sayings of Zen Master Fan-ch'i). In *Zokuzōkyō*.

Chuang Tzu, by Chuang Chou (bet. 399 and 295 B.C.). *See under Nan-hua chen-ching.*

Ch'un-ch'iu (Spring and Autumn Annals).

Chung-yung (Doctrine of the Mean).

Daikanwa jiten (Great Chinese-Japanese dictionary), comp. by Morohashi Tetsuji.

Fan Chün (*fl.* 1134). *Hsin-chen* (An admonition on the mind).

Fan Yeh, *see under Hou-Han shu.*

Feng K'o (*fl.* 1562). *Ch'iu-shih pien* (An essay in search of the right).

Han Fei Tzu, SPTK edition.

Han-hai (Sea of cases of books), comp. by Li Tiao-yüan (1734-1803).

Han Yü (768-824). *Han Ch'ang-li ch'üan-chi* (Complete works of Han Yü), SPPY edition.

Hou-Han shu (History of the Later Han dynasty), by Fan Yeh (398-445), PNP edition.

Hsieh T'ing-chieh, *see under* Wang Yang-ming.

Hsin T'ang shu (New history of the T'ang dynasty), by Ou-yang Hsiu (1007-72), *et al.*, PNP edition.

Hsing-li ta-ch'üan (Great collection of Neo-Confucianism), comp. by Hu Kuang (1370-1418) *et al.*, 1415 edition.

Hsü Heng (1209-81). *Hsü Lu-chai chi* (Collected Works of Hsü Heng), *Cheng-i-t'ang ch'üan-shu* edition.

Hsüan-tsang (596-664). *Ch'eng wei-shih lun* (The establishment of the doctrine of idealism). In *Taishō daizōkyō*.

Hsüeh K'an, *see under* Wang Yang-ming.

Hsün Tzu, by Hsün Ch'ing (*fl.* 298-238 B.C.), SPTK edition.

Hu Kuang, *see under Hsing-li ta-ch'üan, Ssu-shu ta-ch'üan*, and *Wu-ching ta-ch'üan.*

Hua-yen ching (Flower splendor scripture).

Huai-nan Tzu, by Liu An (d. 122 B.C.), SPPY edition.

Huang Tsung-hsi (1610-95). *Shih-shuo* (My teacher's interpretations). In *Ming-ju hsüeh-an.*

————, *also see under Ming-ju hsüeh-an; Sung-Yüan hsüeh-an.*

Huang Wan. *Hsing-chuang* (Biography). In Wang Yang-ming, *Wang Wen-ch'eng Kung ch'üan-shu.*

Hui-neng, *see under Liu-tsu t'an-ching.*

I ching (Book of Changes).
I-wei t'ung-kua-yen (Apocryphal treatise on the *Book of Changes* : on understanding the verification of divination).
Juan Yüan (1764-1849). *Yen-ching-shih hsü-chi* (Supplementary collected works of the room for the study of Classics), 1874 edition.
Jung Chao-tsu. *Ming-tai ssu-hsiang shih* (History of thought during the Ming dynasty).
Kao P'an-lung (1562-1626). *Kao Tzu i-shu* (Surviving works of Kao P'an-lung).
Kawada Kinkyō (1684-1760). *Denshū roku hikki* (Notes on the *Instructions for Practical Living*).
Ku Hsien-ch'eng (1550-1612). *Hsiao-hsin-chai cha-chi* (Notes from the studio of care).
Kuei-ts'ang (Reservoir).
K'ung Tzu chia-yü (School sayings of Confucius), SPTK edition.
Lao Tzu.
Leng-yen ching (Strong character scripture).
Li chi (Book of Rites).
Li Ching-te, *see under* Chu Hsi.
Li Kuang-ti, *see under* Chu Hsi.
Li Tiao-yüan, *see under* Han-hai.
Li T'ung (1088-1158). *Li Yen-p'ing chi* (Collected works of Li T'ung), *Cheng-i-t'ang ch'üan-shu* edition.
Lien-shan (Mountain range).
Lien-teng hui-yao (Essentials of the several lamps combined), comp. by Wu-ming (*fl.* 1189). In *Zokuzōkyō.*
Liu An, *see under* Huai-nan Tzu.
Liu Hsiang (77-6 B.C.). *Shuo-yüan* (Collection of discourses).
Liu I-ch'ing, *see under* Shih-shuo hsin-yü.
Liu-men chi (Six-gate collection), attributed to Bodhidharma (*fl.* 460-534). In *Taishō daizōkyō.*
Liu-tsu t'an-ching (Platform scripture of the Sixth Patriarch), ascribed to Hui-neng (638-713). In *Taishō daizōkyō.*
Liu Tsung-chou (1578-1645). *Liu Tzu ch'üan-shu* (Complete works of Liu Tsung-chou).
———— *Yang-ming ch'uan-hsin lu* (Records of Wang Yang-ming's transmission of truth). In *Liu Tzu ch'üan-shu i-pien* (Supplement to the complete works of Master Liu), 1850 edition.
Lo Ch'in-shun (1465-1547). *Lo Cheng-an chi* (Collected works of Lo Ch'in-shun), *Cheng-i-t'ang ch'üan-shu* edition.

Lu Hsiang-shan (1139-93). *Hsiang-shan ch'üan-chi* (Complete works of Lu Hsiang-shan), SPPY edition.

Lu Lung-ch'i (1630-92). *San-yü-t'ang wen-chi* (Collection of literary works of the hall dedicated to three fish).

Lü Pu-wei (d. 235 B.C.). *Lü Shih ch'un-ch'iu* (Mr. Lü's spring and autumn annals).

Lü Ta-lin (1044-90). *K'o-chi ming* (Inscription on self-mastery). In *Sung-Yüan hsüeh-an* and *Hsing-li ta-ch'üan*.

Lun-yü (*Analects*).

Mao Ch'i-ling (1623-1716). *Wang Wen-ch'eng chuan-pen* (Basic materials for the biography of Wang Yang-ming).

Meng Tzu (*Book of Mencius*).

Ming-chiao (980-1052). *Ming-chiao Ch'an-shih yü-lu* (Recorded sayings of Zen Master Ming-chiao). In *Taishō daizōkyō*.

Ming-ju hsüeh-an (Anthology and critical accounts of Neo-Confucians of the Ming dynasty), comp. by Huang Tsung-hsi (1610-95) *et al.*, SPPY edition.

Ming shih (History of the Ming dynasty), comp. by Chang T'ing-yü (1672-1755) *et al.*, PNP edition.

Ming shih kao (Draft history of the Ming dynasty), comp. by Wang Hung-shü (1645-1723).

Mishima Fuku. *Ōyōmei no tetsugaku* (Philosophy of Wang Yang-ming).

Miwa Shissai (1669-1744). *Hyochu denshu roku* (The *Instructions for Practical Living* punctuated and annotated).

Morohashi Tetsuji, *see under Daikanwa jiten*.

Mu-an, *see under Tsu-t'ing shih-yüan*.

Nan-hua chen-ching (Pure classic of Nan-hua), SPTK edition. Same as *Chuang Tzu*.

Nan Ta-chi, *see under* Wang Yang-ming.

Ni Hsi-en. *Hsiang-chu Wang Yang-ming ch'üan-chi* (Complete works of Wang Yang-ming fully annotated).

Nieh Pao (1487-1563). *Shuang-chiang wen-chi* (Collection of literary works of Nieh Pao).

Ōta Kinjō (1765-1825). *Gimon roku* (Records of questioning), 1831 edition.

Ou-yang Hsiu (1007-72). *Ch'iu-sheng fu* (Prose-poem on the sound of the autumn wind). In *Ou-yang Wen-chung Kung wen-chi* (Collection of literary works of Ou-yang Hsiu), SPPY edition.

————, *also see under Hsin T'ang shu*.

Pa-su (Eight inquiries).

Pan Ku, *see under Ch'ien-Han shu*.

Pi-yen lu (Records of the green cave), by Yüan-wu (d. 1135).

Po-na pen (Choice works).

P'u-chi, *see under Wu-teng hui-yüan.*

Satō Issai (1772-1859). *Denshū roku rangai sho* (Notes and comments on the *Instructions for Practical Living*).

Shao Yung (1101-77). *Huang-chi ching-shih shu* (Supreme principles governing the world), SPPY edition.

Shen Yüeh (441-513). *Yin Hou chi* (Collected works of Shen Yüeh). In *Han Wei Liu-ch'ao i-po-san chia chi* (Collection of works of 103 writers from 206 B.C. to A.D. 589).

Shih chi (Records of the historian), by Ssu-ma Ch'ien (145-86 B.C.), PNP edition.

Shih ching (*Book of Odes*).

Shih Pang-yao, *see under* Wang Yang-ming.

Shih-shuo hsin-yü (New discourses on the talk of the times), by Liu I-ch'ing (*fl.* 421).

Shu ching (*Book of History*).

Ssu-k'u ch'üan-shu tsung-mu t'i-yao (Essential points about the books in the *Four Libraries*), comp. by Chi Chün (1724-1805) *et al.*

Ssu-ma Ch'ien, *see under Shih chi.*

Ssu-pu pei-yao (Essentials of the *Four Libraries*).

Ssu-pu ts'ung-k'an (*Four Libraries* series).

Ssu-shu ta-ch'üan (Great collection of commentaries on the Four Books), comp. by Hu Kuang (1370-1418) *et al.*

Sun Ch'i-feng (1584-1675). *Li-hsüeh tsung-ch'uan* (Orthodox transmission of Neo-Confucianism).

Sun Ch'iang. *Ch'uan-hsi lu chi-p'ing* (Collected comments on the *Instructions for Practical Living*).

Sun Tzu (*fl.* 513-494 B.C.?). *Sun Tzu ping-fa* (Art of war).

Sung I-wang, *see under* Wang Yang-ming.

Sung shih (History of the Sung dynasty), by T'o[q]t'o (d. 1328), PNP edition.

Sung-Yüan hsüeh-an (Anthology and critical accounts of Neo-Confucians of the Sung and Yüan dynasties), comp. by Huang Tsung-hsi (1610-95) *et al.*, SPPY edition.

Ta-chih-tu lun (Treatise on great wisdom), by Nāgārjuna (ca. 100-200).

Ta-hsüeh (*Great Learning*).

Ta-Tai li chi (Book of rites of the Elder Tai), comp. by Tai Te (*fl.* 60 B.C.).

Taishō daizōkyō (Taishō edition of the Buddhist Canon).

Takase Takejirō. *Ōyōmei shōden* (Detailed biography of Wang Yang-ming).

Tan Heng-chin. *Wang Yang-ming ch'uan-hsi lu cha-chi* (Notes on Wang Yang-ming's *Instructions for Practical Living*).

T'ang Shun-chih (1507-60). *T'ang Ching-ch'uan chi* (Collected works of T'ang Shun-chih), 1553 edition.

Tao-te ching. Same as *Lao Tzu*.

Tao-yüan, *see under Ching-te ch'uan-teng lu*.

To[q]to, *see under Sung shih*.

Ts'ai Ch'en (1167-1230). *Shu chi-chuan* (Collected commentaries on the *Book of History*).

Ts'ai Yüan-ting (1138-98). *Lü-lü hsin-shu* (New book on pitch pipes).

Tso chuan (Tso's commentary), ascribed to Tso Ch'iu-ming (6th century B.C.).

Tsou Shou-i (1491-1562). *Tsou Tung-kuo chi* (Collected works of Tsou Shou-i).

Tsu-t'ing shih-yüan (Sayings and anecdotes of patriarchs), comp. by Mu-an (*fl.* 1108).

Tsung-mi (780-841), *Ch'an-yüan chu-ch'üan chi tu-hsü* (General preface to the *Collection of source material of the Zen school*). In *Taishō daizōkyō*.

Tu Fu (712-70). *Tu Kung-pu chi* (Collected poems by Tu Fu).

Wang Chi (1498-1583). *Wang Lung-hsi Hsien-sheng ch'üan-chi* (Complete works of Master Wang Chi).

Wang Hung-hsü, *see under Ming shih kao*.

Wang I-lo, *see under* Wang Yang-ming.

Wang Yang-ming (1472-1529). *Ch'u-k'o ch'uan-hsi lu* (Original edition of the *Instructions for Practical Living*), comp. by Hsüeh K'an (d. 1545).

—— *Ch'uan-hsi hsü-lu* (Supplement to the *Instructions for Practical Living*), comp. by Ch'ien Te-hung (1496-1574).

—— "Hsiu-tao lun" (An essay on the cultivation of the Way). In *Wang Wen-ch'eng Kung ch'üan-shu*.

—— *Hsü-k'o ch'uan-hsi lu* (Supplementary edition of the *Instructions for Practical Living*), comp. by Nan Ta-chi (1487-1541).

—— *Ku-pen ta-hsüeh p'ang-shih* (Commentary on the original text of the *Great Learning*).

—— *Wang Wen-ch'eng Kung ch'üan-shu* (Complete works of Wang Yang-ming), comp. by Hsieh T'ing-chieh (*fl.* 1572), SPTK edition.

—— *Wang Yang-ming chi* (Collected works of Wang Yang-ming), comp. by Wang I-lo (*fl.* 1680).

—— *Wang Yang-ming Hsien-sheng ch'üan-chi* (Complete works of Master Wang Yang-ming), comp. by Yü Lin (1814-75).

—— *Yang-ming ch'üan-shu* (Complete works of Wang Yang-ming). Same as *Wang Wen-ch'eng Kung ch'üan-shu.*

—— *Yang-ming Hsien-sheng chi-yao* (Collection of important works by Master Wang Yang-ming), comp. by Shih Pang-yao (1585-1644).

—— *Yang-ming Hsien-sheng yao-shu* (Important works of Master Wang Yang-ming), comp. by Ch'en Lung-cheng (1585-?).

—— *Yang-ming Hsien-sheng wen-lu* (Literary works of Master Wang Yang-ming).

—— *Yang-ming wen-ch'ao* (Selections from Wang Yang-ming's works), comp. by Chang Wen-ta (*fl.* 1621).

—— *Yang-ming wen-lu* (Literary works of Wang Yang-ming), comp. by Ch'ien Te-hung (1496-1574).

—— *Yang-ming wen-ts'ui* (Collection of literary works of Wang Yang-ming), comp. by Sung I-wang (*fl.* 1547).

Wang Ying-ch'ang (*fl.* 1573). *Wang Yang-ming Hsien-sheng ch'uan-hsi lu lun* (On Master Wang Yang-ming's *Instructions for Practical Living*).

Wei Shou, *see under Wei shu.*

Wei shu (History of the Later Wei dynasty), by Wei Shou (506-72), PNP edition.

Wu-ching ta-ch'üan (Great collection of commentaries on the Five Classics), comp. by Hu Kuang (1370-1418) *et al.*

Wu-ming, *see under Lien-teng hui-yao.*

Wu-teng hui-yüan (Five lamps combined), comp. by P'u-chi (*fl.* 1228-33). In *Zokuzōkyō.*

Yamada Jun. *Yōmeigaku seigi* (Essentials of Wang Yang-ming's philosophy).

——, and Suzuki Naoji. *Denshū roku* (*Instructions for Practical Living*).

Yamazaki Ansai (1618-82). *Zoku Yamazaki Ansai zenshū* (Supplement to the *Complete Works of Yamazaki Ansai*).

Yeh Shao-chün. *Ch'uan-hsi lu tien-chu* (The *Instructions for Practical Living* punctuated and annotated).

Yü Ch'ung-yao. *Yang-ming Hsien-sheng chuan-tsuan* (Collated biography of Master Wang Yang-ming).

Yü Lin, *see under* Wang Yang-ming.

Yüan-chiao ching (Scripture of perfect enlightenment), in *Taishō daizōkyō.*

Yüan-wu, *see under Pi-yen lu.*

Zengaku jiten (Dictionary of Zen).

Zokuzōkyō (Supplement to the Buddhist Canon).

Glossary

Ao	傲
Azuma Keiji	東 敬 沿
Bodhidharma	菩 提 達 摩
Ch'ai Ming-chih	柴 鳴 沿
Chan Jo-shui	湛 若 水
Chan Kan-ch'üan	湛 甘 泉
Chan Kan-ch'üan wen-chi	湛 甘 泉 文 集
Chan, Wing-tsit	陳 榮 捷
Ch'an	禪
Ch'an-kuan ts'e-chin	禪 關 策 進
Ch'an-yüan chu-ch'üan chi tu-hsü	禪 源 諸 詮 集 都 序
Chang	張
Chang, Carsun	張 君 勵
Chang-chou	漳 州
Chang Heng-ch'ü	張 橫 渠
Chang Heng-ch'ü chi	張 橫 渠 集
Chang I	張 儀
Chang Liang	張 良
Chang Lieh	張 烈
Chang Mi	張 密
Chang Po-hsing	張 伯 行
Chang Shu-ch'ien	張 叔 謙
Chang T'ing-yü	張 廷 玉
Chang Tsai	張 載
Chang Tzu-fang	張 子 房
Chang Wen-ta	張 問 達

Chang Yüan-ch'ung	張 元 冲
Chao	召
Ch'e	轍
Chen-chiao	真 覺
Ch'en Chien	陳 建
Ch'en Ch'ing-lan	陳 清 瀾 川
Ch'en Chiu-ch'uan	陳 九 川
Ch'en Hsien-chang	陳 獻 章
Ch'en Kuo-ying	陳 國 英
Ch'en Lung-cheng	陳 龍 正
Ch'en Ming-shui	陳 明 水
Ch'en Po-sha	陳 白 沙
Ch'en Ts'ang-ch'i	陳 藏 器
Ch'en Wei-chün	陳 惟 濬
Cheng (state)	鄭
Cheng (to rectify)	正
Cheng Chao-shuo	鄭 朝 朔
Cheng Hsüan	鄭 玄
Cheng I-ch'u	鄭 一 初
Cheng-i-t'ang ch'üan-shu	正 誼 堂 全 書
Cheng-meng	正 蒙
Cheng-tao ko	證 道 歌
Cheng-te	正 德
Ch'eng (king)	成
Ch'eng (to mention)	稱
Ch'eng Hao	程 顥
Ch'eng-hua	成 化
Ch'eng I	程 頤
Ch'eng I-ch'uan	程 伊 川

Ch'eng-kuan	澄觀
Ch'eng Ming-tao	程明道
Ch'eng Po-ch'un	程伯淳
Ch'eng wei-shih lun	成唯識論
Chi	稷
Chi Chün	紀昀
Chi Wei-ch'ien	冀惟乾
Chi Yüan-heng	冀元亨
Ch'i (state)	齊
Ch'i (material force)	氣
Ch'i-chou	蘄州
Ch'i-tiao K'ai	漆雕開
Chia-ching	嘉靖
Chiao	教
Chieh	桀
Ch'ien	錢
Ch'ien-chou	虔州
Ch'ien-Han shu	前漢書
Ch'ien Hsü-shan	錢緒山
Ch'ien Hung-fu	錢洪甫
Ch'ien Mu	錢穆
Ch'ien-t'ang	錢塘
Ch'ien Te-hung	錢德洪
Chih	至
Chih-tao	志道
Chin	晉
Ch'in	秦
Ch'in-min	親民
Ching (refined)	精

Ching (serious) 敬

Ching-chou 荆州

Ching-shen 精神

Ching-shuo 經說

Ching-te ch'uan-teng lu 景德傳燈録

Chiu-ch'iu 九丘

Ch'iu-sheng fu 秋聲賦

Ch'iu-shih pien 求是編

Ch'iung 邛

Chou (duke) 周

Chou (king) 紂

Chou (compromise) 周

Chou Ching-an 周靜菴

Chou Heng 周衡

Chou Ju-teng 周汝登

Chou-li 周禮

Chou Lien-hsi 周濂溪

Chou Lien-hsi chi 周濂溪集

Chou Mao-shu 周茂叔

Chou Tao-t'ung 周道通

Chou Tun-i 周敦頤

Chu 諸

Chu Ch'en-hao 朱宸濠

Chu Hsi 朱熹

Chu Hui-an 朱晦菴

Chu Hui-weng 朱晦翁

Chu-ko K'ung-ming 諸葛孔明

Chu-ko Liang 諸葛亮

Chu Pen-ssu 朱本思

Chu Te-chih	朱得之
Chu Tzu ch'üan-shu	朱子全書
Chu Tzu ta-ch'üan	朱子大全集
Chu Tzu wen-chi	朱子文集
Chu Tzu yü-lei	朱子語類
Chu Wen Kung	朱文公
Chü-yung	居庸
Ch'u	楚
Ch'u-chou	滁州
Ch'u-k'o ch'uan-hsi lu	初刻傳習錄
Ch'u-shih	楚石
Ch'u-shih Fan-ch'i Ch'an-shih yü-lu	楚石梵琦禪師語錄
Ch'uan-hsi hsü-lu	傳習續錄
Ch'uan-hsi lu chi-p'ing	傳習錄集評
Ch'uan-hsi lu tien-chu	傳習錄點記
Chuang	莊
Chuang Chou	莊周
Chuang Tzu	莊子
Ch'un-ch'iu	春秋
Ch'un-ch'iu fan-lu	春秋繁露
Chung-shuo	中說
Chung-yung	中庸
Chung-yung chang-chü	中庸章句
Chung-yung chi-lüeh	中庸輯畧問
Chung-yung huo-wen	中庸或
Ch'ung-cheng	崇正
Daikanwa jiten	大漢和辭典
Denshū roku	傳習錄
Denshū roku hikki	傳習錄筆記

Denshū roku kōgi	傳習錄講義
Denshū roku rangai sho	傳習錄欄外書
Erh	而
Erh-Ch'eng ch'üan-shu	二程全書
Fa-tsang	法藏
Fan Chao-ch'i	范兆期
Fan Chün	范浚
Fan Chung-yen	范仲淹
Fan Yeh	范曄
Fen	分
Feng K'o	馮柯
Fou-feng	浮峯
Fu-hsi	伏羲
Fu Shang-ling	傅尚霖
Fu-ying	敷英
Fu Yüeh	傅說
Fung Yu-lan	馮友蘭
Gimon roku	疑問錄
Han Ch'ang-li ch'üan-chi	韓昌黎全集
Han Ch'i	韓琦
Han Fei Tzu	韓非子
Han-hai	函海
Han-lin	翰林
Han T'ui-chih	韓退之
Han Wei Liu-ch'ao i-po-san chia chi	漢魏六朝一百三家集
Han Yü	韓愈
Heng-shui	橫水
Ho	和
Ho-p'ing	和平

Ho Shan-shan 何善山

Ho Shu-ching 何叔京

Ho T'ing-jen 何廷仁

Hou-Han shu 後漢書

Hsi 羲

Hsi-ming 西銘

Hsi-yen 希顏

Hsiang (duke) 襄

Hsiang (name) 象

Hsiang-chu Wang Yang-ming ch'üan-chi 詳註王陽明全集

Hsiang-hu 象瑚

Hsiang-shan ch'üan-chi 象山全集

Hsiang Yü 項羽

Hsiao-hsin-chai cha-chi 小心齊札記

Hsiao Hui 蕭惠

Hsieh 契

Hsieh Liang-tso 謝良佐

Hsieh Shang-ts'ai 謝上蔡

Hsieh T'ing-chieh 謝廷傑

Hsien 鮮

Hsin 辛

Hsin-chen 心箴

Hsin-chien 新建

Hsin-min 新民

Hsin T'ang shu 新唐書

Hsing-chuang 行狀

Hsing-li ta-ch'üan 性理大全

Hsiu-tao lun 修道論

Hsiung Shih-li	熊十力
Hsü	須
Hsü Ai	徐愛
Hsü Ch'eng-chih	徐成之
Hsü Heng	許衡
Hsü Heng-shan	徐横山
Hsü-k'o ch'uan-hsi lu	續刻傳習錄
Hsü Lu-chai chi	許魯齋集
Hsü Yüeh-jen	徐曰仁
Hsüan	宣
Hsüan-tsang	玄藏
Hsüeh Hsüan	薛瑄
Hsüeh K'an	薛侃
Hsüeh-pu t'ung-pien	學蔀通辯
Hsüeh Shang-ch'ien	薛尚謙
Hsün Ch'ing	荀卿
Hsün Tzu	荀子
Hu Chü-jen	胡居仁
Hu Hung	胡宏
Hu Kuang	胡廣
Hua-yen ching	華嚴經
Huai-nan Tzu	淮南子
Huan	桓
Huang Cheng-chih	黄正之
Huang Ch'eng-fu	黄誠甫
Huang-chi ching-shih shu	皇極經世書
Huang Chieh	黄節
Huang Chih	黄直
Huang Chih-ch'ing	黄直卿

Huang Chiu-an	黃久菴
Huang Hsing-tseng	黃有曾
Huang Hsiu-i	黃修昜
Huang Hung-kang	黃弘綱
Huang I-fang	黃以方
Huang Lo-ts'un	黃洛村
Huang-lung	黃龍
Huang-mei	黃梅
Huang Mien-chih	黃勉之
Huang Mien-shu	黃勉叔
Huang Shu-hsien	黃叔賢
Huang Shu-tu	黃叔度
Huang Tsung-hsi	黃宗羲
Huang Tsung-hsien	黃宗賢
Huang Tsung-ming	黃宗明
Huang Wan	黃館
Hui (name)	回
Hui (able)	會
Hui-chi	會稽
Hui-neng	慧能
Hung, William	洪業
Hung-tu	洪都
Hyōchū denshū roku	標註傳習錄
I (arts)	藝
I (measure)	鎰
I (righteousness)	義
I ching	易經
I chuan	易傳
I-kuan	一貫

I-min	義民
I-shu	書遺言
I-wei t'ung-kua-yen	遺緯言 通卦驗
I-yen	易遺
I-yin	伊尸
Iki Hiroyuki	猪城 博之
Jan Ch'iu	冉求
Jao Tsung-i	饒宗頤
Jen (humanity, seed)	仁
Jen (man)	人
Jen (name of year)	壬
Ju	如
Juan Yüan	阮元
Jui-yen	瑞嚴
Jung Chao-tsu	容肇祖
Kan-chou	贛冊
K'ang	康
Kao	皋
Kao P'an-lung	高攀龍
Kao Tsu	高祖
Kao Tzu	高告子
Kao Tzu i-shu	高子遺書 卿庵
Kawada Kinkyō	河田琴卿
Keigo Ryōan	桂悟了庵
Ko-wu	格物
K'o-chi ming	克己塘銘
K'o-t'ang	可塘憲
Ku Hsien-ch'eng	顧憲成
Ku Jo-hsi	顧溪

Ku Lin 顧璘

Ku-pen ta-hsüeh p'ang-shih 古本大學旁釋

Ku-sou 瞽瞍

Ku Tung-ch'iao 顧東橋

Ku Wei-hsien 顧惟賢

Ku Ying-hsiang 顧應祥

Kuan Chung 管仲

Kuang-hsiang 光相

Kuang-hsin 廣信

Kuei O 桂萼

Kuei-ts'ang 歸藏

K'uei 夔

K'uei-wai 蕢瞶

Kumazawa Banzan 熊澤蕃山

Kung-hsi Hua 公西華

K'ung Tzu chia-yü 孔子家語

Kuo Hsiang 郭象

Kusumoto Masatsugu 楠本正繼

Kyūshū 九州

Lao Tzu 老子

Lee, Shao Chang 李紹昌

Leng-yen ching 楞嚴經

Li (king) 厲

Li (distance) 里

Li (principle) 理

Li (propriety) 禮

Li chi 禮記

Li Ching-te 黎靖德

Li Hou-pi 李侯璧

Li-hsüeh tsung-ch'uan	理學宗傳
Li Kuang-ti	李光地
Li Kung	李珙
Li Tiao-yüan	李調元
Li-t'ou	涮頭
Li T'ung	李侗
Li Yen-p'ing	李延平
Li Yen-p'ing chi	李延平集
Liang	兩
Liang Ch'i-ch'ao	梁啟超
Liang-chih	良知
Liang Ch'o	梁綽
Liang Jih-fu	梁日孚
Lien-shan	連山
Lien-teng hui-yao	聯燈會要
Lin Ch'un	林春
Liu An	劉安
Liu Ch'ien-chin	劉千斤
Liu Chin	劉瑾
Liu Chün-liang	劉君亮
Liu-hsia Hui	柳下惠
Liu Hsiang	劉向
Liu I-ch'ing	劉義慶
Liu Kuan-shih	劉觀時
Liu-men chi	六門集
Liu-ming chi	六明集
Liu Pang-ts'ai	劉邦采
Liu Po-sung	劉伯頌
Liu-tsu t'an-ching	六祖壇經

Liu Tsung-chou 劉宗周

Liu Tzu ch'üan-shu 劉子全書

Liu Tzu ch'üan-shu i-pien 劉子全書遺編

Liu Yang-cheng 劉養正

Liu Yüan-tao 劉元道

Lo Cheng-an 羅整菴

Lo Cheng-an chi 羅整菴集

Lo Ch'in-shun 羅欽順

Lou Liang 婁諒

Lu 魯

Lu Ch'eng 陸澄

Lu Chiu-yüan 陸九淵

Lu Hsiang-shan 陸象山

Lu-ling 廬陵

Lu Lung-ch'i 陸隴其

Lu Tzu-ching 陸子靜

Lu Yüan-ching 陸原靜

Lü-lü hsin-shu 律呂新書

Lü Pu-wei 呂不韋

Lü Shih ch'un-ch'iu 呂氏春秋

Lü Ta-lin 呂大臨

Lü-tung 閭東

Lü Tzu-yüeh 呂子約

Lüan Hui 欒惠

Lun-yü 論語

Lun-yü chi-chu 論語集註

Lun-yü huo-wen 論語或問

Lung-ch'ang 龍場

Lung-chiang 龍江

Lung-ch'ing	隆慶
Lung-p'eng	籠逢
Ma Ming-heng	馬明衡
Ma Tzu-hsin	馬子莘
Mao Ch'i-ling	毛奇齡
Meiji	明治
Meng Chien	孟簡
Meng Po-shang	孟伯生
Meng Tzu	孟子
Meng Tzu chi-chu	孟子集註
Meng Tzu huo-wen	孟子或問
Meng Yüan	孟源
Miao	苗
Ming	命
Ming-chiao	明覺
Ming-chiao Ch'an-shih yü-lu	明覺禪師語錄
Ming-ju hsüeh-an	明儒學案
Ming shih	明史
Ming shih kao	明史藁
Ming-tai ssu-hsiang shih	明代思想史
Ming-t'ang	明堂
Mishima Fuku	三島復
Miwa Shissai	三輪執齋
Mo Tzu	墨子
Morohashi Tetsuji	諸橋轍次
Mu	穆
Mu-an	睦庵
Nakae Tōju	中江藤樹
Nan-an	南安

Nan-ch'ang　　　　　　南昌

Nan-chen　　　　　　　南鎮

Nan Feng-chi　　　　　南逢吉

Nan-hua chen-ching　　南華真經

Nan Jui-ch'üan　　　　南瑞泉

Nan Ta-chi　　　　　　南大吉

Nan-tzu　　　　　　　南子

Nan Yüan-shan　　　　南元善

Ni Hsi-en　　　　　　倪錫恩

Nieh Pao　　　　　　聶豹

Nieh Shuang-chiang　聶雙江

Nieh Wen-yü　　　　聶文蔚

Nien-p'u　　　　　　年譜

Ning　　　　　　　　寧

Ning-kuo　　　　　　寧國

Ōkubo Toshimichi　　大久保利通

Ōta Kinjō　　　　　太田錦城

Ou-yang Ch'ung-i　　歐陽崇一

Ou-yang Hsiu　　　歐陽修

Ou-yang Nan-yeh　　歐陽南野

Ou-yang Te　　　　歐陽德

Ou-yang Wen-chung Kung wen-chi　歐陽文忠公文集

Ōyōmei no tetsugaku　王陽明の哲學

Ōyōmei shōden　　王陽明詳傳

Pa-su　　　　　　八索

Pan Ku　　　　　　班固

P'an-kung　　　　泮宮

Pen-ts'ao shih-i　本草拾遺

Pi　　　　　　　　費

Pi-kan	比干
Pi-yen lu	碧巖録
Pi-yung	辟雍
Po-i	伯夷
Po-na pen	百衲本
Pu	不
P'u-chi	普濟
Saigō Takamori	西鄕隆盛
Sakuma Shōzan	佐久間象山
San-yü-t'ang wen-chi	三魚堂文集
Sasaki	佐々木
Satō Issai	佐藤一齋
Shang Yang	商鞅
Shao	韶
Shao Tuan-feng	邵端峯
Shao Yung	邵雍
Shen (spirit)	神
Shen (to expand)	申
Shen-nung	神農
Shen Ssu-wei	沈思畏
Shen Yüeh	沈約
Sheng-hsüeh tsung-ch'uan	聖學宗傳
Shih	事
Shih chi	史記
Shih ching	詩經
Shih Pang-yao	施邦曜
Shih-shuo	師說
Shih-shuo hsin-yü	世說新語
Shou-heng	守衡

Shu chi-chuan	書集傳
Shu ching	書經
Shu Fen	舒芬
Shu Kuo-shang	舒國裳
Shu-sun Wu-shu	叔孫武叔
Shuang-chiang wen-chi	雙江文集
Shui-hsi	水西
Shun	舜
Shuo-yüan	說苑
Shushigaku	朱子學
Ssu-en	思恩
Ssu-k'u ch'üan-shu tsung-mu t'i-yao	四庫全書總目提要
Ssu-ma Ch'ien	司馬遷
Ssu-ma Hsiang-ju	司馬相如
Ssu-pu pei-yao	四部備要
Ssu-pu ts'ung-k'an	四部叢列
Ssu-shu chang-chü chi-chu	四書章句集註
Ssu-shu huo-wen	四書或問
Ssu-shu ta-ch'üan	四書大全
Su Ch'in	蘇秦
Sui	雖
Sun Ch'i-feng	孫奇逢
Sun Ch'iang	孫鏘
Sun Tzu	孫子
Sun Tzu ping-fa	孫子兵法
Sun Yat-sen	孫逸仙
Sung	宋
Sung I-wang	宋儀望
Sung shih	宋史

Sung-Yüan hsüeh-an	宋元學案
Suzuki Daisetz Teitarō	鈴木大批貞太郎
Suzuki Naoji	鈴木直治
Ta-chih-tu lun	大智度論
Ta-hsüeh	大學
Ta-hsüeh chang-chü	大學章句
Ta-hsüeh huo-wen	大學或問
Ta-mao	大帽
Ta-Tai li chi	大戴禮記
Tai Hsien	戴銑
Tai Te	戴德
T'ai	泰
T'ai-chi t'u-shuo	太極圖說
T'ai-chia	太甲
Taishō daizōkyō	大正大藏經
Takase Takejirō	高瀨武次郎
Tan-chu	丹朱
Tan Heng-chin	但衡今
T'ang	湯
T'ang Ching-ch'uan chi	唐荊川集
T'ang Chiu-ching	唐九經
T'ang Hsü	唐詡
T'ang Shun-chih	唐順之
Tao-te ching	道德經
Tao-yüan	道原
Te-chang	德章
T'eng	藤
T'ien-chou	田州
T'ien-ch'üan	天泉

T'ien-fei	天妃
Ting	定
Ting-pen	定本
To[q]to	托克托
Ts'ai Ch'en	蔡沈
Ts'ai Hsi-yüan	蔡希淵
Ts'ai Tsung-yen	蔡宗究
Ts'ai Yüan-ting	蔡元定
Ts'ang-chü	倉居
Ts'ao Ts'ao	曹操
Tseng	曾
Tseng Tien	曾點
Tseng Ts'ai-han	曾才漢
Tseng Tzu	曾子
Ts'eng	曾
Tso Ch'iu-ming	左邱明
Tso chuan	左傳
Tsou Ch'ien-chih	鄒謙之
Tsou Shou-i	鄒守益
Tsou Tung-kuo	鄒東廓
Tsou Tung-kuo chi	鄒東廓集
Tsu-hsin	祖心
Tsu-t'ing shih-yüan	祖庭事苑
Ts'ui-yen	粹言
Tsung-mi	宗密
Tsunoda Ryusaku	角田柳作
Tu Fu	杜甫
Tu Kung-pu chi	杜工部集
Tung Chung-shu	董仲舒

Tung Lo-shih	董蘿石
Tung Yun	董澐
T'ung	桐
T'ung-chien kang-mu	通鑑綱目
T'ung-kang	桐崗
T'ung-shu	通書
Tzu	梓
Tzu-chang	子張
Tzu-chih	子之
Tzu-hsia	子夏
Tzu-jen	子仁
Tzu-kao	子羔
Tzu-kung	子貢
Tzu-lu	子路
Tzu-ssu	子思
Tz'u	賜
Wai	外
Wai-shu	外書
Wang An-shih	王安石
Wang Chi	王畿
Wang Chia-hsiu	王嘉秀
Wang Chieh-fu	王介甫
Wang Ch'iung	王瓊
Wang Hsi-chih	王羲之
Wang Hsin-chai	王心齋
Wang-hsüeh chih-i	王學質疑
Wang Hua	王華
Wang Hung-hsü	王鴻緒
Wang I-lo	王貽樂

Wang Ju-chih	王 汝 止
Wang Ju-chung	王 汝 中
Wang Ken	王 艮
Wang Lung-hsi	王 龍 溪
Wang Lung-hsi Hsien-sheng ch'üan-chi	王 龍 溪 先 生 全 集
Wang Mang	王 莽
Wang-men tsung-chih	王 門 宗 旨
Wang Po-an	王 伯 安
Wang Shih-fu	王 實 夫
Wang Shou-jen	王 守 仁
Wang Su	王 肅
Wang Tchang-tche	王 昌 祉
Wang T'ung	王 通
Wang Wen-ch'eng chuan-pen	王 文 成 傳 本
Wang Wen-ch'eng Kung ch'üan-shu	王 文 成 公 全 書
Wang Yang-ming	王 陽 明
Wang Yang-ming chi	王 陽 明 集
Wang Yang-ming ch'uan-hsi lu cha-chi	王 陽 明 傳 習 錄 札 記
Wang Yang-ming Hsien-sheng ch'üan-chi	王 陽 明 先 生 全 集
Wang Yang-ming Hsien-sheng ch'uan-hsi lu lun	王 陽 明 先 生 傳 習 錄 論
Wang Ying-ch'ang	王 應 昌
Wang Yu-chen	王 友 貞
Wang Yü-chung	王 于 中
Wei	衛
Wei Shou	魏 收
Wei shu	魏 書
Wen (duke)	文

Wen (king)	文
Wen (literature)	文
Wen-ch'eng	文 成
Wen-chi	文 集
Wen-chung Tzu	文 中 子
Wen-lu	文 錄
Wu (king)	武
Wu (state)	吳
Wu (surname)	吳
Wu (music)	武
Wu Ch'eng	吳 澄
Wu-ching ta-ch'üan	五 經 大 全
Wu-ming	悟 明
Wu She-li	吳 涉 禮
Wu Shih-li	吳 師 禮
Wu-teng hui-yüan	五 燈 會 元
Wu Ti	武 帝
Wu-ting	武 丁
Wu Ts'ao-lu	吳 草 廬
Yamada Jun	山 田 準
Yamazaki Ansai	山 崎 闇 聖 齋 山
Yanagida Seizan	柳 田 聖 山
Yang	陽
Yang Chi	楊 驥
Yang Chien	楊 簡
Yang Chu	楊 朱
Yang Hu	陽 虎
Yang Lien-sheng	楊 聯 陞
Yang-ming ch'uan-hsin lu	陽 明 傳 信 錄

Yang-ming ch'üan-shu	陽明全書
Yang-ming Hsien-sheng chi-yao	陽明先生集要
Yang-ming Hsien-sheng chuan-tsuan	陽明先生傳纂
Yang-ming Hsien-sheng wen-lu	陽明先生文錄
Yang-ming Hsien-sheng yao-shu	陽明先生要書
Yang-ming hsüeh shu-yao	陽明學述要
Yang-ming-tung	陽明洞
Yang-ming Tzu	陽明子
Yang-ming wen-ch'ao	陽明文鈔
Yang-ming wen-lu	陽明文錄
Yang-ming wen-ts'ui	陽明文粹
Yang Shih-te	楊士德
Yang Tz'u-hu	楊慈湖
Yao	堯
Yeh Shao-chün	葉紹鈞
Yen	燕
Yen-ching-shih hsü-chi	擘經室續集
Yen Hui	顏回
Yen-shou	延壽
Yen-t'an	嚴灘
Yin	隂
Yin Hou chi	隱侯集
Yin T'un	尹焞
Ying	郢
Yōmeigaku seigi	陽明學精義
Yoshida Shōin	吉田松蔭
Yu	幽
Yü	禹
Yü Ch'ung-yao	余重耀

Yü-hang	餘杭
Yü-hsüeh	禺穴
Yü Lin	俞璘
Yü-lu	語錄
Yü-yao	餘姚
Yüan	元
Yüan-chiao ching	圓覺經
Yüan Ch'ing-lin	袁慶麟
Yüan-wu	圓悟
Yüeh (city)	越
Yüeh (name)	說
Yüeh-ling	月令
Yung-chia	永嘉
Zen	禪
Zengaku jiten	禪學辭典
Zoku Yamazaki Ansai zenshū	續山崎闇齋全集
Zokuzōkyō	續藏經

Index